THE COLLECTION FOR THE PROPAGATION AND CLARIFICATION OF BUDDHISM

VOLUME I

BDK English Tripiṭaka Series

THE COLLECTION FOR THE PROPAGATION AND CLARIFICATION OF BUDDHISM
VOLUME I

(Taishō Volume 52, Number 2102)

Translated from the Chinese

by

Harumi Hirano Ziegler

Bukkyō Dendō Kyōkai America, Inc.
2015

First Printing, 2015
ISBN: 978-1-886439-49-8
Library of Congress Control Number: 2014957879

Published by
BDK America, Inc.
1675 School Street
Moraga, California 94556

Printed in the United States of America

A Message on the Publication of the English Tripiṭaka

The Buddhist canon is said to contain eighty-four thousand different teachings. I believe that this is because the Buddha's basic approach was to prescribe a different treatment for every spiritual ailment, much as a doctor prescribes a different medicine for every medical ailment. Thus his teachings were always appropriate for the particular suffering individual and for the time at which the teaching was given, and over the ages not one of his prescriptions has failed to relieve the suffering to which it was addressed.

Ever since the Buddha's Great Demise over twenty-five hundred years ago, his message of wisdom and compassion has spread throughout the world. Yet no one has ever attempted to translate the entire Buddhist canon into English throughout the history of Japan. It is my greatest wish to see this done and to make the translations available to the many English-speaking people who have never had the opportunity to learn about the Buddha's teachings.

Of course, it would be impossible to translate all of the Buddha's eighty-four thousand teachings in a few years. I have, therefore, had one hundred thirty-nine of the scriptural texts in the prodigious Taishō edition of the Chinese Buddhist canon selected for inclusion in the First Series of this translation project.

It is in the nature of this undertaking that the results are bound to be criticized. Nonetheless, I am convinced that unless someone takes it upon himself or herself to initiate this project, it will never be done. At the same time, I hope that an improved, revised edition will appear in the future.

It is most gratifying that, thanks to the efforts of more than a hundred Buddhist scholars from the East and the West, this monumental project has finally gotten off the ground. May the rays of the Wisdom of the Compassionate One reach each and every person in the world.

NUMATA Yehan
Founder of the English
Tripiṭaka Project

August 7, 1991

Editorial Foreword

In January 1982, Dr. NUMATA Yehan, the founder of Bukkyō Dendō Kyōkai (Society for the Promotion of Buddhism), decided to begin the monumental task of translating the complete Taishō edition of the Chinese Tripiṭaka (Buddhist canon) into the English language. Under his leadership, a special preparatory committee was organized in April 1982. By July of the same year, the Translation Committee of the English Tripiṭaka was officially convened.

The initial Committee consisted of the following members: (late) HANAYAMA Shōyū (Chairperson), (late) BANDŌ Shōjun, ISHIGAMI Zennō, (late) KAMATA Shigeo, (late) KANAOKA Shūyū, MAYEDA Sengaku, NARA Yasuaki, (late) SAYEKI Shinkō, (late) SHIOIRI Ryōtatsu, TAMARU Noriyoshi, (late) TAMURA Kwansei, URYŪZU Ryūshin, and YUYAMA Akira. Assistant members of the Committee were as follows: KANAZAWA Atsushi, WATANABE Shōgo, Rolf Giebel of New Zealand, and Rudy Smet of Belgium.

After holding planning meetings on a monthly basis, the Committee selected one hundred thirty-nine texts for the First Series of translations, an estimated one hundred printed volumes in all. The texts selected are not necessarily limited to those originally written in India but also include works written or composed in China and Japan. While the publication of the First Series proceeds, the texts for the Second Series will be selected from among the remaining works; this process will continue until all the texts, in Japanese as well as in Chinese, have been published.

Frankly speaking, it will take perhaps one hundred years or more to accomplish the English translation of the complete Chinese and Japanese texts, for they consist of thousands of works. Nevertheless, as Dr. NUMATA wished, it is the sincere hope of the Committee that this project will continue unto completion, even after all its present members have passed away.

Dr. NUMATA passed away on May 5, 1994, at the age of ninety-seven, entrusting his son, Mr. NUMATA Toshihide, with the continuation and completion of the Translation Project. The Committee also lost its able and devoted Chairperson,

Professor HANAYAMA Shōyū, on June 16, 1995, at the age of sixty-three. After these severe blows, the Committee elected me, then Vice President of Musashino Women's College, to be the Chair in October 1995. The Committee has renewed its determination to carry out the noble intention of Dr. NUMATA, under the leadership of Mr. NUMATA Toshihide.

The present members of the Committee are MAYEDA Sengaku (Chairperson), ICHISHIMA Shōshin, ISHIGAMI Zennō, KATSURA Shōryū, NAMAI Chishō, NARA Yasuaki, SAITŌ Akira, SHIMODA Masahiro, Kenneth K. Tanaka, WATANABE Shōgo, and YONEZAWA Yoshiyasu.

The Numata Center for Buddhist Translation and Research was established in November 1984, in Berkeley, California, U.S.A., to assist in the publication of the BDK English Tripiṭaka First Series. The Publication Committee was organized at the Numata Center in December 1991. In 2010, the Numata Center's operations were merged into Bukkyō Dendō Kyōkai America, Inc. (BDK America) and BDK America continues to oversee the English Tripiṭaka project in close cooperation with the Editorial Committee in Tokyo.

MAYEDA Sengaku
Chairperson
Editorial Committee of
the BDK English Tripiṭaka

Publisher's Foreword

On behalf of the members of the Publication Committee, I am happy to present this volume as the latest contribution to the BDK English Tripiṭaka Series. The Publication Committee members have worked to ensure that this volume, as all other volumes in the series, has gone through a rigorous process of editorial efforts.

The initial translation and editing of the Buddhist scriptures found in this and other BDK English Tripiṭaka volumes are performed under the direction of the Editorial Committee in Tokyo, Japan. Both the Editorial Committee in Tokyo and the Publication Committee, headquartered in Berkeley, California, are dedicated to the production of accurate and readable English translations of the Buddhist canon. In doing so, the members of both committees and associated staff work to honor the deep faith, spirit, and concern of the late Reverend Dr. Yehan Numata, who founded the BDK English Tripiṭaka Series in order to disseminate the Buddhist teachings throughout the world.

The long-term goal of our project is the translation and publication of the texts in the one hundred-volume Taishō edition of the Chinese Buddhist canon, along with a number of influential extracanonical Japanese Buddhist texts. The list of texts selected for the First Series of this translation project may be found at the end of each volume in the series.

As Chair of the Publication Committee, I am deeply honored to serve as the fifth person in a post previously held by leading figures in the field of Buddhist studies, most recently by my predecessor, John R. McRae.

In conclusion, I wish to thank the members of the Publication Committee for their dedicated and expert work undertaken in the course of preparing this volume for publication: Senior Editor Marianne Dresser, Dr. Hudaya Kandahjaya, Dr. Carl Bielefeldt, Dr. Robert Sharf, and Rev. Brian Kensho Nagata, President of BDK America.

A. Charles Muller
Chairperson
Publication Committee

Contents

Translator's Introduction

The *Collection for the Propagation and Clarification of Buddhism* (*Taishō shinshū daizōkyō,* volume 52, number 2102, 1a3–96b3) is a compilation by Shi Sengyou (445–518), a Vinaya master of the Liang dynasty (502–557) consisting mainly of discourses, critical responses to anti-Buddhist discourses, correspondence, reports to the emperor, family codes, and written appeals by Buddhist laypeople and monks, mostly from the Eastern Jin dynasty (317–420) through the second decade of the sixth century of the Liang dynasty. These writings were intended to protect the Buddhist Dharma from interference by those who valued the teachings based on Confucianism and Daoism, and by the political powers of the time, as well as in order to promulgate Buddhism.

Sengyou was deeply concerned about delusions and misinformation held by anti-Buddhists, which he saw as a major cause of negative views toward Buddhism. In his Afterword to the *Collection for the Propagation and Clarification of Buddhism* (in Volume II, forthcoming), he lists six kinds of secular scholars' doubts about Buddhism: (1) what the Buddhist scriptures expound is preposterous and unverifiable; (2) since one's spirit perishes when one dies, it is hardly possible that the spirit will transmigrate in the three periods of existence; (3) no one has ever seen the real Buddha and his teaching has no benefit to state governance; (4) the Dharma teaching did not exist in ancient times and emerged only recently during the Han period; (5) the Buddhist teaching should exist only in the region of the western tribes as its edification is not for Chinese people; and (6) the Dharma was rarely practiced in the Han and Wei periods and began flourishing only during the Jin period.

Sengyou believed that "The Way is propagated by people, and the teaching is clarified by literature." By collecting literary works from distinctive scholars of former ages that were intended to dispel wrong views toward Buddhism, which included expressions to protect Buddhism and were advantageous in protecting the Three Treasures, he hoped to disperse these doubts.

Historical Background

Buddhist teachings transmitted to China before the Common Era were initially practiced only among non-Chinese groups. During the Han dynasty, the Buddhist clergy consisted of *śramaṇa*s from India or Central Asia, and there was not a large number of Chinese followers. Around the middle of the third century we see the remarkable activities of a Chinese Buddhist group led by Zhu Shixing (or Zixing). More conspicuous activities of Chinese monks can be seen during the time of the Eastern Jin dynasty. Thanks to eminent Chinese monks such as Zhi Dun (314–366), Daoan (312–385), and Huiyuan (334–416), who expended great effort to spread Buddhist teachings, the number of Chinese monks notably increased. Intellectuals who were well versed in the Chinese classics, such as the *Zhuangzi* and the *Laozi Daodejing,* and who enjoyed "pure talks" (*qingtan*), became increasingly devoted to Buddhism. By the early sixth century, when Sengyou compiled the *Collection for the Propagation and Clarification of Buddhism* (hereafter, the *Collection*), Buddhism had come to flourish in both north and south China.

The growth of Buddhism subsequently caused serious conflicts between Buddhists and non-Buddhists in political and social arenas and thought. People became more aware that the Buddhist teachings differed significantly from Confucianism and Daoism in many ways. Moreover, lay Buddhists' enthusiasm resulted in the construction of many Buddhist temples and pagodas, which caused financial burden on civil administration and society, and the increasing number of monks who did not observe the precepts and engaged in secular life and business contributed to the deterioration of the sangha. In the north, where non-Chinese groups had ruled continuously since the collapse of the Western Jin dynasty (316), government reaction to the ascendancy of Buddhism resulted in Emperor Wu's persecution of Buddhists between 446 and 452 during the Northern Wei dynasty. In the south, where the Chinese established political power successively, there was no such large-scale Buddhist persecution, but there were longstanding serious conflicts between Buddhists and non-Buddhists. Accordingly, Buddhist groups became the target of criticism from anti-Buddhist groups and were compelled to explain their positions and protect Buddhism at the same time.

Characteristics and Significance

The *Collection* is widely known as an invaluable source to examine the early development of Chinese Buddhism. It offers much insight into how Buddhism, a foreign religion, was accepted in Chinese society, mainly by intellectuals of the southern dynasties, and how these early adopters understood the Buddhist tenets in relation to their abundant knowledge of the Chinese classics. In fact, we find various issues encountered by Buddhists to be deeply rooted in Chinese society and belief: whether or not the spirit perishes after death; the causality of reward and retribution in the three periods of existence; the differing viewpoints of the sovereign and of monks; Chinese monks' beliefs and Chinese customs and thought on such notions as filial piety, taking the tonsure, and styles of personal deportment (such as manners of sitting, eating, and dress); lay Buddhists' religious practices; a ruler's attempt to recruit monks for his brain trust; and criticism of Daoism.

A notable aspect of this work is that Buddhist tenets are explained using Confucian and Daoist terminology. It is widely known that *geyi,* a way to interpret Buddhist scriptures by means of the philosophy asserted in the *Laozi Daodejing* and the *Zhuangzi,* was popular during the Eastern Jin period. It began with Zhu Faya and Kang Falang who studied with Daoan under Fotudeng. Even though Daoan criticized *geyi,* it is known that he allowed only Huiyuan, his eminent disciple, to explain Buddhist doctrines using non-Buddhist texts. We see many examples of this tendency in this work.

In addition to *geyi,* throughout the *Hongmingji* authors quote from the Chinese classics and historical records to support their arguments. Wherever possible I have tried to indicate in the notes the sources of these quotations together with available English translations.

Moreover, the *Collection* is a valuable source to examine the early stage of Daoism in the south, particularly the Daoist school called the Way of the Five Pecks of Grains (Wudoumidao), or the Way of the Celestial Master (Tianshidao). For instance, in fascicle eight (in Volume II of this translation, forthcoming), in Shi Xuanguang's criticism of Daoism, Daoist practices, and rituals such as the "unity of the *yin-yang* vapors" (*heqi*) and the "mud and ash fête" (*tutanzhai*) are described. In addition, we find the titles of each position of the organization together with their derivations. A scarcity of clearly dated Daoist sources for studies of early Daoism is a crucial problem in current scholarship. Although the *Collection* is a Buddhist work from chiefly the fourth and fifth centuries, it also serves well as a primary source for contemporary Daoism.

Finally, it should be noted that this text served as inspiration for Daoxuan (596–667), who took Sengyou's compilation as his model in compiling his own *Extensive Collection for the Propagation and Clarification of Buddhism* (*Guang Hongmingji*) in 664.

Questions on the Compilation

The text of the *Collection for the Propagation and Clarification of Buddhism* currently circulated consists of fourteen fascicles, with fifty-eight headings. Sengyou, however, lists this work as consisting of ten fascicles together with a table of contents, with thirty-three headings, in his compilation *Collection of Records Derived from the Tripiṭaka* (*Chusanzangjiji*), completed around 515 in the last years of his life. The Buddhist catalogue *Zhongjing mulu* compiled by Fajing in 593 lists this text as being comprised of ten fascicles as well, but Fei Changfang's catalogue *Lidai sanbaoji* completed in 597 records the *Collection* as consisting of fourteen fascicles. Questions about the completion of the fourteen-fascicle text are still controversial and require further research.

Note on the Translation

Citations from the *Taishō shinshū daizōkyō* are listed in this form: Taishō serial number; volume number; page; register (a, b, or c); line number(s). For example, *Taizi ruiying benqi jing,* T.185.3:472c1–483a13.

Transliterations of Chinese language follow the Pinyin system. Japanese Romanization follows the modified Hepburn system as employed in *Kenkyūsha's New Japanese-English Dictionary* (third and later editions).

THE COLLECTION FOR THE PROPAGATION AND CLARIFICATION OF BUDDHISM
VOLUME I

Compiled by Shi Sengyou at Jianchu Temple in Yangdu during the Liang dynasty

Fascicle One

Preface

The awakening [of the Buddha] is as boundless as the ocean. The wisdom [of the Buddha] is as completely illuminating as a mirror. The edification [of the Buddha] ingeniously spreads throughout the universe; in fact, it created [the sage kings] Yao and Shun, as if molding ceramic art or casting metal. The law [of the Buddha] dominates beyond the world in which we cling to language; therefore it created the Duke of Zhou and Confucius, just as if fashioning clay into figures. 1a3

Nevertheless, the greater the Way is, the more difficult it is to believe; the higher the tone of the music, the fewer there are who can sing it harmoniously. Mount Sumeru is lofty and steep, where very strong winds (Skt. *vairambhaka*) arise. Treasures accumulate in a depository and then theft occurs. Once upon a time, when the Tathāgata resided in this world, his edification shook the trichiliocosm, and yet the four devils harbored grudges and the six masters embraced poisonous thoughts;[1] not to speak of today, the last phase of the period of the Semblance Dharma.

Almost five hundred years have passed since the time the Great Dharma reached the east. When conditions are good, people have faith [in Buddhism], but when conditions are not, they do not; the fortune [of Buddhism] has its ups and downs as well. Those who have right views propagate and support [the teaching], and those who are evil and deluded slander [it]. As for perverse Confucianists who abide by literature, they keep their distance [from Buddhism] because it is considered heathen. The honey-tongued heretics (i.e., Daoists) adopt [Buddhism] in their teaching and consider both to be the same teaching. Those who keep their distance [from Buddhism] suffer drastic delusion, and those who adopt [Buddhism in their teaching] experience confusion about the colors of vermilion and purple.[2] As a consequence, sophisticated arguments have gradually become more complicated and corrupted forms of words have exceedingly flourished.

The *hedan* bird screeches in the night [in search of daybreak], yet it cannot split the darkness for broad daylight. The legendary *jingwei* bird holds pebbles in its mouth [and drops them in the sea in order to fill it up], yet it fails to mar the natural features of the blue ocean.[3] Nevertheless, if brightness is disturbed by darkness and greatness is slandered by smallness, even though nothing can be changed at all, it would pollute people's eyes and ears. This will cause those of weak and infirm natures to follow false debates and go astray for a long time, and those who have disordered logic to pursue heretical doctrines and indulge in everlasting [delusion]. This is why it is easy to fall into hell and difficult to ascend to the pure state.

I, Sengyou, am of superficial learning, but I am deeply bent on propagating and guarding [Buddhism]. I resent in my mind flattering statements and groundless customs. Thereupon, making use of short intervals of medical treatment or spare moments while dwelling in the mountains, I have compiled intelligent writings of ancient and modern times and collected polished essays by Buddhist clergy and laypeople. Among them, I made use of all those [writings] that painstakingly eliminate evil [teachings] and are irrefutable expressions to protect the Dharma, regardless of the length of the works. In addition, among written records and literature by distinguished scholars of former ages, I have compiled all those that are advantageous [for the Three Treasures] as well. They are classified and arranged in fourteen fascicles.

The Way is propagated by people, and the teaching is clarified by literature. [This work] is [intended] to propagate the Way and clarify the teaching. Therefore, it is called the *Collection for the Propagation and Clarification* [*of Buddhism*] (*Hongmingji*). At the same time, led by my shallow thought, I append my own discussion at the end. I pray that by a drop of water and a particle of dust I will be able to help increase the water of the ocean and raise the height of Mount Dai. However, my learning is solitary and uncultivated and my knowledge is limited. I am ashamed of being narrow-minded. Well-versed expert gentlemen, please grant your aid to enlarge this compilation.

Mouzi's [*Discourse on*] *the Elucidation of Delusions* (*Lihuolun*), or the Exposition by Mouzi Bo, Governor of Cangwu Prefecture[4]

Mouzi has already studied the Classics, commentaries on them, and all philosophers' works. Regardless of the size or length, there was no book he did not like. Although he was not delighted with books on the art of war, he still read them. He read books on the immortals and immortality, but restrained himself and never believed [in these things]; he considered them to be preposterous. 1b

In the time after Emperor Ling (r. 168–189) [of the Later Han dynasty] had passed away, the world was in turmoil. Only Jiaozhou was relatively peaceful. People of the heterodoxy moved en masse from the north to settle there. Many practiced the art of the immortals, abstaining from [eating] grain to prolong their life spans. There were many contemporary people who learned [the art of the immortals from these people]. Mouzi always rebuked them by [referring to] the Five Classics. None among the Daoists and practitioners of the heterodox arts dared respond to [his rebuke]. [People] compared this with the case where Meng Ke (i.e., Mencius) drove off Yang Zhu and Mo Di.[5]

Before this, Mouzi fled with his mother to Jiaozhi (present-day Vietnam). At the [Chinese] age of twenty-six he returned to Cangwu and took a wife. The governor [of Cangwu prefecture] heard that Mouzi abided by learning, and visited him to ask him to become a civil official. At that time, [Mouzi] was just in the prime of his youth, and had intensely set his heart on learning. Moreover, he saw that the world was in chaos and he had no intention of entering government service. He did not accept the offer after all.

During this period, all the provinces and prefectures were suspicious of each other and isolated from one another, without communication. Since [Mouzi] had profound learning and great knowledge, the governor [of Cangwu prefecture] wanted to send him as a diplomatic envoy to pay homage to Jingzhou (in present-day Hubei province). Mouzi believed that while it is easy to decline honor and rank, it is difficult to shirk a mission. Consequently he dressed properly and was about to go. As it happened, the regional governor of the province [learned that] Mouzi was a well-educated recluse and summoned him. Again Mouzi feigned illness and excused himself.

A younger brother of the regional governor, the governor of Yuzhang prefecture (in present-day Jiangxi province), had been murdered by the Leader of Court Gentlemen Ze Rong (d. 195). The regional governor then planned to send the Commandant of Cavalry Liu Yan, who commanded troops and who was about to head to [Yuzhang]. [But the regional governor] was afraid that [this action] would provoke reciprocal suspicion from the outer world and the troops would not be able to proceed. So he asked Mouzi, "My younger brother was killed by a rebel. My great indignation about this, [as his brother who shares] the same flesh and bones, arises from the bottom of my heart. I am about to send the Commandant of Cavalry Liu there, [but] I am afraid that the outer world is in turmoil and travelers cannot get through. You are well learned in both literary and military arts and especially talented in diplomacy. Now I would like you to oblige us by giving your consent to going to Lingling and Guiyang (in present-day Hunan province) and to making their roads available for our passage. What do you think?"

Mouzi replied, "Just like a horse that has been fed and waits at your stable, I have been treated [kindly] for a long time. [When the moment arrives], a patriot forgets himself and hopes to devote himself as much as he can." Accordingly, [Mouzi] dressed and was about to depart. At this point, his mother suddenly passed away and he was not able to make the trip.

For a long time [Mouzi] reflected, "Since I have a fluent tongue, I am handily appointed for a mission. Just now the world is in disturbance, and it is not a time to distinguish myself in the world." Then he lamented, "Laozi wrote, 'Exterminate sagacity and reject knowledge.'[6] If one cultivates himself and maintains truth, all of nature does not take away his ambition, the world does not deny his pleasure, a son of Heaven cannot subjugate him, and feudal princes cannot befriend him. Therefore, he finds approval as noble."

Then Mouzi had the earnest intention [to learn] the Buddhist Way, and concurrently studied Laozi's *Five Thousand Words* (i.e., the *Daodejing*). He took in the profound subtle meanings as if they were wine and drink, and played on the Five Classics as if they were [musical instruments like] the Chinese zither (*qin*) and the reed organ. Many common people condemned him, thinking that he had gone against the Five Classics and turned to a heterodox way. Even if he wished to engage these people in disputation, it was not [in accordance with] the [Buddhist] Way. Even if he wanted to keep silent, he was unable to do so. Consequently, he spent time with brush and ink to briefly cite the words of the sages and wise ones in order to make a testament of [his response to the condemnation of Buddhism] with explanations. This is called Mouzi's [*Discourse on*] *the Elucidation of Delusions* (*Lihuo*[*lun*]).

A person asked, "From whom was the Buddha born? Does he or does 1c
he not have ancestors and a country [to which he belonged]? What does he bestow on all people? What does he look like?"

Mouzi replied, "You have big questions. I am dull, but I will roughly explain the outline [of the biography of the Buddha]. I have heard the state of the Buddha's transformations. It is impossible to record his [entire] chronicle, since he accumulated moral conduct for several hundreds of billions of years. Nevertheless, when he came into [the existence in which he would become] the Buddha, he was born in India, in the provisional form of the son of [Lady Māyā], the queen of King Śuddhodana. Once, while taking a midday nap, she had a dream that she rode upon a white, six-tusked elephant. She was very delighted and accordingly felt that she had become with child. On the eighth day of the fourth month, [the child] was born from the right armpit of his mother. He landed upon the ground, took seven steps forward, and said, raising his right arm, 'There is no one in Heaven and Earth who goes beyond me.' At that time, Heaven and Earth quaked tremendously and the palace became bright all over. On the same day, a servant of the royal family also gave birth to a child, and a white horse in the stable bore a white colt. The [servant's] baby was called Chandaka and the white colt was named Kaṇṭhaka. The king instructed them to always attend the prince.

"The prince had thirty-two major marks and eighty minor marks of physical excellence. He was one *zhang* and six *chi* tall, and his body was of a golden color all over. He had a protuberance (*rouji;* Skt. *uṣṇīṣa*) on the top of his head. His jaws were just like those of a lion. His tongue [was so long that it] could cover his face. His palms had the pattern of a thousand-spoked wheel. The light radiating from the top of his head illuminated everything for ten thousand *li.* This is a rough description of the major marks of the Buddha.

"When [the prince] was seventeen years old, his [father,] the king, chose as [the prince's] consort a girl from a neighboring state. Whenever the prince seated himself, he moved his seat away from her. When he slept, he did not share a bed with her. The Way of Heaven is, [however,] quite evident; *yin* and *yang* had relations [with each other]. Consequently she conceived a son, who was born six years later. The king regarded the prince as invaluable and extraordinary, and he built palaces for him and arranged female entertainers and precious amusements in a row in front of him. But the prince did not wish for worldly pleasure; his intention lay in morality.

"At midnight on the eighth day of the fourth month of the year [the prince] turned nineteen years old. He called Chandaka, had him put the bit and bridle on Kaṇṭhaka, and mounted the horse. Spiritual beings helped them, lifting them up, and [they all] flew out of the palace.

"The next day [the prince's quarters] were found empty and no one knew where [he] was. There was none among the king, the officials, and the people who did not sob, [missing him]. They pursued [the prince] and caught up with him in a field. The king said [to the prince], 'Before you were born, I prayed and asked the gods [for you]. Now I already have you, you who are just like a precious stone or a jade tablet. You must succeed to the throne, and yet you have left [the palace]. What are you going to do?' The prince replied, 'All things are impermanent; any existence will pass away. I would like to learn the way [to enlightenment] and liberate all sentient beings in the ten directions.' The king realized that [the prince's resolution] was steady and firm. So the king rose and returned [to the palace]. The prince promptly departed. He contemplated the Way for six years, and finally attained buddhahood.

"The reason [the Buddha] was born in the first month of the summer season is because it is the time of the fourth month of the year (*zhonglü*),[7] when it is neither [too] cold nor [too] hot, when grasses and trees bloom, and when people take off the fox-fur robes and put on linen clothes. The reason he was born in India is because it is located in the center of the universe, which maintains its justice and peace. There are altogether twelve kinds of scriptures he authored, eight hundred and forty million fascicles in all. Among them, a large fascicle contains less than ten thousand words and a small fascicle consists of more than a thousand words. The Buddha gave the teaching all over the world and liberated the people. Accordingly, on the fifteenth day of the second month, he entered nirvana.

"His teaching and precepts continuously exist. If we follow [the teaching and precepts] and are capable of practicing them, we will be able to attain 2a *wuwei* as well, and happiness will be passed on to later generations.[8]

"Those who observe the five precepts have six purification days in a month. On the day of purification, one concentrates his or her mind, repents, and turns over a new leaf. *Śramaṇa*s observe two hundred and fifty precepts and have purification every day. Their precepts are not what laymen (Skt. *upāsaka*) are not able to learn. Their proper deportment and course of action are not different from those of the [Chinese] classical rites of antiquity. Throughout the day and night, they talk about the [Buddhist] Way and recite sutras, and do not take part in worldly affairs. Laozi said, 'Deportment [of those who] have exceeding virtue is just to follow the Way.'[9] This is what he meant [about *śramaṇa*s]."

A person asked, "For what reason precisely is he called the Buddha? What is the meaning of '*buddha*'?"

Mouzi replied, "The word *buddha* is a posthumous title, just as the Three Augusts are called gods and the Five Thearchs are called sages [in China]. The Buddha is the founder of morals and the originator of divinities. The term *buddha* means awakened. [The Buddha] is beyond our sensory perception; he can transform into and manifest as various entities; he sometimes appears and sometimes disappears; he can become smaller or larger; he can be a round or a square shape; he can become old or young; and he can hide and reveal himself. He goes through fire without being burned. He steps on a sword without being injured. He can be in filth without being soiled. Even if he experiences a calamity, it has no effect on him. When he wants to travel, he flies through the air, and when he sits, he emits light. Therefore, his title is Buddha."

A person asked, "What is called the 'Way'? What category is the Way?"

Mouzi replied, "The term 'Way' means to lead. It leads people to *wuwei*. Pull it forth and it does not advance. Pull it back and it does not retreat. Lift it and it does not ascend. Lower it and it does not descend. Look at it and it has no shape. Listen to it and it has no sound. Outside of the visible world is vastness, [but the Way] meanders beyond it. A breadth of a hair is minute, [yet the Way] is full of twists and turns within it. Therefore, it is called the Way."

A person asked, "Confucius considered the Five Classics to be the teaching of the Way, which should be recited while folding one's hands before one's breast and practiced. Now, the [Buddhist] Way you explain is the absolute vacancy (*xuwu*) and beyond our sensory perception. It does not expose its significance and does not direct its performance. Why is it different from what the sage (i.e., Confucius) said?"

Mouzi replied, "You cannot consider what you are familiar with to be important and what you are unfamiliar with to be trivial. You are confused by matters of the outside world and lose yourself in the mind. In doing something, you should not lose morality. It is just as in the case that one should not lose *gong* and *shang* [of the fundamental notes] when tuning the strings of a musical instrument.[10] The Way of Heaven is regulated with the four seasons and the ways of human beings are regulated with the five cardinal virtues. Laozi said, 'There was something mixed, coming into existence before Heaven and Earth. It can be considered as the mother of the world. I do not know its name, but if I dare to give a name to it, it is called the Way.'[11] The Way helps people in being able to serve their parents at home, helps those who govern the state in ruling over the people, and helps those who establish themselves [in the world] without the assistance of others in harnessing themselves. If you practice [the Way], it will fill the universe. If you reject and do not practice it, it will disappear and yet will not leave you behind. You do not understand this. Why [do you think] it is different from [the Way of which Confucius speaks]?"

A person asked, "The greatest reality does not look adorned, and the highest level of expression has no polished [words]. [An expression of]
2b concise words that is comprehensible is elegant. Things that require less work and yet achieve a goal are clever.

"Therefore, pearl and jade are rare and yet valuable, while rubble is common and worthless. The sages [of China] established the foundation of the Seven Classics, which consist of less than thirty thousand words and within which all issues are treated. The Buddhist scriptures are numbered at some ten thousand fascicles, whose words are in the hundreds of millions, which is more than one person is able to sustain. I think they are troublesome and unimportant."

Mouzi replied, "The reason large rivers and oceans are different from a pool of water on a street is because they are deeper and wider. The reason the Five Sacred Mountains are dissimilar to mounds is because they are taller and bigger. If [the Five Sacred Mountains] are not extremely higher than [ordinary] mountains and hills, even a crippled sheep could climb up to the peaks. If [large rivers and oceans] are not extremely deeper than small streams, even a small boy could take a bath in the abysses. Qiji (a legendary fine horse capable of covering a thousand *li* in a day) does not live in a garden, and a fish that [is capable of] swallowing a boat does not swim in mountain streams that are several *ren* deep. If you break open a three-*cun* large oyster to look for a pearl [that is as large as] a bright moon, or if you try to find a brood of Chinese phoenixes in a nest of thorny brambles, it will certainly be difficult to find them. This is because the minor cannot contain the great.

"The Buddhist scriptures expand issues for hundreds of millions of years in the past, and still state main points for all ages. When the primordial substance had not yet arisen, when the primal beginning had not yet been produced,[12] and when Heaven and Earth began to rise, their slightness could not be grasped, and their minuteness could not be entered. [But] the Buddha governed over them all, even the vast world outside [of the universe], analyzed within the profound and subtle world, and missed nothing to record about them. Therefore, the scriptures are counted in some ten thousand fascicles, with words in the hundreds of millions. The more [words there are], the closer to completion [it is] and the richer [the content is]. Why [do you think] it is unimportant? Even though [the scriptures] cannot be sustained by one person, it is like the case where you drink water when arriving at a river. When you have drunk enough and you feel satisfied (i.e., your thirst is quenched), would you then care about the remaining water?"

A person asked, "The Buddhist scriptures are numerous. I would like to master their main points and dismiss the superfluities Please simply discuss their essence and eliminate embellishments."

Mouzi replied, "No. The sun and moon are both bright, but each has its own time to shine. Each of the twenty-eight constellations has its own place over which it rules. Multifarious medicinal herbs grow equally, but each of them has its own effect to heal sickness. Fox-fur robes are worn to protect against coldness, while linen clothes are worn to keep out heat. A boat and a carriage travel different routes from each other, though both of them transport travelers. The reason Confucius did not take the Five Classics to be perfect and further wrote the *Spring and Autumn Annals* (*Chunqiu*) and the *Canon of Filial Piety* (*Xiaojing*) is simply because he wanted to propagate the means of the Way by which people may act freely. Even though Buddhist scriptures are numerous, [they all] result in one. Although the Seven Classics are different from each other, the esteem in which they hold morality, benevolence, and righteousness results in the same, too. The reason why filial piety is explained in numerous ways is to give instruction according to people's conduct. It is just as when both Zichang and Ziyou asked the same question about filial piety Confucius gave each a different answer to correct their individual shortcomings. Why [do you think] there is something [in Buddhist scriptures] to dismiss?"

A person asked, "If the Buddhist Way is the most august and the greatest, why did [Emperor] Yao and [Emperor] Shun, the Duke of Zhou, or Confucius not cultivate it? No expression [of the Buddhist teaching] is found in the Seven Classics. Master, you have already indulged in the *Book of Odes* (*Shijing*) and the *Book of History* (*Shujing*), and have been delighted with the *Book of Rites* (*Liji*), and the *Book of Music* (*Yuejing*). Why are you also fond of the Buddhist Way and happy about this foreign method? How could [Buddhism] surpass the Classics and their commentaries and be better than the sages' works? If I were you, I would not accept it."

Mouzi replied, "It is not necessarily that only books of the words of Con-
2c fucius are [useful], just as medicines do not have to be prescribed by the great doctor Bian Que [to be efficacious]. Whatever meets righteousness is followed, and whatever heals sickness is good. Gentlemen extensively take all that is wholesome in order to complement themselves. Zigong said, 'What necessity was there for my master to have a regular master?'[13] Emperor Yao served Yin Shou, Emperor Shun served Wu Cheng, [the Duke of Zhou] Dan studied with [Taigong Wang] Lü [Shang],[14] and Confucius studied with Lao Dan (i.e., Laozi), but none of these are found in the Seven Classics. Even though these four masters [Yin Shou, Wu Cheng, Lü Shang, and Lao Dan] are sages, when compared with the Buddha they are like white deer compared with a *kylin,* or swallows compared with a Chinese phoenix. [Even so,] Emperor Yao and Emperor Shun, the Duke of Zhou, and Confucius still studied with them.

"Moreover, the Buddha has the marks of physical excellence, he can transform, he has supernatural powers, and he has no set pattern. How can you reject and not study Buddhism? In the items and meanings of the Five

Classics, there are some lacunae. As for the fact that the Buddha is not mentioned [in the Seven Classics], how worthwhile is it to be doubtful and suspicious?"

A person asked, "It is said that the Buddha has thirty-two major and eighty minor marks of physical excellence. Why is he so different from [ordinary] people? I am afraid that this is an extravagant expression and a description of unreality."

Mouzi replied, "As the saying goes, 'The fewer chances to see, the more suspicious [one is].' A man sees a camel and says that it is a horse with a swollen back. [We also say that] Emperor Yao's eyebrows were of eight different colors, each of Emperor Shun's eyes had double pupils, the mouth of Gao Yao (a chief judical officer for Emperor Shun) was [just like] a crow's beak, King Wen [of the Zhou dynasty] had four nipples, [the legendary ruler] Yu had three orifices in each ear, the Duke of Zhou was hunchbacked, Fuxi had a nose [just like] a dragon's, and Confucius had a depression on the top of his head. Laozi had a sun-shaped lump and the mark of a moon on his forehead, and two nose bridges. He held the Chinese characters of the Ten [Celestial Stems] in his hands, and treaded upon the two [principles of *yin* and *yang*] and the five [primary elements] (i.e., metal, wood, water, fire, and earth).[15] These men are not different from [normal] people, are they? How worthwhile is it to be doubtful of the Buddha's marks of physical excellence?"

A person asked, "The *Canon of Filial Piety* says, 'Your body, hair, and skin are received from your parents. Do not dare to damage them.'[16] When Zengzi was about to die, he said, 'Uncover my feet, uncover my hands!'[17] Now, *śramaṇa*s shave their heads. Why do they go against the sage's words? They do not follow the way of filial piety. You are always fond of discussing right and wrong and correcting wrong to right, yet on the contrary, [you think] it is alright [for *śramaṇa*s to shave their heads], don't you?"

Mouzi replied, "It is not benevolent to slander sages and virtuous people. It is not intelligent that correction is not much to the point. How can you cultivate virtue being neither benevolent nor intelligent? If you are not going to cultivate virtue, you are the same as those who are stubborn and stupid. How can I easily discuss [these matters] with [such a person]?

"Once upon a time a man of Qi crossed a large river by boat, and his father fell into the water. He bared his hands, grasped his father's head, turned his father upside down, made him regurgitate the water, and so was able to bring his father back to life. It is the gravest impiety to grasp the head of one's own father and to turn him upside down, but by doing so this man helped his father escape death. If he had cultivated himself as is usual for a filial son, folding his arms [and doing nothing], his father would have died by drowning. Confucius said, 'If you can be faithful to the Way with them, you may not yet take measures suited to the occasion with them.'[18] This refers to acting in what is considered a proper manner at the time.

"Moreover, the *Canon of Filial Piety* says, 'Kings of previous times had the highest virtue and the essential points [of what is good and appropriate].' Taibo, however, had his hair cut off and his body tattooed following the custom of the Wu-Yue region [of southern China], disregarding the righteousness toward one's body, hair, and skin [stated in the *Canon of Filial Piety*]. Nevertheless, Confucius praised him [and said], '[Taibo] may be said to be a man of the highest virtue.'[19] Confucius did not defame Taibo for having his hair cut.

3a "Seeing this, if one has great virtue, he will not be tied down by trifling [faults]. It can be said that the utmost concessions are that *śramaṇa*s give up their family property, abandon their wives and children, do not listen to music, and do not look upon [beautiful] worldly things. Why [do you say that] they go against the sage's words and do not follow [the way of] filial piety? Yu Rang [of Jin] swallowed charcoal and lacquered his body [for a vendetta]. Nie Zheng flayed the skin of his face and punished himself [after committing a successful assassination]. Princess Bo [of Lu state, who was married to the Duke of Gong of Song state], in order to follow the way of womanhood stayed in the flames [when a fire broke out in her mansion]. Gao Xing, [a widow of Liang state,] mutilated her [beautiful] appearance [by cutting her nose off]. Gentlemen consider that these people were brave and died for righteousness; I have heard no one slander their self-mutilation or suicides. Compared to the actions taken by these four people, *śramaṇa*s' shaving their beards and hair is not far removed from them."

A person asked, "There is no happiness beyond having posterity, and there is no impiety greater than having no posterity. *Śramaṇa*s abandon their wives and children and give up wealth, or they never marry for their entire lives. Why do they carry out [such a] practice against happiness and filial piety? They themselves suffer and yet they have nothing wonderful. They exhaust themselves and yet they have nothing marvelous."

Mouzi replied, "One who is strong on the left must be weak on the right. One who formerly had the extensive must later have the narrow. [Confucius says,] 'Meng Gongchuo is excellent as a chief retainer of [the powerful families such as] the Zhao or Wei [of Jin], but he is unfit to be a high official of [a small state such as] Teng or Xue.'[20] Wives, children, and belongings are extra in secular life. Purity and *wuwei* are the wonders of the Way. Laozi said, 'Fame or body, which do you hold more dear? Body or wealth, which do you think more valuable?'"[21]

Again [Mouzi] said, "One may observe customs handed down from the three preceding dynasties (i.e., Xia, Yin, and Zhou), read the arts of the ways of Confucians and Mohists, recite the *Book of Odes* and the *Book of History,* cultivate etiquette, respect benevolence and righteousness, and consider cleanliness [to be important]. The people of the world will hand down [this person's] virtuous works to the next generation and he will brim over with fame.

"Such [acts] are what mediocre people perform, and what people of peace and non-worldly desire do not seek. Therefore, if in front of you there is a pearl like that of the Marquis of Sui[22] but there is a tiger behind you, even though you may see [the pearl] you will run away. Why do you dare not take the pearl? [It is because preserving] your life comes before profit.

"Xu You lived in the nest of a tree. [Bo]yi and [Shu]qi starved on [Mount] Shouyang. The sage Confucius praised their virtues and said, 'They are the ones who sought benevolence and attained it.'[23] I have never heard them ridiculed for not having posterity or property. *Śramaṇa*s cultivate morality instead of having worldly pleasures, and return to [the ways of] virtuous wise people, having given up the joys of having wives and children. If this is not wonderful, what can be wonderful? If this is not marvelous, what can be marvelous?"

A person asked, "The Yellow Emperor [sat] with his garments hanging down and established rules for clothing and ornaments.[24] The Viscount of Ji recited [to King Wu of Zhou] the *Great Model* (*Hongfan*), in which deportment is the most important of the five issues (i.e., deportment, language, looking, listening, and thinking).[25] Confucius authored the *Canon of Filial Piety*, in which [he considers that the regulation of] clothing is the beginning [of] the three virtues (i.e., the regulation of clothing, the regulation of manners, and virtuous acts). In addition, [Confucius] said, '[A gentleman] adjusts his clothes and cap, and imbues his appearance with dignity.'[26] Even though Yuan Xian was poor, he did not take off his cap made of birch bark. When Zilu encountered danger, he did not forget to tie the chin-straps of his cap. Today *śramaṇas* shave off their hair and wear undyed cloth. When they come across other people, they make no decorum of kneeling and standing up. They have no proper manners in their course of action. Why do they go against the code of deportment and clothing, and denigrate the adornments of the official class?"

Mouzi replied, "Laozi said, 'Those who possess the highest degree of virtue do not consider that they are virtuous, and therefore they possess virtue. Those who possess the lowest degree of virtue [seek] how not to lose it, and therefore they do not [actually] possess virtue.'[27] During the times of the
3b Three Augusts, the people ate [raw] meat, wore animal-skin clothing, and lived in nests in trees or caves. They valued the simple and unadorned life. Why would they need *zhangfu* caps or furs woven with adornments?[28] [Without those things,] the people of that time are said to have been virtuous, honest, trustworthy, and [possessing] *wuwei*. The conduct of *śramaṇas* is similar to theirs."

A person said, "If things were just as you say, such people as the Yellow Emperor, Emperor Yao and Emperor Shun, the Duke of Zhou, and Confucius would be rejected; they would not be worthy of being emulated."

Mouzi replied, "If you see things extensively, you will not be confused. If you have a good faculty of hearing, you will not be deluded. Emperor Yao and Emperor Shun, the Duke of Zhou, and Confucius cultivated worldly affairs, while the Buddha and Laozi pursued *wuwei*. Confucius traveled to more than seventy states. Xu You heard that there was to be an abdication of the throne [for his sake], and he then washed his ears in a gulf [because he thought the abdication was so foul that it polluted his ears]. The way to be a gentleman is sometimes to go out [for official service] and sometimes to remain in seclusion, or to sometimes remain silent and to sometimes speak out. He does not let his emotions overflow and he does not give full sway to his nature. Therefore, the reason why the way [of a gentleman] is noble lies in the purpose for which it is employed. What reason is there in rejecting them (i.e., the sages)?"

An inquirer said, "In the Way of the Buddha, it is said: 'People die and then must be reborn.' I do not believe this is true."

Mouzi asked, "When a man is about to breathe his last, a family member goes up to the roof and calls his name. He has died. What then is [his family] trying to call back?"

A person replied, "[That person] tries to call the spirit of the dead (*hunpo*) back [to rejoin the body]."

Mouzi asked, "If the spirit (*gui*) returns, he revives, [but] if it does not return, what is the spirit then called?"

[A person] replied, "It becomes a spiritual being (*guishen*)."

Mouzi said, "That is correct! Without doubt, the spirit (*hunshen*) does not perish. Only the physical body decays and becomes rotten. The body is just like the roots and leaves of the five major grains, and the spirit is compared to the seeds and kernels of the grains. The roots and leaves come into existence and then inevitably die. How could the seeds and kernels have a termination? [People] attain the Way and only their bodies perish. Laozi said, 'The reason we have great calamity is because we have a body. If we did not have a body, what calamity would we have?'[29] He also said, 'When the work is done, retiring into obscurity is the Way of Heaven.'"[30]

Someone said, "Those who practice the Way die and those who do not practice the Way also die. What difference is there [between the two]?"

Mouzi replied, "[Your question is], so to speak, to ask for a lifetime honor without performing good conduct for even one day. If one attains the Way, even if he dies, his spirit returns to Heaven. If he has committed evil conduct, after death his spirit inevitably receives retribution. Ignorant people are in darkness about the established facts, while intelligent people foresee things that have not yet germinated. Comparison between practicing the Way and not practicing the Way is just like that between gold and grass. Having wholesomeness and being given happiness are [as clear as] the comparison between white and black. How could there not be a difference? Nevertheless, you ask what is the difference [between the two]."

A person asked, "Confucius said, 'While you are not able to serve human beings, how can you serve the spirits? While you do not know life, how can you know about death?'[31] The sage declined to answer this [question on spiritual beings and life and death]. Now Buddhists always speak of matters of life and death, as well as of the affairs of spiritual beings. I am wondering if this goes against the words of sages and saints. Those who follow the Way ought to make the mind absolutely vacant and simple, and return to the principle of simplicity. Why, then, do [Buddhists] disturb our will by talking about life and death? Why do they speak unnecessary words about spiritual beings?"

Mouzi replied, "It appears that your words are, so to speak, like those
who observe the outside and yet are not aware of the inside. Confucius
deplored the fact that Zilu did not consider the whole issue from beginning
3c to end. [Therefore,] he merely restrained [Zilu] with those words. The *Canon
of Filial Piety* says, 'Build the ancestral shrine [for one's departed parents].
Present offerings to them in the same way as you would worship spiritual
beings. Offer sacrifices in the spring and autumn, thinking of them.' It continues, 'Devote yourself to loving and respecting them while they are alive.
Devote yourself to mourning after their death.'[32] Did [the sage] not teach
people to serve the spiritual beings and to know about life and death?

"The Duke of Zhou begged [spiritual beings] for Emperor Wu's life and said, 'I, Dan, am versatile and able to serve spiritual beings.'[33] What does this mean? Isn't the tenor of life and death stated in the Buddhist scriptures of this kind? Laozi said, 'If one who knows the child (i.e., the phenomenal world) proceeds to guard the child's mother (i.e., to preserve the One), he will be free from all peril to the end of his life.'[34] [Laozi] also said, 'If he who employs the light reverts to its [source of] brightness, no disaster will befall him.'[35] These statements are about the tenor of life and death and the positions of good or bad fortune. The essence of the highest Way is to truly esteem solitude. Why would Buddhists be fond of debate [about life and death]? It is only that they cannot ignore it when someone comes to ask questions. Can there be a bell or a drum that makes a sound by itself? They only produce sounds when struck."

A person asked, "Confucius said: 'The barbarians of the east and north have their rulers, but they are still not as good as the states without rulers in our great land.'[36] Mencius ridiculed Chen Xiang, who was learning more of Xu Xing's teaching, saying, 'I have heard of people using [teachings of] our great land to change the barbarians' [customs], but I have never heard that our customs were changed by the barbarians' teachings.'[37] You learned the way of Emperor Yao and Emperor Shun, the Duke of Zhou, and Confucius at an early age, but you abandoned it and are learning more about the barbarians' teaching. Are you continuously deluded?"

Mouzi replied, "[Words like] this sound only like the idle talk of the time when I did not yet understand the Great Way. It may be said that you see the elegance of ceremonial forms and yet lack knowledge about the truth of morality, or that you catch a glimpse of the light of a torch or candle but you have not yet seen the sun in the sky. What Confucius spoke of are the ways to correct social customs or practices. Why Mencius spoke thus is merely that he deplored [that Chen Xiang] concentrated his attention on [Xu Xing's teaching]. Formerly wishing to live in the region of the nine barbarian tribes of the east, Confucius said, 'If a gentleman dwelled among them, what vileness would there be?'[38] When Confucius could not find an official position in the states of Lu and Wei, and when Mencius was not employed in the states of Qi and Liang, how could they have taken service in the states of the barbarian tribes of the east and north?

"[The legendary ruler] Yu is from Qiang, the barbarian tribe in west China, and yet he was a sage. Gusou is the father of [the sage king] Shun and yet he was foolish. You Yu was born in [the barbarian state of] Di [to the north of our great land], and yet [he helped] Qin establish hegemony. Guan[shu Xian] and Cai[shu Du] (i.e., the Duke of Zhou's brothers) came from the basin between the Yellow River and the Luo River, but they spread a false rumor [to cause trouble for the Duke of Zhou]

"A commentary says, 'The polestar is located in the middle of the sky, in the north above us.' Seen from this point of view, the land of Han (i.e., China) is not necessarily the center of the universe. According to what the Buddhist scriptures state, all sentient beings of the entire universe belong to the Buddha. Therefore, I heartily esteem Buddhism and study it. What reason do I have to abandon the way of Emperor Yao and Emperor Shun, the Duke of Zhou, and Confucius? Gold and pearl never impair each other. The Marquis of Sui's pearl and emerald never hindered each other. You say that other people are deluded, yet it is you yourself who is deluded!"

A person asked, "It cannot be said to be charitable to give away one's father's property to a stranger. It cannot be said to be benevolent to sacrifice oneself for others while one's parents are still alive. Nowadays a Buddhist scripture states that Prince Sudāna gave his father's property to complete

strangers, granted a precious elephant belonging to the state to its enemies,
4a and [gave away] his own wives and children to others.[39] It is said to be uncivil to not respect one's own parents and yet to respect others. It is said to be immoral to not love one's own parents and yet to love others.[40] Prince Sudāna was neither filial nor kind, but Buddhists respect him. Isn't this peculiar?"

Mouzi replied, "In the doctrine of the Five Classics, the first son [from the legal wife] is designated as heir. Yet the Great King [of the Zhou dynasty] saw [his grandson] Chang's ambition. [So] he moved his youngest son [Jili, who was Chang's father, up in the succession] to become his heir. Consequently, the enterprise of the Zhou dynasty was achieved, and by means of this a peaceful world was realized. In the custom of marrying a woman, a man must inform his parents [to obtain their approval]. [Nevertheless,] Emperor Shun married [two daughters of Emperor Yao] without telling [his parents]. By this means, he achieved the important relation of husband and wife. People of integrity must be invited for service and talented vassals wait to be drafted for public services. Yi Yin, [however,] carried a heavy three-legged caldron on his back and besought King Tang [of the Yin dynasty for an official position]. Ning Qi knocked on [his ox's] horns to beseech [Lord Huan of] Qi [to grant him an official position]. With [the help of Yi Yin,] King Tang won the throne, and with [the help of Ning Qi,] Qi state attained hegemony.

"According to etiquette, a man and a woman should not put their hands on each other, [but] if the wife of one's elder brother is drowning, it is an expedient way in [such an] emergency to put one's hands on her [in order to pull her out of the water]. If we can comprehend the greatness of things, then we should no longer pay attention to minor details. Why should a great person comprehend ordinary matters? Prince Sudāna saw that the world is impermanent, and money and property were not real treasures for him. Therefore, he donated at his will, and by doing so he achieved the Great Way. His father's kingdom received the blessings, and enemies were unable to invade [his father's kingdom]. When [Prince Sudāna] attained buddhahood, his parents and brothers were all able to attain liberation as well. If this is not a filial and benevolent [act], then what is benevolent and filial?"

A person asked, "In Buddhism, *wuwei* is of value, giving alms is pleasurable, and observing the precepts requires as much caution and attention as if one were approaching an abyss. Today, *śramaṇas* give themselves up to wine. Some have wives and children, or purchase [goods] at a low price and sell [them] at a high price [for profit]. They devote themselves to such swindles. This is a great hypocrisy in the world.[41] Is this what is called *wuwei* in Buddhism?"

Mouzi replied, "Gongshu [Ban, a master carpenter in Lu state during the Spring and Autumn period,] was able to give people a hatchet, an ax, and an ink line [with which to do construction], but he was not able to make them as skillful as himself. Sages are able to impart their ways to others, but they cannot make others follow and perform them. Gao Yao was able to punish thieves, but he couldn't make greedy people become [as upright as] Boyi and Shuqi. The five penalties can punish villains, but they cannot regenerate such evil people to be [as virtuous as the disciples of Confucius,] Zeng Shen and Min Ziqian. Emperor Yao was not able to educate [his son] Dan Zhu, and the Duke of Zhou was unable to admonish [his brothers] Guan[shu Xian] and Cai[shu Du]. Wouldn't Tang's (i.e., Emperor Yao) teaching be clear? Wouldn't the Duke of Zhou be possessed of morality? [Yes, they were.] Nevertheless, there was no help for bad people.

"Figuratively speaking, if people who are well versed in the Seven Classics are smitten with money and women, can it be said that the six arts [that these people have mastered] are depraved and lustful? Hebo, even though he is the god [of the Yellow River], cannot drown people who stay on land. A violent wind, though it blows swiftly, cannot fling dust onto the surface of deep water. You must be worried about the fact that people are unable to practice. How can you say that Buddhism has vice?"

A person asked, "Confucius said, 'Luxury leads to haughtiness, and frugality to meanness. It is better to be mean than to be haughty.'[42] Shusun [Qiaoru] said, 'Frugality is respectful. Luxury is the worst among evil acts.'[43] Today Buddhists consider donating all one's property to be honorable and giving all one's money to others to be valuable. How can there be merit [in doing so]?"

Mouzi replied, "'That was one [critical] time, and this is another.'[44] This 4b
expression by Confucius [indicates that] he detested luxury and impoliteness, and Shusun's comment [is intended] to admonish the arrogance of Lord [Zhuang], who carved pillars. Neither case prohibits making donations. When

[Emperor] Shun tilled on Mount Li, his benevolence did not reach even the neighboring area. Taigong [Wang Lü Shang] butchered cows [to make a living],[45] but his kindness did not extend to his wife and children. After these two men were employed, their benevolence flowed all over the world and their kindness was bestowed upon the world. For those who have abundant property and plenty of money, it is valuable to give alms to others. For those who live in poverty and who are often poor, it is valuable to follow the Way.

"Xu You was not greedy to ascend the throne. Boyi was not contented to take the reins of the state. Yu Qing gave up a fief of tens of thousands of households, and gave relief to destitute people in a crisis. These are all [acts of] their goodwill. Xi Fuji [of Cao state took his wife's advice and] gave a pot of food to [Zhong'er, who defeated Cao], and his kindness helped keep his community intact (i.e., Zhong'er did not attack the community).[46] Xuan Meng (i.e., Zhao Dun) saved his most important life and body in return for a meal [he had given to Ling Zhe].[47] If you have done good in secret, without expecting return, you will receive a positive reward as bright as the sun. Needless to say, if you sink in fortune in order to give rise to good intentions, your merit and virtue are as lofty as Mount Song or Mount Tai, and as vast as a great river or the ocean. Those who embrace a compassionate heart are rewarded with happiness, and those who harbor evil receive misfortune as retribution. It has never happened that those who have planted rice will harvest wheat, or that those who have caused disaster will obtain happiness."

A person said, "Among qualities, nothing surpasses sincerity; in speech, nothing goes beyond truth. Laozi eschewed artful expressions and showed respect for simple words. Buddhist scriptures, [however,] do not directly indicate the matter and yet extensively take allegories in vain. Allegory is not the essence of reason. It is a combination of different matters in order to express one thing, which is not an excellent explanation. Even though [Buddhist scriptures] have numerous expressions and extensive words, they are similar to a cart full of fragments of jade pieces, which are not considered to be treasure."

Mouzi responded, "Things that both [a speaker and a listener] have seen can be explained with the real thing, but things that only a speaker has seen are difficult to explain in exact words. Formerly a person who had not seen a *kylin* asked someone who had seen one, 'What kind [of animal] is a *kylin*?'

The one who had seen it answered, 'A *kylin* is just like a *kylin.*' The questioner said, 'If I had seen a *kylin,* then I would not have asked you the question. Nevertheless, you said only that a *kylin* is just like a *kylin.* How can I understand this?' The one who had seen a *kylin* said, 'The *kylin* has a body like a roe deer, a tail like a cow, hooves like a deer, and a back like a horse.' The questioner understood right away.

"Confucius asked, 'Is one not like a gentleman when he does not feel depressed even though people do not know of him?'[48] Laozi said, 'Can the space between Heaven and Earth not be compared to a bellows?'[49] Moreover, he said, 'How the Way is in the world is compared to waterways between mountains that flow into large rivers and oceans.'[50] Would these be considered artful expressions? The *Analects* (*Lunyu*) of Confucius states, 'He who takes the reins of government by means of virtue can be compared to the north polestar.'[51] Here, a celestial body is referred to and compared to a human being. Zixia said, 'It is just as all plants have differences [in their growth].'[52] The three hundred chapters in the *Book of Odes* [were compiled], collecting events and arranging them into each category. In writings by the thinkers of the numerous schools [in the late Zhou dynasty] and books about the occult, up to books classified for sages, there is none that does not employ allegories or use parables. Do you maliciously say that when he expands the teaching, the Buddha alone uses allegories and parables?"

A person asked, "There is no one among the people who, while conducting 4c
themselves in life, does not like wealth and high position, does not hate poverty, is not pleased by joy and leisure, or does not avoid troubles. The Yellow Emperor considered the five kinds of meat (i.e., beef, lamb, pork, fish, and venison) to be the best to keep us in good health. Confucius said, 'He does not detest finely cleaned rice and finely minced meat.'[53] Nowadays *śramaṇa*s put on red robes, have only one meal a day, and shut off their six sense organs throughout their lifetimes. If they are like this, what fun do they have?"

Mouzi replied, "[Confucius said,] 'Wealth and high position are what people desire, but if a gentleman does not obtain them in the proper way, he would not place himself there. Poverty and meanness are what people detest, but if a gentleman cannot avoid them in the proper way, he would not abandon them.'[54] Laozi said, 'The five colors (i.e., blue, yellow, red, white, and black) cause people to become blind. The five notes [of traditional Chinese music] (i.e., *gong, shang, jue, zhi,* and *yu*) cause people to become deaf. The five flavors (i.e., sweet, sour, bitter, pungent, and salty) cause people's tastebuds to be paralyzed. Going at full speed in the wild while hunting makes people crazy. Rare goods distract people from having [proper] conduct. [As a result,] sages take care of their bellies and not their eyes.'[55] How could these words be false? Hui of Liuxia [of Lu state] did not change the way he acted even after he was offered a position as one of the three highest-ranking officials.[56] Mu of Duangan did not barter his body for the wealth offered by Lord Wen of Wei state.[57] Xu You and Chaofu lived high up in a tree, which they said was more peaceful than the imperial palace. Boyi and Shuqi starved on Mount Shouyang, but they said they were more satisfied than King Wen and King Wu. Probably they were satisfied just with their resolutions. Why [do you say that *śramaṇa*s] have no fun?"

A person asked, "If Buddhist scriptures are profound and extravagant, why do you neither talk about them at court nor discuss them with your superior and father? You cultivate only at home and relay [the teaching] to your friends. Why do you also study the Classics and commentaries and read various philosophers' works?"

Mouzi replied, "You have not yet reached the origin, and yet you ask about the streams [that emanate from the source]. I do not mean that it is not magnificent to set out a sacrificial stand and pot at a camp gate, to hoist military flags and banners in a palace hall, to cope with [the heat of] the fifth month by wearing a fox-fur robe, or to ward off [the coldness of] the eleventh month by putting on a hemp garment. These actions are perverse in their orientation of time and place.[58] Therefore, if you sustain the teaching of Confucius and become a disciple of [the Legalist Gongsun] Yang, the lord of Shang, or if you have the theory of Mencius [who advocated the rule of right] in your mind yet call on Su Qin or Zhang Yi [who advocated the rule of might], you will have no accomplishment at all but you will have made a big mistake.

"Laozi said, 'When scholars of the highest class hear about the Way, they diligently practice it. Scholars of the middle class, when they hear about the Way, keep only half in their mind. Scholars of the lowest class, when they hear about the Way, have a great laugh at it.'[59] Since I am afraid that [scholars of the lowest class] will burst into laughter, I will not talk [about Buddhism]. When one is thirsty, he does not necessarily drink the water of a large river. But how can he be dissatisfied with the water of wells and fountains? For this reason, I study the Classics and commentaries as well.”

A person asked, “What is the history of the land of Han (i.e., China) hearing about Buddhism for the first time?”

Mouzi replied, “Many years ago, Emperor Xiaoming (r. 57–75) saw in a dream a holy man who had sunlight on his body and who flew in front of the palace. [The emperor] was greatly delighted with this. Next day, he asked of the entire body of ministers, ‘What god is this?’ Fu Yi, a well-read, greatly experienced person, answered, ‘I have heard that in India there was a man who had attained the Way. He is called the Buddha. He could fly in the air and had sunlight on his body. I am worried that [you saw] that god.’ Then 5a
the emperor came to realize this and dispatched [to the west] eighteen people, including the Inner Gentleman Cai Yin, the Gentleman of the Palace Guard Qin Jing, and the Disciple of the Erudite Wang Zun. They copied the Buddhist scripture [called] the *Sutra of Forty-two Chapters* (*Sishierzhang*), in [the country of] Dayuezhi [in Central Asia]. The sutra was deposited in the fourteenth cubicle of the Lantai stone chambers [in Luoyang]. Then, outside the Yong gate to the west of Luoyang a Buddhist temple was built. On the walls [of the temple] was painted an illustration of a large military group of mounted soldiers circumambulating a pagoda thrice clockwise. Furthermore, buddha images were made and placed on the Qingliang Tower of the southern palace and on the Kaiyang Gate of the city wall. During his reign, Emperor Ming had his mausoleum called Xianjie (“Prominence and Uprightness”) constructed in advance. Illustrations and images of the Buddha were made and placed on it as well. At that time, the nation was rich, the people enjoyed peace, and barbarians in distant regions admired our morality. Hence, the number of those who studied Buddhism increased.”[59]

A man asked, “Laozi said, ‘Those who know do not speak, while those who speak do not know.’[60] He also said, ‘He who is greatly eloquent speaks with a stammer, and he who is greatly skillful looks clumsy.’[61] [Just as Confucius said,] ‘A gentleman is ashamed that his words are greater than his conduct.’[62] Supposing that *śramaṇa*s have attained the highest Way, why do they not practice it instead of sitting [and doing nothing]? Why do they talk about right and wrong and take up right and wrong for discussion? I think that these [*śramaṇa*s] commit the theft of virtue.”

Mouzi replied, "Suppose you are afraid that next spring there will be a serious famine, so you do not eat in the autumn [in order to save food]. Or, fearful that it will be cold in the eleventh month, you wear two fur robes, one over the other, in the fifth month. Although these actions are taken in order to be fully prepared beforehand, it is unavoidable that you look stupid. Laozi's maxim refers only to those who have attained the Way. What do those who have not attained the Way know? When the Great Way is explained in one word, the whole world is joyful. Isn't this great eloquence? Didn't Laozi say that 'When the work is done, to retire into obscurity is the Way of Heaven'?[63] When a person has already retired into obscurity, what more does he have to say? *Śramaṇa*s of today have not yet attained the Way. How can they help but to speak? Even Laozi, [who said 'those who know do not speak,'] still made speeches. If he remained silent, [as he taught,] how could he give the account of the *Five Thousand Words* (i.e., the *Daodejing*)?

"It is all right if one knows [the Way] and does not speak it. But if one is unable to know [the Way] and furthermore unable to speak it, he is just stupid! Consequently, he who is able to speak [the Way] but unable to carry it out is the teacher of the nation. He who is able to carry out [the Way] but unable to speak it is the force of the nation. He who is able to carry out [the Way] and also speak it is the treasure of the nation. Each of these three types of people has an applicable point. How then could they commit the theft of virtue? Only those who are unable to speak and also unable to carry out [the Way] can be said to commit the theft [of virtue]."

A person asked, "If things are just as you say, we should only have to learn how to progress in our debates and study speeches and discussions. Why do we have to regulate our minds and follow morality as well?"

Mouzi replied, "How slow to understand you are! Spoken language and discussion have their own proper and adequate times. It is said about Qu Yuan [in the *Analects* of Confucius], 'When the Way prevails in the world, he is straightforward. When the Way does not prevail in the world, he can roll up [his principles] and keep them close to his heart.'[64] About Ning Wuzi, it is said [in the *Analects*], 'When the Way prevailed in the world, he displayed his intelligence. When the Way did not prevail in the world, he behaved like a stupid person.'[65] Confucius said, 'Not to talk to one with whom you may talk is to waste a person [of talent]. To talk to one with whom you may not talk is to waste your words.'[66] Therefore, to be intelligent or to behave like a stupid person both have their proper times. [Based on time and place,] speech and discussion serve several purposes. Why [do you say that] we [only have to learn how to progress in] debates and discussion without carrying out [the Way]?" 5b

A person asked, "Why do you say that Buddhism is the most esteemed and the happiest teaching of *wuwei* and freedom from avarice? Many people and scholars in the world slander [Buddhism], saying that 'Its words and theory are vague, difficult to take up [for practice], and [the notion of] absolute emptiness is hard to believe.' Why [do they say this]?"

Mouzi replied, "The most delicious food does not satisfy every palate. Great music is not familiar to every ear. Even if [the noble music] *Xianchi* [composed by the Yellow Emperor] is played, [the refined music] *Dazhang* [composed by Emperor Yao] is set forth, [the lofty music] *Xiaoshao* [composed by Emperor Shun] is set out, and the music is sung nine times, no one joins in the chorus. [On the contrary,] if music from a stringed instrument of [the ruined states] Zheng and Wei is played, or if current popular songs are sung, [many people] unexpectedly clap their hands on the beat without fail. Therefore, Song Yu, [replying to King Xiang of Chu state,] said, 'A visitor sang in Ying, [the capital city of Chu]. When he performed simple and crude folk songs, those who joined in the chorus numbered a thousand people. When he played [highbrow music], making the [refined] note *shang* and stringing up to the clear note *jue,* no one in the audience responded.'[67] This indicates that all the people were pleased with vulgar music and did not understand well-cultivated [music].

"Han Fei criticized Emperor Yao and Emperor Shun from a narrow viewpoint, as if looking at [the sky] through a tube. Jie Yu reproached Confucius with a view as small as a [strand of] hair.[68] They all stand pat in their inferior [views] and disregard great [views]. To hear the clear note *shang* and say that it is the note *jue* is not the fault of the player but due to the listener's poor faculty [of listening]. To see [Bian] He's jade and call it a stone is not because the jade is ignoble but due to the beholder's lack of knowledge.[69] A snake with supernatural powers can regenerate its body into one even if it is cut into many pieces, but [the snake] cannot cause people not to cut it apart. A turtle with mysterious powers appeared to Lord Yuan of Song state in a dream, but [the turtle] could not evade the net of [the fisherman] Yu Qie.[70] The Great Way is *wuwei,* which is neither what ordinary people understand, nor what may increase its value by praise, nor what may lose its value by slander. Whether or not it is employed is up to Heaven. Whether or not it is practiced is up to the turn of time. Whether or not it is believed is up to fate."

A person asked, "You interpret the Buddha's teaching with the Classics and their commentaries. Your expressions are rich, and the meanings are clear. Your compositions are energetic and the explanations are beautiful. Isn't this due to your rhetorical skill rather than being the truth?"

Mouzi replied, "No, it is not. Since I have a broad view of things, I am simply not deluded."

A person asked, "How did you come to have a broad view of things?"

Mouzi replied, "Through the Buddhist scriptures. When I did not understand Buddhist scriptures, I was more deluded than you are. Even though I recited the Five Classics, I just considered them to be flowery and had not come to realize their truth. Now I see the doctrines of the Buddhist scriptures, read the essentials of the *Laozi* [*Daodejing*], abide by the nature of tranquility without worldly desires, and contemplate the practice of *wuwei.* When I come back to view the affairs of the world, I feel as if I am stealing a glance at a gorge from high above the earth,[71] or as if I am ascending Mount Song and Mount Dai to look over the small foothills. The Five Classics are just like the five flavors and Buddhism is just like the five grains (i.e., staple foods). Since I heard the Way, I have been in a condition that is just like clouds opening up to reveal the sun, or entering into a dark room holding a torch."

A person asked, "You said that [the Buddhist] scriptures are [as deep as] great rivers and seas, and the words are [as beautiful as] brocade and embroidery. Why do you respond to my questions referring to [the Classics such as] the *Book of Odes* and the *Book of History* instead of using Buddhist
5c scriptures? Do you intend to combine different categories in one?"

Mouzi replied, "A thirsty man does not need [the water of] a large river or the sea to quench his thirst. A hungry man does not need the granary of Mount Ao to fill his stomach. The Way is established for the wise. Debate is well constructed for knowledgeable people. Books are transmitted for those who understand them. Things are clarified for people of insight. I refer to phrases [of the Classics] since I think that you know the meanings. If I speak with the words of Buddhist scriptures and discuss the essentials of *wuwei,* it would be like explaining the five colors to the blind, or playing the five notes [of traditional Chinese music] for the deaf. Even though [music] master Kuang [of Jin state] was artful, he could not strum a Chinese zither that had no string. Although fox and badger furs are warm, they cannot warm the dead.

"Gongming Yi [of Lu state] played the musical piece *Cao* in the note *qingjue* for a cow, but the cow just bent her head down and ate [grass] as before. This does not mean that she did not listen to [the music], but [the music] did not meet her ears. On the other hand, if there were the buzz of a mosquito or gadfly or the lowing of an orphaned calf, she would promptly swish her tail, strain her ears, and stamp on the ground, listening to it. This is why I only respond to your questions referring to the Classics."

A person asked, "Once when I was in the capital, I entered Dongguan Library and studied at Taixue National University, where I saw what talented scholars regulated and I listened to what the circle of Confucian scholars discussed. However, I never heard that to cultivate Buddhism is considered valuable and that to damage one's appearance by oneself is considered superior. Why do you indulge in [Buddhism]? When you get lost, alter the route! When you exhaust all methods, return to the old [method]! Don't you think so?"

Mouzi replied, "One who excels in dealing with extraordinary matters cannot be deceived. One who is versed in the Way cannot be surprised by strange things. One who discerns tones in words cannot be deluded by words. One who understands righteousness cannot be swayed by profit. Laozi said, 'Fame harms oneself. Advantages debauch one's behavior.'[72] He also said, 'If deception is set up and power is established, the absolute vacancy spontaneously becomes valuable.'[73] To cultivate the art of the inner chamber, to go with the current of the times, and to strive to tune oneself to the present time, taking advantage of unguarded moments, are actions taken by scholars of the lowest class and rejected even by scholars of the middle class.

"It is needless to speak of the highest Way, which is vast and what sages of the highest class practice. [The highest Way] is as expansive as the sky and as deep as the sea. It is not suitable for people who peep over a wall or for those who consider a several *ren*-high wall to be tall. This is proper, as a matter of course. [These people] see the gate (i.e., outer factors), while I see the room (i.e., inner factors). They pluck the flowers (i.e., worldly glory), while I take the fruit (i.e., truth). They seek perfection, while I preserve the One. You should change course immediately! I ask you to follow [Buddhism]. You have not been aware of what the causes of fortune and misfortune are like."

A person asked, "With the words of the Classics and their commentaries and the splendid doctrines, you praise the Buddha's conduct and extol his virtue, which [you say] is lofty, as it rides the high clear clouds, and is wide, as it goes beyond the end of the earth. Can it be that [your praises] exceed the essential qualities and surpass the reality [of the Buddha]? Accordingly, my taunt considerably touches Buddhism on its disadvantage and hits the vitals."

Mouzi replied, "Alas! My praises [for the Buddha's virtue] are just like adding a speck of dust to Mount Song and Mount Tai, or collecting the morning dew and throwing it into a large river or the sea. Your slanderous words [against Buddhism] are like using a ladle and goblet to attempt to reduce [the volume of water in] a large river or the sea, or plowing by foot to attempt to lower Mount Kunlun, or raising a hand to block the sunlight, or lifting a lump of earth to block the flow of the Yellow River. My praises cannot make the Buddha loftier and your slander cannot bring him low."

A person asked, "Is the issue of longevity stated in the talisman registers of Wang Qiao, Chisongzi, and the eight immortals, and in the one hundred and seventy fascicles of [Gan Ji's] *Divine Book* (*Shenshu*), the same as that
6a in the Buddhist scriptures?"

Mouzi replied, "A comparison [between these texts of the immortals and the Buddhist scriptures] in category is just like comparing the five powers (i.e., the five states of Qi, Song, Jin, Qin, and Chu in the late Zhou dynasty) with the Five Thearchs [who ruled in accordance with virtue], or comparing Yang Huo, [who looked like Confucius,] with Confucius himself. A comparison [between them] in shape is just like comparing foothills with Mount Hua and Mount Heng, or small creeks and ditches with large rivers and seas. A comparison [between them] in elegance is just like comparing a tiger hide with a sheepskin, or mottled hemp with brilliant and beautiful embroidery. There are ninety-six different teachings, but the most esteemed among them is none other than Buddhism. The texts of the immortals, when we listen to their words, sound great and fill our ears, but when we seek their efficacy, it is like grasping at wind or trying to catch a shadow. Hence, [the texts of the immortals] are not upheld in the Great Way and are not valued in *wuwei*. How could they be the same?"

A person asked, "Some among the practitioners of the Way [of the Immortals] avoid grain and do not eat it, yet they drink wine and eat meat. They say also that this is the way of Laozi. In Buddhism, however, to drink wine and eat meat are the heaviest violations to the precepts, and yet [Buddhists] do eat grain. Why do they contradict each other?"

Mouzi replied, "There are extant about ninety-six various teachings in total. So far as having no worldly attachment and *wuwei* are concerned, nothing is more esteemed than Buddhism. I have inspected the two volumes of the *Laozi* [*Daodejing*] and have learned that this scripture prohibits the five flavors, but I have never seen any word to proscribe against the five major grains. The sage (i.e., Confucius) formulated the writings of the seven canons in which there is no mention of a prohibition against eating grain. Laozi wrote the *Five Thousand Words* (i.e., the *Daodejing*) and yet the issue of abstaining from grains is not indicated. The sage (i.e., Confucius) said, 'Those who eat grain are intelligent. Those who eat grass are silly. Those who eat meat are violent. Those who eat vapor have a long life.'[74] The people of the world do not understand this matter; they see that the six kinds of birds stop breathing and do not eat in the autumn and winter seasons, and then they try to imitate them. They do not know that each thing or being has its own true nature. It is just as a magnet attracts [a heavy piece of] iron and yet it cannot pull a [light strand of] hair."

A person asked, "Should we rather stop eating grain or not?"

Mouzi replied, "Before I understood the Great Way, I once learned [the way of abstaining from grain] too. There are several thousand and several hundred methods to abstain from grain. When I practiced them, they were not effective at all; when I performed them, there were no [good] signs at all. Therefore, I just gave up [these methods]. I observed the three teachers with whom I studied. They described themselves to be seven hundred, five hundred, and three hundred years old [respectively], but in less than three years after I had begun to study with them, they all died. The cause of their deaths is probably that they abstained from grain, did not eat it, and [instead] ate various fruits; they went back for second and third servings when they enjoyed meat; they had an entire barrel of wine when they drank; their spirits

were muddled and delirious; the energy of grain did not fill [their bodies]; and their ears and eyes were deluded and were not debarred from lewdness and evil. When I asked them why they did this, they replied, 'Laozi said that
6b he reduces and again reduces till he comes up to *wuwei.*[75] We need only to reduce day by day.' As far as I observed them, however, they just increased [their self-interest] day by day and did not reduce [anything at all]. Thereupon, they all died before reaching the age at which one may know the decrees of Heaven (i.e., fifty years old).[76] Even Emperor Yao, Emperor Shun, the Duke of Zhou, and Confucius were all unable to live to a hundred years of age. Nevertheless, foolish and deluded people of these latter days want to seek inexhaustible longevity by [the alimentotherapy of] ingesting drugs and the avoidance of grain. How sad!"

A person asked, "Those who practice the Way [of the Immortals] say that they can prevent disease and do not get sick, or that they can recover from illness without acupuncture and medicine. Is this true? Why do Buddhists recommend acupuncture and medicine when someone becomes ill?"

Mouzi replied, "Laozi said, 'When things reach their prime, they begin aging. This may be said to be the deviation from the Way. Anything that deviates from the Way soon comes to an end.'[77] Only those who have attained the [Buddhist] Way will not be reborn. Since they are not reborn, they will not be in the prime, either. Since they are not in the prime, they will not age, either. Since they do not age, they will not become ill. Since they do not become ill, they will not decay. For this reason, Laozi considered having a body to be a great calamity.[78] When King Wu was ill, the Duke of Zhou begged for [King Wu's] life,[79] and when Confucius was ill, Zilu asked leave to pray for [Confucius].[80] I see that all the sages became ill, but I have never seen that they did not fall into illness. Shen Nong tasted [the flavors of the various] grasses and he was about to die several tens of times.[81] The Yellow Emperor bowed with his head to the ground and received acupuncture from Qi Bo. How could these three sages be inferior to Daoist practitioners of the present time? When I examine [these points], your words are also worthy of rejection."

A person asked, "All teachings are the same in [regard to learning] *wuwei*. Why do you distinguish them from each other, arrange them, and indicate their differences? Furthermore, you cause those who learn the teaching to be suspicious. I am afraid that this is wasteful and futile."

Mouzi replied, "Although we call all of them 'grass,' the natures of various grasses cannot be distinctively explained. We call them all 'metal,' but the natures of various kinds of metals cannot be distinctively explained. Even in the same category, there are differences in their natures. All things are just so. Why would this not be so only in regard to teachings? In bygone days Yang [Zhu] and Mo [Di] blocked the path of a group of Confucianists. Their carts could not advance, and people could not make progress. It was not until Mencius opened up [the path] that the people came to know what to follow.[82] [Music] master Kuang played his Chinese zither, waiting for someone who could understand his tune to appear in later ages.[83] Sages formulated the model decorum, hoping that gentlemen would see it in the future.

"Seeing that a jade and a stone were put in the same chest, Yi Dun turned pale.[84] Seeing that purple overpowered vermilion when the two colors mixed, Confucius sighed in lamentation.[85] [The light of] the sun and moon is not unclear, yet numerous clouds obscure it. Buddhism is not incorrect, but numerous private teachings obscure its justice. Thereupon, I distinguish and differentiate [Buddhism from other teachings]. The intelligence of Zang Wen [Zhong] and the uprightness of Weisheng [Gao] were what Confucius was very stern about.[86] All of his words were [spoken in order] to correct [the vices of] the world. Why is it wasteful and futile [to distinguish teachings from each other]?"

A person asked, "It is all right if you slander the immortals, repress unusual things, and do not believe that there is a way to immortality. Why do you believe that it is only Buddhism by which one should attain liberation? The Buddha lived in a foreign land. You have not set foot on that soil, and have not yet seen the place. You have only read the writings and trust in what [the Buddha] did. He who sees [only] a bright aspect is unable to know the 6c
reality. He who sees a shadow is unable to discern the form. [What you believe] is almost untrue."

Mouzi replied, "Confucius said, 'See what a man does, observe what he has done, and examine with what he is content. How could he conceal his character?'[87] Formerly, [Taigong] Wang Lü [Shang] and the Duke of

Zhou asked each other about their administrations, and each knew how [the states of Qi and Lu] would end up.[88] Yan Yuan, on the day when he rode on a carriage drawn by a team of four horses, observed Dongye Bi's way of handling the horses and he knew [that the horses] would break down.[89] Zigong witnessed the meeting of [Prince Yin of] Zhu state and [Prince Ding of] Lu state, and intuited the reasons for their death [based on their behavior].[90] Confucius heard the notes of strings played by [music] master Kuang and recognized that it was King Wen's musical composition.[91] Jizha [of Wu] listened to music and saw the customs of various countries.[92] Why is it necessary to set foot on [that soil] and see [that place]?"

A person asked, "I once traveled in Khotan country where I often met *śramaṇa*s and Buddhist followers, whom I reproved, referring to my [Confucian] doctrines. None could respond to me and they all backed down. Many of them corrected their resolution and changed their intention. Why do you alone have difficulty reforming yourself?"

Mouzi replied, "When light feathers meet with wind high above, they are blown away. When fine stones get into the flow of water from a mountain stream, they are carried down[stream]. Mount Tai alone remains unmoved in a whirlwind. Massive rocks are not swept away even by a rapid current. When plum trees are nipped by the frost, they become leafless, but pines and cypresses are hardly withered. The Buddhist followers you met were certainly not of broad experience and knowledge and did not have extensive insight. Consequently, they humbly backed down. You, [however,] are not going to vanquish even a stupid person such as myself, not to speak of those who are well versed in the [Buddhist] Way. You do not reform yourself and yet want to change others. I have never heard that Confucius followed the robber Zhi, or that King Tang [of the Yin dynasty] and King Wu [of the Zhou dynasty, who are known as sages,] modeled themselves after [the tyrants] King Jie [of the Xia dynasty] and King Zhou [of the Yin dynasty]."

A person said, "In the Way of the Divine Transcendents, one does not eat in autumn and winter, nor does he shut himself up in a room for dozens of days. This can be said to be the [condition of] the most content, free from avarice. I think that this should be considered respectful and valuable, and I am afraid that Buddhism is not as good as [the Way of Divine Transcendents]."

Mouzi said, "Pointing to the south when it is in fact the north, one says to himself that he is not confused. Considering west to be east, he says to himself that he is not stupid. Being a [humble] owl, he laughs at [a noble] phoenix. Holding [insignificant creatures such as] mole crickets and earthworms, one ridicules turtles and dragons. Cicadas do not eat, but gentlemen do not value them. Frogs and pythons hibernate, but sages do not attach importance to them. Confucius said, 'Of all [beings who have] life between Heaven and Earth, human beings are the noblest.'[93] I have never heard that he respected cicadas and pythons. Nevertheless, among the people of the world there are inherently those who eat sweet flag [grass] and discard cinnamon and ginger, and who decline to drink sweet dew but sip unrefined vinegar. The fine hair on the skin, although it is small, can be examined if you look at it [closely enough]. Mount Tai's loftiness cannot be seen if you turn your back on it. It is a matter of whether or not you pay attention to it, or whether or not you are careful. In Lu state the Ji family was respected and Confucius was vilified.[94] In Wu state, Great Steward Pi was considered to be capable and [Wu]zi Xu was not considered to be good.[95] So, [given these situations,] your questions [may be seen to be] reasonable."

A person asked, "The school of Daoism says, 'Emperor Yao and Emperor Shun, the Duke of Zhou, Confucius, and seventy-two of his disciples did not die and became immortals.' The school of Buddhism says, 'All people die 7a
and no one can avoid death.' Why?"

Mouzi replied, "These are absurd statements, not what the sages said. Laozi said, 'Even Heaven and Earth cannot last long. How much less can human beings?'[96] Confucius said, 'Furthermore, [the virtuous] withdraw from the world.[97] Those who are benevolent and filial permanently exist.' For as long as I have read books of the six arts and looked at biographies and records, Emperor Yao passed away; Emperor Shun was [buried] on the mountain of Cangwu; there is Emperor Yu's mausoleum at Guiji; Boyi and Shuqi have their tombs on Mount Shouyang; King Wen died before he could put King Zhou (the last emperor of the Yin dynasty) to death; King Wu could not wait for King Cheng to grow to adulthood but he passed away; there is a chapter [in the record] regarding the reburial of the Duke of Zhou; Confucius had a dream [in which he sat between] two pillars [receiving an offering];

there is a record for the age of Bo Yu, when he died before his father (i.e., Confucius); there is a record that Zilu's [body] was salted; there is the expression of [Confucius], 'It is fate!' for [Ran] Boniu;[98] there is Zeng Shen's expression [before his death], 'Uncover my feet!';[99] and there are the records for Yan Yuan that [Confucius] said, 'Unfortunately, he was short-lived'[100] and then composed the parable of a young plant that does not go on to flower.[101] All these [examples] are written in the Classics, and are the utmost significant words by sages. I consider the Classics and their commentaries to testify [to my words]. The people of the world take [the Daoist assertion] as testimony and say [that these sages] did not die. Are they not deluded?"

A person asked, "Your interpretation is indeed perfect! Certainly it is not what we can understand. I wonder, however, why your responses are arranged in thirty-seven sections. Is there any model for this?"

Mouzi replied, "[Taking a hint from] rolling mugwort, wheels were invented, and [observing floating] driftwood, boats and oars were devised.[102] [Picking up an idea from] spider's webs, nets [for catching birds] were invented. [Seeing] bird tracks, [the Chinese] written language was created. Therefore, it is easy to accomplish something if there is a model, while it is difficult to accomplish anything without a model. I read the essentials of the Buddhist scriptures, which list thirty-seven elements [for enlightenment].[103] The *Laozi Dao[de]jing* consists of thirty-seven chapters as well.[104] Thereupon, I modeled [my responses] after these [examples]."

Then the deluded people who heard [Mouzi's explanation] became reverent and nervous; they turned pale. They stood up, folding their hands in salute. They haltingly prostrated themselves and said, "We are ignorant, and we were born in a benighted place. We dared to make stupid statements without worrying about fortune and misfortune. Now we have heard your instructions and [our doubts have been dispelled] very rapidly, just as hot water melts snow. We tell you now that we will be able to repent, clear our minds, and admonish ourselves. We wish to receive the five precepts and become Buddhist laypeople."

The *Discourse to Correct Faulty Accusations [against Buddhism]* (*Zhengwulun*) by an Anonymous Writer

There was an idiosyncratic person who brought a false charge against the Buddha. He said, "Yin Wenzi is a man who possessed supernatural power. He sympathized with the northern barbarians [since they are like] a deer whose father shares a doe with his son, they are avaricious and cruel, they are profiteers, they are shameless, they encroach upon [neighboring lands], they do not tire of massacring people, they cannot be persuaded by means of the virtue of modesty, and they cannot be admonished by means of talk. Therefore, [Yin] managed all things for them, and so forth. Moreover, he had a disciple (i.e., the Buddha) who had attained the Way to transform, and so on. Moreover, he made [the disciple] prohibit [the northern barbarians] from destroying life, forbade their style of marriage, and proscribed them from having offspring. As a measure to smite the barbarians, what is better than this? And so forth."

I corrected this, "The accuser already said that the Buddha does not 7b
exist. Furthermore, he said that Wenzi had supernatural power. He also said that there was a disciple who attained the Way, who could transform, who was broadminded, and who completed the marvelous principles. These are superficial and heartless words. Now, Yin Wenzi is precisely a disciple of Laozi. Laozi is namely a disciple of the Buddha. Therefore, it is stated in the sutra, 'I have heard it said that in Zhugan there was an old teacher who thoroughly entered nirvana and who eternally and everlastingly remains there without beginning or end.'[105] [The Chinese word] Zhugan means India. [The term] nirvana is a barbarian word; the Chinese [equivalent] is *wuwei*. If the Buddha was not [born] before Laozi, how could [Laozi] call [the Buddha] the one who was born before himself (*xiansheng*)? If Laozi was not [born] before Yin Wen, how could [Yin Wen] ask [Laozi] for the *Daodejing*? Inferring from this, [we see that] the Buddha was formerly Wenzi's ancestor, and the original of all sages. How could it happen that a disciple can supernaturally transform and his teacher cannot?

"Moreover, when a sage governs the world, he certainly rules over it with morality. If the people in remote regions do not submit [to his rule], he pacifies them with [the influence of] civil culture and virtue. He uses weapons only if compelled to out of necessity. He is one who will remove violence, stop fighting, save the people, and carry out a minor killing in order to stop mass murder. Consequently, in the Spring and Autumn period, when feudal lords subjugated [other states], they took actions relying on [the principles of] justice and order. If their hostile state had a fault, they assuredly beat a drum in order to make [the fault] known, and assembled troops of justice in order to deal with those who caused the fault. They did not punish others for ambiguous reasons. Therefore, when their enemies were subjugated, they soothed [them] in a soft and gentle manner, and neither inflicted punishment indiscriminately nor used armed force excessively beyond all reason. When they won, they performed the rite of mourning [for those who had lost their lives in battle]. When they killed, they wept with grief for those who had been killed. Accordingly, to arrest by means of temptation was severely censured, and causes of extermination were strongly restricted.

"To appease evil in order to quell injustice, and to use the road [of the other state] in order to carry out an atrocity [against its own enemy],[106] are variants of [stories found in] the Classics and their annotations. Innumerable derisive comments and condemnation about them can be found. Therefore, when [Zhao Meng of Jin state] met the feudal lords at [the west gate of] Song state for a treaty of alliance, the reason [Zhao Meng] gave priority to Jin state and restrained Chu state is because he hated [the people of Chu,] who were deceptive and wore armor under their clothes [in order to wage a surprise attack on the people of Jin], and he respected the virtue of honesty.[107]

"Resentment and benevolence toward an enemy should not affect the descendants [of the enemy]. Vice is put to an end within one generation. Heavy punishment should not be recklessly dispensed. This is a clever system for all rulers to follow and an excellent law for governing a country. Generals and jingoistic fellows of later ages, when they were troubled by the degeneration of morals, began to compete with each other depending on their cunning powers, and indulged their ravenous minds with deceptive plots. When they did battle in a field, they were unrestrained in attacking and killed everything in sight. When they annihilated a city, they completely buried [the inhabitants] alive, to the last person. Therefore, Bai Qi (?–258 B.C.E.), [who had buried alive many people of Zhao state who had surrendered,] cut off his own head at Duyou.[108] Dong Zhuo (?–192), [a tyrannical vassal of the Later Han dynasty,] was slaughtered at a palace gate.[109]

"Gentlemen know that such [immoral people] inevitably come to ruin. The whole world grieves when [innocent people] are slaughtered. The harm of armed might reaches this point. This is what we should be distressed by, and why we should sigh deeply [in sorrow]. How could there be a sage who wants to indulge in cunning and exterminate common people? Moreover, [even in a small village of only] ten households a wise person can be found, not to speak of a vast area, mile after mile. Zhonghua (i.e., Emperor Shun) was born in [the region of] the eastern barbarians. Wenming (i.e., King Yu) was from [the region of] the western barbarians. How could there be a fixed place from which sages and wise people emerge? Either articulating [the teaching] here or teaching in silence there, styles of teaching are myriad, and 7c
yet the thread of the principles does not differ. Examining the reason why the Buddha manifested his trace in Central India and illuminated miracles in Central Asia, there are probably very profound meanings that cannot be explained in detail.

"How could there be a sage who hates the enemies' power and wants to exterminate them without even a single survivor? [If there were,] how different is this from the case where once a pestilential vapor runs rampant, it cannot be purged by any clear and good thing, or that once a fire is set in the center of a field, [fragrant] orchid and *caryopteris divaricata* (a water plant with a foul smell that lasts very long) are both burned? Wasn't the tyranny of King Jie and King Zhou just like this? Even if the northern barbarian states really do commit many treacherous acts, if you displace violence with violence,[110] this goes against the purpose of leading [the world] by an expedient means. To engage in argument referring to these [examples] is sufficient to abuse others with slander and to confuse ignorant and inexperienced people. How could it be a rebuke [by someone who] is kindhearted, logical, and thoughtful?"

Again, the accuser said, "Yin Wenzi deceived [the people]; he told them that there are thirty-two levels of Heaven, and so on. Moreover, he recklessly quoted [a phrase of] the *Loutanjing,* '[Each of all] heavenly palaces is two hundred and forty thousand *li* in circumference. One side [of the heavenly palace] has a hundred gates, and the gate is ten thousand *li* wide,' and so on."[111]

I replied, "The Buddhist scriptures state that in realms of the heavens and the earth there are stages from high to low. The [scriptures] all present [an analysis of] the sections [of the heavens and the earth], which are systematically described in good order and with logic. Nevertheless, the accuser has exaggerated [the descriptions] and either fabricated a false statement or was confused and misled and could not investigate the reality. How could there be a land two hundred and forty thousand *li* in circumference, containing gates four million *li* wide in total? This case serves as an example for the rest [of the accuser's statement], and it is enough to clarify that he made many mistakes. Even slaves and herders may know that this is not so, not to speak of intellectuals. [The accuser] wants to show his erudition and yet only reveals his stupidity."

Again, the accuser said, "The Buddha also went all around the five realms of existence [before he became a buddha]. He committed many transgressions and atrocious acts, yet he still attained buddhahood. This is not a law to frighten those who do evil. Moreover, in counting people, there are few good people but many bad people. When bad people die, they would fill up the realm of the six domestic animals. It has been a long time since the creation of the world up to the present day. [If this were the case], then animals would occupy nine-tenths [of the world] and the human race would already be rare."

I corrected this, "It is indeed as you said that the Buddha was once evil, too. The reason he attained buddhahood is because he corrected his mistakes and followed what is good. If he had grown [even more] evil, if he had never reformed himself, and if he had been deluded and consequently had kept going [the wrong way], he would have received [the retribution of] suffering for a long, dark period; he would have transmigrated in the five realms of existence without the means for liberation. [The Buddha, however,] was able to dig up the saplings of various evils, extinguish the ember of the three poisons, cultivate the wholesomeness of the five precepts, and accomplish the excellence of the ten wholesome acts.[112] He practiced like this *kalpa* after *kalpa*. Even when he was tired, he never stopped. He completely understood the ultimate state of things and clarified that the three periods (i.e., past, present, and future) are empty. Thereupon, he was able to liberate himself from the illusory world of birth and death, and go beyond to the place of *wuwei*.

"In counting the number of insects in the world, we cannot reach a calculation. [The number of] people who reside in China are like [the number 8a
of] extremely small fine hairs that grow on a horse's body. How could it be said that [animals occupy] nine-tenths [of the world]? 'Of all [beings who have] life between Heaven and Earth, human beings are the noblest.'[113] The reason Rong [Qi]qi was content with the three kinds of happiness is because he thoroughly understood the clear distinction between the noble and the humble.[114] Furthermore, if one does not depend on [the fact that] he is of the human race and is not repulsed by animals, if he considers hay and water to be delicious food and does not think [wearing] a bridle is a punishment, and if he is content with [his circumstance], then there is nothing too difficult for him."

Again, the accuser said, "There is the *Sequel Scripture of No Spirit* (*Wuling xiajing*)."[115]

[I corrected this,] "The *Sequel Scripture of No Spirit* is merely a bizarre book. It is not a book like those [written by] the Three Augusts and the Five Thearchs, or words of instruction and admonition. It is something that people of great talent and learning do not [consider worthy of] study and reading. The words of the ancestors older by three or five generations [recorded in the *Sequel Scripture of No Spirit*] are similar to those of the petition to the Celestial Thearch. This itself nearly reveals a fabrication, without question. I will now deal with it for the time being.

"Generally people of the world frequently say, 'If a person dies, he will perish without the numen (*ling*) and the spirit (*gui*).' In that case, if there is no numen, there is no Celestial Officer; and if there is no spirit, then there is no place where [the spirits] gather. If one's descendant who believes in the Buddha traces back to what his ancestor did and finds fault to reproach, even if one's ancestor was a wise person or gentleman, if he did not necessarily do the same thing as his descendant (i.e., believe in the Buddha) while he was alive, then the Celestial Officer will take him into custody. [The Celestial Officer] orders the corpses of [virtuous people like] Yan [Hui] and Ran [Boniu] to suffer the pain of slaying, and benevolent ancestors to have powerful poisons added to their esteemed bodies. How could this be done by an intelligent, upright, and honest spiritual being (*shen*)? Then, if [such a thing] could not be done [by an intelligent, upright, and honest spiritual being], it must be done by a fox, a badger, an evil spirit of mountains and rivers, or a lewd and fierce ghost. How could such a being overpower the spirits of both kindhearted and wise people, and trouble those who observe the Buddhist precepts? In this way, [the *Sequel Scripture of No Spirit*] brings a false charge against [Buddhism]. It is a shallow and disgraceful text!"

Again, the accuser said, "Buddhist monks exploit the common people immorally, and build beautifully decorated Buddhist temples on a great scale. This is extravagant and futile, and so on."

I corrected this, "In teaching [people] there are both depth and shallowness. [The teaching should] be given in a timely manner and respond to people. All of this was already stated completely in the beginning section. Let me repeat it. No one surpasses Yao and Shun in being respectful to others and humble about themselves. They had fine hemp robes embroidered [with a design of] a mountain, a dragon, a pheasant, and axes [to distinguish official rank]. Therefore, the *Spring and Autumn with Commentary* (*Chunqiu zuoshizhuan*) by Zuo Qiuming states, 'The bells of a carriage horse make [excellent virtue by the sound] known publicly. The banners and flags patterned with sun, moon, and stars make their brilliance known publicly. The images comparable to each other by the five colors make the differences of things known publicly.'[116] Therefore, the residences of monarchs require the Gate of Gold (*jinmen,* i.e., the gate for the emperor), the steps of white jade leading to the throne (*yubi*), an astronomical observatory for the emperor (*lingtai*), and a gate of the imperial palace (*fengque*) in order to distinguish them from [the dwellings] of the common people and make clear [the difference] between the noble and the humble.

"Regarding human feelings, affections of the mind arise following what people see. Consequently, 'when [the ruler] hears the sound of his drums and tambours' and sees the shape of a feather banner, 'he thinks of his leaders and commanders.' 'When [the ruler] hears the sound of the Chinese zithers (*qin se*)' and sees stately manners, 'he thinks of his officers of the court.'[117] When we change standpoint and viewpoint, both our internal feeling and external appearance become different. Now, of the fellows who spend days in leisure, those who see forms and yet do not reach the Way all respect noble
8b status and disregard humble status. Therefore, all Buddhists admire and respect [the Buddha's] relics and try to keep the image of him in their hearts.

"Consequently, they inscribe and display illustrations and images [of the Buddha], extend respect to him, and donate curios of great value in order to enhance the temple of worship. So when a person of the highest class goes there, he disregards the adornments [such as the building, the illustrations, and the Buddhist images] and experiences various unfathomable tastes. When a person of the lowest class goes to the temple, he praises the beautiful decorations and amuses himself with the splendor. First his ears and eyes are pleased, and gradually he may be led to the principles of justice. [Sentient beings] are pulled out from the three lowest realms of existence, and no one is left behind. It is just as when a container is filled with water; it adapts to the volume [of water]. If a hole is bored into the bottom [of a container], or if it has no bottom, it simply cannot hold [the water].

"Moreover, [the accuser] persistently makes a false charge that [the teaching of] weal and woe was made by the Buddha. It should be said that he does not understand the foundation [of the teaching]. I will again briefly explain it.

"[The relation between] good or ill fortune and virtue or vice is similar to [that between] shadow or sound and form or voice. It is a natural consequence, from which no one can escape. To [choose your own] actions is up to you; but from reason a profound response will arise. The Buddha, the Duke of Zhou, and Confucius, however, all clarified [the principles of] loyalty, filial piety, truthfulness, and obedience. Those who follow these principles have good fortune and those who go against them experience bad luck. When the way to cross over water has been shown, [it is possible] by using a boat and oars, but it is impossible to cross over [the water] by foot. The way to instruct people and the skill to save people from distress and death are also similar to [the facts that] Shen Nong ate grain to satisfy his hunger and the Yellow Emperor hung down his garments in order to control coldness and heat. If someone wishes to be sated while his mouth is closed, or if he asks for warmth while he remains naked, we cannot grant [such favors] upon him by force. The reason Bian Que was called a good physician is because he prescribed medicine according to the disease, and simply did not lose the proper way. No one blames him for causing people not to die. Furthermore, Bian Que said, 'I am able to cause people who ought to live not to die, but I am unable to cause people who ought to die to live longer.'[118]

"If the master (i.e., the accuser) were in the position of a son, he would be impious to his parents, and if he were in the position of a vassal, he would be disloyal. He has a serious disease but he is not aware of it. He is offered good medicine but he does not take it. Accordingly, he experiences woes, and on the day he dies he will further blame the sages and deeply resent the good physician. [What he is doing] is just like '[an insane person] who runs toward the east' and through his own force throws himself into a trap."[119]

Again, the accuser said, "Among *śramaṇa*s, those who reside in the capital city and Luoyang are numerous, but I have not heard that they could lengthen the emperors' life spans. To a great degree, [Buddhists] cannot harmonize *yin* and *yang* in order to cause a year of abundance, enrich the people, prevent calamities, cure epidemics, overcome and suppress disturbances, and so on. To a lesser degree, [they] cannot avoid [eating] grain in order to breathe pure [vapor], protect life, surmount difficulty, prolong life, stay young forever, and so on."

I corrected this, "That is not so. Zhuangzhou (i.e., Zhuangzi) says, 'Those who thoroughly understand the conditions of life do not strive after what they cannot do in life.'[120] This is a case of having ascertained that the life span cannot be changed. If one's lot in disposition and life could be sought by means of wisdom and virtue, then that of the two sons Fa (King Wu) and Dan (the Duke of Zhou) would have been sufficient to cause their father [King] Wen to live until a thousand years old. When Yanzi (i.e., Yan Yuan) died, [Confucius] said, 'Heaven is destroying me!'[121] [Confucius] lamented greatly over [Yanzi's death]. He simply had nothing with which to prolong [Yanzi's life].

8c "Furthermore, the degree of *yin* and *yang* is governed by a turn of fate. The misfortune that happens once every one hundred and six years will occur whenever the time arrives. Therefore, [Emperor] Yao had a big flood, as if water had filled the sky.[122] [King] Tang [of the Yin dynasty] had a drought. In [the battlefield of] Zhuolu there was bloodshed enough to float a large shield.[123] In [the battle of] Banquan [the soldiers'] corpses covered the wilds.[124] Why did [these monarchs] not dispel [the disasters] while sitting on their thrones, and rescue [the people] before [such calamitous events] happened? Moreover, people may climb up a tree like a bear, stretch their legs like a bird, guide [the breath], expel [old vapor], ingest [fresh vapor], stop taking a variety of millet, use petals, and inhale wind and dew instead of food. To anticipate a long life doing these things is a sort of 'there was still something for which he had to wait' (i.e., necessitating resorting to a long life).[125] Yet even if [they practice] like this, it is still possible to die young when the time comes. No one can live forever. From a *śramaṇa*'s viewpoint, [immortals such as Chi]song[zi] and [Wangzi]qiao are just like infants who have not yet become young boys.

"[*Śramaṇa*s] are just extending their ambitions to the outer realm of the two polarities (i.e., Heaven and Earth), and prolonging their life in the place of eternal life. Why, for the sake of longevity, would they rack their brains, perform [practices] at the common level, and compete with Juan[zi] and Peng[zu, who enjoyed a long life]? The one who criticizes [Buddhism] improperly wants to develop the debate by covering his fault. He stands on an aggressive position and refuses to listen to counsel, [but] his words have no constancy, and his memorial to the throne makes no distinction between sovereign and subject. Alas! The *Beili,* [the amorous court music composed by King Zhou of the Yin dynasty,] disrupted graceful [music]. I hate that [the compound color] green takes over [the fundamental color] yellow.[126] That excessive noisy sound has never been arranged. I will exclusively follow the example set by my late teacher (i.e., Confucius), who did not answer [questions about life and death]."

Again, the accuser said, "At the end of the Han dynasty, there was Ze Rong (?–195), who gathered an army and became a dependent of Tao Qian (132–194), the governor of Xuzhou. Qian had him supervise the transportation. Nevertheless, although Rong earlier believed in Buddhism, he dared to seize government freight for his own profit, he built Buddhist temples, and so on. He gave away wine and food to all passersby, and so on. He was later attacked by Liu You and killed, and so on."

I corrected this, "This criticism does not need a rope to bind [the accuser]; he is bound by himself. The Buddha's teaching leads [people] with benevolence and humanity, not killing; faithfulness and honesty, not boasting; incorruptibility and virtue, not stealing, as the most important principles. Laozi said, 'Arms are ominous instruments.'[127] Those who are close to them are evil. [Ze] Rong relied on arms, committed brutal acts calmly, conspired with others, and rose in revolt. He committed murders, [which is a violation of] the first [precept]. He accepted a mission [from others], took advantage of it, and did not repay [the kindness of] his master, [Tao Qian]. [These are acts of] deceiving others, [which is a violation of] the second [precept]. He seized government property in order to profit himself. [This is] stealing, [which is a violation of] the third [precept]. The Buddhist scriptures state not to give wine as charity, but [Ze] Rong did so freely. [This is] drinking intoxicants, [which is a violation of] the fourth [precept]. If one violates all the precepts, he is working toward death. This can be compared to the case where a [former] official, who perverts and tyrannizes without restraint after resigning from office, can be easily put down by a five-foot-tall boy. Ze's tragic death is just an appropriate and sufficient example to help [our clear understanding] that evil [people] incur misfortune."

Again, the accuser said, "Shi Chong (249–300), [who was extremely wealthy,] also strongly believed in the Buddha, but he could not prevent the execution of his entire family and relatives [for his personal offense], and so on."

I answered, "I know all about Shi Chong's nature. He was arrogant and indulged in a luxurious life above his status. He was addicted to drink and arbitrarily exceeded his authority without restraint. He amassed tremendous wealth and collected much [property], but he did not offer relief to those who were helpless, without kith or kin. Speaking of his natural abilities, he had an average advantage. Regarding his virtue, he did not have any at all. Although he acquired influence by making use of [the Buddha's] name and
9a following [the Buddha], he observed no precept in the least. He is just like a worldly person who appears virtuous and yet whose mind is wicked, whose appearance is stern and yet whose innermost heart is weak, whose mouth praises [the virtuous kings] Yu and Tang and yet whose acts match those of [villains such as] King Jie and [the robber] Zhi. He brought disaster on himself. Again, whose fault would it be?"

Again, the accuser said, "Zhou Zhongzhi believed in the Buddha and was diligent, too. Nevertheless, he did not receive any fortune [in return] after all, and so on."

I corrected this, saying, "Now that I think of his words, [the accuser] seems to rejoice in others' calamities; [his words] are not logical. Even though Zhongzhi had an inclination toward the [Buddhist] Way, he did not make the decision to receive the precepts and become a disciple [of the Buddha]. As for his natural disposition, he was brilliant and fair. He had a superiorlevel of talent but he also had a streak of obstinacy. He had not yet been united with the Daoist principle of [returning to the state of] an infant.[128] On this account, it is reasonable that he was defeated and suffered a downfall when he met a powerful man who was jealous of those better than himself. Even if [the situation] were just as the accuser says, there are those who, even though they are diligent, are still killed. How does this differ from the case of Yan [Yuan] and Xiang [Tuo, a genius who at only seven years old was a teacher of Confucius,] both of whom died young; or the case of [Bo]yi and Shu[qi], who starved to death; or the case of Bi Gan, who was faithful to [King Zhou of the Yin dynasty], yet sank to the misfortune of having his heart cut out;[129] or the case of Shen Sheng, who was very filial and yet ended in the sorrow of [committing suicide by] hanging? Comparisons like these are too many to mention. Confucius said, 'The virtuous are long-lived[130] and people of justice are prosperous.' Nevertheless, even they cannot escape [from death]. Be sure to be aware of the testimony of your former lives. It is the most revered! It is truthful!"

Again, the accuser said, "Families who serve Buddhism are pleased with death and hate life. On the day when they place cotton [near the nose and mouth of a dying person to determine when the breath ceases,] waiting for his death, they all think that happiness and wealth will come [to the dying person], no one looks sad and sorrowful [about his death], and so on."

I corrected this, saying, "Can the accuser save up things without shutting his mind? If he cannot, why does he speak conversely? A Buddhist scripture states, 'He who considers himself to have attained the [Buddhist] Way is capable of abstrusely seeing that others are the same as himself, and of equalizing merits and demerits.' When such a person experiences the change from life to death, [everything] is indistinct and there is no emotional sign [for him]. When he walks in the land of weal and woe, he remains calm and is not distressed. He is delighted with the laws of nature, and he knows his life. He is simply content with the time and comfortable with the place.[131]

"Those who have not realized this [state of mind] grieve over [death] and have the thought to exercise caution in their last moments. This is why [they try] to enhance their sincere [faith in the Buddha]. Therefore, [the

Buddha] has the justice of the universal vow of great compassion. We feel sympathy and sorrow even for an enemy's death, recompense his enmity with virtue, and forgive his past misdeeds. Could it be possible that there is no sorrowful and mournful feeling, since the heartbreak of our own flesh and blood spontaneously flourishes? Those who love their parents and relatives do not dare hate others [because] they are deeply afraid to put others in the same situation as themselves. Here we see that [the accuser's words] go against [our natural] feeling and are contrary to reason."

End of Fascicle One of *The Collection for the Propagation and Clarification* [*of Buddhism*]

Fascicle Two

The *Discourse to Clarify Buddhism* (*Mingfolun*) by Zong Bing of the Jin Dynasty

The most subtle Way must be assuredly revered in respect to leading people
[to virtue]. Many people of the world, however, see Buddhism as absurd. 9b
Everyone thinks that he cannot examine himself [even in the present world], and has no time to be concerned about himself in regard to a later existence. [People think that] anything that is as far as ten thousand *li* from here or that happens more than one hundred years from now is all uncertain; much less certain are that Mount Sumeru is great, that the Buddha's realm is extraordinary, that our spirits do not extinguish [after death], that people can attain buddhahood, that the mind creates all phenomena, that all things of the world are transient, and that the conditions created in former existences last for one hundred million *kalpa*s and cause retribution. [Nevertheless,] these are all outstanding, wonderful, transcendent, clearly seen, true in reason, and real phenomena. How could those who have become accustomed to hearing [a folk song such as] "Yellow Flowers" enjoy the melody of "Cloud Gate," [which was composed by the Yellow Emperor]?

Moreover, people of the world value classical books written by the Duke of Zhou and Confucius. From the time of Emperor Yao to the Han period, [however,] the nine provinces (i.e., China) never influenced foreign regions. What was it that moved Emperor Ming (r. 57–75) of the [Later] Han dynasty? What virtue did he possess that he alone was illuminated by supernatural light? All people's feelings like these are entirely involved with long-established custom, and people cannot be free of worries and petty notions and cannot see by means of the profound eyes. Consequently, truth is not far away, but people give rise to suspicions and sink in [delusions]. How sad it is!

Gentlemen of the Middle States (i.e., China) are versed in [the subjects of] ceremony and righteousness, but they are inexperienced in knowing the human mind.[132] How then could they know the mind of the Buddha? Now in worldly affairs and familiar matters—not to speak of in your spirit, the self—if your plan is not good, you will still be visited by vicissitude. If you are successful [in dealing with] the spirit, you will be ennobled without limit. If you are unsuccessful, you will eternally fall [into the world of delusions] without end. Shouldn't you then seek [as cautiously as if] you were standing on the edge of an abyss, or think [as carefully as if] you were stepping onto thin [ice]? To plan one's chances in the game of *go* (*yi*) is easy, but has the mind of the great *go* player Qiu ever been understood?

Moreover, [people of the world] want to follow the [narrow] view, [just like] a frog in a well, and they recklessly repress the Great Way. They end up only entrapping their spirits at the bottom of the heavenly snare. Don't you think this is too frightening? Now, with unenlightened knowledge, they try to illuminate what is profound. Therefore, they cannot find even their own failure by themselves. How then could they clarify what they have to attain? They should clarify the direction in which their dark spirits [are going] and seek the wholesome way. They should firmly cultivate themselves, taking Buddhist scriptures as their guide.

Those Buddhist scriptures contain the virtue taught in the Five Classics; they are deeply enhanced with very promising reality; they include the void (*xu*) [advocated] by Laozi and Zhuangzi; and they completely emphasize the teaching that all phenomena are empty (*kong*). With lofty words and real principles, [the Buddhist scriptures] reverently move one's spirit. They shine as brightly as the sun and they are as clean as wind. Except for a sage, who can expound them? I will sincerely look into the views of people of the world, juxtapose those views with the Buddhist doctrines, and clarify [Buddhism].

The *Discourse* states: Now if [the operation of] the mind leaves one's whole body from the heels to the crown of the head and goes up through the
9c air, it will go on without stopping. Then the four directions and the upper and lower directions are all boundless. Life is not created all by itself. It certainly transmits what has been saved up. If we trace what is transmitted, there is non-beginning. What is produced repeatedly without ceasing for successive generations is non-ending. Regarding the body, every day we all make use of the essence [of the body] that is limitless and came intimately from non-beginning, and that will, furthermore, be ceaselessly transmitted into the future. Then, into the immeasurable and boundless vastness for eternal time

from non-beginning to non-ending, people originally throw themselves one after another and spread out. Thereupon, [the Chinese people] situate China (*chixian*) in [the middle of] the whole wide world and they have no doubt about it.

[Buddhists] declare that there are three thousand suns and moons, and twelve thousand worlds arranged in the universe. They count as many countries as there are grains of sand in the Ganges River and put in order as many *kalpa*s as there are flying particles of dust. They disperse widely what the profound edification contains, and [see] very small things to be the same as inexhaustible things. Why do [non-Buddhists] doubt the other side (i.e., Buddhists), while being content with themselves? If a very tiny thing is placed upon a blue sea, the two differ from each other [in size by a great degree], but there is still limitation there. When the principles of human relationships [of Confucianism] are joined with the Grand Void (*taixu*) [of Buddhism], how can we express the difference [between them]? Therefore, what people of the world think great is what the [Buddhist] Way considers to be minor. What people think is distant is what Heaven considers to be near. What has been said, "The time before Xuanyuan (i.e., the Yellow Emperor) is remote antiquity,"[133] possibly seems like yesterday in the lofty view of those who have mastered the Way of Heaven.

It is said [in the *Liji*] that [the teaching of] the *Book of History* is to know distance, but it is not beyond the time of [Emperor] Tang [Yao] and Emperor Yu [Shun]. Phrases composed in the *Spring and Autumn Annals* are limited to kingcraft. There is piety in the *Book of Rites,* goodness in the *Book of Music,* warmth in the *Book of Odes,* and cleanliness in the *Book of Changes* (*Yijing*). Now, in infinitude, if we display three thousand shining suns and moons and correctly see the twelve thousand arranged worlds, then we will know that what the Duke of Zhou and Confucius wrote are possibly just like responses to the vulgar demand to rule over [the masses] in a region [as small as a snail's tentacles, where] Chu state and Man state [fought for hegemony].[134] Moreover, [the responses] would be rather insufficient and only about the matters of one's present life. What exists beyond [the present] life has been left as it is, and never discussed. If this is not the case, why do they emphasize having a physical body as the beginning and leave out being a spirit after death? "[Confucius] climbed up Mount [Eastern] Meng when Lu state looked small [to him]. [He] went up Mount Tai when the world appeared small [to him]."[135] These [comparisons] mark the boundaries between [Confucianism and Buddhism].

In addition, the [*San*]*fen* (i.e., the books written by Fuxi, Shen Nong, and the Yellow Emperor) and the [*Wu*]*dian* (i.e., the books by the Five Thearchs) have already been lost. Compilations by scholars of shallow learning are exclusively comprised of tracts on governing [the nation]. If there were transcendent remarks [in Confucianism], some were scattered and lost in historical records, and some were destroyed at [the time of the incident of] burning [the books on the Chinese classics] and burying [Confucian scholars alive]. The ways of Laozi and Zhuangzi and the arts of all the perfected, such as [Chi]song[zi] and [Wangzi]qiao, can truly cleanse our minds and nourish our bodies, but none of these are collected in the Six Classics, either. Accordingly, scholars merely stick to the incompleteness of [Confucian] literature, which relieves only trifles. They consider the *Book of History* and the *Book of Rites* as the line to draw, and abstain from hearing the lofty teaching to probe into the very root of the spirit over *kalpa*s. They are blinded by immediate matters and forever disregard [the lofty teaching]. This, too, is sad! Alas! They are just like those who, when walking under a stratus cloud, do not believe that the sun and moon exist.

The expressions "[The successive movement] in alternating *yin* and *yang* is called the Way" and "The unforeseen movement in alternating *yin* and *yang* is called a spirit"[136] possibly mean that the ultimate of nonexistence is the Way, where both *yin* and *yang* are integrated. Therefore, it is said "[The successive movement] in alternating *yin* and *yang*." That which descends from the Way enters into [the realm of] vigorous spirits, which exists beyond
10a *yin* and *yang,* and which is not examined by these two factors. Hence, it is simply said that "The unforeseen movement in alternating *yin* and *yang*." [Yan] Junping's theory that "'one produces two' refers to the spiritual intelligence" indicates this.[137] If these two phrases do nothing to clarify [the spirit], then with what is the vigorous spirit clearly defined?

Moreover, although the spirits of all sentient beings are ultimately equal, [each] transmigrates following the conditions they met, and forms a [correspondingly] dull or ingenious consciousness. In addition, [this consciousness] and its root (i.e., spirit) are free from decay. Now, even though [the sage]

Shun was born as the son of [an ignorant man,] Gu, the spirit of Shun is certainly not something that Gu passed on to him. Nor is the spirit of [Shun's unworthy son,] Shangjun, what Shun gave to him, either. Before birth, there is generally [the difference] of dullness or ingenuity [of the spirit]. Since the root is established before birth, we know that [the spirit] is immortal after death. Furthermore, if [the spirits] are immortal, they are different from each other. Accordingly, the stupid and the sacred are distinct from each other. We know that the distinctions between the stupid and the sacred and between birth and death do not change the immortal status of the spirits. Therefore, it is said that "The vigorous spirit receives a physical body and transmigrates all over the five realms of existence while Heaven and Earth are formed and destroyed innumerable times."[138]

The physical body [of Shun] had the [auspicious] double-pupil eyes when he was born [the son of] the ignorant man Gu. Unintelligent [Shang]jun received his physical body from the gentleman (i.e., Shun) who had virtue within. The stupid and the sacred naturally should separate from each other. By what perceptible law, then, did [these two] incorporate? Wouldn't it be that the spirit of Zhonghua (i.e., Emperor Shun) was dull a long time ago, but he established a [good] cause *kalpa*s ago and consequently conditions met [the cause] after a myriad of transformations? Now his [lofty] spirit solitarily separates from others, but in remote antiquity there was a chain of transmigrations of the dull spirit. Accordingly, [Shun's lofty spirit] is the completion of the refinement [of his formerly dull spirit]. These three issues: the immortality of the spirit, the law that conditions meet [the primary cause], and the sagehood attained through deep-rooted practice, are examined here.

If the formation of a physical body [corresponds to] the formation of the spirit, and if the cessation of a physical body [corresponds to] the cessation of the spirit, then when the body is injured, the spirit should be damaged as well, or when the body falls ill, the spirit should also be fatigued. It is reported that there are people whose bodies are perishing, or who are about to die, and yet whose spirits and consciousnesses are calm and perfect. When [Confucius] took hold of [Ran Boniu's] hand through the window,[139] [Ran Boniu] was extremely ill. Nevertheless, there was no change [in Boniu] as a person of virtue. This is simply a testimony to the immortality [of the spirit]. If it is certain that the spirit is produced with the body and it is originally not [what is produced by] conditions meeting [a direct cause], I am now engaged in "taking examples from various things for distant matters, and then examples from various human beings for familiar matters."[140]

It is said that there is no spirit in the Five Sacred Mountains and the Four Holy Rivers, but such a conclusion is premature. Even if we accept that there is spirit there, the mountains are simply large piles of soil and the rivers are merely accumulated water. How could "the spirit that attained the One" (i.e., the origin of all phenomena) be produced from such coarse materials as water and soil?[141] [The spirit] works upon rocks and streams and entrusts itself there, and is solemnly united with them. If the mountains fall to pieces or the rivers dry up, [the spirit] certainly does not go to ruin together with the water [of the rivers] and the soil [of the mountains]. The spirit is not what the form makes. It incorporates with [the form] and yet it is immortal. So it is in the case of human beings. "The spirit is the word to express [something] more ingenious than all things under the sun."[142] If [the spirit] is created availing of the form and perishes following the form, the form is considered to be the origin [of the spirit]. How could it then be called "ingenious"? "The vigorous spirit goes forth in all directions, flowing on boundlessly, reaching to Heaven above, and wreathing round the Earth beneath."[143]

Sages "search out exhaustively what is deep" and wise people "investigate what is the minutest."[144] As for [virtuous] people such as Zai [Wo], Zi[gong], Zhuang[zi], Ji [Kang], [Ji]zha of Wu, and [Zhang Liang] Zifang, wherever the operation of their vigorous [spirits] directs their course, [their spirits go fast even though] they do not hurry, and [they arrive at their destination] without going;[145] they penetrate the universe from their own place. [All these sages, wise people, and virtuous people] are the same as common foolish
10b people in that their bodies rot and stink [after death] or that they delight in tasty food. Could there be a reason why [their spirits] receive the bodies [of common people] to be born, and perish following [the decay of their bodies]? We must think of this, too.

The Duke of Zhou offered a sacrifice to Heaven and Earth for [Minister of Agriculture] Houji, and performed a sacrifice to the ancestors for [his father,] King Wen. Some people of the world say that this was a waste of filial piety. If I were to ask those who say so why they understand that this act was indeed a waste [of filial piety], there would certainly be no reason for their understanding. If there is no reason for it, the spirits of King Wen and Houji cannot be said to have perished. "If [gentlemen] perform purification for three days, they must see those for whom the purification has been performed."[146] Can we conclude that the Duke of Zhou did not see [King Wen and Houji], since ordinary people do not see them? When [Jizha of Wu] buried [his son] between Ying and Bo, he said, "[My son's] bones and flesh have returned to earth, but his spiritual vapor goes wherever it likes."[147] He meant [by this] the immortality [of the spirit].

The most virtuous administration follows Heaven. Great turmoil fills Heaven. This is essentially what the mind and the spirit do. Emperor Yao discerned all principles, and he was completely free from avarice, since his spirit was exquisite. King Jie indulged in all vices, since his spirit was contrary to virtue. It does not mean that Jie did not know Yao's virtue. He was aware of his vice, which would ruin him. The desires of his physical body went against his spirit. The consciousness capable of knowing [the virtue of] Yao and his ruin from vice was always contained in his spirit. If [Jie] had not taken the throne and lived a thousand years, when he did evil, he might be visited by pain successively, or when he did a minor good act, he might become somewhat magnanimous. Couldn't he have overthrown his evil and cultivated his virtue little by little? What his spirit contains, as [mentioned] before, includes the consciousness to know [the virtue of] Yao, which must have had at least a chance to be used. Moreover, if [Jie's] life span had increased to a thousand years and he had not ceased [cultivating his virtue], it would be possible that his desires would have all been pacified and his spirit would have become as exquisite as that of Yao.

When an unusual movement of the sun, moon, or stars occurs, a sound becomes off-tune. As the new moon and the full moon take turns, oysters and clams respond to each of [these cycles] [by becoming lean or fat]. According to the seasonal days—the spring and autumn equinoxes, the winter and summer solstices, and the first days of spring, summer, fall, and winter—the swallows, wild geese, dragons, and snakes nimbly appear and disappear. For all these, mysterious changes come first and later reveal themselves in phenomena. Generally all beings are equally created by mysterious changes.

How could it be [possible] that only several matters are so, and myriad changes are exactly not so?

Therefore, those who are put to death on the charge of murder, who are punished on the charge of inflicting injury upon others, who are put in jail, who do not commit a crime now, or who are guilty and yet are [as free from punishment as those who are innocent], have all first established conditions in the unseen world and now the reason of the human world reveals [the results of these conditions]. Hiding and revealing are one and the same. If a sin is formed in hiding, an abomination reveals itself clearly. There is nothing at all strange in this. He who has done evil evidently gets the worst of it in hiding. Why is this strange?

With the immortal spirit that contains the consciousness to know [the virtue of Emperor] Yao, [human beings] appear and disappear in countless generations. Suffering initiates evil, and pleasure leads to good. In addition, there is the foundation of the sun and moon that bestows light to shine brightly. What reason would there be for a person not "to reach the Way by one change,"[148] effacing himself and studying intensively with respect? Rather than being afraid of being [like] Jie and Zhou in remote antiquity, all people should [strive to] gradually become [like virtuous kings such as] Tang and Wu in the future, not to mention the young people of refined taste who let
10c their minds float on a limpid stream. When you see from this standpoint, it is clear, too, that people are able to become buddhas.

Life arises entirely from the germination of feeling (*qing*).[149] [The expression] "when a male and a female unite their essences (i.e., sexual union), all creatures are incarnated" completely refers to [the fact] that their essences are united through feeling.[150] When feelings meet selves, various spirits receive physical bodies. It greatly appears as if feeling is the foundation of life. Even though [sages such as] the Five Thearchs and the Three Augusts transcended feeling and probed into the spirit, they still have to follow all principles. Even [sages] met the conditions a long time ago, and now they have to condescend to enter [the realm of] incarnation through the essence, be born mutually following [the principles], and produce numerous offspring, to say nothing of [ordinary people whose] feelings are linked to their spirits, and whose bodies become extinct. How would it be possible that they will not receive bodies again and will not go through the transmigration of birth and death innumerable times?

If the consciousness is able to clear the foundation of immortality, receives the training of diminishing one's actions from day to day, "diminishes it, and again diminishes it, and certainly arrives at *wuwei,*"[151] there will be no feeling to lead to desire. Only the spirit will shine and then there will be nothing equivalent to life. When there is no life, there is no body. There is no body and yet there is the spirit. This is the meaning of *dharmakāya.*

The Yellow Emperor, Yu Shun, Duke Ji (i.e., the Duke of Zhou), and Confucius are admired and trusted by the people of the world. When we see that [the Yellow Emperor] ascended to Heaven [on the back of dragon that] was given the reins, that [Emperor Yu Shun] was like a hidden dragon and [later ascended to the throne] like a soaring bird, that [the sincerity of the Duke of Zhou] raised a headwind that lifted up the fallen rice plants, and that [Confucius] sang a song with stringed accompaniment while he had nothing to eat, [we can see] that all [four sages] took their ultimate spirit as their essence, and consequently became what the function of their spirits manifested as responses of a free and easy manner. Even though the law of manifestation is external, it just appears and disappears following the movement [of numinous powers]. There must be also something beyond the human tether.

The chart emerged from [the Yellow] River, and writing came out from the Luo [River].[152] The bush of luck-tea grew vigorously without being planted [in the garden of Emperor Yao when he ascended the throne]. The mystic jade tablet was completed without being polished [in the time of Yu].[153] [During the reign of Emperor Wu Ding of the Yin dynasty], two kinds of mulberry trees suddenly grew together in the garden. [Within one night the trees grew so large around that] one could encircle them with both arms, and then [they] suddenly vanished.[154] [When Emperor Wu of the Zhou dynasty was subjugating King Zhou of the Yin dynasty,] a fireball flew over the palace and became a raven.[155] A large three-legged caldron became light, while a small one became heavy, [in accordance with the virtue of the rulers].[156] All these events suddenly happened and the changes occurred, being affected by numinous powers. This is truly a group of evident [phenomena] of mystery.

At the culmination of *dharmakāya,* numinous powers ingeniously touch sentient beings and transform in order to manifest. [The *dharmakāya*] shines upon the spirit and its achievement brightens all things. What wonder could it not exhibit? What change could be limited? Why would it merely ascend to the nine heavens, walk like a dragon in the underworld, inhale wind, or abstain from grain? Generally, the greatness of [the *dharmakāya*'s] glorious deportment and auspicious omen [can be found in instances of] the transformed bodies separated from a buddha and a bodhisattva, springing out from the earth,[157] moving the [great] world,[158] and pouring the water of a huge ocean into a [single] pore.[159]

Compared with [the instances of] the Yellow Emperor, Yu [Shun], the Duke of Zhou, and Confucius, its mysterious changes have no set rules. Regarding the obscure appearance and disappearance of various auspicious omens, which were mentioned above, they have already left [the realm of] form and entered into [the realm of] the spirit, and they are the same as the profound metaphysical agency. Why do the people only believe in this (i.e., Confucianism) and restrain themselves from that (i.e., Buddhism)? The Dharma King (i.e., the Buddha) who was deeply awakened is pure, just, lofty, and bright. Truly there is testimony for this. He is just in front of you, without the least distance, yet ignorant people are not aware of it. How sad it is!

The "various signs" stated in the *Hongfan* chapter [of the *Book of History*], that is to say, the corresponding auspicious and inauspicious [manifestations], are all derived from the mind. The sorts [of unusual phenomena], such as a white rainbow piercing the sun, Venus entering into the Pleiades, a variety of millet plants growing in a cold ravine, city walls [suddenly] collapsing, or frost falling [in summer], are entirely caused by human feelings and remotely presented as natural phenomena. Originally [human mind and natural phenomena] are mutually related, just as is a form and its shadow. And just as
11a there is no shape without shadow or no voice without sound, there is no human feeling without reward or retribution. How could [the law of reward or retribution] apply only to the sorts [of unusual phenomena like a white rainbow] piercing the sun or frost falling [in summer]? All minutely respond to various human feelings; no one can escape from phenomena [that manifests due to the law of reward and retribution].

Sometimes, however, [retribution] is formed over and above one's physical body, and sometimes it is cast on incidents. [It manifests] directly or indirectly in a confused manner, apparently or obscurely, and is endlessly long or vast. Who can see the edge of [the manifestation of retribution]? Various extraordinary things fill the world and numerous phenomena reach our eyes. All these result from the movement of the numinous powers that have gathered after countless generations. Therefore, the Buddhist scriptures state that the forms of all existences are produced from thought. Moreover, [the scriptures] say that the mind is the origin of existences; the mind makes Heaven and the mind makes Hell. The meanings derive from those [mentioned above]. Hence, those who have a virtuous mind and pure feelings will certainly be reborn in the outstanding and magnificent state. Those who have corrupt feelings and who commit impure acts will be eternally deluded in the region of the three lowest realms of existence. How far-reaching and subtle this advocacy is! Isn't this what has the law of truth yet is straightforward, cleanses our spirits, uplifts our thoughts, and causes us to sincerely make up our minds with awe [to pursue the teaching]?

Even though a myriad of feelings all mutually constitute conditions and form consciousnesses that move and make phenomena, in fact the nature [of feelings] is nonexistence. Since the time [the Buddha] opened the ferry for enlightenment, his solitary voice enables us to extinguish worries in a flash, but no one has reached this point. I will further explain and clarify it.

Sacred spirits shine abstrusely and yet they have no consciousness for thinking. This is because there is severance between the mind and things and only the spirit exists there. Accordingly, the foundation that is void and intelligent remains permanently, and is never exhausted. Now, if the mind and things interact and it is not the state of spirit only, even if you are as subtle as was Yanzi (i.e., Yan Yuan), [a person usually free of avarice,] you will certainly be intent on looking up to [Confucius], be fond of benevolence, be delighted with mountains, "nearly attain to [perfect virtue], and be often empty of avarice,"[160] [but you will not be in the state of spirit only]. This is all because the mind is exerted and gives rise to consciousness. For sure, the functions [of the mind] subtly make contact with each other, and the consciousnesses cleverly follow one after another, just as flames come together, resulting in a big blaze.

If by means of the realization of emptiness the mind is set at rest, the function of the mind ceases and feeling and consciousness become exhausted, and the spiritual intelligence is perfect. Since feeling meets consciousness and new [feelings and consciousnesses] cleverly follow the old, all this is not the state of [the spirit] only. How could [the state of the spirit only] constantly exist? [It is similar to the case of] the good cook Ding, who was shown an ox, yet he certainly was not looking at the whole body of the ox [when he butchered it].[161] It is what the Buddhist scriptures state: the law of changes and dispersions, and the nature of phenomena and consciousness, are empty; [they are just like] a dream, an illusion, a shadow, an echo, a bubble, or the [image of the] moon reflected on water. Isn't this so? Yanzi was aware of [laws] like this. Therefore, he dealt with existence just as he did with nonexistence, he touched a real thing just as he did an unreal thing, and he did not perceive existence to offend him and consequently did not respond to it.[162]

Now, when we observe Yanzi's "being often empty of avarice," we see that in fact existence is nonexistence. Moreover, those below the level [of Yanzi] lose the truth further away. Although they go toward the Great Way in haste, they are called insane, just the same as those who pursue a demented person who is running toward the east.[163] They all defy the principles, trespass against the beneficial activity [of unseen divine beings], go against Heaven, and act recklessly. [Moreover, this] is not true existence, not to speak of touch, taste, sound, and color and shape (*se*); they are also mere shadowy apparitions falsely made by feeling. In addition, even if a boat is hidden in a narrow ravine, [both the boat and the ravine] can be moved [by a person of great strength].[164] Changes happen more quickly than lightning. The future has not yet come, the past has already vanished, and the present does not stay. Even in the instant of the blink of an eye or an intake of breath, nothing
11b can be grasped. What are you going to abide by and consider as existence? It is astounding that false existence covers up the spirit!

[Suppose] there is a mirror. When it is covered with dust, if there is only a little [dust] [the mirror] shines fuzzily, but when [more dust] accumulates it shines dimly; when [the dust] piles up more thickly [the mirror] still shines but it is rather dark. Since [the mirror's] original nature is bright, even if [the mirror] is covered by dust it still shines. Although from dimness to darkness the essential point (i.e., the function of shining) follows [the outer state of] the mirror, it is not extinguished. When we discern things with [such a dusty mirror], it is certain [that we will] lose [their original nature] more and more, according to the amount of dust [on the surface of the mirror], and make mistakes. The principle of the spirit of a human being is similar to this. When the false existence implicates the spirit, exquisite or coarse consciousness arises. The consciousness clings to the spirit. Consequently, although [a person] dies, [the consciousness attached to the spirit] does not perish. If it (i.e., the consciousness attached to the spirit) is permeated with emptiness, the repeated permeation certainly leads to the exhaustion [of the consciousness], and then the original spirit is probed. This is the meaning of nirvana.

Therefore, wise sayings are as abundant as clouds. We follow [them], and open [our minds] and clear them with emptiness. If rocks and forests are beyond perception and wind and water are unreal, when we go [to such places] full of thoughts, we will become free from worry and petty notions, not to speak of the sages who are peaceful, respectful, and empty (*kong*) and who teach the void (*xu*) to people. How could those people with pure minds not be delighted by the exhaustion [of the consciousness]? Therefore, in ancient times [there were many people who] took advantage of the void and entered the Way. Even if those who have attained buddhahood are as numerous as grains of sand in the Ganges River, [their number] has not yet reached the point where they are too numerous.

A person asked, "The spirit is originally the acme of the void. Why is it imbued with all things in the phenomenal world and why does it make a relationship with them? Furthermore, [the spirit] is equal in being primarily void. Why is it divided into the ignorant and the sacred? Again, it has already been said that the mind makes all things in the phenomenal world. Before all things in the phenomenal world were created, what implicated the mind and made it move to produce them?"

I answered, "The spirit is subtle while the physical body is coarse, but both make interactions. Since the subtle [spirit] forms a relationship with the coarse [body], we know that the void establishes a relationship with existence. Now, although an ignorant person is mean, he is essentially able to know about the past in the present and to think of other places while being here. All this is due to the fact that the spirit [related to the body] has functions, so if we can completely train [our minds], we will know that [the spirit] is basically equal and void. I have explained that the mind makes all things in the phenomenal world. When we observe reality based on this view, [we can understand] that these three issues are assuredly true. The reason they are so is, however, derived from non-beginning. How could there be the beginning of non-beginning? This is also 'the deepest profundity.'[165] Zhuangzi says that when Ran Qiu asked [Confucius] if it could be known how it was before Heaven and Earth came to exist, Confucius replied, 'It was just like the present.'[166] He probably meant that although there was [an origin] before non-beginning, if one makes inquiry into the very origin, from the first it is just as indistinct and indistinguishable as 'Ran Qiu today.'[167] The original creation of spiritual intelligence and the first ancestor of sentient beings are all indistinct, and they are beyond our grasp. How could it be an issue whether or not those who learn [Buddhism] understand?

"A sage is indeed a coagulum [of the spirit], who simply gives up [the physical body], and who 'is simply moved and later responds.'[168] [The issue] is beyond our comprehension, namely outside of the universe, where there is nothing by which we are moved. Therefore, [sages] left it intact and did not discuss it. How could ordinary people comprehend an issue about which even sages do not speak?

"Now we live together, treading upon Earth under the canopy of Heaven. Outside of [the Earth] upon which we tread and [Heaven] under which we reside, could there be finality? The reason Yu assisted the five regions (i.e., Dian, Hou, Sui, Yao, and Huang) and governed no more than the nine
11c provinces probably means that [they are] simply the areas that are reached by worldly influences. The region outside the farthest land, the land from where the sun rises, and the land where the sun goes down, are not participated in by the human principle, and were not clarified by holy people and sages, to say nothing of the place further away where it is chaotic and obscure. How could such borderlands be discussed? Now, we inferred from [the Earth] upon which we tread and [the Heaven] under which we reside, and have finally reached what we cannot discuss. [Your question] is, therefore, the same as this. In the case where we infer the function of the spirit of the present, seek the beginning point in the past, and finally reach what the sage left intact and did not discuss, an element of truth simply threads together, too. How could we discuss it alone?

"All [phenomena] are derived from conditions made in the unseen world and following [the law of] the universe they are eternal, but [we cannot comprehend all of them] because what people's senses feel is limited. People's minds receive the sacredness by which they form the consciousnesses. It is just as when people's eyes meet with sunlight, by which they come to see. The reason Li Zhu could examine a [very tiny] autumn hair on an animal's body a hundred *xun* away from him is because he just looked with his keen eyes, availing of the sunlight. Now, if very tiny hairs are spread a thousand steps away from us, weak-sighted people [among us] cannot see them even availing of [the sunlight], yet they have no shortcomings in perceiving the tiny hairs and avoiding danger. Why is the tiny hair a hundred *xun* away questioned on the basis of the vagueness of a thousand steps away? Those who do not master the foundation of conditions that give rise to phenomena and who lack feeling have no chance to meet sacredness, but they have no shortage in knowing and reaching the ferry that leads to the [Buddhist] Way. Why is the teaching that was already clarified questioned due to the vagueness of the beginning of conditions that give rise to phenomena?"

A person asked, "People of today say that since they do not understand the beginning of conditions that give rise to phenomena, they cannot believe in the Buddha. Is this not affections of the mind? Why doesn't the sage clarify it?"

I answered, "What is called affections of the mind is a state of harboring [something in the mind] or of exciting [the mind], and there is still an incomprehensible point in reason. We ought to avail ourselves of the sacredness in order to understand it thoroughly. This is real affections of the mind based on reason. Therefore, if people enjoy themselves being impeded by existence, then [the Buddha] clarifies [people's minds] with the significance of suffering and emptiness. If [the teaching of] love without distinction is not propagated, then he shows [the teaching of] benevolence [to save sentient beings] through the act of diving into [the jaws of hungry tigers]. Those [who practice the teaching] do not necessarily reach [the goal] all together. Accordingly the three vehicles are established. Since acts [that cause reward and retribution] vary, cultivations differ from each other. So the six *pāramitā*s are elucidated. There is not even a single lack in the [Buddha's] responsive activity for the ferry and the bridge to [enlightenment]. It can be said '[the Buddha] is simply moved and later responds.'[169]

"Consequently, the heavenly beings who listened to the teaching on Vulture Peak were entirely relieved. [Among them,] those who arrived at the ultimate state were numerous. Would they have further questioned the beginning of conditions that give rise to phenomena and later (i.e., after they understood) arrived at the principle? The clear instruction is adequate. If you cultivate as [the Buddha] said, what would be deficient? Otherwise, how different are those who still certainly do not believe in [the Buddha] and in the end have excessive doubts about what is beyond our comprehension from those who get a fatal disease and yet do not take medicine that is offered, or from those who are struck by a stray arrow and yet do not take the shaft out, bearing the pain, and who demand to know the basics of the construction of the arrow and the medicine, and so on, and end up in death?

"This is entirely because those who have cultivated [the Buddhist Way] from ancient times and yet have not attained great good fortune (i.e., enlightenment) cause the people who believe in [the Buddha] today to absurdly doubt [the teaching]. How could this be considered to be real affections of the mind based on reason? The unreasonable movement of the mind [full of] absurd doubt assuredly has nothing to move the sacredness and to be able to elucidate. [The *Book of Changes* states:] 'I do not [go and] seek [the youth-
12a ful] and inexperienced, but he comes and seeks me.'[170] We certainly ought to efface ourselves, and our acts ought to comply with the profound teaching. If we sincerely go with faith, awakening will come later in accordance with the response. Once we attain awakening, what is aroused can finally reach the acme of the unseen world. Those who stick to absurd doubt, who do not return to purity, and who do not straighten themselves out will precisely fall into the disaster of delusion for a long time. Can there be a tomorrow [for them]? To turn one's back on [the Buddhist teaching] differs slightly from facing it, but to go up [to Heaven] is greatly separated from falling into [Hell]. Shouldn't you be careful?"

A person asked, "Confucius teaches: '[People with lofty ideas] will not seek to live at the risk of injuring their virtue. They will fulfill justice at the cost of their own life.'[171] [This is] the culmination of virtue. In the Buddhist scriptures, too, the practices for bodhisattvas are prescribed. Laozi elucidates the utmost of *wuwei,* that is to say, the culmination of nirvana. However, [Confucius and Laozi] have never spoken about supernatural power and the attainment of buddhahood. Could there be something Confucius and Laozi have left out? By clarifying the [Buddhist] Way, do you want to stir up [trouble] among people and cover up the real [practices] for attaining the Way? How can I stop giving rise to the question that there is no reality [in Buddhism]?"

I answered, "In the origination of edification, each teaching depends on to what it responds. As people hoped for peace to reign in the world, [the teachings of Confucius] promulgated in the region of the Zhu and Si Rivers was the response [to the people's entreaty] in order to govern the Way. When the pure wind [of edification] became becalmed, the two chapters [of the *Daodejing*] were compiled in order to stop the movement. If Yan [Hui], Ran [Boniu], Zai [Wo], Zigong, Yin Xi, and Zhuangzi were externally commended in the conduct of Confucianism and the profound learning in order to lead [the world] to the height of what people of the world feel, and they internally received the learning of nonarising (i.e., Buddhism) in order to specialize in seeking the principle of the spirit, who in the world would know it? As for the class of people such as Ran Qiu, Ji Lu, Zixia, Zisi, Mencius, [Guo] Linzong, [Zheng] Kangcheng, Ge Gong, Yan [Jun]ping, Ban Si, and Yang Wang[sun], some played their part within ethical education, some ended up by themselves, living an easy life free from worldly matters, and they were not delighted with the Buddhist teaching. All [of these people] stopped within their scarce conditions and finally did not go any further. Therefore, Confucius and Laozi spoke out and instructed. The objective sphere of affections of the mind reached by these [people] was consequently neither beyond what they asked for nor more than what they responded to.

"Confucianism promulgates benevolence and Daoism restrains activity. [Confucianism and Daoism] have already affectionately taught and come to the verge—[these teachings] have all arrived at their culmination. Even though the benevolence and good [of Confucianism], the inactivity [of Daoism], and what the Buddha spoke of are common, regarding the *dharmakāya* and nirvana [both Confucianism and Daoism] express nothing. Therefore, [these terms] are simply obscure. Moreover, generally it is said that '[The Way] does nothing [always for the sake of doing it], but there is nothing that it does not do'[172] and 'The *dharmakāya* has no form and universally enters into all things.'[173] Aren't [these two] the same in tenor? Thereupon, even though the three teachings of Confucius, Laozi, and the Tathāgata are different courses from each other, they are all of a piece in learning wholesomeness."

A person asked, "From the time of the Three Augusts and the Five Thearchs up to the time of Confucius and Laozi, there must have been people who cleansed their minds by the Buddhist teaching. We, however, have heard no trace of the exchanges [of their discussions]. Why is this?"

I answered, "I have already made clear my intention about this in my previous discussion. Scholars of shallow learning exclusively compiled the vestiges of political affairs. If there were otherworldly statements, some were dispersed into historical records, and some vanished at the time of burning [the books on the Chinese classics] and burying [Confucian scholars alive]. Now I will repeat and express what I have in my mind.

"[It is stated in Kong Anguo's preface to the *Book of History* (*Shangshu xu*) that] the writings by the Three Augusts are called the *Three Ancient*
12b *Books,* which speak about the Great Way. At that time filial piety and benevolence were fully practiced. Why would they have had to teach humanity and justice [to the people]? The people did not leave behind simplicity and honesty. How could [philosophers] such as Laozi and Zhuangzi incite them to do so? If it is not clarified that the foundation of the spirit is nonarising and the nature of all things is empty in order to illuminate the culmination, what is considered to be the Great Way? This writing [of the Great Way] has disappeared. Who in the world could know about it?

"The historian [Sima] Qian talks about the Five Thearchs. In all [his remarks], he says, '[The Yellow Emperor] was a born genius,' 'He was able to speak as an infant,'[174] '[Emperor Gaoxin, a born genius,] spoke his own name (i.e., he named himself),'[175] '[Emperor Gaoyang] was serene and profound and well versed in all things,'[176] and 'His (i.e., Emperor Yao's) intelligence was just like that of spirits.'[177] [These remarks] are already similar to those about the birth of the Mahayana bodhisattvas who manifest in various kinds of transformations. [The Yellow Emperor] resided on the hill of Xuanyuan, climbed up Mount Kongtong, and ascended Mount Wan and Mount Dai.[178] [Emperor Gaoyang] went to Youling and Panwu,[179] and his outstanding vestige is beyond waves (i.e., the secular world). How could we know that [their activities] were not derived from the Way of the Tathāgata?

"During the long-lasting period of the Five Thearchs, Yao reigned for one hundred years and Shun for only seventy years. In the style of Guang Cheng, Dawei, Hong Yai, Chao[fu], Xu [You], Zhifu, the northerner [Wuzhai], and the four immortals of Mount Gushi, the profound manners were accumulated and brimmed over at that time. Of the books by the Five Thearchs, however, there are only two compositions extant: the *Tang*[*dian*] and the *Yu*[*dian*] (i.e., the *Canon of Yao* and the *Canon of Shu* in the *Book of History*), which are not complete. Furthermore, in Zichang's records (i.e., the *Shiji,* compiled by Sima Qian) it is said that 'Thinkers of the various schools wrote about the Yellow Emperor, but their writings were neither elegant nor instructive. Even government officials do not easily express in words about [the writings].'[180] The historical records only adopted the vestige of bloody matters of rule, and did not record even a single [word about the truth] in a million [words]. How can we accept that it is entirely false [that there were Buddhist practitioners in ancient times] just because the flourishing of the highest path (i.e., Buddhism) is not found in these incomplete compositions?

"Now, here we see the ruler of spiritual intelligence who roamed in the great and vast world, the seven sages who all together went to Mount Juci,[181] and a holy man seen on Mount Gu Ye.[182] They were beings in transformation. Why do we have to explain much about them? How could we know that what [these] sublime words elucidate is not [the manifestation of] the spirit that went to extremes beyond numerous *kalpa*s? Guang Cheng said, 'The essence of the ultimate Way is deeply obscure.'[183] He means [by this] the 'heroic valor concentration' (*shoulengyan sanmei;* Skt. *śūraṃgama-samādhi*). [His statement] 'He who attains my Way will be the August at the highest, or a king at the lowest' means that one can ascend or descend according to the edification; he is similar to the Flying Emperor, [that is to say,] the wheel-turning noble king (Skt. *cakravartin*). [His statement] 'He who fails in attaining my Way will see the light for the highest, or he will become the earth for the lowest'[184] refers to those who transmigrate in Heaven and in the human realm.

"[When the Yellow Emperor met a herder,] he sensed the great lofty air [of the boy], called him the Heavenly Master, and withdrew from that place.[185] [The Heavenly Master] is also [one of] the ten epithets [for the Buddha].

This is probably the teaching of nonarising (i.e., Buddhism). The [Buddhist] Way was deeply practiced at that time. The practice spread among [people of] profound and distinguished [knowledge], but this fact went into oblivion in ancient times, and the [Buddhist] doctrines were concealed behind writings. Thereupon, what the various schools of thinkers collected seems understandable but it is obscure. Furthermore, the learned among government officials do not say that [their writings] are elegant and instructive. Consequently, the result is that those who follow the worldly way and who do not deeply master the Way depend on history books that restrain them from reaching the [Buddhist] doctrines, disregard the profound edification complying with immediate feelings, and put their vigorous spirits in eternal trouble. Isn't this sad?

"Boyi said in the *Book of Mountains and Seas* (*Shanhaijing*), 'In the country of Tiandu the people are very dear to others and love each other.'[186] In Guo Pu's commentary on the book it is said, 'The country we formerly called Tiandu is Tianzhu (i.e., India) where Futu (Buddhism) originated, and the expression "to be very dear to" means "to love."' [This is] also a model
12c of the Tathāgata's great benevolence. Originally [Buddhism] was known in the times of the Three Augusts and the Five Thearchs. Although the national statute records do not impart [this information about Buddhism], this is insufficient to cause doubt.

"Generally, how can we surmise things that happened from the three dynasties (i.e., Xia, Yin, and Zhou) to the time of Confucius and Laozi, which were not recorded in books of history? Confucius asked about rites and Laozi responded to [his questions]. [Complying with] the request of the Prefect of the Pass Yin [Xi], [Laozi] elucidated the Way for him [by compiling the *Daodejing*].[187] If the two chapters [of the *Daodejing*] had disappeared and his words remained only in the *Book of Rites,* people of later ages would have said that the old man of the imperial censor (i.e., Laozi) knew only about rites. Wouldn't this old scholar have mastered what is profound? Now, when the existence of various writings for a hundred generations is uncertain, [with some being extant and others having been lost,] there is nothing fully complete in reason. How could we judge solely by our observation that Confucius and Laozi had no exchange [with Buddhists]?

"Replying to a question of Emperor Wu of the Han dynasty, Dongfang Shuo advised him [to ask a man from Central Asia about the black ashes he had obtained, which, Zhu Falan later said, were the remains] burned in fire at the time of the exhaustion of a *kalpa*.[188] Liu Xiang's *Biographies of Arrayed Transcendents* (*Liexianzhuan*) states that seventy-four men [of the Transcendents] are found in the Buddhist scriptures. These are [views of limited scope] of scholars. Again, it was not [during the reign of] Emperor Ming of the [Later] Han dynasty that [Buddhism] began [in China]. Nevertheless, those who exercise their spirits and stick to mundane matters are many and evident, while those who form sincerity in the tranquil and subtle state are rare and inconspicuous. Therefore, the fact to secretly be grateful [for the Buddha] is simply not exposed in sentient beings.

"The eminent Buddhist monk Fotudeng was a kindhearted sage at the time of Shi Le and [Shi] Hu. [Fotudeng] told Shi Hu that 'In the city of Linzi county (in present-day Shandong province) there is the old site of the King Aśoka Temple where there is still a [buddha] image, and the dew basin is buried in the earth, twenty *zhang* under a big tree in a deep forest.'[189] An envoy of [Shi] Hu looked for them, relying on the illustration, and found everything [Fotudeng] had mentioned. Recently, when Yao Lüe's uncle was a king of Jin, he saw a bright light at the site of the King Aśoka Temple, so called by the elders, in Puban of Hedong. Seeking [the origin of the light], he had [his men] dig there and obtained relics of the Buddha in a silver case inside a stone container. The brightness was extraordinary. Following [Yao] Lüe, [the king of Jin] came out onto the bank of the Ba River to see [the relics arrive]. Today *bhikṣus* live in a new temple [where the relics are worshiped].

"From the observation of these facts, [we can see that] a long time has passed since Buddhist practices were transmitted to the land of Qi and Jin. The reason [the transmission of Buddhism] was not mentioned in the three commentaries [on the *Spring and Autumn Annals*] (i.e., the *Chunqiu Zuoshizhuan,* the *Gongyang,* and the *Guliang*) is similar to the reason why in the history books written by Gan Bao and Sun Sheng (i.e., the *Jinji* and the *Jinyangqiu*) there are no remarks about the Buddha. The subtle [Buddhist] edification is, however, really obvious. During the Jin period, [Buddhism] flourished in the Jiangzuo area (present-day Jiangsu province)."

A person asked, "If all buddhas actually exist, understand thoroughly all phenomena, and are able to do all things freely with their awesome supernatural powers, why do they not brightly manifest themselves today? Why do they not cause those of exquisite [faculties] and those of weak [faculties] equally to have faith and awaken them to the truth? Why do they not disperse their spiritual functions over [people] in distress in order to remove them from the fate of being accused with a false charge? Why do they not make the class of gentlemen see Buddhism?

"Accordingly, people do not equally believe in [Buddhism], and they fall down together into the suffering of an *icchantika*. Among the people of the states of Qin and Zhao, six hundred thousand were buried by Bai Qi and Xiang Ji in a day.[190] Actually, all people of good ethics of all ages, and all those who were buried neither necessarily have the conditions from previous lives for great wholesomeness, nor do they accumulate great evils without any [good] conditions. Nevertheless, [the buried people] had no chance to see the Buddha's mercy and were buried together on the same day. Sadly, this misery is completely equal [for all of them]. [All buddhas] watched this
13a extremely cruel [incident] from their seats, and never responded. What can be considered to be their mercy?

"The condition [advocated in Buddhism] does not overturn one's fate, and [Buddhist] virtue does not cause people to leave the [miserable] world; that is to say, [Buddhism] cannot save people. On what basis can it be considered that [the Buddha's] supernatural power is free and wonderful? Marquis Yang of Lu state put off the sunset [by guiding the sun with a spear when he fought Han state].[191] Geng Gong [of the Later Han dynasty] welled out water [by adjusting himself and vowing twice in the land of the Xiongnu].[192] Song [Jun of the Later Han dynasty, the governor] of Jiujiang, [governed well]. [Therefore], tigers [who had harmed the people there] kept out of Jiujiang and locusts were held back at the state boundary.[193] Since they all thoroughly employed the power of their minds freely, they could mysteriously move non-human beings [and phenomena, such as the sun, water, tigers, and locusts]. It goes without saying that the Buddha's supernatural power to pacify [Bai] Qi's mind and tame [Xiang] Ji's mind is in order to save the lives of a million people. [To save their lives] is much easier than to put Mount Sumeru into a poppy seed and much more benevolent than to sacrifice one's physical body for [a hungry] tiger and a dove.[194]

"Nevertheless, if we think this now and yet it is unrealizable, if we relate this and yet it is not complied with, or if we entreat and yet there is no salvation, then it is desolate, no different from a bare, empty sky. Moreover, among Buddhists, there are those who become *śramaṇa*s and burn their bodies, those who renounce moral laws and cut the six feelings, and those who suffer from labor, or squander their fortunes in order to serve a temple and [buddha] images. It is pitiful that their present [existence] is promptly carried away and they do not see what they have attained. Alas! It is a pity!

"If it is said that the response (i.e., retribution and reward) will come in the future, [this does not make sense because] the six hundred thousand people mentioned previously were different [in terms of] the goodness and evil of their actions, and yet they were equally killed through injustice. Even if good and evil acts differ from each other, why is there difference only in what they undertook after death? Differences between good and evil acts made in the present life become one and are not graded. The future is vast and restless. What are we supposed to expect there? Are we supposed to be afraid that there is really no future?

"A sutra says: 'As [the Buddha's] toes touch the earth, all triple-thousand buddha lands appear, and all people, even to the extent of the blind, the deaf, the dumb, prisoners, and those who are suffering, attain peace.'[195] Regardless of distance, life or death, and observance of the precepts (i.e., Buddhist or non-Buddhist), the Buddha is equally benevolent to everyone. If [the Buddha] has the benevolent mind, he should see people's suffering, and he should give peace to them in the same manner as [is related] in this [passage of the sutra]. Moreover, Buddhist scriptures have many words like this, to make us happy. In fact, somewhat unexpectedly there is no immediate response. How can we know that this is not the case of an outstanding person in a foreign land whose ability was superior to his contemporaries, who made this fictitious teaching, who used threat and conciliation, whose words had subtle and profound tastes, and who [expounded] matters that have the gracefulness of clarity and solemnity, and consequently [those of a simple heart] easily believed in him, submitted themselves to [his teaching], and then undertook unfathomable matters one after another, and the situation does not stop?"

I answered, "You do not see the path [of the Buddha]. That is why you take a smooth path to be rocky. If you actually look at the path from above, you will not see anything difficult. Nothing, in its regular course, is the Way.[196] The Buddha simply established the [Buddhist] Way by means of the spirit.

Hence, virtue and the Way are one. The spirit and the Way are two [different issues]. Since they are two [different issues], they illuminate [sentient beings] in order to lead to [myriad] transformations. Since [virtue and the Way are] one, they always have causality and yet nothing to create.

"Each of myriad transformations certainly follows causality, and is created in the Great Way. The reason we call him the Buddha is because he is free from all existing things and is beyond comprehension; it is not because he can save people absurdly, apart from [the causes and] conditions they created in their previous existences. Sentient beings are innumerable. Guidance of the spiritual function entirely pervades, just like complying with [the unevenness of the surface of] a precipice. What part is illuminated is simply unthinkable. For instance, [the great] flood and the four villains [during the reign of Yao], the ignorance of [Shun's father] Gu, and the haughtiness of [Shun's
13b brother] Xiang are entirely the true aspects of nature, which even [the sage kings] Yao and Shun could not change. Nevertheless, it is certain that in each case [the problem was solved] complying with its precipice (i.e., case): [Yao and Shun] controlled the flood and exiled the [four] villains. This is as sufficient as being able to meet their virtue. Wouldn't it be great?

"The [Way of the] Buddha is probably none other than the Way of sages. [The Buddha] does not only accomplish salvation for sentient beings but also expounds the teaching for those of the realms beyond this mundane world. It is just as with Yao's distinguished corresponding manifestation that when causality is ripe, even without doing anything, his achievement spontaneously manifested [in phenomena]. The reason the tones of a bell move non-humans, [just as the tunes of Zou Yan's music caused a variety of millet to grow in a cold ravine,] is because the [human] mind profoundly corresponds [to the non-human's],[197] not to mention [how every being is moved by] ingenious sages who consider the principle of the spirit as virtue.

"Generally, all those who have encountered each other in a far buddha land have a strong will and a pure spirit that have increased in brightness through many *kalpa*s. Thereupon, they are able to take in [the Buddha] and understand him thoroughly. The result is that Śākyamuni emits light that shines throughout the ten directions, Prabhūtaratna [Buddha] caused a [seven-treasure tower] to spring up [whenever the *Lotus Sutra* was expounded],[198] and the world of Merupradīparāja Tathāgata was moved into Vimalakīrti's [ten-foot-square] room [in an instant].[199] How could the Buddha manifest himself alone [without causality]? [Those who are capable] can see [the Buddha].

"As for people like the gentlemen here today, they were not born in the fortunate [world] of the Arhat (i.e., the Buddha) but live within the land governed by Yu (i.e., China). Since in sincerity they all went against [the Buddha] in their former [existences], they meet perversity in their present [existences]. Even if a person is as upright as [Bo]yi and [Shu]qi, or as dutiful as [Hui of] Liu[xia] and Ji[zha], as long as what he sets his mind on is against [Buddhism], how can he feel and see the Buddha? It is even [more difficult] for those who are presently called gentlemen or those below them [in status]. Although these people perfume their bodies with decorum and emit the fragrance of fame in the world, they have strong sensual desires and their ambitions do not adhere to the [Buddhist] Way. 'The gentleman among men is, in fact, the small man of Heaven.'[200] On what basis could one who contains the highest spirit respond to the affections of their minds? How could there be a case where the Buddha unfairly hides from them? They themselves do not see [the Buddha].

"If some people were born following [a cause and] a condition and have the sincerity to practice the six *pāramitās* due to acts made in their previous life, they feel and see [the Buddha] brightly by themselves. There must be such people time after time. If so, and if there are Buddhist clergy and laypeople side by side, how do we know the difference between them? In this case, coarseness and excellence lie in oneself. Hence, whether or not one sees [the Buddha] is due to the difference in the response [they would receive]. How could you doubt the existence of the Buddha because you are not clear about the glorious appearance [of the Buddha]?

"There are numinous beings between Heaven and Earth. It is clear that the vigorous spirit is not perishable. Now, the spirits of the [buried] people of the states of Qin and Zhao arose together with the universe. Even if Heaven and Earth are settled and corrupted, [the spirits] are imperishable. How could the two generals [Bai] Qi and [Xiang] Ji destroy six hundred thousand spirits at once? Spirits are unable to be exterminated; what are exterminated are physical bodies. Just as the Buddha says, what is usually perishable are the physical bodies of sentient beings. Since the bodies [of six hundred thousand people] perished, wouldn't they all have used up their natural life spans [when Bai] Qi and [Xiang] Ji [buried them]? How can we make this clear?

"[The *Book of Changes* states:] 'The method of Qian (i.e., Heaven) is to change and transform, so that everything obtains its correct nature as appointed [by the mind of Heaven].'[201] All lives, extending to those of birds, pigs, dogs, and sheep, are treated equally in the hexagrams (six-line diagrams) and the six diagrams for divination [in the *Book of Changes*]. People eat other living creatures in order to support themselves. They are as cruel as spiders that spin their webs [in order to catch and eat other insects]. Hawks and tigers cannot survive unless they catch and eat [other animals], but people can [subsist] on cooked grain and vegetables. Even so, [people still kill and eat other living creatures]; they are very ferocious. The Way of Heaven is extremely fair; what it disseminates is life. How could it allow people to oppress the lives [of others] and suppress a response from the unseen world?
13c Even though the [buried] six hundred thousand people must have been dissimilar to one another in character—some were good and some were bad—I am afraid that they did not differ in mercilessly eating other sentient beings. The good is different from the bad. Therefore, [the reward and retribution] they received in their lifetimes should have certainly been dissimilar. [However,] they were all equal in harming sentient beings. Consequently, they should assuredly have received detriment on the same day.

"Daoist sayings and what people of the world say are nothing new. Regarding Lord Yu [of the Han dynasty, a virtuous man who administrated fair justice,] and Bing Ji, [who rescued and raised Emperor Xuan of the Han dynasty,] their virtuous conduct of rescuing and making others happy was later rewarded.[202] On the other hand, Yan Yannian [of the Han dynasty], Tian Fen [of the Wei dynasty], and Emperor Xuan of the Jin dynasty murdered [innocent people] and received retribution in turn. These [examples] are all found in books of history of the Han and Wei dynasties as what was believed in the world.

"[One's acts] to save the lives of others will pass on blessings to his descendants, not to speak of the case where one's vigorous spirit becomes the subject to save or destroy others' lives; he will have reward or retribution in his later existence. If we destroy or save others' lives, we ourselves will certainly receive retribution or reward. Needless to say, if one satisfies or frustrates the spirit of others, he will ascend or fall in his own spirit. Those killed by [Yan] Yannian were all ordinary small people, while Dou Ying, [who was killed by Tian Fen,] and Wang Ling, [who was driven to commit suicide by Sima Zhongda, who later became Emperor Xuan,] were talented people; [the former was] a prime minister and [the latter] a loyal official [of the Wei dynasty]. [These victims] were dissimilar in their intelligence and social status, but [their killers] were equal in receiving retribution.

"In respect of receiving retribution, it is [meted out] regardless of excellence or humbleness; there is no difference between a general, a minister, and an emperor of the Jin dynasty. Isn't it the case where the Way of Heaven is extremely fair, [all people are equally] the children [of Heaven] regardless of the distinction of their mental faculty, or where the principle lies in a person's life, not in their nobility or humbleness? Even though a hog and a fish are humble, each of their lives is correctly based on the Way of Heaven. When we observe a large bird circling in the air, a small bird chirping, the ox whose lowing Gelu [of Jie state] recognized,[203] and the deer who moved Xi Ba [of Qin],[204] [we know that each of these animals] is deeply affectionate toward the fellow animals of its kind.

"[Suppose] there are a pregnant woman and a young child. If a person cuts open [the woman's belly] and scoops out [the fetus], or roasts [the young child], this is called an unjust and grievous offense, one at which Heaven shudders. To hunt pregnant animals in spring or to roast or salt down a lamb and a young bird are the same [as the case mentioned above] in the Way of Heaven. How could there be no retribution? Nevertheless, following the proper [ancient way of living] in which people drank blood, we now cannot suddenly stop hunting and fishing.

"Therefore, a sage king educated [people] by 'keeping away from the slaughterhouse and kitchen.'[205] This is probably because he tried to lessen the harm, submitting to the fact that people slaughter [animals for food]. If one walks into a slaughterhouse and hears [the animal's dying] cries, he cannot bear [to eat the meat]. To set up hunting [and fishing] seasons in accordance with the wolf, [who sacrificed its prey in the ninth month,] and the otter, [who sacrificed its fish in the first month,] is done because it is hateful to injure pregnant animals [by hunting] at the inappropriate time. To hunt [in spring] without a net shows clearly that the lives of living creatures are important. Mencius showed great appreciation [for King Xuan of Qi state, who could not bear to see an ox, a large animal, killed] in order to anoint bells with its blood [for worship, and who ordered the use of the blood of a sheep, a small animal, instead].[206] It is because Mencius knew that the king was so virtuous to abandon destroying life.

"Since the former kings relieved the masses and helped meet an urgent need, they had very deep benevolence, but they could not exercise strict control over [the destruction of life] immediately. The Tathāgata traced to the very source of spirit and elucidated its apex. Therefore, he values equally the lives in the five realms of existence, and set forth the abandonment of the destruction of life as the first of many precepts. King Bimbisāra received retribution [for killing] a white hare. [King Liuli of] the Śākya clan was ruined because [he had killed] yellow fish.[207] [These] indicate the natural features of retribution. [The law of causality] is entirely deep, profound, and inconceivable, yet evident.

"If [the people who were buried] had been able to listen to the [Buddhist] Way and had cultivated the teaching and the precepts with respect, they would certainly not have fallen into a pit at Changping and been buried alive [as were the soldiers of] Lord Mafu (i.e., Zhao Kuo) [of Zhao state].[208] Even after falling into the pit, if they had believed in the teaching [and had been able to practice] thoroughly, they would have surely transcended their impending
14a difficulties. If the sin caused by the condition [one created] in a previous existence is heavy, it is hard to receive the reward for his former [good conduct], but the virtue he earns by observing the precepts arrives later, and he will surely not be buried alive again in his next existence. What you said about dispersing the spiritual function over the distressed in order to remove them from suffering injustice is just such a case as this. It is the highest benevolence. If one who is good in secular values and yet who does not have faith in the [Buddhist] Way destroys the lives of many living creatures, retribution exposes him to danger. This is just as it should be.

"The Buddha avails himself of the principle [of causality], lives up to the very nature of things, and saves people through the Dharma. He cannot unreasonably save those who do not follow the Dharma and the principle. How could the Buddha be unreal? This can be compared to the case of Bian Que, [a great doctor of ancient China]. Even though he tried to cure a sick person with medicine, if [the sick person] did not trust him and did not take the medicine, the disease would not be cured. Wouldn't Bian Que still be considered an excellent [doctor in such a case]?

"The reason [Marquis] Yang of Lu state put off the sunset [by guiding the sun with a spear when he fought Han state], Geng Gong [of the Later Han dynasty] welled out water [by adjusting himself and vowing twice in the land of Xiongnu], and the distant ancestor [Song Jun of] Jiujiang had virtue by which locusts and tigers were kept out of the area, is entirely because their strong sincerity moved [the Way of the Spirit]. That the Way of the Spirit is moved is precisely the same as that the Buddha is moved. If [those who could have moved the Way of the Spirit] had been in the states of Qin and Zhao, they would surely not have fallen into trouble. That is to say, all those who fell into trouble had no sincerity. By what [force] could they have moved the Buddha and harmonized and softened [the minds of Bai] Qi and [Xiang] Ji?

"Since those who possessed supernatural power congregated at the hall of a thoroughly educated one (i.e., Vimalakīrti), it was possible to see Mount Sumeru in a mustard seed. Moreover, although they were now a tiger and a dove, they might have been human beings in their previous existences. They had once had the formation of a [good] condition. Therefore, they met the Buddha and received the good fortune of [the Buddha] sacrificing his physical body to save the [starving] tiger and cutting off a piece of his thigh to give [to a hawk] instead of [letting] the dove [be eaten by the hawk]. If it were not that [the Buddha] was moved and able to take action to sacrifice himself for them, how could the miracle to harmonize and soften [atrocious beings] recklessly happen? 'The cessation of blowing sounds from the myriad apertures completely attributes to each of their own causes.'[209] Why do you doubt the Buddha?

"If your determination [to take refuge in the Buddha] is firm, when you think of him, you will see him, and when you speak to him, he will listen to you. Confucius met the Duke of Zhou in a dream.[210] [Emperor Gaozong of the Yin dynasty] saw the figure of Fu Yue [in a dream,] and [after a search] Fu Yue in fact came to him.[211] [In the former case] there is a long interval between the time of the Duke of Zhou and that of Confucius, and [in the latter case] Fuyan, [where Fu Yue was found,] is a long distance away [from the capital]. [The separation in time and distance,] however, did not obstruct these profound meetings. When we presume from this point, we should believe that if we purify our thoughts and perceive [the west], we will see Amitābha Buddha beyond myriad worlds without any effort. Why do you say that there is no difference [between the Buddhist teaching] and the bare, empty sky?

"The Way lies in training the spirit, not in having the physical body exist. Hence, *śramaṇa*s shave their heads, burn their bodies, encourage their spirits, and cut off association [with the secular world]. The spirit is imperishable, and it is capable of traveling quickly to wherever it is going. Is there any contradiction?

"[People of the secular world] strive for principles of human relationships and are distressed with their six feelings. What can they find within themselves seeking agitation in their spirits? If they sincerely take the tonsure by themselves and cut off [association with the secular world], they will diminish [their actions] from day to day, and through the purification they will actually draw close to the Way. Even if they made strenuous effort to make a good reputation for themselves or expended all their fortune to build a fabulous residence, if they die soon after that, what they receive in name and reality does not go beyond 'robbers and boasters,' [just as is stated in the *Laozi Daodejing*].[212] If they construct a mansion where images of deities are placed and where it is profound, tranquil, and solemn, their physical bodies will comply with its subtlety and their spirits will follow the profundity. If [the physical body] is subtle, the response [they receive] will be pure. If [the spirit] is profound, the bliss [they receive] will be wonderful. Which is better: to be 'robbers and boasters' or to be close to the Way? 'Their present existence is promptly carried away,' [as you said previously,] because they rise to [Heaven upon death]. If they go secretly and are united with the spiritual intelligence, happiness and prosperity will manifest in their later existences. How can we see what they will obtain [in the present existence]?

"Activities in human affairs are certainly linked to the Way of the Spirit. In the phenomenal world nothing exists irrationally; everything must have
14b a reason to exist. If profound and unseen reward or retribution is not like what I have said above, for what reason were the six hundred thousand people buried alive? Since they were buried alive due to retribution, there must have been people who escaped from being buried alive due to reward. Now, among

people of the Warring States period, there were those as ingenious as An Qi[sheng], those as profound as the four white and bright men [of Mount Shang], and the man who became an emperor by having a noble face and who became a monarch by giving a part of his fiefdom to feudal lords (i.e., Emperor Gaozong of the Han dynasty). People of fame and talent were innumerable. They were as equally [in danger as] if they were within the target range of the skillful archer Yi,[213] but why would they alone be so [famous]? Wouldn't this be a corresponding manifestation of reward from each person's previous existence?

"Inasmuch as happiness in this existence is the result of actions made in a previous existence, it is clear that the actions one makes in this existence will result in reward and retribution in his next existence. Now, the difference of personality (i.e., good or evil) in this existence is made clear by the previous existence, so why is only what one accepts in his next existence allowed to be exceptional? According to what a sutra expresses, 'To take the chance to see the Buddha's edification is entirely due to the fact that there was originally an excellent condition [in the previous existence]. Therefore, when one meets [the Buddha], he feels as if he has met [the Buddha] before.'[214] [Nevertheless, you said that] there has been no sudden corresponding manifestation of response and all faults have nothing to do with [retribution]. On the contrary, you falsely accuse that the highest teaching [of the Buddha] is a fictitious idea. Alas! Divine examination is very evident. You should fear the offense of disgracing the Sage. I venture to ask you: Is the one who made up the fictitious idea a sage, a wise person, or a small person?

"The Sage does not have an invariable mind of his own. It is probably because he educates the masses, following their natures, and has them fulfill [what they have been taught]. If the spirit perishes when the body dies, [people] should just devote themselves to do their best with the Confucian teaching to the ends of their lives. Again, what is the matter? [Buddhists] try to delude people by saying that the spirit is immortal, and deceive them by telling about the attainment of buddhahood. [Buddhism] induces people to take the tonsure and burn the skin, and causes married couples to divorce. There are innumerable people who have refrained from having offspring. Moreover, distinguished sages have no fixed place to educate [people]; some are hiding and some are isolated [from the world]. What are these fictitious ideas good for? The harm they cause is much more painful. We know that this is not what sages and wise people did.

"If the person [who founded Buddhism] belongs to a group of [small] people like Fan Xu, [about whom Confucius lamented,][215] he restrains himself out of fear that the Duke of Zhou and Confucius may consider him a heretic and does not venture to act recklessly. If he is below the level of that group, he is merely one of the good-for-nothings. How can such a person found a school, in addition to the nine schools, be more honorable than Laozi and Zhuangzi, and illuminate [the world of] a thousand years later?

"Five hundred years [after Śākyamuni passed away], people like Nāgārjuna, Āryadeva, Aśvaghoṣa, Kātyāyanī, Dharmaṣresthin, Vasubhadra, and Dharmatrāta respectfully explained the teaching of the [Buddhist] Way in the *Dazhidulun,* the *Zhonglun* (Skt. *Mādhyamaka-śāstra*), the *Bailun,* and a group of the Abhidharma discussions. These people had a genius for supernatural powers. The eight wise men, such as Jīvaka and Jiantuole,[216] about whom Sun Chuo (d. ca. 370) recently composed a hymn, and those whose portraits Zhi Daolin (314–366) drew together with a eulogy, such as Dharmarakṣa, Yu Falan, [Yu] Daosui, and Que Gon[ze], have the spirit that shines over the Chinese nation. Zhu Faxing of China (i.e., the Western Jin dynasty) was compared to the Director of the Imperial Secretariat Yue [Guang] (d. 304) by his contemporary [Sun Chuo]. Śrīmitra of the Jiangsu area [during the Eastern Jin dynasty] was highly evaluated for the outstanding and lofty state of his mind by all the princes. Guo Wenju was broadminded, profound, and sincere, and he had faith only in Buddhism.

"Generally [speaking,] since the time of Nāgārjuna, could there be people who entirely incur danger caused by the deceit of those good-for-nothings mentioned above? In that case, wouldn't the matter of Master Yellow Face (i.e., the Buddha) be undoubted?

"The image, relics, teeth, hair, other articles, and remaining footprints
14c of the Buddha are still luminous in his homeland. This fact is also evidence of the [Buddhist] Way. There are many people in the foreign land (i.e., India) who have keen natures for examining things and who are intelligent. In addition, their sensual desires are generally deep. Since the time their ancestors stood in front of the Buddha, all of them have accumulated [faithful] acts,

intimately transmitted [Buddhism] in the world, and relied on the [undeniable] facts. The image, the relics, and the legacy [of the Buddha] brightly educate the people, and their harmonious relationship [with the Buddha] is clear. Hence, the descendant kings bade the whole nation to observe the precepts. The four kinds of Buddhist disciples devote themselves wholeheartedly to ascetic [practices]. They will have no regret even if they were to die [from these practices]. If the [Buddhist] doctrines are peculiar and vague, and if there is nothing real and wonderful in these events, would [the people of India] be willing to exert themselves to control their carnal desires in order to respect the Invisible One? If the image and the articles [left behind by the Buddha] are not real, and if [groundless] rumors are circulating, why do people, both of the past and of present times, torment themselves to leave behind carnal desires in order to make progress toward the goal? [Some people] must be discouraged in the process of cultivation, but almost everyone becomes more serious. We can briefly infer [from this point that the Buddhist Way is indubitable].

"I would like to argue [the following]. The reason why from former times [the fruition] is not evident for those who study the [Buddhist] Way is because [their intention] lies in holding onto life, but suffering arises from [holding onto] life. Ignorant people are not aware of this. Therefore, all buddhas enlighten them by means of [teaching the causes of] suffering, and lead them by means of [teaching] non-birth. [The idea of] non-birth cannot be quickly realized. Then the people are led by means of reward and retribution in their existences. If one collects merit and sublimates himself more and more, he can be led to the clear, serene culmination. For this reason, the [Buddhist] Way is as vast as a blue sea. No matter how small, there is nothing that is not ferried across, and no matter how large, there is nothing that is not led.

"Even though [the Buddhist Way] is very much opposed to [the teaching of] striving after making a living and holding onto life, it also teaches the five cardinal duties and induces people to practice and assist ethical education. The reason why people of the world say that weal and woe are not well timed in the Way of Heaven is similar to the reason why the historian [Sima] Qian had deep emotion about [the unhappy death of] Boyi.[217] First of all, why would the sage Confucius have made a reckless statement? Confucius said, 'If one accumulates enough good deeds, his family will have more than enough blessings to spare, but if he accumulates enough evil deeds, his family will have more than enough misfortune to spare.'[218] Nevertheless, Yan [Hui] died young and Ran [Boniu] had a disease. We have never heard about their descendants. [On the other hand,] Shangchen (i.e., King Mu of Chu state) died a natural death in old age, [even though he had murdered his father, King Cheng,] and his son King Zhuang was sagacious and assumed the hegemony. Generally these matters cannot be entirely understood in reason, but could there be anything that is not understood in reason?

"We cannot help believing the teaching that [if one accumulates enough good deeds,] he will have blessings in his later existence, and [if he accumulates enough evil deeds,] he will have misfortune in the three lowest realms of existence. Even though the physical body has life and death, the vigorous spirit will certainly receive responses (i.e., reward and retribution) to [what one has done in his lifetime]. How is this different from the case where the responses to one's conduct manifest in their present existence? Causes and conditions, however, have a sequence. Therefore, the manifestation of reward and retribution has timing: early and late. It is just as there are early or later manifestations of fortune or misfortune in one's lifetime. In this case, the Confucian teaching supports the Buddhist [teaching] and both meet on common ground. [The Buddhist teaching] can really be said to be the extremely profound and unalterable Way.

"Human beings are just like dust floating in the air; life and death are illusory. If [life and death] are encompassed within the framework of one hundred years, there is no one, wether young or old, who is not included. Even [elderly people] whose hair has faded and turned to yellow and whose back is hunched over [with age] and covered with spots, like the blowfish, still feel that the time they have lived is fleeting, not to mention those who have lived for a shorter time. Moreover, time never stops and the movement [of heavenly bodies] is everlasting. The time that has already passed is incalculable and limitless. Each moment is as brief as the blink of an eye or a glance, and it has simply come down to the present time. Why is it difficult to come up to one hundred years by accumulating moments that are as brief as the blink of an eye? There are, however, few people who are able to reach even half [of one hundred years].

"People's attachment to their physical bodies, which are [as short-lived as] morning dew, has mostly nothing in the reality of the clean and remote [world]. Why do they content themselves [within the brief period of time of] a water clock with [the physical body, which will eventually] become rotten and stink, abuse the eternally existing (i.e., immortal) spirit, and not themselves cast obstructions to the remote wind? Although the Nominalists and the Legalists are statesmen, why would they alone have nothing to do with [this fact] in the Great Way? Since they merely wander in the realm of human beings, and are noisy on the worldly path, they simply feel that the human way is prosperous and belittle the idea of spirits. If we turn ourselves around in the center of the world and ascend a high mountain, we have wonderful views far away: the clear spaciousness of the universe and the wonder of the sun and moon shining through. Could it be possible that there is no dignity of awesome numinous beings of various sages there, and there is only a multitude of people who busy themselves with worldly matters? Certainly, we will think of the eternal [world] in order to open the thought of the Way of the Spirit, and feel tranquility in order to elucidate the corresponding manifestation of numinous beings. 15a

"In the past in Lu state Confucius wrote the Five Classics, by which he educated the people of the world. When he looked down from the top of Mount Tai and Mount Meng, both the world and Lu state appeared small [to him].[219] Doesn't this indicate that his spirit united with the universe and consequently he transcended this world? If this is so, the Five Classics were probably written merely to respond to trivial requests [of the world] for a momentary lifetime. How is it possible that the people of the world block the Buddhist Dharma and do not believe in it?

"I would like to ask you: Is the reason you do not believe in [the Buddhist Dharma] because [you think] there is no spiritual intelligence but the multitude, or because [you think] that there is spiritual intelligence but there is no buddha? If there is no spiritual intelligence at all but the multitude, then who ordered the swallow to cause [Xie, the founder of] the Shang dynasty to be born into the world?[220] Who left the footprints of a giant that caused [a lady] to have a feeling and give birth to Qi (i.e., Houji)?[221] The Han, Wei, Jin, and Song dynasties all had an auspicious decree from Heaven [for the establishment of the dynasty]. Therefore, we know that beyond the world of visual and auditory senses the Way of the Spirit brightly exists. If there are the principles of spirits, there must be the subtle zenith. If 'he who is marvelous since he has gotten the One' is not the Buddha,[222] who else could he be? The spiritual being profoundly responds according to each case. It does not respond in predetermined ways. Following a fact, it offers teaching. Why are you worried that it is not complete? Why is it necessary to deceive the people and later teach them? In that case, it is not open to question that the Dharma is real and the teaching is truthful.

"I would like to discuss and say that all sentient beings take the vigorous spirit to be primary. Therefore, by [natural] law all beings respond to the spirits who have reached the profound culmination. In the case of Yao, various kinds of animals that lived far away danced, being impressed with his virtue.[223] Isn't this the manifestation of moving [and responding between Yao and the animals]? The Buddha is the foundation of various manifestations of moving and responding. For the sun, moon, the seas, and the high mountains, there are the morning and evening rites and the significance of the worship of viewing the mountains and rivers from a distance, not to mention the Buddhist Way that many people cultivate; those of high rank trace to the very source of spirits beyond the realm of arising, those of middle rank receive a physical body in the subtle realm of arising (i.e., the realms of heavenly beings and human beings), and those of low rank can be exempted from the three lowest realms of existence.

"What the worldly teaching propagates is to attain peace and order in the whole course of one's life. Those who deeply master [the Way] are rare, while those who [chase after] the world are numerous. How could they have ever participated in [the Buddhist Way]? They just follow worldly trends and say that if one dies his spirit perishes. Consequently they do not strive for a lofty aspiration in the pure and distant [world], and utilizing every spare moment, many people comply with worldly trends. Therefore, the way of gentlemen is seldom practiced. If we examine with the Buddhist Dharma, our physical bodies are not ourselves; probably they are only like an inn in which to rest
15b for awhile. The spirit is the part of ourselves [that remains permanently]. It exists boundlessly and eternally, and has no end (i.e., is immortal).

"The virtue of those who have the best virtue pervades over them limitlessly. Those who are good in the middle rank are slowly led to purity, are promoted, and attain the exhaustion [of defilement]. Those who are least virtuous in the low rank just have a chance to reform their evil acts, and they may make up for mistakes they have made to move to an upper rank. Therefore, from ancient times, regardless of sharp and dull faculties, there are innumerable people who keep themselves pure, hold a lofty aspiration, behave prudently in the present existence in order to shape karma in the next existence, and go on to supreme virtue. This is the efficacy of the Buddhist Dharma. These are all what worldly customs and traditions block and what the Buddha opens up. As for the category, isn't it the vast bright way to the wondrous existence? Why do you disregard it and not uphold it?

"Wind, after passing through a flame, is warm, and it is assuredly fresh when it blows through a forest. Water becomes muddy in a rapid stream, and when it becomes purified the rocks can certainly be clearly seen. Gains and losses in the function of the spirit also lie in to what the spirit entrusts itself. Not having faith in the Buddhist Dharma is not necessarily due to one's temperament but is probably because of one's frame of mind. If you try to keep your mind away from worldly affairs and move what is projected [in your mind] to the pure and subtle [state], the Buddhist doctrine will be clear and all matters can be believed. It is really wonderful to frame one's mind [in this way]!

"If you avail yourself of this clear token of [what the Buddha taught] in the past, you will eventually be able to become a ruler in the Way of the Spirit. Since you can eternally save all the karma of your ancestors, both evident and hidden, up to a hundred past generations, it is the great filial piety. Since all sentient beings benefit from benevolence, it is the highest mercy. Since the spirit concentrates and becomes subtle, it is the culmination of the Way. Since it penetrates brightly without hindrance, it is the completion of brightness. If what began even in the mind of an ordinary person is placed on the right track at the beginning, even if many *kalpas* pass, for sure it will directly gather at the profound culmination [of the Way] in the end. [Buddhism] is wonderful like this. Equally, if the same [ordinary] person fails to get onto the track [of Buddhism] and goes astray, he will aimlessly go a long way and eternally sink into the nine realms [of the transmigration of birth and death]. How sad it is! If what I said above is not true, why in the world do virtuous sages suddenly appear, why are stupid and humble people born and brought up, and why are there all buddhas in the upper stratum and flying and wriggling insects at the bottom? All of these are the natural features of the gains and losses of the spirit.

"People have a physical body of seven *chi* and grow old and die in several tens of years, of which half is entirely occupied by nighttime. Since there are many days to go into mourning or to get sick, [people] suffer for half [of their remaining time, not counting nights]. Even if someone has prosperity in his life, or if he attains his aim in enjoying prosperity, how [valuable] is this? In addition, the prime of life passes [quickly], and when one has honor and fame he is certainly afraid of being disgraced. Pleasure really comes together with distress, and there is no perfect peace. [People,] however, strive with each other in entering the steep path of popular custom, and hate to advance on the spacious path of the Buddhist Dharma. What do you think of their intelligence? There are really many people in the world who are troubled about the Buddhist doctrine since they cannot understand the beginning of the conditions that give rise to phenomena. [The realm of] conditions that give rise to phenomena is vast and limitless, and it is not reached by our recollections. What gains and losses are concerned with cannot be perceived through [understanding] the doctrines; namely, it is beyond the universe. Therefore, the Buddha left it intact and did not discuss it, as I have already presented in my previous discussion. I would like to repeat and explain this.

"'The sage created the *Book of Changes*.'[224] [Consequently we] can practice divination by interpreting the sun, moon, and heavenly bodies that hang down from the sky, and know good or bad luck, peace or upheaval. Nevertheless, when we investigate why it results in such a situation, [we find that]
15c
we are unable to know anything, since the sage did not clarify it. Now, if we give up what we can know because we do not know [why it results in such a situation], and take actions contrary to divination or against the signs of the sky, would anything be lost? To go against the Buddhist Dharma because the beginning of conditions that give rise to phenomena is not clear is similar to this. Moreover, people say that the spirit originally does not exist since they do not remember what they thought in their former existences.

"If a person [does not remember anything] from the time he was a fetus to the time his milk teeth were replaced with permanent teeth, it cannot be said that he had no spirit. This happens only within his [present] life. When he thinks of this he has a vague feeling and remembers nothing, not to mention one who has experienced the transmigration of birth and death and who has gone through different bodies. Why wouldn't the memory of his former existence have faded away? Even if his memories fade, it does no harm to the eternal existence (i.e., immortality) of the spirit. If he does not understand about the beginning of conditions that give rise to phenomena, why is it an obstruction to its doctrine that is continually clear?

"When Zilu asked about death, the Master (i.e., Confucius) said, 'While you do not know life, how can you know about death?'[225] When he asked about serving spiritual beings, [Confucius] said, 'While you do not know about serving men, how can you know about serving spirits?'[226]

"Wouldn't it be that although [Zhong] You (i.e., Zilu) was completely fond of bravery and sincerely served his master, he should have originally asked questions about matters within his lifetime? Even though [Zilu] had questions about birth and death and the origin of spiritual beings, they are not from real affections of the mind based on reason. Therefore, [Zigong said,] '[The Master's discourses about] man's nature and the Way of Heaven cannot be heard.'[227] In Buddhist statements there is the phrase 'The fourteen questions regarding the issue of [permanency] of sentient beings or the issue on whether or not [the world] has boundaries are entirely left intact and not answered by all the intelligentsia.'[228] If answering [such questions] indeed has no benefit, [it causes people] to fall into viciousness. Then the Way to respect sages and to believe in the Buddha should decline what it renounces and should take what it is granted, just as when a thirsty man goes to drink water from a river and scoops up water from the stream [with his hands] to satisfy himself. Would it be necessary for him to trace the very source [of the water] on Mount Kunlun? Generally, in the Buddhist Dharma, unreasonable things like disobeying Heaven and hindering the principles can be doubted. Now, [in Buddhism,] there is no unreasonable hindrance and there is truth to follow the mandate of Heaven and purify the spirit. Wouldn't this really be so?

"When a person is born, he is born with anxieties. Trouble and misfortune happen in events every now and then. Natural disasters rise in force imperceptibly. Even refined and noble people or those who have a million followers spontaneously have a physical body and a spirit at the beginning, and wait for impermanence (i.e., death), just sitting there. Even though 'the members of the household are with stern severity' or 'the wife and children are to be smirking and chattering,'[229] they suddenly become downcast and absent-minded. How much less can we rely adequately on people's minds? Therefore, in as brief a time as [a man glimpses a white colt as it] passes by a crevice,[230] people just compete with each other. They wastefully slander the profound teaching and indulge themselves in wanting to harm it uselessly, but the spirit is immortal. Even if they desire its morality, they cannot have it, and they must receive a body because of a sin they have committed. Sentient beings who have no redeeming features and various kinds of insects of the present time are all examples of this. Those who try to seek [a better rebirth] should consign themselves only to sincerity, believe in the Buddha, rely on the mind, and observe the precepts in order to reinforce their vigorous spirits.

"If you receive the aid of numinous beings in your lifetime, you will be pure and peaceful after death. If you are pure and peaceful endlessly, then you will directly attain buddhahood. The Buddha is originally said to be this state, but people disparage it. On what basis do you judge that people are better than the Buddha? They are not better [than the Buddha]. They cannot stop falling into the evil realms where they eternally receive intense suffering. Alas! It is beyond our control in the secular world that there are people who
16a are born into the six extreme evils. Those who are diligent in what they hear and see, when they are about to die they mostly have a stable mind on their deathbeds. Even if those in urgent and desperate situations chant the name of Avalokiteśvara with wholehearted devotion, there is almost no one who will not be favored with salvation. I mentioned previously that these are all an auspicious omen: 'If you receive the aid of numinous beings in your lifetime, you will be pure and peaceful after death.'

"The emperor and feudal lords [are busy with administration and] have no time to eat leisurely even in the early afternoon, [but] the masses depend on [these people's hard work] only within their lifetimes. How can they increase [the strength of] their spirits and manage myriad cycles [of existence]? If you rely on the Duke of Zhou and Confucius to educate the masses, and taste the Buddhist Dharma to nourish the spirit, you will be an intelligent ruler in your lifetime and a bright spirit after death, and you will always manage [myriad cycles of existence]. How could the Tathāgata deceive me? [What he says] does not lead to wasting money and harming people by worshiping a pagoda, making luxurious images, and supporting incapable monks with tolerance.

"Those who do not see the profound reality of things and yet look at immediate disadvantages will unrestrainedly insult the Dharma. If, however, you revere the Way, believe in the teaching, become aware of impermanence, empty the realm of form, have benevolence, set in order the edification, do not take people's lives easily by abusing a position of nobility and power, and do not let a good-for-nothing person secretly avail himself of treatment beyond his lot, wouldn't it be possible that leading the masses by means of virtue and setting them in order by means of decorum would result in a world whose prosperity is attributed to benevolence? Why do both people of a rank with which they feel self-satisfied and those of low status who work in the fields and marshes value it highly enough, by which they can not relieve their vigorous spirits by themselves?

"Formerly Master Huiyuan purified his karma on Mount Lu. I went there and stayed for fifty days. [Master Huiyuan] was lofty and virtuous. His study of the [Buddhist] doctrine was exquisite. It was certainly a noble style. His teacher, Master Daoan, had spiritual virtue that was spontaneously wonderful. He was a *bhikṣu* such as is rarely encountered. They both kept purity themselves. Both were originally of wide knowledge in the [Buddhist] Way, and later lived in isolation on a mountain. Hence, [Huiyuan's] spiritual teaching is more profound than a solemn forest. [Master Huiyuan] often talked with me under the trees on a cliff or in a valley. [His words] were philosophical, but there was spontaneously something to admonish people in their expression.

"Generally, my discussion up to now is only what Master [Huiyuan] spoke in accordance with the tenor of the Buddhist scriptures. What is well confirmed refers to that [Cang Jie] created a written language on the basis of bird's footprints, that he who traced the very source of the spirit could hear people's songs, [which led him to truth,][231] or that [Emperor Wen of the Han dynasty] who recovered the power took Tiying's word (i.e., petition) and consequently corporal punishment was permanently abolished.[232] Certainly phenomena suddenly come out of the affections of the delicate mind and finally shoot up into the sky. With my confused, ignorant, and humble words I have warned of affections of the mind. If I suddenly die, how could I not know that I am transcending to [Heaven]?"

End of Fascicle Two of *The Collection for the Propagation and Clarification* [*of Buddhism*]

Fascicle Three

The *Discourse to Explain the [Buddhist] Way* (*Yudaolun*) by Sun Chuo

There was a person who was doubtful of the highest Way (i.e., Buddhism). I explained to him thus. The universe is immense and abundantly full of various kinds of things, in which a multitude of things abundantly exist and kaleidoscopic changes endlessly form a harmonious whole. Hence, those of limited knowledge expect what emerges within what they each view. [For instance, aquatic animals such as] fish and mollusks do not understand anything on the land near marshes, and those animals that have fur and feathers are not aware of the force of a stream and waves. Those who feel satisfied even while [caught] in a snare are suspicious about the capability of those who swim around in an ocean. Those who can fly only to a height of several *ren* doubt the ability of those who can soar high into the sky. 16b

People bound by the worldly teaching and who indulge in looking at the traces of the Duke of Zhou and Confucius say that the highest virtue reached its culmination with Yao and Shun, and that sublime words were completed in the *Laozi* [*Daodejing*] and the *Book of Changes*. How could they see the excellent tenor of that transcended world and what profoundly illuminates the darkness? It is sad! The [Confucian cap called] *zhangfu* is abandoned by people who customarily wear almost nothing, and [Emperor Shun's musical composition] *Dashao* and [Emperor Yu's] *Daxia* are ignored in rural areas. The highest truth is declined in unsystematic practices, and the Great Way is discontinued by scholars of limited views. If these people are extremely deluded and cannot be improved, they will not be moved by words and explanations. [Nevertheless,] I will try to clarify the tenor [of Buddhism, hoping that] there may be someone who will come to be awakened in due course.

The Buddha is the one who has realized the Way. The Way is what leads sentient beings. It responds to the affections of their minds and leads them by means of following them. "It does nothing, but there is nothing it does not accomplish."[233] Since it does nothing, it is free from preoccupation, peaceful, and spontaneous. Since there is nothing it does not accomplish, it spiritually educates all beings. In what all beings seek, there is the variety of low and high. Therefore, of the methods to transmit the teaching, some are precise and some are less exact. The foundation of the teaching is given to those of superior faculty. Misfortune is visited upon those who do not follow [the teaching]. Those who indulge in wine are imposed with a penalty. Those who commit adultery are punished heavily. Those who steal are meted out appropriate punishment [for the crime they committed]. There are the criminal laws established by the three dynasties, [the Xia, Yin, and Zhou,] and the five penalties.[234] People who violate the law are not pardoned. This is the rulers' common institution, of which prime ministers and governors take charge. If a sage king rules over the world and officials are intelligent and broad-minded, the criminals mentioned previously will certainly be thoroughly inspected, and there will be no hope of avoiding punishment. If vicious people are not allowed [to indulge] their self-interest, there will be no violators in the state, and wise and virtuous people will certainly be cited and evaluated for reward.

Moreover, when the ruler is bright, his vassals are honest, the world is pure, and the law prevails; we can especially distinguish good and bad from each other and not be confused about right and wrong. Needless to say, in
16c the place where deities are present, regardless of distance and obscurity, they are intelligent, upright, and honest in punishing the evil and helping the good. Hence, reward and retribution will visit even an extremely small merit and a very small demerit [respectively,] without the slightest aberration.

When we go over the testimonies of weal and woe of all ages, they all have derivations and are recorded in evidence. How could they be concealed? The reason [they cannot be concealed] is because in a family that has plotted a crime, its descendants will not flourish.[235] Daoists clearly proscribe that a family can inherit the position of general beyond three generations.[236] Isn't this because weapons are evil, and warfare is a perversion that leads to killing many people? Wei Ke followed [his father's] initial will and attained [the reward of] the grass trap.[237] [Bao] Zidu was faithful and received the conferment [with the help of] a very fast horse.[238] After Prince Xiang of Qi state pinned the blame on [Pengsheng], the disaster of falling from a vehicle befell him.[239] Prince Hui of Jin state ignored courtesy. Consequently, he was at a disadvantage and had difficulties [at the battle of] Hanyuan.[240] This is all corroborative evidence that the dead retaliate against or reward the living.

With regard to [the stories] that Xuan Meng had pity for a starving man, [Ling Zhe,] at Yisang[241] and an old lady who beat cotton in water sympathized with the weariness of [Han Xin, the Marquis of] Huaiyin,[242] these all show that with a meal one who had suffered from starving was saved. Moreover, Zhao [Dun] (i.e., Xuan Meng) received help from [Ling Zhe,] who betrayed his master [to save Xuan Meng's life], and the old lady [who beat cotton] received the reward of a thousand pieces of gold. These are [examples] of obtaining a large return by doing a minor favor. The reward did not go beyond their lifetimes. Therefore, when you achieve virtue secretly, blessing is revealed in all things. If you make an action implicitly, [the response to the action] shines explicitly. This is the natural course of events. It is compared to sowing grain seeds in the soil, and then reaping a harvest one hundred times greater [than the original quantity of seeds]. The earth and the grain have no feeling toward human beings, yet a natural advantage comes to them [from the earth and grain].

A person criticized this, saying, "If the issue of reward and retribution indeed entirely has signs, why does the teaching of the Duke of Zhou and Confucius not proscribe killing? Why was Shaozheng Mao executed [by Confucius]?[243] Why did [the Duke of Zhou] put his two younger brothers [Guan and Cai] to death?"[244]

I answered, "I can say that you understand the words of the teaching but you have not mastered the heart of the teaching. Do you think that the sages had the intention of killing [from the beginning]?"

The person answered, "No."

I continued, "You are really aware that they had no intention to kill. However, they killed [the three men] because it was simply the intention of the masses."

"As the times go and the world changes, insincerity and simplicity arise in human beings. Prior to the time when records were made by tying knots, the world was happy and very peaceful. In the time of Tang and Yu, decorum occurred for the first time. Accordingly, in the three dynasties, the net of criminal law became more evident. Even though executions were strictly carried out, this still did not prevent [crimes] as heinous as a ruler and his vassals exterminating each other, or fathers and sons killing each other. The law of the jungle was more violent than in the case of jackals and tigers. Sages were aware that the people's feelings were indifferent to killing and it was impossible to swiftly put an end to it. Therefore, they gradually restrained the people [from killing] and had them seek the appropriate manner.

"This is compared to the case where a viper bites a man's leg and he must have the leg cut off in order to save himself from death, or a man who has a malignant tumor in the body must gouge it out in order to save his life. To lose one in order to keep ten is to weigh the significant over the less significant. Hence, the reason criminals are executed in fall and winter is because they take life according to the seasons [when all things wither and decay]. The reason hunting is performed in spring and summer is to select and leave out pregnant animals and nursing baby animals. In the politeness of providing a way of escape,[245] if a bird or beast [unwittingly] comes toward [a hunter], he sheathes his bow [and does not shoot]. If you have heard the cries [of animals] or seen them alive, when their meat is served to you, you will not eat it. 'If you go fishing, you will not use a net. If you hunt birds with bow and arrow, you will not shoot those at roost.'[246] You have compassion for each and every insect.

"As for discussions of lawsuits, you will reprieve the death sentence, and in a time of natural disasters you will grant amnesty. If [the application
17a of punishment] is open to question, you will apply the less harsh one; you would sooner acquit someone of a charge [than mete out unjust punishment]. If you must pass a sentence of death, you will do so with tears in your eyes, feeling sympathy and never joyful. This shows that one's gratitude for having been given birth and raised is deep. It is the utmost in the way of humanity. This is what is called 'It does all and yet does not rely on them; it excels and yet it does not preside over all.'[247] This virtue covers [all things] and yet one does not think its merit lies in oneself. It is exercised daily and yet [all beings] are unaware of it.[248] When we take these points into consideration in order to seek [verification], it is sufficient for us to comprehend what [the teaching of the Duke of Zhou and Confucius] returns."

A critic said, "The Duke of Zhou and Confucius taught people to take life at the proper time, but the Buddha would like to stop [all killing] at a stroke. How can we punish brutal men, restrain wicked people, and exercise control over the masses?"

I answered, "This is not so. The Duke of Zhou and Confucius are nothing other than the Buddha; the Buddha is nothing other than the Duke of Zhou and Confucius. Probably, they are simply different names for non-Buddhism (*wai*) and Buddhism (*nei*). Thus, one who holds the reigns of the August is the August, and one who is on the throne of a king is a king.

"'Buddha' is a Sanskrit term; the Chinese translation is Jue. The meaning of the term *jue* is to enlighten people. It is compared to Mencius, who considered sages those who are first awakened [and then later enlighten others].[249] The purport is the same [in the Buddha and sages]. In responding to [the demands of] the world and serving as a [good] model for people, they probably comply with the time. [The teaching of] the Duke of Zhou and Confucius relieves the extremely corrupted world, while the Buddha's teaching simply clarifies the fundamental law [to save the corrupted world]. Both [teachings] are consistent; they do not differ as to the goal. Namely, it is just as the sages of non-Buddhism differ in the depth of their deeds. At the time of Yao and Shun, the world was peaceful. Hence, the two rulers nobly abdicated from the throne. Since the time of King Tang and King Wu was difficult, both rulers led troops into battle [for the throne]. There is a big difference between these people's actions, keeping silent [about handing over their reigns] and using force in their wrath.

"Nevertheless, as for the essential qualities of these actions, how much difference would there usually be? Therefore, those who consider retrogressively see one as two always, while those who understand properly have nothing to go to other than one."

A critic said, "In the teaching of the Duke of Zhou and Confucius, filial piety is considered to be the root. Filial piety is the culmination of virtue and the foundation of all actions. 'When this foundation is established, the way [of human relations] arises'[250] and '[utmost piety] reaches to spiritual intelligence.'[251] Consequently, in cases where children serve their parents, they attend to their parents with devotion while [the parents] are alive, and they offer worship to their parents after [they have] passed away. Among three thousand offenses, there is nothing heavier than having no offspring.[252] Our bodies are [received] from our parents, and we must not presume to injure or wound them.[253] Thus, Yuezheng [Zi Chun] was injured in the leg and was overwhelmed with shame for the rest of his life.[254]

"However, the way of the *śramaṇa* is to leave his native place recklessly, to abandon his parents, to stay with strangers, to shave his beard and hair, to damage his natural appearance, to have no sign of supporting [his parents] while they are alive, to discontinue the rite of ancestor worship after [his parents'] death, and to consider his parents by blood to be the same as mere passersby. In going against good conscience and hurting human feelings, nothing is worse than this. Nevertheless, [Buddhists] say we should propagate the [Buddhist] Way, spread benevolence, and extensively save all sentient beings. How is this different from mowing down the roots [of a tree], trimming the branches and trunks, and then saying that [the tree] will be distinguished and grow tall and thick? I have neither heard nor seen such a thing. If skin did not exist, how could hair attach to it? This greatly contradicts the worldly teaching. How are you going to reassure us about this matter?"

I answered, "This is really a serious delusion of the extremely vulgar and a great error caused by your wrong view. Alas! I cannot remain silent.

"Parents and child are one body, and they cast their lots together. Therefore, if a mother hurts her finger, her child feels a flutter in his heart [even if he is away from her]. It is because their common vapor causes him to feel
17b and respond to it. Their unity leaves no space between them. Therefore, to curry favor with one's parents is the utmost of filial piety. If a father is prosperous, his son will rise to a high position. If a son attains high rank, his father will be respected. Therefore, filial piety is valuable. It is valuable because we can rise in the world, practice the way [of humanity], and glorify our parents for a long time.[255] Even if we were to prostrate ourselves before our parents, cherish them, and offer them a feast of the three different kinds of meat (i.e., beef, mutton, and pork) every day, we would still not be able to cause all people to respect us. [On the other hand, if we have an achievement of] being relied upon by the whole world, this is close to the glory of nourishing our parents.

"'To be in accordance with the central element [of our nature] is the regular path.'[256] 'To maintain gentleness is considered to be unchanging [teaching].'[257] Both the physical body and fame should be renounced. We should dismiss from our minds both our parents and ourselves. These are the ways to nourish our parents. I have already elucidated the foundation [of filial piety]. I will talk to you further about the next issue.

"The two types of fame, being loyal [to one's country or master] and filial to one's parents, are incompatible with each other. [Kao] Shu of Yin opposed the ruler, [Lord Zhuang of Zheng state, and organized a meeting for Lord Zhuang and Lord Zhuang's mother, who had had a conflict with her son,] yet [Kao Shu] was praised as faithful and filial in a history book.[258] Shi Que killed his son [because he had kept company with Zhouxu, who had ascended the throne by killing the heir of Wei state], and displayed integrity as a loyal military man.[259] The [*Chunqiu*] *Zuoshizhuan* states that when a son [reaches the age when he] can enter government service, his father teaches loyalty to him; once [the son's] name is recorded on the orders of appointment and he is commissioned, it is considered an offense to serve two masters.[260] In this case, those who tie the chin straps for holding the cap at court have to give up the way of filiality. Why? Because if he sees [that his master] is in danger, he will sacrifice his life [to save his master] but will pay no attention to his parents.

"All these people's names are recorded in history books and their services are glorified as the highest of the teaching [of human ethics]. How could the recorders of history consider their impiety to be a sin? Therefore, as the proverb says, 'When you look for a loyal subject, you must go to the clan that produces filial sons.'[261] This indicates that even though there is a minor fault on one hand, there is a great favorable aspect on the other hand.

"Moreover, Gun was exiled to a border region, but [his son] Yu did not ask for permission to leave office.[262] If [Yu] had abandoned Yao's decree in order to look for his father, he would have placed the highest government affairs [below] his personal sorrow. This is mere minor wholesomeness, neither great nor lofty.

"Taibo of the Zhou dynasty left his relatives in the distance, sought escape in a strange land, cut his hair, and tattooed his body, [complying with the customs there,] and never returned to his homeland in his lifetime or even after his death.[263] Nevertheless, he is praised for having the highest virtue in Confucius's *Analects,*[264] and recorded as a man of great morality in the history books. This is actually because he was indifferent to the honorable throne and maintained the nobility of effacing himself; the merit he made by trying to give the throne [to his brother] three times is lofty, and the fault he committed by damaging his body [through cutting his hair and tattooing his skin] is minor. Consequently, he was able to make great changes to the barbarian customs and leave his teaching to history.

"[Bo]yi and [Shu]qi, who starved together on Mount Shouyang, did not consider the fact that [their father,] the lord of Guzhu, would lose his heir, yet Confucius considered them to be benevolent and wise.[265] Could there be critics who would say that these two people were immoral? Gao Xing of Liang state damaged her [good] looks and kept her chastity. Princess Bo of Song state followed righteousness and neglected her life. Both their names are ranked among those women who died to defend their chastity, and their virtue is considered a model for all women. If you keep in mind the morality of these two ladies, you will simply escape the charge of being stupid and immoral. When we speak in accordance with these points, we can see that [our judgment] is in order of the importance of the [standard] by which we abide.

"Formerly, the Buddha was a crown prince, but he abandoned his country and studied the way [to enlightenment]. He wanted to keep the original feature completely and enter the Way. [Nevertheless,] he was afraid that he would not be able to escape from being detained [in the palace]. So he cut his beard and hair and changed his court dress of a crown prince [to a common robe]. He showed [his will] to not return [to the secular world] outwardly and tried to govern himself in simplicity internally. Thus, he gave up the palace and stayed in a vast forest. He took off the clothes of imperial emblem in order to put on a [hermit's] robe of deerskin. Then, he took as his dwelling a place where tree branches hung down and a mat of grass as his cushion. He saved himself the trouble of combing his hair. He avoided the nuisance of taking a bath. He tightened the reins of running after [empty fame, power, and wealth], and closed the gate of carnal desires. His eyes were restrained from [the five colors such as] black and yellow. His ears were closed to lewd
17c sounds. His mouth forgot [the five tastes such as] sweet and bitter. His thought was released from joy and sorrow. His mind left behind nuisances.

"He stuck to the One (i.e., truth) and controlled his wandering spirit. He entered the breath-counting meditation (Skt. *ānāpāna*): (1) counting [from one to ten], (2) following [the breath on inhalation and exhalation], (3) abiding in tranquility (i.e., stopping mental activities), (4) contemplating [the breath], (5) transferring [the fruition to the wholesome faculty], and (6) becoming pure [and entering the way of insight]. He let his mind play in the three groups of the four stages of meditation, and he went in and out of the twelve gates of meditation. While he meditated, he folded his hands over the navel, was silent, remained still like a mountain, and was as serene as deep water. His spirit was just like cold ashes and his body was like a withered tree. He sat upright for six years. Then, enlightenment was achieved and he was called the Buddha.

"He is equipped with the three transcendental knowledges and the six supernatural powers. He attained right, perfect enlightenment. His graceful body, which is [one] *zhang* and six [*chi*] tall, has a golden glow. Its light suppresses that of the sun and moon. His voice is in harmony with the winds that blow from the eight directions. His body has the thirty-two [major] and eighty minor marks of physical excellence. He surpasses all beings. His spirit is completely free. Thus, he saunters beyond the three realms of existence, transforms freely in boundless realms, and makes the sky revolve, the earth dance, the mountains fly, and streams meander. He appears and disappears suddenly. His supernatural transformation is unceasing. Wherever his mind is directed, nothing can hinder him. By the great doctrine, he reformed a great number of evil beings to correct their courses. None among the numerous demons and those who had followed minor teachings did not adhere to [the teaching of the Buddha].

"At this point in time, Heaven became pure and Earth was made prosperous. 'The various things obtain their full development.'[266] Living creatures, even wriggling [insects], were immersed and nurtured in mysterious liquid. Withered and dry [trees] were refreshed and bloomed. [The Buddha] returned to his native country in glorious radiance, where he extensively expounded the teaching. His father, the king, was moved, became awakened, and ascended to the place of Buddhist practice, too. In this way, [the Buddha] brought honor to his father. What [ordinary] filial piety can be compared to this?

"Thereupon later generations receive and propagate the teaching. They resolve to revere the lofty path. They all follow their parents; they hold nothing other than what [their parents] esteem. They simply please their parents and then take the action [to become a monk]. If they have brothers, their parents' support is not abolished. Since they are able to cultivate the great work immensely, their gratitude to their parents is not neglected. Moreover, [Buddhist monks] enable the dead to attain happiness in order to be reborn in Heaven. They do not have to be concerned about offering ancestor worship. Isn't this the way to the Great Pervader (*datong*) that concurrently holds wholesomeness?[267]

"[The *Book of Changes* says] that the neighbor of the east side butchers an ox [in order to make an offering to a god], while the neighbor of the west side offers [simple] sacrifices to a god.[268] In [the religious rites of] the Yin dynasty, a variety of millet was considered to be good [for offering], but in [the rites of] the Zhou dynasty, the highest virtue was more esteemed [than offerings]. On this point the period of the rise and fall [of these two dynasties] is apparent.

"There are twelve kinds of scriptures in Buddhism. Four among them exclusively hold that exhorting people to be filial is important. The attentive intention [of these scriptures] can be said to be perfect. Nevertheless, ordinary people do not know the details of their origin. They have not gotten involved in the place concerned with [the Buddhist teaching], but then make wild talk and reckless speech; they wholeheartedly attack and criticize [Buddhism]. With a view as small as the light of a firefly or candle, they doubt [the teaching] that is as abundant as the light of the sun, moon, and stars. With [knowledge as shallow as] a drop of dew on the tip of a blade of grass, they doubt the quantity of water in a deep ocean. They consider false accusations to be eloquence and having [unreasonable] determination to be an honor. They can be said to be those who are disrespectful to great men and disgrace the ordinances of Heaven."[269]

Response to He Chengtian's Letter by Layman Zong Bing: The Criticism on the *Discourse on Buddhist Laymen and Clergy* (*Baiheilun*)

He's Letter to Zong

Recently I received a letter from you, virtuous Gentleman for Palace Attendant, which says that you are diligent in Buddhist rituals for [rebirth in] the Western Paradise. The determination of a person of virtue and talent [like you] is great. How could I regard [a lifetime as long as] ten thousand *kalpas* to be extravagant? However, I regret that our life span is short and

we have nothing to measure [the life span of the tree called] Mingling.[270] 18a
Huilin, a monk of Zhicheng Temple, wrote the *Discourse on Buddhist Laymen and Clergy,* and he was expelled from the sangha. Fortunately, he had the chance to gain the benevolent help of the brilliant sovereign (i.e., Emperor Wen of the Song dynasty), and he was able to escape from [permanent expulsion due to one of] the four gravest offenses (Skt. *pārājika*). Since those who become monks ought not to clarify this issue, why do we, lay Buddhists, keep silent? Could you please try to determine which is better, the clergy or lay Buddhists? I am very ignorant, but I hope you will have good ideas to enlighten me.

Sincerely yours,
He Chengtian

Zong's Response to He's Letter

Monk [Hui]lin's *Discourse on Buddhist Laymen and Clergy,* which you sent to me, is clear in writing and excellent in its points of argument. I am, however, in the dark about the explicit principles and I have not yet understood thoroughly the intention of [his discourse].

[The *Discourse on Buddhist Laymen and Clergy*] already states: "The principles of the unseen world are not based on human affairs alone. The Duke of Zhou and Confucius were doubtful of them, but they did not provide an explanation. Śākyamuni gives an explanation, but it is not true."

In this case, [which standpoint does Huilin take regarding his advocacy of] the principles of the unseen world beyond human affairs—are they vast and simply empty, or is there still the spiritual intelligence? If they are vast and simply empty, why do all sages, including Zhuangzi and Laozi, say that there are spirits? If there is the spiritual intelligence, on what basis did [Huilin] judge [that the principles of the unseen world are vast and simply empty] is really not like what the Buddha says?

Now we are altogether within the confines of ordinary people. Even when we infer familiar matters, we still make many errors and mistakes, through which we fall into disaster. Even in crude games like *go* and encirclement chess, we pay attention and examine them. Sometimes we think that it is alive but it turns out to be dead; or that it is dead but in fact it is alive. In all of our familiar matters, we have never seen those who always gain and never lose. On what basis does [Monk Huilin] determine [matters] outside of Heaven and Earth, beyond hundreds of million of *kalpa*s, and of the imperceptible [world], and say with certainty that what [the Buddhists] debate is not true? If we infer according to facts and are not allowed to obtain the reality, then we may have doubt.

The physical body of a human being is very coarse while the spirit is quite subtle. If the physical body follows the spirit, how could both equally die? [What happens when the nature] responds to the affections of the mind is [seen in these historical facts]: the city wall collapsed [when the wife of Qi Liang cried], frost fell [when Zou Yan cried out toward Heaven], a white rainbow pierced the sun [when Jing Ke attempted to assassinate the First Emperor of the Qin dynasty], and Venus went into the Pleiades [when Bai Qi sent provisions to King Zhao]. [Furthermore,] when a doctor [practicing the medical science] of admonishing the vapor makes water or fire in the mind, [the patient's body] always responds to it by becoming cold or warm. Needless to say, if we are exclusively sincere and ingeniously cultivate with the most brilliant wisdom and the highest energetic will, [the Buddha] is moved and responds, and we will receive a body; moreover, we will be reborn in the land of the seven treasures. How could this be not true?

Furthermore, [the *Discourse on Buddhist Laymen and Clergy*] states: "Even if we try to reduce the existence of a tree by analyzing it into smaller pieces, nothing harms the luxuriant [growth of the tree that] hangs down its leaves to make shade. Even if we try to separate materials from a room and empty it, nothing damages the majestic beauty of the room. Precious brocade produces splendor by various colors. Good thick soup attains deliciousness by seasonings such as salt and plum (i.e., vinegar)."

By means of this, [Huilin] tries to block the tenet of fundamental nonexistence (*benwu*), but this is not so, either. What is called fundamental nonexistence stated in the Buddhist scriptures does not mean that everything, [including phenomena in which] various conditions come together in unity, is empty. Existing things such as [the luxuriant growth of a tree whose] leaves hang down and make shade and [the majestic beauty of a room] can simply exist as they are. Therefore, this is called the truth of existence (*youdi*)[271] [in Buddhism]. Since nature is fundamentally nonexistence, it is called the truth of nonexistence (*wudi*).[272] Although I do not know the Buddhist doctrines

completely, I think that this advocacy is explicit and very stable. Ever-changing existence from ancient times suddenly ends up in emptiness. Just at the time of its peak of efflorescence, wouldn't it be in permanent existence? Since its 18b
nature is inevitably empty, it suddenly becomes empty, doesn't it? This can be also compared to Huizi's (i.e., Hui Shi's) expression, "All creatures may be born and may die at the same time. The sun in the meridian may decline at the same time."[273]

The fact of death and decline is constantly clear prior to the time before its birth and the meridian. Ignorant people do not see the reason; they merely see its existence. Hence, the Marquis of Qi state who usurped the place of [the legitimate ruler of] the Shuangjiu family wept falsely and longed for their happiness.[274] Wise people have the mind that is one with truth. Thus, Yanzi often was nearly empty[-minded]; he appeared to have no [ability] although he had it, and seemed lacking although he had real [capacity]. Everyone under the level of Yanzi appreciates emptiness according to the depth [of their competency]. Additionally, if we look at those in the level further below, even if they are not capable of purifying themselves with the most virtuous words [of the Buddha] in order to exhaust the delusion of attachment and competition, how could there be nothing similar to a little bit [of this appreciation of emptiness]? Why should it be to the contrary, like fire that increases coldness, and further cause [people] to have the desire to feel persistent attachment to their preferences?

Moreover, [the *Discourse on Buddhist Laymen and Clergy*] says: "To clarify [the tenet of] impermanence increases the feeling to crave for the shelter [of the Buddha]. To speak of suffering and falsehood deepens the people's anxiety to compete with time." This statement is a mistake.

Furthermore, [the *Discourse on Buddhist Laymen and Clergy*] states: "Arguments such as that of a boat hidden in a ravine [that is taken away by a man of great physical strength][275] or an empty marketplace [where one searches for a horse to buy][276] are already fully heard in the Middle Kingdom, [but] they are not the main theme of the truth. Consequently they were not adopted for the foundation of the teaching. I think that we can analyze the reason for this as easily as pointing to the palm of our hand."

"The boat that was hidden in a ravine and was secretly carried away" means that the present time does not stay, as it is stated in the Buddhist scriptures. If this [truth] can actually be clarified, [we will know that both] things and self are permanently unreal. How could it not be the main theme of the truth? Probably there were not many who understood it. Therefore, it was simply not considered to be the fundamental teaching. The eminent Zhi [Dun] was not yet the same as the Buddha, as it is said. Why does [Huilin] slight these most virtuous words just because they have frequently been spoken in the Middle Kingdom?

In addition, it is said [in the *Discourse on Buddhist Laymen and Clergy*]: "If mysterious light is examined, there is no light as small as one *cun* in diameter. If mysterious transformation is analyzed, there is not even a very small amount of reality. If you repeat the word 'the immeasurable life' in vain, who has seen a hundred-year-old man? All these kinds of things are entirely said to be inconsistent with actual facts."

Supernatural light, mysterious transformation, and immeasurable life all derive from sincere faith, which is profound and wonderful. Hence, people [of sincere faith] are simply going to be reborn in the buddha land, and to be closely illuminated by [the Buddha's] light, and their life will be immeasurable. Those who sink in evil views and who are absurdly disrespectful to mysterious transformation are indeed widely separated in the principles from [those who have sincere faith]. How could they see auspicious omens in the actual phenomena [such as supernatural light and mysterious transformation]?

The mind without greed is the foundation of the ten wholesome acts. Thus, we can cut off Hell facing down and be reborn in Heaven looking up. This is also what [the *Discourse on Buddhist Laymen and Clergy*] means by saying, "If you obey righteousness and follow the Way, the principles correct your mind." Since we hold sincere reverence in mind, we worship and repent our sins. Since we are aware of impermanence, we have no stinginess in the mind, abandon wives and children, and make donations. How could there be [the case stated in the *Discourse on Buddhist Laymen and Clergy* that] "to ask for one hundred times [more than one gives]"? Moreover, how could it be said without going through the intention to be respectful "to not take advantage of the feeling to not be stingy"? Nirvana is considered as having no happiness to be happy. The *dharmakāya* is considered as having no body to be the body. If you neither long for [happiness and the *dharmakāya*] nor determine [to pursue] them, it can be "to increase the thought to indulge in idleness and give rise to the mind of curiosity." If you sincerely praise and revere [Buddhism], indulgence in idleness will gradually be removed, and you will obtain the benefit in no [secular] benefit. Would this be concerned 18c with "the custom of competing for a benefit" [as is stated in the *Discourse*]?

Again, [the *Discourse on Buddhist Laymen and Clergy*] says: "The Way lies in freedom from avarice, but [Buddhists,] being avaricious, demand [things]. Even in a very short time if [something] is not beneficial [to themselves], they do not move."

How serious a false charge against Buddhists does this bring? In the great purpose of Buddhists, the eight kinds of sufferings derive entirely from craving. They clearly express the twelve causations, and simply have lofty people clarify the spirit in nonarising. Those who hope for this path can be said to have desire for non-desire. With regard to instructing and leading ordinary people, Heaven and Hell have the reality [of reward and retribution, just as] shadow [follows a form] and sound [responds to a voice]. Similarly, because of Yu Gong's benevolent work, [his descendants] were invited to officialdom and given a fief.[277] Yan [Yannian] was fond of killing people and consequently he was executed.[278] Those who are afraid of being executed and who want to be given a fief will certainly reject killing and cultivate benevolence. Even though those who practice with wonderful determination in order to hope for [rebirth in] Heaven and who attentively [observe] the five precepts in order to keep away from Hell have desire for necessary desire, they practice the pure path to reduce themselves day by day [until they attain *wuwei*]. This is also like heading west in order to seek Ying (i.e., the capital of Chu state), [which is in the south]. Why would you worry that they will not arrive there?

Furthermore, [the *Discourse on Buddhist Laymen and Clergy*] shows dislike [and says that] "The red and blue colors dazzle the eyes that appreciate colors. Buildings [like a Buddhist temple] cause the mind that likes splendor to boast of them. [Buddhists] build up private power and organize sectarian influence. They demand the fame of pursuing cultivation with determination and dedication and indulge in the desire of excelling and competing."

This is assuredly the ugliness of a black locust; or it can be merely said that even if the [tax] law was set at a low [rate], by the misapplication [of the law] a higher tax [than the proper rate] is demanded. How could the

Buddha then be treated rudely and said to have created the law for greed? Wang Mang (45 B.C.E.–23 C.E.) stole the Six Classics in order to seize the emperor's throne. The First Emperor of the Qin dynasty built Afang Palace under the pretext of having an audience. Would we put the blame [for these actions instead] on the ethical education given by their predecessor kings?

Again, [the *Discourse on Buddhist Laymen and Clergy*] states: "We should reject the tracks of the exoteric and esoteric [teachings], but keep their important purposes. It cannot be helped that what indicates one's next existence was concealed and treated unfairly in Daoism and Buddhism."

Please tell me what importance [Huilin] wants for the purposes. Certainly he wishes for people to pursue their advantages and reform their minds in order to reach their natures. The sage has no invariable mind of his own; he simply accommodates himself to others' minds, which he takes to be his own mind. If it is the true nature of living creatures that the body dies and the spirit perishes, in conformity with the nature of mortality [the sage] would have surely just transmitted the teaching in cooperation with the Duke of Zhou and Confucius. Then, if people have received nothing [like the teaching of the immortality of the spirit], the reality of reforming their minds would have been pure.

Why is it necessary [for Buddhists] to deceive [people] by [speaking of] the immortality [of the spirit] and imposing the Buddhist doctrine upon them, [to indulge in] shaving their hair and burning their skin, and to cut off the marriage relationship? The number of [potential] descendants extinguished by them is incalculable. If they harm themselves like this and injure the virtue of fulfilling their natures, why wouldn't Śākyamuni prevent them from doing such things? Fellows who lack faith are not willing to cultivate their advantages and reform their minds. Those who have faith are indeed the peers of Jīvaka, Jiantuole, Gītamitra, Zhu Fasheng, Bo Fazu, Dharmarakṣa, Yu Falan, Zhu Faxing, Yu Daosui, Que Gongze, Fotudeng, Śrīmitra, Guo Wenju, Shi Daoan, Zhi Daolin, and Master [Hui]yuan. In spiritual operation, character, and behavior, these people do not seem really to fall behind Bhikṣu [Hui]lin. Why should they have recklessly damaged human principles and taken the tonsure [merely] for the edification of the insincere man (i.e., the Buddha)?
19a These are all simply because the reality of spiritual wonder attracts [people's]

minds from a distance and achieves the enterprise of supernatural power and pure truth.

You sent this discourse [to me] from afar on the pretext of your lack of faith [in Buddhism]. Moreover, people of the world who doubt [Buddhism] all think [the *Discourse*] to be wonderful, too. Therefore, I have tried to answer by myself in order to offer some help for people [to understand Buddhism]. The issue that people of the world judge whether or not Buddhism is good is entirely a great [question affecting] the destinies of human beings. Why can we take a noncommittal position on it? Therefore, I have exhausted my ignorant thoughts and composed the *Discourse to Clarify Buddhism* in order to present what I have in my mind. It has just now been completed. I am having copies made, [but] a copy is not yet ready to send with this letter. When I write to you again later, it will be included.

Sincerely,
Zong Bing

The Elucidation of the Criticism on [the *Discourse on*] *the Equality of Good* (*Junshanlun*) (i.e., the *Discourse on Buddhist Laymen and Clergy*) by He Chengtian

I formerly sent you the *Discourse on the Equality of Good* together with an inquiry about your opinion. I received your thoughtful response. You think that the purpose of this is [a great question affecting] the destinies of human beings and we should clarify it, but we cannot take a noncommittal position on it. Although I cannot submit to all [of your opinions], I do not hold fast very much to biased views, either. I am, however, seeking a jade that glows in the night in a vast sea and I have simply not yet obtained it.

I think that the Buddhist scriptures are from a school that is a good branch of the nine schools, including Daoism and Mohism. In benevolence and giving alms, [Buddhism] is no different from [the teaching of] the Middle Kingdom. Great people and gentlemen consider benevolence to be their duty. They have nothing to bear in mind. They just harmonize ordinary people's ears and eyes by images and adornments. If it is still a slight that [Buddhism] wastes and harms [our country], the benefit it propagates will probably be apparent. Thus, [Buddhism] exists together with [the nine schools]. People of fantastic taste having appeared, [Buddhism] is then considered to be better than Confucianism, to surpass [the teaching of] Laozi, and to alone be noble. This [indicates] that people have not been able to seek the foundation of the worthy words left [by the Buddha] and yet they are misled by a nonessential theory. To know [the true meaning of] the words, you must wait for one who understands beyond words. If you have faith only because of the reward and retribution of Heaven and Hell and the testimony that causes and conditions are not destroyed, control your feelings, take coarse food, are completely diligent in worship, and hope that you will probably be sheltered under the jeweled canopy [offered by Ratnaśikhi] or that you will ascend to the [lion] seat of Merupradīparāja [Tathāgata], this is just nothing but Chunyu Sheng's big joke.[279]

Your discussion says, "[If they are vast and only empty, why do] all the sages, including Zhuangzi and Laozi, say that there are spirits? [If there is the spiritual intelligence,] on what basis did [Huilin] judge [that the principles of the unseen world are vast and simply empty] is really not like what the Buddha says?"

I would like to respond to this. There are rites and music in the world in which we live, while there are spiritual beings in the netherworld. What sage kings consider to be the teaching is not obscure about its existence from the beginning. If there are reward and retribution in the next life, could it be the case that the Duke of Zhou and Confucius just keep silent and do not have even a few words about it? If an infant is approaching a hole in the ground, ordinary people are frightened by this. Wouldn't sages still be merciful?

Moreover, you said, "The physical body of a [human being] is very coarse while his spirit is really subtle. If the physical body follows the spirit, how could both equally die?"

I answer: The body and the spirit mutually support each other. People of ancient times compared them to a torch. When firewood burns down, the flame becomes weak. When the firewood completely burns, the flame dies out. Even though [the spirit] is subtle, how could it alone be transmitted?

19b Again, you said, "[What happens when the nature] responds to the affections of the mind is [seen in these historical facts:] the city wall collapsed [when the wife of Qi Liang cried], frost fell [when Zou Yan cried out toward Heaven], a white rainbow pierced the sun [when Jing Ke attempted to assassinate the First Emperor of the Qin dynasty], and Venus went into the Pleiades [when Bai Qi sent provisions to King Zhao]. [Furthermore,] when a doctor [practicing the medical science] of admonishing the vapor [makes water or fire in the mind, the patient's body] always responds to this by becoming cold or warm. If we are exclusively sincere and ingeniously cultivate, [the Buddha] is moved and responds, and we will receive the body; moreover, we will be reborn in the land of the seven treasures. How could this be not true?"[280]

I will respond to this. [The events of] the city wall collapsing, frost falling, [a white rainbow] piercing the sun, and [Venus] going into the Pleiades are not examples that elucidate the next life. They should not be referred to in the present discussion. Furthermore, to see [the medicine of] admonishing [the vapor] with water or fire and to wish to be able to be reborn in the country of the seven treasures can be compared to the case of having observed a blacksmith decorate with gold, [the gold] then wishes to be able to mold and cast itself [into a sword like the Moye].[281] You will know at last that this is impossible.

Again, you say regarding the truth of existence and the truth of nonexistence, "[Although I do not know the Buddhist doctrines completely,] I think that this advocacy is explicit and very stable. Ever-changing existence from ancient times suddenly ends up in emptiness. Just at the time of its peak of efflorescence, wouldn't it be in permanent existence? Since its nature is inevitably empty, [it suddenly becomes empty, doesn't it?]" and "Ignorant people do not know the reason; they merely see its existence."

I will answer this. If, as you say in the discussion, just at the time of its peak of efflorescence it already inevitably has the reality of emptiness, in that case, things are permanently empty, and emptiness and things are the same. If emptiness and existing objects are no different from each other, why are the wise and the ignorant so called in different ways? The Way, so called, in former times has no form in shape and no [worldly] affairs in function. It is peaceful, undisturbed, empty, and perfect. It nourishes wisdom and inspires peace and harmony in one's mind. Would it alone be afraid of conditions from former lives, [just as Buddhists are,] before removing clinging and attachment? You say, "[Ignorant people] merely see its existence," but are they superior to

[Buddhists] in this point? To laugh and sneer at the Marquis of Qi state [who was satirized by Chunyu Sheng] is just like the case where those who retreated fifty steps [in a battlefield] laugh at those who retreated a hundred steps.[282]

Furthermore, you say, "'The boat that was hidden in a ravine is secretly carried away' means that the present time does not stay, as is stated in the Buddhist scriptures. If this [truth] can actually be clarified, [we will know that both] things and self are permanently unreal."

I will respond to this. Regarding the issue that leaving secretly means not staying [in Buddhism], wouldn't it mean to enter death from life, or to enter nonexistence from existence? There is a passage [in the *Zhuangzi*]: "[Mengsun] will be frightened in his body [by death], but there will be nothing to harm his mind. He takes [his body] as a temporary dwelling, so he has no resentment of death."[283] Jia Sheng (i.e., Jia Yi) also said, "We simply transform to the dead. What further worry do we have?"[284] This is one who has achieved awakening of the change from life to death. Nevertheless, [Buddhists] act frivolously. While they are alive, they are anxious about the afterlife. They attach their minds to immeasurable life and have ambition to be reborn in Heaven. Our permanent void (*changxu*) is different [from their emptiness] on this point.

Moreover, you say, "Supernatural light, mysterious transformation, and immeasurable life all derive from sincere faith, which is profound and wonderful. Hence, people [of sincere faith] are simply [going to be reborn in the buddha land, and to be closely] illuminated by [the Buddha's] light. . . . Those who sink in evil views and who are absurdly disrespectful to mysterious transformation indeed are widely separated in the principles from [those who have sincere faith]."

I will now respond to this. I do not follow [your opinion on this], either, because those who are disrespectful to the wonderful edification are seeking the light of [the Buddha], but you simply seek it in sincere faith. When we ponder the teaching of Śākyamuni, [we see that] it delivers people by means of expedients. If there is the corresponding manifestation [of the Buddha] like this, why does he not show its mysterious transformation in order to cause people of evil views to understand? Why doesn't he value several tens of millions of talks [of the teaching] and yet is sparing of momentary supernatural light? He speaks eloquently with the voice of the phenomenal world in vain, and he has come to an end without clarifying the true wisdom. [Sentient beings] are exhausted throughout life and do not know in what to take refuge. Isn't this sad?

Again, you say, "Since we hold sincere reverence in mind, we worship 19c
and repent our sins. Since we are aware of impermanence, we have no stinginess [in the mind], abandon wives and children, and make donations. How could there be [the case stated in the *Discourse on Buddhist Laymen and Clergy*,] 'to ask for one hundred times [more than one gives]'?"

I will answer this. To be complicated and skillful in order to begin a matter is not as good as to remove greed and cease competitiveness. To observe the precepts in order to cleanse [the mind of] penitence is not as good as annihilating a glorious hope in order to accomplish simplicity, to say nothing of inviting what one prefers and praying for a benefit or forgeting one's blood relations and desiring fame. If you say there is no [case] of asking for [a hundred times more than one gives], I do not believe it.

Furthermore, you say, "Nirvana is considered as having no happiness to be happy. The *dharmakāya* is considered as having no body to be the body. . . . If you sincerely praise and revere [Buddhism], indulgence in idleness will gradually be removed, and you will obtain the benefit in no [secular] benefit."

I am responding to this. Nirvana is considered as leaving behind suffering to be happy. The *dharmakāya* is considered as taking the suffering [of sentient beings] to be the body. That is just the reason people who praise and revere [Buddhism] are unable to cut off [hope]. If it results in no [secular] benefit, what do those who diligently cultivate it attain, and why do you say they attain it in no [secular] benefit? This is the testimony that both the body and the spirit are exhausted. I am afraid that this is not what you should articulate in your discussion.

Moreover, you say, "Those who hope for this path can be said to have desire for non-desire. With regard to instructing and leading ordinary people, [heaven and hell] have the reality of [reward and retribution, just as] a shadow [follows a form] and sound [responds to a voice]. Similarly, because of Yu Gong's benevolent work, [his descendants] were invited to officialdom and given a fief. Yan [Yannian] was fond of killing people and consequently he was executed. Even though those who practice with wonderful determination in order to hope for [rebirth in] Heaven and who attentively [observe] the five precepts in order to keep away from Hell have desire for necessary desire, they practice the pure path to reduce themselves day by day [until they attain *wuwei*]. This is also like heading west in order to seek Ying, [which is in the south]. Why would you worry that they will not arrive there?"

I would like to answer this. It is very good that you mention that ordinary people are instructed and led and you compare reward and retribution with shadow and sound. What was caused by shadow and sound, however, must be matched to the original form and voice. How can a form of usual [length] produce a shadow of eighty thousand *yojana*s? To be stagnant, just like to have desire for non-desire, is still usually to stagnate in the object of desire. The ears and eyes preside over different [senses]. Engineering and art craft are different kinds of work. Even in such minor fields, thought and faith are not on the same level with each other. Thus, even if the [sounds of] metal and stone are able to harmonize,[285] Mount Tai would not be able to reveal its height. Even if wild geese and swans get together, the deep autumn is not able to transmit its intention. [This is because they originally have nothing to do with each other.] Accordingly, you want to achieve non-desire by means of having desire, and you hope to undergo reducing day by day [to reach *wuwei*]. Even though you say to head west [in order to seek Ying, which is in the south], you have traveled this far from Ying. What can you do about it?

Furthermore, you say, "If it is the true nature of living creatures that the body dies and the spirit perishes, [in conformity with the nature of mortality the sage] would have surely just transmitted the teaching in cooperation with the Duke of Zhou and Confucius. . . . Why is it necessary [for Buddhists] to deceive [people] by [speaking of] the immortality [of the spirit] and imposing the Buddhist doctrine upon them, [to indulge in] shaving their hair and burning their skin, and to cut off the marriage relationship? If they harm themselves like this and injure the virtue of fulfilling their natures. . . ."

I am responding to this. Chinese people and non-Chinese people naturally have differences. What are [these differences]? Chinese people receive the vapor that is pure and peaceful, and they have benevolence and righteousness in their minds. Therefore, the Duke of Zhou and Confucius elucidate the nature [of the Chinese] and the teaching in which they learn [their natures]. People of foreign countries receive a nature that is tough and strong, and

they are greedy, angry, and perverse. Therefore, Śākyamuni was strict with the rules of the five precepts. In the discussion you sent to me, this is called 20a
"the sage has no invariable mind of his own; he simply accommodates himself to other people's natures."[286] In the admonition to chastise cruelty, there is nothing more painful than Hell. In the exhortation to lead to good, there is nothing better than Heaven. It is not the meaning of the golden mean (*zhongyong*) to exhaust the root of heartlessly causing injury. The Duke of Zhou and Confucius do not do so. They follow its natural temperament and leave behind its very [evil elements].

Misconduct in sexual behavior and stealing are set forth in the five penalties. The crime related to wine is clarified in the section called the *Announcement about Drunkenness* (*Jiugao*), in the history of the Zhou dynasty (a chapter of the *Book of History*).[287] "[The ruler of a state,] in the spring hunting, will not surround a marshy thicket" [in order not to harm young animals].[288] When we see living creatures, we cannot bear their death. [We established] the laws for the five offenses in hunting and chasing game from only three directions [so that the animals have a chance to escape].[289] We fish without a net. Hence, benevolence is extensively diffused, and benefits reach even to pigs and fish.

For a gathering on a happy occasion, there is always [meat] on a cutting board. Even old people are able to have meat [because there is enough]. We till land in spring and gather the harvest in fall. Sericulture and weaving are done in a timely manner. The three numinous beings have come,[290] and a hundred deities are all worshiped. When we compare these with what they (i.e., Buddhists) do, wouldn't these be [considered] great?

Furthermore, we make clear the praise of offering a libation in worship, while we are strict in the punishment about dubious laws. To give an account of the questions asked by the chief magistrate of Pu (i.e., Zilu) is the foundation to exhort the teaching.[291] To expound [Confucius's] answer, "the fume rising as the vapor,"[292] clarifies the testimony of our next life. Those who wear a black [monk's] robe and stare in anger, and who are emulous of me in this discussion, have a wrong frame of mind.

In addition, you state in your discussion, "people like Jīvaka, [Jian]tuo[le], and Śrīmitra . . . do not fall behind Bhikṣu [Hui]lin in spiritual operation, character, and behavior." You have already clearly mentioned that we, ordinary people, are not able to infer familiar matters. On what basis do you now conclude the superiority or inferiority of people who lived a hundred years ago or who live several thousand *li* away? One such as Bhikṣu [Hui]lin is a monk in appearance, but has [the mind of] disinterestedness like Heaven. He seems to discern truth or falsehood profoundly. Particularly, he is not willing to fear the scriptures, to protect his master, and to garnish illusory remarks. For this reason, I respect him. It is said in Sun [Chuo] Xinggong's *Discourse* [*on the Way and the Wise*] that Dharmarakṣa is erudite and intelligent and Yu Falan is sincere and knowledgeable. With whom of the Middle Kingdom do you want to compare these two people?

Moreover, Ying, the king of Chu, built a Buddhist temple. Ze Rong offered relief to starving travelers. How could they have pure character and behavior? Formerly when I was in the eastern capital city (i.e., Jiankang), Śramaṇa Daohan visited me from Wuzhong and exhorted [Buddhism to] me. He was very earnest and sincere. Because of this, he stayed for three nights. He talked for my sake about the [causes and] conditions of refining the body and purifying the spirit, and the testimony of the arising and extinguishing of sin and merit. All of this makes sense. I folded my hands before my breast and listened to his outspoken remarks without sleeping from night till morning.

I withdrew and thought. The reason a person rises in the world, becomes famous, has faith, and practices the Way really relies on the teaching of the Duke of Zhou and Confucius. Zilu says, "When I hear [well-intentioned advice], if I cannot carry it out in practice, I am concerned only that there is [something else] I have yet to hear."[293] I have to do many things. Why should I suddenly abandon this and attend to that (i.e., Buddhism)? In addition, I sought [the reason why] the written form [for the three-year mourning], which is well matched to human feelings, had been established, and I came to know that the next life is above my means. Having investigated thoroughly the endless grief [about death] throughout our lifetime, I have realized that it is difficult to receive this body again.

Sages are my teachers. How could the Duke of Zhou and Confucius deceive me? As I was overcome by your generosity, I have fully presented the ins and outs [of my opinions]. Hoping that the aged and respected person of great intelligence instructs others without being wearied, I have simply not yet kept silent here. You said formerly you had already sent the *Discourse to Clarify Buddhism.* I am looking forward to receiving it. I hope you will be clear in your thinking. 20b

Sincerely,
He Chengtian

Response to He of Hengyang, the Criticism on the Elucidation of the *Discourse on Buddhist Laymen and Clergy* by Zong Bing

I have respectfully read the discussion you sent to me. You repress the edification of Buddhism and set forth your aspiration in the teaching of Confucianism. [In your discussion,] significant matters are collected and expressed, and your talent in literature and argument examines and clarifies [these issues]. It may very much be a key writing that enlivens people of the world's feelings, and it is really an instructive discussion of the central region (i.e., China).

Having observed your intention, I see that you do not mean that the one who established Buddhism is not a sage, but [you say that] the teaching is an expedient [way], without truth. I, [however,] have not completely appreciated on what basis you base your belief that [Buddhism] has no truth. Now, when we determine and see a long-range plan of things together, the gains and losses are about on par. The marvelous edification [of Buddhism] arose outside the acme of profundity and its cause is bound together with the unseen world. Couldn't it be that we have had holy people who talk to each other [as easily as] pointing at their palms? You vainly believe in the incomplete historical records [compiled] after the incident of burning books [carried out by the First Emperor of the Qin dynasty], and then, with [these incomplete records,] you want to reject and stop the supernatural edification [of Buddhism]. It makes my blood run cold.

Sages "make an exhaustive discrimination of what is right, and effect the complete development of every nature, till they arrive at what is appointed for it [by Heaven]."[294] If there are those who do not attain [the appropriate] points, [sages feel] as if they have cast those people into a moat. Now [Buddhists] delude people [by the tenet of] the immortality of the spirit, and deceive them [by the tenet of] the attainment of buddhahood. They indulge in shaving the head, wearing red robes, and burning their bodies and fingers.

In addition, they do not employ their natural gifts in order to support their parents and the way of husband and wife or father and son. From the time Buddhism was introduced to the thirty-six states west of the Sha River (near Turfan) prior to the time of its introduction to China, those who cut off [familial] relations [of husband and wife or father and son] number in the hundred millions or hundred billions. It is quite possible that there are sages and wise people among the eastern and western barbarians. If we think of those [who were born in barbarian tribes] and who came to [China], such as You Yu and Jin Ridi, there were more people who were about to be born and yet who could not [be born]. If Buddhism has no truth, wouldn't the cruelty of casting people into a moat, [just as Bai Qi and Xiang Wu did,] be unspeakable?

Regarding the expedient [stated] in the Buddhist scriptures, what kind of way do you think it is in accord with? Do you say you want it in order to exceed the proper limits in righting a wrong, or in order to govern foreign people whose natures are "tough and strong" and who are "angry and perverse"? The sort of people who are angry and perverse will still not believe and will not be frightened if you bind them with the three-article [provisional] law [promulgated by Emperor Gaozu of the Han dynasty], or punish soon after rewarding. Would it be possible to rule over them by means of the tenets "[emptiness is] nothing other than form," fundamental nonexistence, nirvana, the *dharmakāya,* the twelve causations (Skt. *pratītyasamutpāda*), and *kalpa*s as numerous as the minutest particles of dust?

Those who receive this instruction are what you call people who "receive the vapor that is pure and peaceful, and who have benevolence and righteousness in their minds." Since we avail ourselves of [the vapor that is] pure and peaceful in order to explicate the sublime words, and encourage the righteous nature in order to learn the subtle practice, we are consequently able to purify our illumination and contemplate the Dharma. When [we realize that] the Dharma and illumination are all empty, we reach the [Buddhist] Way (i.e., awakening). These are entirely stated in the Buddhist scriptures, and are what you believe. As to people in modern times who are superhuman and have excellent virtue, such as the eight wise men for whom Sun [Chuo] Xinggong made eulogies and the five thinkers praised by Zhi Daolin, they are all considered to be lofty by their contemporaries. Therefore, the two (i.e., Sun Chuo and Zhi Daolin) could make a composition about them. How can this be called wild talk?

Sun [Chuo] praises Dharmarakṣa as erudite and intelligent, and Yu Falan as sincere and knowledgeable. I do not have relationships with the sophisticated and the simpleminded. [Therefore] I have no idea with whom I should compare these *bhikṣus*. [Yu] Falan's disciple, [Yu] Daosui, however, has not yet caught up to his master. When Sun [Chuo] comments on him, [Sun said,] 20c
"[Intelligent people] equate him with noble people."[295] I would say that I think [one of these noble people] is Yu Wenbing. The two eminent monks, Dharmarakṣa and [Yu] Falan, must have been even more outstanding than this person. I do not know of Bhikṣu Huilin at all. Moreover, I have no idea about public opinion. If you say that [Bhikṣu Huilin] is as good as [Yu] Wenbing, he may not naturally fall behind [Yu] Daosui, but he must still be below Dharmarakṣa and [Yu Fa]lan. The comment I made previously is not an impropriety of speech. If [Huilin] has the appearance of a Buddhist monk who is sincere and capable, [the mind of] disinterestedness like Heaven, and profound knowledge [to discern] truth and falsehood, why is it not certain that Śakra-devendra will transform and willfully urge him to attain buddhahood? The *Discourse on Buddhist Laymen and Clergy* cannot yet be considered upright.

In the discussion I received, you express a doubt: "If there really are reward and retribution in the next life, why did the Duke of Zhou and Confucius keep silent, without even a few words about it?" This is indeed a common question, based on prejudice. This is truly something we should clarify together.

The sacred spirit originates profoundly. As it is moved, then it responds. It is not something that leads people prior to a necessity. During the declining years of the Shang and Zhou dynasties, the people fell into great misery, and regicide was rampant. The reason the masses moved the sages to action is [because the world was in] disorder. Consequently, the responses found in the Six Classics are only about governing [the state]. Therefore, there is no word of the Buddha.

Liu Xiang says that the nine provinces mentioned in the *Yugong* (i.e., the earliest known book of the geography of China) probably follow what is recorded in the *Book of Mountains and Seas,* which states: "The people of India (Shendu) are very dear to others and love each other."[296] Guo Pu says that India (Tianzhu) is the place where Buddhism originated. Even though this is a barbarian region [from the Chinese point of view], countless domains spread out like stars in the sky. Somewhat to our surprise, we do not know which domain [is the center of] glory. Since the people extend their feelings of dearness and love, the edification of Buddhism [was founded] responding to this. The coarse people of that region (i.e., India) are petty and numerous. Some of them are confused and ferocious and the relations between sovereign and subject are not controlled properly.

The exquisite people of this region (i.e., China) used to cherish the Way at all times, and Buddhist services existed, too. Even though they might have received the Dharma-nature [as a natural endowment] near the Yi and Luo Rivers, or they might have experienced the ultimate reality near the Zhu and Si Rivers, Shi Yi, [the historiographer of the Zhou dynasty,] carelessly did not record [these events] because they had nothing to do with the way of governance, and Bu Shang (i.e., Zixia) did not compile them because they go against the Confucian way. Even if there were some [Buddhist documents] in the non-Buddhist canon hidden in the double wall [of Confucius's house], they would have also been burned by the king of Qin (i.e., the First Emperor of the Qin dynasty). It is not yet necessarily known whether or not the Duke of Zhou and Confucius kept silent about [reward and retribution in the next life]. There is no case where the way of the profound absolute vacancy and issues of the mysterious immortals have not been mentioned in worldly books. The words of Confucius regarding the Way are found in chapters of Zhuangzi's book, [the *Zhuangzi*,] of the remote age. [The record of] the feast [of the Queen Mother of West] at Yaochi was discovered from a high grave of Ji county (in present-day Henan province). In that case, through the Five Classics that are concerned with state administration, we cannot yet fill in the wonderful edification beyond this world [due to the lack of records].

You also say in your criticism, "Things are permanently empty, and emptiness and things are the same. If emptiness and existing objects are no different from each other, why are the wise and the ignorant so called in different ways?" What Buddhist scriptures state is that form is empty; there is nothing other than emptiness. It is not said that there is no existence. There is existence but it is simply empty. There is existence, so there are two different

appellations: the wise and the ignorant. It is empty, so all differences are altogether empty. Form is naturally not form. Even though form is empty, conditions join together and become an existence. From the beginning, existence is naturally not existence. All [phenomena] are just like those things that are produced by illusion, or revealed in a dream. They exist, but they do not. The future has not yet come, the past has already gone, and the present does not stay. There is no fixed existence, either. Generally these several principles 21a
are the laws all profound sages attained ultimately. It is really difficult to make them clear by indicating them with language. When I observe things from this point of view, I truly realize it is evident. Therefore, I feel free from worries and petty thoughts, and so I increase purity [of mind] by washing away [defilements]. How can you be content with it?

Furthermore, you say, "The body and the spirit mutually support each other. People of ancient times compared them to a torch. When firewood burns down, the flame becomes weak. When the firewood is completely burned, the flame dies out. Even though [the spirit] is subtle, how could it alone be transmitted?" Well, fire is produced from firewood, [but] the spirit is not made from the body. Of thoughts, there are both exquisite and coarse ones. They are moved and obtain the bodies that follow them. When the [exquisite] spirit reaches its acme, it transcends the body and becomes independent of it. There is no body, but the spirit exists. This is called the eternality of the *dharmakāya.* Hence, we begin as an ordinary person, and will become a tathāgata at last. Even though our life is coarse until now, if we have a view that turns upward for countless *kalpa*s without exhaustion, we will certainly learn [Buddhism] in order to ascend to the pure world. [It is said in the *Book of Odes* that] "A mulberry insect has a child, which a wasp carries on its back [as its adopted child]."[297] If we compare [this unusual matter] to those in the spiritual world, where we "will be sheltered under the jeweled canopy [offered by Ratnaśikhi], or we will ascend to the [lion] seat of Merupradīparāja [Tathāgata]," why would we have no hope?

In addition, you have doubt and say, "[The teaching of] Śākyamuni delivers people by means of expedients," "Why doesn't he value the several tens of millions of talks [of the teaching] and yet is sparing of momentary supernatural light?" and "[Why] does he not show its mysterious transformation in order to cause people of evil views to understand?"

Although it is called "expedient" as a term, [the degree of manifestation] of people's receptivity and the Buddha's response, either dim or apparent, complies with evil acts and meritorious deeds variously. In former times the Buddha expounded [the Dharma] and emitted light for sentient beings, [because] they all usually accumulated wonderful sincerity. Consequently they could make a spiritual journey [to the world of buddhas]. In addition, at that time the Buddha's words were already evidently expedient. Therefore, even negligent people could hear them. The light is emitted and it illuminates us through contemplation. People of wrong views do not have the conditions to look at [the light] even if it envelops them. Now if we see Buddhist scriptures and yet do not repent of our negligence, even if we are enveloped [by the light] in advance, how beneficial would it be? People such as wise men of sincere faith are able to clearly perceive supernatural illumination by themselves. On what basis do you know this and always say that [supernatural light] is simply wild talk? [It is stated in the *Chunqiu Zuoshizhuan* that] "The regular stars are not visible, yet it is a bright night."[298] When I examine what year and month [this happened], I see it corresponds to the night when the Buddha was born and emitted a light. Guan Youan set sail on the sea on a windy night. All his companions sank [with the boat], but Youan saw a light in the darkness. Heading toward the light, he [and his family] reached an island, and only he and his entire family were saved.[299]

The Buddha has no discrimination. He responds only to good. There are too many cases to mention in which the Buddha's responses were given to people like Wang Xiang or Guo Ju.[300]

These are also auspicious omens of seeing the light. Couldn't there be the Buddha even if you have not seen [the Buddha's response]?

In addition, you explain the prosperity [of the teaching] of the Duke of Zhou and Confucius, which you compare to and consider to be greater than [the teaching of] the Buddha. The regime of this country is, however, merely the prosperity of sovereigns. But the exquisite spirit still never perishes and transmigrates in the unseen world. Our life is as short as a breath, in which the eight kinds of suffering are abundant. Even though we strive for the Confucian teaching in order to rectify ourselves momentarily, we will soon die. In the disaster of the three superintendents, the uncle and nephew distrusted each other, and the brothers killed each other.[301] Even though among the seventy-two of disciples

[of Confucius] some "ascended to the hall and some passed into the inner apartments" (i.e., attained mastery),[302] those who lived until the age of fifty were few. Yan [Hui] died young, Ran [Boniu] was afflicted with disease, [Zhong] You (i.e., Zilu) was cut apart [as a punishment], [Zai] Yu was executed together with his relatives, and Si (i.e., Zigong) lost his beard. Was not the suffering [of 21b
Confucius] in the Kuang and Chen regions unspeakable?[303] He spread the teaching abroad while suffering hunger, and wandered from state to state. How many people could he save after all? When we observe this alongside the Buddhist teaching, we see only his lament there. Isn't this the result of the congregation of causation from the previous existences of people of the world?

Moreover, the truth spread by [Confucius] has not yet been deep and great at this point. If we outwardly act in accordance with [Chinese] rites and music, and cultivate inwardly with [the teaching of] nonarising (i.e., Buddhism), purify the spirit in the state of nirvana, and consider thousands of millions of *kalpa*s to be bygone years [of our lifetime], wouldn't it be really great? Events are not transmitted [accurately] to later generations and we have not been able to know the principles [sufficiently]. I hope you will not say that based on crude evidence the Duke of Zhou and Confucius were not so. All people say that the Buddha makes wild talk, but the *Book of Mountains and Seas* says that those who died and who were reborn are very numerous.[304] In the immortal realm such as Mount Kunlun, the field of Guangdu [where Houji was buried], and the mound of Xuanyuan, the weather is neither cold nor hot, phoenix's eggs are eaten, sweet dew is drunk, the inhabitants are sheltered by jade trees, they sip the water of the Zhu fountain, and they do not die even though they reach a thousand years of age. Regarding such stories as [the spirit of Gun, Emperor Yu's father,] being transformed into a yellow bear and entering an abyss under Mount Yu,[305] [the spirit of] Shen Sheng, [the crown prince of Jin state, talking with Hu Tu, his former attendant,][306] and Boyou [of Zheng state becoming a ghost and avenging himself on the people of the state],[307] not a few [of these stories] are found in what [Zuo] Qiuming related.[308] All of these can be inferred from the crude [traces] of this [country] (China) in order to believe the exquisite [talk] of that [country] (India).

I was told that in former days you had [a chance to hear] the [Buddhist] Way. I can see that one who hears the Buddhist Dharma and straightens himself is indeed [equal to] a daring soldier of Pucheng (in present-day Shanxi province).[309] Is it because what you have heard is not yet lofty? If what you heard is lofty, it is still possible [for you] to change your mind, just as a leopard changes [its spots]. Human beings are creatures of exquisite spirit. If we, however, take refuge in the culmination of numinous beings (i.e., the Buddhist Way) and roughly receive the teaching and precepts, it is enough to move even an insignificant amount of [the Buddha's saving power]. If we move it, we will rise higher. Wouldn't it be an eternal good plan to leave behind delusions?

In former days, the fact that the spirit is immortal was just as the Buddha says, but the spirit casts away, the mind is wounded, and we go against the government of the unseen world by ourselves. How could we know that suffering and difficulties in this existence would not be due to [sins we committed in] previous existences? If we imprudently despise the teaching of the respectful spirit with our own view, I am afraid that we may pass on this difficulty to [our next existence]. A Buddhist scripture states: "Once when Śākyamuni was a *bhikṣu* of the Hinayana, he slandered the Mahayana. Because of this, even he fully underwent hardships, passing through hells for a very long time." [Even Śākyamuni fell into Hell,] to say nothing of those who have no faith at all. Moreover, on what basis can we determine that this Buddhist scripture must be false?

The words used in your previous letter rebuking me are merely in accordance with Bhikṣu [Hui]lin's chapters and sentences. My intention has already been roughly told. I could not reply to each [of your questions], but everything has already been thoroughly covered in my composition, the *Discourse to Clarify Buddhism.* Now I will attach it [to this letter] and send it to you. I ask you to please do your best, make a thorough investigation properly, and tell me completely whether I am right or not. I am old and about to die. I would like only to continue this until my last day. When you have received this letter, please write your frank response to me.

Sincerely,
Zong Bing

He's Second Response to Zong

21c I read your second letter together with your great discourse. The tactical deployment you took up [for the discourse] is just like what Xiang Ji (i.e.,

Yu) [of Chu state] did [for his campaigns]. You have already made [his rival,] Emperor Gaozu, [the founder of the Han dynasty,] look humble, not to speak of a less capable person [like me]. The testimonies and examples [you showed] are solid and clear. The language and expressions [you used] are erudite and rich. You really wish to spread your benefit and kindness and your instruction is extended to even ordinary people. I deeply acknowledge that this is due to a gentleman's consideration. [Nevertheless,] you just intend to make the teaching mysterious by means of [abstract discourse, just like] shadow and sound. Therefore, I had better keep silent and help fulfill your cherished hopes. I, however, always think that foreign matters may not be what the Chinese are engaged in. Thus, I simply made the previous statement. If China and foreign countries should now surely be the same, I am simpleminded. I venture to apologize for my slowness. In spite of it, I still have a thought. Those who are versed in the nature of Heaven and Earth are not misled by unrealistic, peculiar matters. Those who discern the way to prosperity or decline do not employ their minds for unreasonable, illogical matters. Otherwise, if your discussion is not on the basis of an expedient, and the general instruction is entirely expressed from your feeling, wouldn't this be the ignorance of a well-read, experienced person? I have not yet had a chance to meet and talk with you. I send my letter in lieu of a meeting with you.

Yours truly,
He Cheng[tian]

End of Fascicle Three of *The Collection for the Propagation and Clarification* [*of Buddhism*]

Fascicle Four

The *Discourse on the Full Understanding of Life* (*Daxinglun*) by He Chengtian

The two polarities (i.e., Heaven and Earth) were already positioned, and a sovereign joined them. In the universe, there is nothing nobler than [these three]. [The Way of] Heaven has two divisions: *yin* and *yang;* Earth has two functions: toughness and gentleness; and human beings have two foundations: benevolence and righteousness. People are born only when there is Heaven and Earth, while Heaven and Earth become supernatural only when there are people. The three powers (*sancai*) are a single and interdependent unit. Consequently, the one who can receive the vapor that is pure and peaceful, whose spiritual intelligence is particularly prominent, whose feeling is in overall charge of all ages, whose wisdom encompasses all things, whose ingenious thought traces to the very source of the deep and dark world, whose production is equal to that of Nature, and who results in benevolence and capability, is a sovereign. When he nurtures the common people and helps Heaven in propagating virtue, the sun and moon are clear and bright; the four kinds of supernatural animals (i.e., *kylin,* Chinese phoenix, turtle, and dragon) appear; the auspicious wind has the same tune; the four seasons are harmonious; various types of foods, including the nine kinds of grains, animals that feed on grass or grain (i.e., cattle, sheep, and dogs), products of the soil, aquatic products, and foods of various flavors such as sour or salty are served at the table; and a house, a boat, a vehicle, things decorated with gold, pottery, and dark yellow fabrics made of silk or linen are supplied for equipment, implements, or clothes. The culture follows rules of decorum and entertainment follows the eight kinds of musical sounds [produced from the calabash and musical instruments made of earthenware, stretched hides, wood, stone, metal, silk strings, and bamboo]. All things are protected, and living creatures reproduce. There is nothing that is not provided.

If people are careful in spending, it is easy to be sufficient. If it is easy to be sufficient, there will be a surplus of power. If there is a surplus of power, the people's will and feeling will become extravagant. Then, the mind
22a delighted with governance will arise. If things are concise, nothing will be disturbed. If nothing is disturbed, the spiritual intelligence will be sharp. If the spiritual intelligence is sharp, one will make plans carefully. Then, the business to save and govern [the people] is accomplished. Therefore, Heaven and Earth instruct the people with [the virtues of] thrift and simplicity. [The two diagrams] *qian* and *kun,* [the opening sections of the *Book of Changes,*] teach the people with [the way of] ease and concision. This is why instructions are attentive and generous like this. How can [human beings] be sentient beings on the same level with birds, fish, snakes, and insects?

Sentient beings have appropriate seasons in which to be caught and [pertinent means] of employment. To start a fire [in a field for a winter hunt], we wait for a gale to blow. For hunting and fishing, we inquire into [the activities of] the wolf and otter.[310] This is because we follow the seasons of nature. A real man neither hunts a fawn nor takes eggs. The common people do not use a fine-meshed net [for fishing]. The song "Rushes" (*Xingwei*) was composed.[311] We bestow good influence even upon the fish. This is because we love what we human beings use. [Gentlemen] stay away from the kitchen. We are cautious not to commit the five offenses in hunting.[312] Emperor [Tang] of the Yin dynasty took a new prayer.[313] When Confucius fished, he did not use a net. This is because we define the way of benevolence.

All living things must die. The physical body is destroyed and the spirit scatters, just as [all things] become luxuriant in spring and decay in autumn, and the four seasons change, one after another. How could there be further [rebirths] to receive another body? The *Book of Odes* states that "Happy and easygoing gentlemen seek a blessing by no crooked ways."[314] This means that the propagation of the Way lies in oneself. [The *Book of Odes* also says:] "The three sovereigns (i.e., Dawang, Wang Ji, and Wen Wang) reside in Heaven."[315] This denotes that the exquisite spirits ascended far to [Heaven]. Nevertheless, one harbors sensual desires in the mind while outwardly fearful of the expedient teaching (i.e., Buddhism), or one deeply considers his present life while giving donations in hopes of a reward in the next life. Our predecessor Confucian masters in former times said nothing about these issues. I am originally deficient in intelligence and vigor, and I do not know how to make it my business to practice [this teaching].

The Expatiation of the *Discourse on the Full Understanding of Life* of He of Hengyang by Yan Yanzhi (384–456)

I formerly obtained your discourse, in which with deep views and extensive thought you take the human way to be lofty and degrade other living creatures. The content is clear and subtle, and the subject does not lose significance. This is really helpful for the [Confucian] teaching, and good enough to wipe out the heretical school. There is no need to speak of those who seek [the Confucian teaching] equally. How could they forget what they rely upon? I am merely concerned that if [music played only with] Chinese zithers is monotonous, it will lose the clear harmony. Thereupon, I will briefly and broadly write several articles, and take all your responses, [which I expect to] receive later.

You say that he who is in one unit together with the two polarities and who becomes the three powers with them must be a name of the virtuous one, but this is not a category of people in general. Generally, however, various species [of living creatures] are equally called sentient beings; this is the name for those who bear consciousness. How could it be the title for sages and wise people? In that case, to comment on the three powers has nothing to do with the masses. How does calling them sentient beings abuse sages and wise people? Even though I have the feeling to depend upon [the importance of] order, I am not worried that [calling them sentient beings] causes disorder. If both registers (i.e., sages and ordinary people) can be taught and all can be lifted up, understand the principles thoroughly, make a restriction to leave language behind, adopt this, and share reality, then it is possible [to be harmonious], just as when the notes of *beilü* and the note *gong* naturally harmonize, or just as two separated pieces of a tally join together.[316] Why do you discontentedly stick to *lü* [of the *yin* notes] and slander *lü* [of the *yang* notes]?[317]

Moreover, [it is said in the *Book of Changes* that] "the great virtue [of Heaven and Earth] is called life."[318] [In life,] there is a common feature of all things, which is the same as what differentiates all things. How could it be distinguished to attain life? The life that is not different for each living

creature should be [known as] sentient beings. In the ranks of sentient beings, however, there are a great many differences between the ignorant and the wise. People employ other living creatures in order to nourish themselves, and other living creatures are put to work in order to support people. Even though at the beginning [people] may follow [the law of Heaven], they come
22b to kill [other living creatures] at last. Various causes sprout. Sensual desires are not repressed. Life is harmed in increasing and miserable ways. The law of Heaven will be pent up and destroyed.

Emperors and sages lament this situation, but they cannot suddenly take away [the habits that] remain entrenched [in the world]. Therefore, they set up the teaching to plan seasonal hunting and the scriptures to prudently follow the seasons. It is simply to nourish those who bear consciousness by opening up [the way of] benevolence and to gradually return to the cessation of extremities. Those who take the Way to be the mind will probably stop [evils] before they come to [the worst] like this.

Furthermore, you understand that in the great law of Nature the life and death [of all creatures] are equal in rising and falling. Various existing things are really suitable for this. In the truth of spirits, however, the issue of remaining in existence or not might differ from the issue of the withering of grass or the fading away of [living creatures]. If [the spirit] is the same as trees and plants, then it will disappear like smoke. Moreover, you say that the three sovereigns ascended far and their exquisite spirits reside in Heaven. If the exquisite spirits indeed exist, and they are surely different from trees and plants, then there is nothing to support your opinion regarding the doctrine of receiving a body. Is it that because the three sovereigns were purely good, they were rewarded and reborn in Heaven? You intended to denounce [the doctrine of] future life, but on the contrary you established [the concept of] ascending far [to Heaven]. Since you undertook to denounce [the doctrine of the future life] and yet established [the concept of ascending far to Heaven], I understand without doubt that this is not what is removed by the power. If there is merely the exquisite spirit, which does not have any form and appearance, I have no idea what it relies upon to establish itself in Heaven. I am too cowardly to make a conclusion. Therefore, I strive for and depend on your opinion. So, [my thoughts go] back and forth, but I have not yet attained contentment.

Generally, within [the realm of] fate there is nothing that does not move [others] without response. Actions and the way of reward and retribution inevitably tally with each other. Even if it is said that they inevitably tally with each other, why do you suspect we have hope [for a reward]? Consequently, those who forget kindness have no demand [for a reward] and those who keep merit have hope [for a reward]. Cherishing merit while hoping [for a reward] is not yet wholesomeness. When kindness is removed, this will be the highest level [of virtue]. There are wise people and those who are not so wise among human beings, and then there are public and private in our thoughts. In this physical world it cannot be said that since some people expect rewards, those who establish their virtues all wish for [a reward]. Moreover, according to the common talk of those who reign over the world, people who value giving donations have no recollection [of their act of giving], and when government officials conduct righteousness, they still show kindness to others without thinking [that what they are doing is wholesome], not to speak of those who listen to the essentials of the [Buddhist] Way. Wouldn't it be possible for them to be disinterested? Would they never fail to have sensual desires when they take actions? Wouldn't they be afraid of the expedient teaching at every chance? You have never been able to promote [Buddhism], and you always put it down. Even though you deeply reproach, correct, and upbraid [Buddhists], please cease your arrogant speech and do not attack them. You usually firmly entrench yourself in a castle, and it is difficult to send a letter [to convince you]. Furthermore, I have been cooped up with worries and distresses in my house, and I had no chance to entrust my feelings and reasoning to you. Recently I received a graceful and great letter from you. I wanted to express my intention and judge your former explanation. I worry that it may not be worthy.

Sincerely yours,
Yan Yanzhi

Response to Yan of Yongjia

I respectfully read your esteemed letter and examined repeatedly your deep intention. You draw a line between each of the three powers. Your inference of testimonies is refined and pure. You declare your aspiration for the [Buddhist] Way and praise and admire Buddhists. You take account of all through this world (*ming*) and the other world (*you*). You act in sincerity and reach out to [all] things. When you practice it in yourself, it is excellent. When you expound it in the teaching, it is magnanimous. It is faultless. [Nevertheless,] when I take a step backward and seek what your good instruction came from, [I feel as if] you want me to inspect the Big Dipper and the North Pole, but you get even more lost and your thoughts may become obscure. You have not yet understood completely. Therefore, I will relate my original intention once again.

You said, "[You say that] he [who is in one unit together with the two polarities and] who becomes the three powers with them must be a name of the virtuous one. Why are sages and wise people also so?" [I am afraid that you misunderstand my words.]

22c The way of human beings was established incorporating various benevolences and righteousness. Natural compassion is a manifestation of the virtuous. To feel ashamed for evils is the beginning of a chivalrous mind. [Nevertheless,] the trees of Mount Niu were cut with scythes and axes [and lost their beautiful] nature.[319] A peaceful and quiet state of mind is put into disorder by the thought of interests. We should really nourish the initial stage [of a wholesome heart] and help its growth. Then, can there be no mistake [if it is said that a wholesome heart] exists but it is not counted?

In addition, you say, "To comment on the three powers has nothing to do with the masses. Why does calling them sentient beings abuse sages and wise people?" I have already heard your instruction, but I have still not understood on what basis the two roads [of sages and ordinary people] are judged [separately]. Would Yi [Yin] and Yan [Hui] belong to the lower stratum [of sentient beings]? Would [Sun] Qiao (i.e., Zichang of Zheng state) and Ji[zha of Wu state] belong to the upper stratum? If we people hope for [sagehood] tirelessly, in order to dispel what we have not yet understood, we certainly raise both registers [of sages and ordinary people]. If [the notes of *beilü* and] *gong* [naturally] harmonize and two separated pieces of a tally join together, wouldn't this be the highest wholesomeness?

Moreover, you say, "The great virtue [of Heaven and Earth] is called life. [In life,] there is a common feature of all things, which is the same as what differentiates all things. How could it be distinguished to attain life?" I do not say that this is not so. Even though people are born and equally placed under the great virtue (i.e., life), they cannot be called sentient beings. It compares to the case that although sages equally receive the five primary elements, they cannot be called the people. What merit is there in considering that the life that is not different from each other must be sentient beings?

In the letter received, you say, "People employ other living creatures in order to nourish themselves, and other living creatures are put to work in order to support people." If you broadly judge like this, then you have the same thought as my humble view. As to passion and sensual desires, if we do not restrain them, we will destroy life and be brutal to other living creatures. We will be the so-called one of excessive [desire] or the arrogant one. Sages assuredly remove this.

Furthermore, you say, "Those who take the Way to be the mind will probably stop [evils] before they come to [the worst] like this." I would like to ask you a question. Are those who stop [evils before they come to the worst like this] not going to kill [animals] with their own hands? Or do they make all [people] equally receive the teaching [of not killing]? If you mean that they do not kill with their own hands but go to a market [to buy] a necessary amount [of meat], the issue is originally the [same] intention as that [gentlemen] should stay away from the kitchen. If you want to recommend it to families entered in the household registers (i.e., common people), I see that your discussion does not hold water.

Moreover, you say, "If [the spirit] is the same as trees and plants, then it will disappear like smoke. What does the exquisite spirit rely upon to establish itself in Heaven?" Well, the disembodied spirits are dim and faint. Wandering spirits become evil spirits. When [the spirit] is glorified and [its departure from the body] saddens others, it will go somewhere. Zhongyou (i.e., Zilu) received [no answer from Confucius] when he wanted to know about death.[320] Si (i.e., Zigong) was also unsuccessful in getting an answer [regarding the nature of human beings and the Way of Heaven].[321]

As for the matter that we will never again receive a body, I clearly stated this in my previous discussion. Regarding the matter of what the spirits rely upon to exist in Heaven, I ask you to depend on Confucius's answer. Regarding [the comment,] "Actions and the way of reward and retribution inevitably tally [with each other]," I should say that the Yu family [of the Han dynasty] made a gate higher and waited for the merit of the accumulation of their virtuous deeds,[322] and Lord Boyang, [who rescued Emperor Xuan when the emperor was still an infant,] did not attack [any enemy] yet he was blessed with the rank of marquis.[323] How are these concerned with the next life?

In addition, you say, "According to the common talk of those who reign over the world, people who [value] giving donations have no recollection [of their act of giving], and when government officials conduct righteousness, they still show kindness to others without thinking [that what they are doing is wholesome]." This statement is true. There is, [however,] something to slightly regret [about this]. To require kindness in order to plan for a reward is what a preacher exhorts. To be kind in order to be delighted with a reward is a common affair of the world. If one doubts [the Buddhist] scriptures, he will suffer hardships for successive *kalpa*s. If he diligently makes donations, he will obtain rewards accumulated many times over. These issues are not likely to be included in the teaching of our school. Thereupon, I am simply discontented.

23a I know that you want to draw it (i.e., Buddhism) to the upper stream. This is also something for which I do not begrudge supporting immensely. Those who place themselves in reality, however, considerably take the splendor of foreknowledge to be vile. Therefore, I do not [draw Buddhism to the upper stream]. If donations are not made as aid in an emergency and if kindness is given [only in order to receive] merit and fame, when these are all evaluated by a wise person [like you], we feel ashamed. Thus, I have acted in accordance with my perseverance for a long time, but I have never improved myself. I feel inwardly ashamed at [Qu] Boyu [of Wei state, who continually tried to practice good conduct].[324] I have not spared the time to censure others.

Sincerely,
He Chengtian

The Second Expatiation to He of Hengyang

I have been occupied in farming for a while. I was [busy] personally gathering the crops in a rice field among the hills. In spare moments from my farming, aged rustics are my companions. The topic of our conversation is limited to crops. My work is entirely to plow land and pasture animals. We talk about ripening, and plan how to plough side by side. I did not hear anything of intelligent significance. I received a subtle argument from you, by which I am brightly consoled. The content of your letter is very detailed, and I feel more ashamed of my obstinacy. [Nevertheless,] I now again forget [my obstinacy] and write to you of what I cherish in my mind, in order to convey to you what I have not yet expressed.

In investigating the principles, to rely on our intentions is not as good as to analyze it from the sacred literature. The discussion on the three powers must be originally based on all three lines (*hua*) [of the *Book of Changes*]. When the three lines are displayed, the middle line refers to the virtue of a sovereign.[325] Therefore, it is so supernatural that it can reach the uppermost, and so lofty that it can unite with the head of the state. Consequently, I said formerly that if one is not suitable to Heaven and Earth, he has nothing with which to originally respond to the knowledge of these things. Even if you broadly examine your clear thought, you have not been willing to remain in agreement with me.

You still take [all people] without discarding [anyone] in [the three powers]. You carry them extensively without leaving anyone out. Your resolution to be generous to people is really ample. I am, [however,] afraid that your arrangement of positions is disordered and consequently there will be numerous ambiguous issues. If wherever natural compassion arises you exhaust the capacity of universal love, and if wherever the feeling to be ashamed of evils arises you accomplish the righteousness of [divine] help for honest people, you are the most benevolent and the most righteous. I can find no flaw [in this], but those who care about [benevolence and righteousness] are few and those who use them for their own benefit are many. Those people who possess their lot [of benevolence and righteousness] in advance and have not reached its apex simply cannot be a match for the two polarities (i.e., Heaven and Earth) [of the three powers].

Now, if one who renders himself at the apex [of benevolence and righteousness] is a teacher, if those who have not [yet reached the apex of benevolence and righteousness] are [his] disciples, if their minds of respect and yielding are helped [to develop], if their minds of jealousy and conflict are removed, if we cause the blades of scythes and axes [with which the trees of Mount Niu were cut down] to be melted down [and made useless], if [we cause] the arising of the thought of merit and demerit to stop, and if we urge the people of a hundred generations to go out and get onto the path of sincerity and kindness, why doesn't a bud [of the wholesome mind] grow? Why isn't the wholesome mind invoked? Nevertheless, you falsely accuse that "[a wholesome heart exists but] it is not counted." I have not yet evaluated your intention. Even if the three powers are equally arranged in a line, we cannot bring people of superficial talent into the line. Even if they are called sentient beings, we cannot mix them up recklessly with the man of nonarising (i.e., the Buddha). Therefore, in this land, those of humble birth are not counted in [the three powers]; and in [the Buddhism of] that land, sages and wise people are clearly distinguished. The purpose of recommending all [members] of both registers [of Buddhism and Confucianism] lies in this.

Regarding people like [Sun] Qiao (i.e., Zichang) and [Ji]zha, their virtue is not able to be one with [that of] emperors and kings. How could they belong to the upper stratum? Yi [Yin] and Yan [Hui] still rely on birth [through receiving] the natural vapor. They ought to belong to the lower stratum. The judgment of the two paths [of sages and ordinary people] is easier than giving instructions to one's servants by merely gesturing with one's chin.

Moreover, I am aware that you say, "Even though people are born and equally placed under the great virtue, they cannot be called sentient beings. It is comparable to the case that although sages equally receive the five primary elements, they cannot be called people."

The reason [sages] cannot be called people is that [sages] are more vigorous than people in spiritual intelligence. Now, [sages] are equally placed under [the great virtue] in the same way as [ordinary] people. Why do you avoid [the idea that sages] and people are the same? Certainly, we must differentiate them on the basis of their extraordinary spirits, but we should not distinguish them based on the life they received. You avoid in vain the name of the people, but the reality of the people is not damaged.

23b [What you are doing] cannot help but resemble the case that if one is afraid of a single-plank bridge and tries to avoid [stepping on] it, in the end he will not be able to avoid [crossing over to the other side]. As for my statement, "People employ other living creatures in order to nourish themselves, and other living creatures are put to work in order to support people," I intend to mean that the ignorant and the wise restrict each other, and the confused and the intelligent control each other. This matter, [the difference between human beings and animals,] derives from human intellect; it does not derive from the laws of Heaven. Therefore, at the beginning we are compassionate to its emergence, and lament its stagnation and [eventual] disappearance in the end. Would your [feast of] various types of food including livestock serve the same purpose as this?

Generally, moving and flowing well are the nature of those of the lower stratum, while making judgments in transformation and shaping (i.e., change) is the work of sages of the upper stratum.[326] If one carefully builds a fence [around a house], he is still worried that a thief may come over the fence, not to speak of [his worry when] he completely sets up everything in order to satisfy extravagant desires. This is precisely the beginning of extremities. How could we discuss abandoning excessive [desires]? Therefore, I know that in your discussion of "to destroy life and be brutal to other living creatures" I cannot share anxieties with heartless people [like you]. The intention to be fond of killing is found in some people, but the feeling to love life is abundant. "Those who take the Way to be the mind," which I said refers to having abundant feelings of loving life, rejecting unreality, casually fulfilling [life], stepping on reality, and having no premature death, and yet it is not considered to be benevolence whose benefits and favors reach Heaven. Why would kindness be limited to just fawns and eggs? Why would the issue emulate only [the activities of] wolves and otters?

Judging from this, we should simply not [kill] with our own hands, but we should also not put the blame on the market or the kitchen [where animals are butchered]. Moreover, this does not mean that outside of the market and the kitchen there is nothing to be offered [as food] to nourish us. The writing of Shen Nong is explained by Zhongsan (Ji Gang, 233–262) [in the *Discourse on Health Care* (*Yangshenglun*)]. Gongli (i.e., Zhong Changtong of the Later Han dynasty) praised this matter (i.e., health care), and Zhongyang (i.e., Jiao Shen of the Later Han dynasty) worked hard at the practice [of guiding the breath (*daoyin*)].[327] This shows exactly that formerly there was a biography of that person and we now hear of him. Why is it necessary to take carving meat to be the nature of people who received [a vapor of] harmony, or to take broiling and boiling meat to be a means to help wholesomeness? If you worry that my shallow argument does not hold because it is difficult to recommend equally to common people, [it is just like] your concern that since the two men [Guan]shu and [Cai]shu were not intimate [with the royal family of the Zhou dynasty], the virtue of the Zhou dynasty would be lost in the future. If we can set forth a far-reaching prospect and seek [a good result] for a long period of time, we will be able to fulfill it in a short period of time and to expect merit in a long period of time.

If the exquisite spirit is exactly distinguished from grass and trees, your answer, "Wandering spirits [become evil spirits. When the spirit is glorified and its departure from the body saddens others, it will go somewhere]," is the theory that exquisite spirits [exist]. If [you say] that even though there are [spirits] and they have no form, then could there be beings without form in the world? This, indeed, is the question. You ought to show the assured view. The reason Confucius did not answer [the question about the spirits] is because he had not discerned whether or not [spirits] exist. [Nevertheless,] you have already accounted for their existence. How could you align yourself with him in not giving an answer [to the question]? Even though you are fond of studying, I am afraid that you have not gotten to what you rely upon. Otherwise, this is because the paths of understanding and of obscurity are very much separate from each other, and the mysterious issue and the evident are far removed from each other; these facts consequently cause the bright moon to stop shining on the world, and [worldly] knowledge restricts your mind from understanding [Buddhism].

You say that if my words, "[Actions and the way of reward and retribution] inevitably tally with each other" are embodied, it is the Yu family at an end. Wouldn't it be that my discussion was too elaborate and yet, against my intention, I ended up with a noncommittal opinion? Or, [it is like] a worldly person who has an unpolished gem and displays it in a market is censured. Otherwise, [it is like] an officer in charge of translation who is affected by the customs [of his own state] talks even more about the conditions of that state. If I have not completely taken care of the matter, please let me again present my recent explanation in minute detail.

[The relation between] reward and retribution and actions is primarily called fate. I think that there are no absurd things. Each one is moved with good virtue. Among those who are moved [with good virtue], the minds of human beings are the greatest. The movement of one's thought cannot be perceived by servants practicing divination. When it is extended to its accumulated point, we are not competent enough to determine its origin and we must give up [examining it]. I will take the popular view, and based on this I will show clear evidence.

Zhuangzhou (i.e., Zhuangzi) says that if the land is tilled in a careless and haphazard manner, the reward (i.e., the harvest) is poor, too.[328] Lord Sun (i.e., Xunzi) says that the force of reward or retribution falls on a person according to each category.[329] These statements are set forth to admonish us for our future 23c
lives. Shouldn't we respect them? Since merciful people deeply saw this fate, they made the correct statement of its foundation. This is not to invite its end.

[The Buddhist teaching] is to increase good qualities, prevent evils, return the people to the grand submission [to the natural course],[330] deliver sentient beings [from evils], and cause them to enter into the land of eternal life. It brings about widespread blessings for everyone, and [the Buddha] is the highest of a hundred deities in nobility. Why should it be merely that blessings are extended to one's descendants and happiness is limited to being ranked as a high official or minister? If we continuously save [others] with good [intentions], a good [result] will also follow. That force is just like that of a sundial. Without any exercise of thought, it will occur naturally.

Why do you say, "To require kindness [in order to plan for a reward is what a preacher exhorts]," "[To be kind in order] to be delighted with a reward [is a common affair of the world]," "If one doubts [the Buddhist scriptures], he will suffer hardships [for successive *kalpa*s]," and "If he diligently makes donations, [he will obtain rewards accumulated many times over]"? It appears that this is because you verify the parsimonious feeling familiar to you, and you doubt the virtuous teaching with which you are unfamiliar. Consequently, you just punish those who boast about achievements, but are recklessly censured for forgetting about wise people. The difference in significance between "those who forget [kindness]" and "those who keep [merit]" and the distinction in thought between public and private have already been fully explained in my previous letter. I will not repeat it here. You, who thinks that "those who place themselves in reality, [however, considerably] take the splendor [of foreknowledge] to be vile," tend to simply stay in kindness and leave behind coldheartedness. If there are people like those who make donations not in order to give aid in an emergency, or who are kind only expecting fame [in return], then you will be ashamed of them and I will also be ashamed of them.[331]

The Second Response to Yan of Yongjia

I have believed in my narrow view from the time I was young. The older I grow, the deeper [this tendency] becomes. If I scruple to say what I have already begun to say, I [feel] that my heart will become clogged and rotten. Hence, I was hoping to float relying on a stream or to soar entrusting myself to a female *kylin,* when you expressed your thoughts with good intention and again kindly gave explanations. The way you investigated and testified is thorough and clear. Your beautiful expression is extensive and abundant. If sometimes good jade has a flaw, even a humble person may point out the flaw. When there is a waning moon, even a rustic looks askance at the part that is lacking. How could I, such a [rustic] person, be fond of arguing? However, I cannot stop talking. Again, I will take a step further and ask you questions to get [your instructions], with which I will examine completely what brings me to a standstill.

In your letter you say, "The discussion on the three powers must be originally based on all three lines [of the *Book of Changes*]. When the three lines are displayed, the middle line refers to the virtue of a sovereign. Therefore, it is so supernatural that it can reach the uppermost, and so lofty that it can unite with the head of the state."

If, just as your point of argument, we consider the three lines [of the *Book of Changes*] to be the three powers, the first (bottom) line is intended to be the line of Earth and the third (upper) line is said to be the rank of Heaven. [The *Book of Changes,*] however, [says,] "The one can live in seclusion without regret."[332] This does not mean a category of [things like the Earth] which supports and contains all things in its largeness. [It is also stated in the *Book of Changes*] that "Gentlemen are active and vigilant [all the day]."[333] This does not refer to the deep blue [sky] (i.e., Heaven).

As a matter of fact, as long as the two polarities, [Heaven and Earth,] have no consigning basis, how can we take [the second line] to designate the establishment of [the way of] people? Since the line is located between justice and harmony, it is simply suitable to correspond to sovereign virtue.

Moreover, you say, "[If] wherever natural compassion [arises] you exhaust the capacity of universal love, and [if] wherever the feeling to be ashamed of evils [arises] you accomplish the righteousness of [divine] help for honest people, you are the most benevolent and the most righteous." This indicates that you admit that those who practice benevolence and righteousness become the three powers.

Again, you say that Zichang and [Ji]zha cannot belong to the upper stratum, and Yi [Yin] and Yan [Hui] ought to belong to the lower stratum. People who are qualified to put on yellow lower garments (i.e., ranking officials such as Zichang and Jizha) still fall below [the sovereign virtue of the three powers]. Although you said [the judgment of the two paths of sages and ordinary people is easier than] giving instructions to one's servants by merely gesturing with one's chin, since there is no warrant for high and low (i.e., sages and ordinary people), a deluded one [like me] has not yet comprehended this.

Yin and *yang* nourish the vigor [of people], while toughness and gentleness give them their natures. They each have a round head and rectangular feet; they do not differ in their appearance. They have much natural compassion and the feeling to be ashamed of evil. So does everyone. For those who take part in and accept the two polarities [in order to be in the three powers], however, it is necessary to hold benevolence and righteousness as the first step. I feel that you want to limit [the qualification of human beings] with rank or proper equipages such as vehicle and clothes that [the emperor] should carefully bestow upon his vassals. Consequently you cause the nature of kind people and incorruptible scholars [such as Zichang and Jizha] to be compared with that of beasts, and you see the wise, [such as Yi Yin and Yan 24a
Hui,] who are capable and virtuous, as having the same physical energy as shellfish. Would the meaning to develop the symbolism of the hexagrams be like this?

Furthermore, you say, "[Now, sages] are equally placed under [the great virtue] in the same way as [ordinary] people. Why do you avoid [the idea that sages] and ordinary people are the same? Certainly, we must differentiate them on the basis of their extraordinary spirits, but we should not distinguish them based on the life they received."

Such extraordinary spirits are already different from [the spirits of] other living creatures. Why would they all suddenly be the same under the law of receiving life? Life is based on the law and the law differentiates [between sages and other living creatures]. Then, on what basis is the same name, "life," given to other living creatures? If you stick to this name "life" and cause the people to certainly follow it, then is something undefined and complete (*huncheng zhi wu*)[334] [that came into existence before Heaven and Earth] also included in this instance?

Again, you say, "If one carefully builds a fence [around a house], he is still worried that a thief may come over the fence, not to speak of [his worry when] he completely sets up everything in order to satisfy extravagant desires. This is precisely the beginning of extremities. How could we discuss abandoning excessive [desires]?"

You said at the beginning [of this series of arguments] that emperors and sages set up the teaching to plan seasonal hunting and the scriptures to prudently follow the seasons; in this way [they tried] to gradually return to the cessation of extremities. Now, you criticize with the statement, "This is precisely the beginning of extremities." I have not known in detail whether this rebukes my view or ridicules sages.

Furthermore, you say, "Outside of the market and the kitchen, why can there be nothing to be offered [as food] to nourish us? The writing of Shen Nong is explained by Zhongsan. . . . Why is it necessary to take carving meat to be the nature of people who received [a vapor of] harmony, or to take broiling and boiling meat to be a means to help wholesomeness?"

Well, in offering to Heaven and Earth, calf's horns [are used]; in the state offering the three domestic animals, [cows, pigs, and sheep,] are sacrificed; and the thick soup of beef or pork is served in a wooden vessel on a painted wooden stand to offer to guests of honor. An old man of seventy years is not satisfied until he eats meat. Why can you merely display herbs and medicines and reserve them as the best remedy? The reason I am worried that [your argument] does not stand up is not that it is difficult for me to support your great discussion, but I take a step back and doubt this matter; simply, [such dietary habits] cannot be suddenly removed from the world.

Moreover, you say, "If [you say] that even though there are [spirits], they have no form, then could there be beings without form in the world? This, indeed, is the question. You ought to show the assured view."

I examined the intention [of this point] in your letter, as [I feel] it seems you do not reject that there are spiritual beings. Just on the point in which you say that spiritual beings should have some substance, isn't it possible you are confused, since Indian books state that spiritual beings become other living creatures? People of former days considered spiritual beings to be [the foundation of] the teaching. Moreover, they wrote it down in books and scriptures, and it is widely found in written materials. [Lord Sun] Qiao (i.e., Zichang) of Zheng state and [Ji]zha of Wu state considered this so, too. Therefore, when music is played six times [with the Chinese zithers made out of wood from] Mount Yunhe, the spirits of Heaven really descend [from Heaven], and when it is played nine times [with the Chinese zithers made out of wood from] Mount Longmen, the manes of people all come and gather.[335] You often adhere to the *Rites of Zhou* (*Zhouli*), but recently you disregard this meaning. Just now you berate beings without form. It is an incoherent argument!

Again, you say, "These statements (i.e., Zhuangzi's and Xunzi's) are set forth to admonish us for our future lives. Shouldn't we respect them? Since merciful people deeply saw this fate, they made the correct statement of its foundation."

You have not made it clear about so-called merciful people. What are they? If you depend on the doctrine of reward and retribution [in accordance with] actions that is stated in books other than [Confucian texts], it is entirely the teaching of expedients to which I refer. In investigating the utmost doctrine, you have not analyzed with the sages' words and yet you have adopted many crafty and strange [words] in order to support [your argument]. Can it be to give the impression of rescuing by means of water from disasters caused by water?

Furthermore, you say, "I think that there are no absurd things. Each one is moved with good virtue," and "If we continuously save [others] with good [intentions], a good [result] will also follow. That force is just like that of a sundial. Without any exercise of thought, it will occur naturally."

If these words are certainly so, those who are moved with good virtue 24b
must be equal in degree of seriousness, just as the force of a sundial must have a certain extent in length. As to decorations in building or construction, they are not initiated by a benevolent mind. Even though hunting is done according to the [appropriate] seasons, the extremely cruel nature [of human beings] has not been uprooted. For what is a person rewarded to ascend to Heaven, which is splendid and joyful? For what is one punished to fall into hell, which is dark and full of suffering? Excellent words come to an end in

differentiating high from low, and the law is made without a scale (i.e., measure or standard). All things have come to this point!

Moreover, a guardian attendant who teaches and loves [his master] encourages [his master] to abstain from eating the intestines of dogs and hogs, [which resemble those of human beings].

A good cook who wields a knife [to butcher cattle for meat] feels afraid whenever he comes to a complicated joint.[336] The sage is as bright as the sun and moon, and his edification can open the three powers (*santong*).[337] If [actions and the way of] reward and retribution inevitably tally, how does it hinder the teaching? Why was it sealed in the ages of [Fu]xi and Tang [Yao]? Why was it buried in the time of the Duke of Zhou and Confucius? In the beginning, nets [to catch animals and fish] were made and this has given rise to a number of sins. [The practice of] offering animal sacrifices was established and opened the punishment of the long night [of spiritual darkness] (Skt. *dīrgha-rātram*). The heavenly kitchen (i.e., food naturally collected) is abandoned, and those animals fed with grass and grain are considered delicious. There has been no benevolence to save people from drowning [in extreme misery]. The cruelty of putting people into a dry moat was carried out without restraint. In order that these acts not be repeated, you should sincerely consider the issues deeply. If you think that the intelligence of the exquisite spirit [of sages] is not yet complete in some points, even though you are thoughtful and love strange ideas, you have not come to disgrace the sages.

When you talk about benevolence and righteousness, you say, "those who care about [benevolence and righteousness] are few and those who use them for their own benefit are many." However, when you speak of doing kindness, you approve that men of virtue and talents who are left neglected forget a reward. Since those who care about [benevolence and righteousness] are few, who are able to be those of virtue and talents yet who are left neglected? Since those who use [benevolence and righteousness] for their own benefit are many, how can you say to forget a reward? If you can encourage people who are willing to give [to the poor], expect companions who want to be benevolent, expound the meaning of forgetting reward and retribution, and lead the people toward a mind of righteousness, then righteousness is truly here and you are not far [from the goal] in seeking benevolence.

As to your statement, "[The Buddhist teaching is to increase good qualities, prevent evils, return the people to the grand submission to the natural course,] deliver sentient beings [from evils], and cause them to enter into the land of eternal life. It brings about widespread blessings for everyone, and [the Buddha] is the highest of a hundred deities in nobility," the intention of this is nonsense, and it is not what I am concerned with in this discussion. Isn't this like the case when the Qin army was about to escape and their messenger talked nonsense?[338] How could I continue to press you? Please take a seat. I will explain it to you.

Sages are [originally] placed above, and they do not have to strive for supremacy against a hundred deities. If there is a beginning, there is an end. How can you be in the land of eternal life? Well, the other world and this world are distinguished clearly from each other. Various things are investigated completely. From early times, when [people kept records by] tying knots, up to the later period, when culture and education flourish, [sages] lead the nature of human beings by means of the Way. Therefore, they cut off the intimacy and fame of being praised. They manage Nature within the proper rules. Nothing hurts the capacity of universal love. By hunting and fishing, both the wise and ordinary people are nourished. Game for its threefold use [in hunting] is served to guests as a practical matter.[339] Gold and precious stones illuminate splendidly. A panpipe with thirteen reeds (*sheng*) and a short flute (*yue*) harmonize the rhythm. Getting drunk and being satisfied with kindness, one is benefited in this way for ten thousand years. Recluses [who do not serve the government] broaden new works every day, while officials expound the teachings of ancient sage sovereigns. Sincerity is apparent in bright rulers. Benefits spread to all people. The dragon seal [of emperors] manifests [magnificent] views. Musical stones create harmonious rhythms. These are for the paradise of Yao and Confucius.

During the time of obscurity, a man lives in seclusion on a hill or near a mountain stream in order to attend to his own virtue. He kills chickens, makes a variety of millet, and entrusts somewhat his ambition; or, [just like Yi Yin,] he carries a heavy three-legged caldron on his back to cook, becomes famous and immortalizes his fame; or a man [like Taigong Wang Lü Shang] butchers sheep, uses a knife [to cook], and lets his lofty aspiration ride the 24c
drifting clouds. These are the ways for gentlemen to set the mind. Why is it

necessary to consider the future blessings of the family that has accumulated enough good deeds to be vile, to hope for the blessings of the next existence of which there is no proof, to turn one's back on the real pleasures of one's own lifetime, and to be tired of working in vain, without a place to return to? [To practice something elusive like] trying to harness [shapeless] wind or catch a shadow is not the grace of the golden mean of the Confucian school. To admire a barbarian and to be confused by absurd things go against the goal of a masterly mind. [A Buddhist monk's] squatting or kneeling upright in worship and [the Chinese style of] bowing complaisantly are inconsistent with each other after all. I personally wish that you would give up practicing both [Buddhism and Confucianism] and abide by [Confucianism] alone.

Metaphors such as a single-plank bridge, the two men [Guan]shu and [Cai]shu, a person in the world [who keeps an unpolished gem and displays it in a market], and an officer in charge of translation, have nothing to do with the original meanings. Therefore, I say nothing about them.

The Third Expatiation to He of Hengyang

Sacred thought is difficult to investigate, and a mysterious response is unforeseen. It is as the courtier [Ji Kang] said, "No matter how hard mediocrity devotes himself, he cannot catch even a clue of it."[340] How could superficial and obstinate people search and draw out [an answer]? I vainly think that [the inscription of Emperor Wen of the Wei dynasty, which denied the existence of] the cloth that could be washed in fire (*huohuanbu*), was [engraved in stone, but it was] cut down in a later generation,[341] and Teng Xiu felt ashamed of himself throughout his life [for his ignorance] about the barbels of a shrimp.[342] Therefore, I simply fear to judge with my own speculation anything outside my consideration.

You have already discerned the truth or falsehood [of Buddhism]. The scriptures of doctrines (*fangshu*) are everlasting,[343] and their unique insights are strong, durable, and skillful. It is difficult to have doubts about them. I will write a little more about what I think and explain it, itemizing in accordance with your responses. Since fortune and misfortune are mingled in the matter, and foreign and Chinese [thoughts] are mixed in the meaning, although

I tried to make a brief and concise statement, it ended up becoming a petty composition. After I send this out, I would like to maintain my silence.

You respond and say, "If, just as your point of argument, we consider the three lines [of the *Book of Changes*] to be the three powers, the first (bottom) line is intended to be the line of Earth and the third (upper) line is said to be the rank of Heaven. [The *Book of Changes,*] however, [says,] 'The one can live in seclusion without regret.' This does not mean a category of [things like the Earth] which supports and contains all things in its largeness. [It is also stated in the *Book of Changes*] that 'Gentlemen are active and vigilant [all the day].' This does not refer to the deep blue [sky] (i.e., Heaven).

"As a matter of fact, as long as the two polarities, [Heaven and Earth,] have no consigning basis, how can we take [the second line] to designate the establishment of [the way of] people? Since the line is located between justice and harmony, it is simply suitable to correspond to sovereign virtue."

My explanation is this: According to former scholarship I have heard, the simple symbol of the diagrams (*xiang*) begins with three lines (*sanhua*) and the sixty-four hexagrams (*jiangua* or *zhonggua*) end with six lines (*yao*).[344] With the three lines the foundation of the position of the three powers is set up. [In the hexagram *qian,*] before the six lines change [each line shows] what a group of dragons pass through.[345] Hence, after the sixty-four hexagrams, the significance of one's course of action is clarified. Therefore, [it is stated in the "Explanation of the Words and Sentences" (*Wenyan*) in the *Book of Changes* that] "The one can live in seclusion [without regret]," "[Gentlemen] are active [and vigilant all the day]," "[This is 'the dragon'] lying hidden," and "[Gentlemen] advance together with the movement of time]."[346] These are the meanings for sages to adapt to the circumstances of their times and the way to unite [the diagrams]. If we consider that the two polarities [Heaven and Earth] have no consigning basis, and we do not take the second line to be designated for the establishment of [the way of] people since the first line is not intended for Earth and the third line is not positioned for Heaven, then I do not understand on what basis your previous assertion that "the three powers are one unit" arises.

If you still accept the theory found in the "Commentary of Appended Judgments" (*Xicizhuan*) [in the *Book of Changes*] and you do not surpass the instruction received from your teachers, why do you take only the meaning of the hexagrams correctly and decline the meaning of the simple symbol of the diagrams? If there is [a theory of] the three powers other than [those formulated by Fu]xi and King Wen, this is "a new thought of spring and autumn," about which I have no idea.[347] Moreover, although "The one can live in seclusion [without regret]" and "[Gentlemen] are active [and vigilant all the day]" are not described for Heaven and Earth, the connotation for low and high has not been lost overall. How could you reject the significance in setting up the foundation [of the three powers with the three lines] on the basis of the treatises that are variations [of the original text]?

In addition, I know you say, "Since the line is located between justice and harmony, it is simply suitable to correspond to sovereign virtue." If there
25a are merely the lines for justice and harmony and rather unexpectedly there is no person of justice and harmony, to what are the lines going to be applied? If justice and harmony lie in [sovereign] virtue and all ordinary people cannot have justice and harmony, my discussion that one is suitable to [Heaven and Earth] cannot be seen as extravagant.

You respond, "[Moreover, you say,] '[If] wherever natural compassion [arises] you exhaust the capacity of universal love, and [if] wherever the feeling to be ashamed of evils [arises] you accomplish the righteousness of [divine] help for honest people, you are the most benevolent and the most righteous.' This indicates that you admit that those who practice benevolence and righteousness become the three powers."

Again, you say that "Zichang and [Ji]zha cannot belong to the upper stratum, and Yi [Yin] and Yan [Hui] ought to belong to the lower stratum. People who are qualified to put on yellow lower garments (i.e., ranking officials such as Zichang and Jizha) still fall below [the sovereign virtue of the three powers]. Although [you said the judgment of the two paths of sages and ordinary people is easier than] giving instructions to one's servants by merely gesturing with one's chin, since there is no warrant for high and low (i.e., sages and ordinary people), a deluded one [like me] has not yet comprehended this."

My explanation is this: The so-called most benevolent and most righteous are designations only for those who have completely reached the acme of benevolence and righteousness and who can receive [the virtue] standing on an equal footing with Heaven and Earth. [By this] I do not mean that anyone who has even a little bit of the feeling of shame for evils and of universal love is in the three powers. As I have already explained this in my previous discussion, I am surprised that you still have a question about this. In the four [great elements] (i.e., the Dao, Heaven, Earth, and the Sage King) of the universe,[348] only the sovereign is an entity [among sentient beings]. We know that those who make the two polarities [of Heaven and Earth] the three [powers] are none other than sages. The *Book of Changes* and the *Laozi* [*Daodejing*] come to the same [standpoint]. You should have no more doubts.

According to the grading of the Eastern Lu, [where the Duke of Zhou and Confucius are from,] [Sun] Qiao (i.e., Zichang) and [Ji]zha do not fully equip righteousness. Why are they placed higher to occupy the highest rank? In the light of the basis of the western land (India), since Yi [Yin] and Yan [Hui] have not attained the *dharmakāya,* they must be placed lower, in the rank of living beings. In the discussion you gave me, you comment on Śākyamuni's [teaching] with the view of the Duke of Zhou. Therefore, my intention was taken contradictorily. I hope you will understand this. I have become rather verbose.

Sages become sovereigns or teachers, while wise people become subjects or assistants of the teachers. When they approach supernatural achievement smoothly, and are influenced by the great work, they can share the course of action, and keeping silent and speaking are also achieved at the same time. If one masters a part [of the virtue of Heaven and Earth] to this point, how could he turn his back to become a ranking official of the yellow lower garment? You vainly see that there are those who cannot be ranked equally with sovereigns, unreasonably and resentfully blame it on them, and do not know to raise [the people in the three powers] up to the highest point. Furthermore, it is not the feeling of sticking to principles. If you pointed out and concluded like this, why do you say there is no warrant [for high and low] (i.e., sages and ordinary people)?

You respond, "*Yin* and *yang* nourish the vapor [of people], while toughness and gentleness give them their natures. They each have a round head and rectangular feet; they do not differ in their appearance. They have much natural compassion and the feeling to be ashamed of evil. So does everyone. For those who take part in and accept the two polarities [in order to be in the three powers], however, it is necessary to hold benevolence and righteousness as the first step."

My explanation is this: If it is assumed that those who have a round head and rectangular feet, and who most certainly have the sincerity of feeling shame for evils and natural compassion in the same way, and who do not differ in their appearance, can all take part in and accept the two polarities [in order to be in the three powers], then is a group of people like Jiao (a younger brother of King Zhuang of Chu state) and Zhi [who are known as robbers] reckoned among those in the three powers? If this is actually impossible, we cannot place them on the same level with great people, if the only reason for this is that they are equally human. It is difficult for ordinary people to become equal to [great people] in dignity and capacity. It has already been stated that "The benevolent rest in benevolence and the wise seek benevolence,"[349] "To practice energetically is close to benevolence,"[350] and "The one who is afraid of vice strives to be benevolent."[351] If we regard those [who try to be benevolent for benefit] in the same light as the one of the principal seat, truth and falsehood become mutually indistinguishable. Zhuangzi says, "In the world, the good people are few and those who are not good are many."[352] If [the people] are divided like this, how can you say, "So does everyone"?

25b You respond, "I feel that you want to limit [the qualification of human beings] with rank or proper equipages such as vehicle and clothes that [the emperor] should carefully bestow upon his vassals. Consequently you cause the nature of kind people and incorruptible scholars [such as Zichang and Jizha] to be compared with that of beasts, and you see the wise, [such as Yi Yin and Yan Hui,] who are capable and virtuous, as having the same physical energy as shellfish. Would the meaning to develop the symbolism of the hexagrams be like this?"

My explanation is this: The reason to limit the qualification [of human beings in the three powers] with ranks or proper equipages such as vehicle and clothes is indeed that [some people's] natural dispositions do not qualify them [to be equal to Heaven and Earth]. Although they want to avail themselves of [ranks or proper equipages], what can be done about those who are suspicious or deceitful? We bear a numinous being in ourselves and become a human being, which cannot be equated with beasts. In receiving vapor to be born, even incorruptible scholars cannot have divergences. The symbolism of the hexagrams shows numinous beings. It does not symbolize life. If you see [a numinous being and life] as the same, would it not be rather a reckless false accusation?

You respond, "[Furthermore, you say, 'Now, sages] are equally placed under [the great virtue] in the same way as people. . . .' Such extraordinary spirits are already different from [the spirits of] other living creatures. Why would they all suddenly be the same under the law of receiving life? Life is based on the law and the law differentiates [between sages and other living creatures]. Then, on what basis is the same name 'life' given to other living creatures? If you stick to this name 'life,' and cause the people to certainly follow it, then is something undefined and complete (*huncheng zhi wu*) also included in this instance?"

My explanation is this: I said previously, "[In life, there is a common feature of all things,] which is the same as what differentiates all things. How could it be distinguished to attain life?" You responded to this, "I do not say that this is not so." Furthermore, you asked, "What merit is there in considering that the life that is not different from each other must be sentient beings?" This indicates that you contradict my [opinion] that [those who attain life] are sentient beings, yet you accept [my opinion that life] is not different. Could there be anything that is not different and not sentient beings? Therefore, I again simply said: "Certainly, we must differentiate them on the basis of their extraordinary spirits, but we should not distinguish them based on the life they received." You responded this time, "Why would they all suddenly be the same under the law of receiving life? Life is based on the law and the law differentiates [between sages and other living creatures]." May I ask you about the law of receiving life? Is it originally *yin* and *yang*? I do not see the difference [between sages and ordinary people in the law of life], but you said that you have suddenly not been the same. If there are differences in the law, isn't it that [*yin* and *yang*] escape in vapor? Then, beyond *yin* and *yang* there is moreover a realm [of transmigration of birth and death] where one receives life. How should the three periods, [past, present, and future,] be firmly founded? If the life of the undefined and complete existence [before the formation of Heaven and Earth] has a common vapor with that of people, would this be the meaning of the undefined and complete [that Laozi uses]? If vainly in the name of life you do not see the truth of life, it does not match your previous statement. If you say that life is not life, this means that people are not people. Venerable Sir Li's (i.e., Laozi) theory about this, [namely that something undefined and complete that came into existence before Heaven and Earth,] probably has such meaning. To censure something that exists by means of a nonexistent thing is somewhat unprecedented.

You respond, "[Again, you say,] 'If one carefully builds a fence [around a house], and so on.' You said at the beginning [of this series of arguments] that emperors and sages set up the teaching to plan seasonal hunting and the scriptures to prudently follow the seasons; in this way [they tried] to gradually return to the cessation of extremities. Now, you criticize with the statement, 'This is precisely the beginning of extremities.' I have not known in detail whether this rebukes my view or ridicules sages."

My explanation is this: Formerly I read your original discussion, [the *Discourse on the Full Understanding of Life*]. Regarding the section from "the nine kinds of grains" up to "When Confucius fished, he did not use a net," I came to understand for the first time that you meant in your discussion that whatever is governed and produced originates entirely from the sages, who are personally good teachers, in order to lead common people. In my solitary, humble, and clumsy opinion, I would say that whatever [sages] do,
25c there must be reasons for their actions. Sages manage and control [their actions], and do not let them go to excess. This is the great point of two views, yours and mine, in deciding the issue, and the point on which you and I differ. Since I am going to control its excessiveness, I have a theory of stopping excessiveness. On the other hand, you just clarified [the sages'] preparing and providing. You, however, have not been aware in what way [the sages] leave behind excessiveness. In your response, you said again, "We will be the so-called one of excessive [desire] or the arrogant one. Sages assuredly remove this." I do not understand your intention here. Therefore, recently I asked you about the issue of excessiveness. You replied and said, "I have not known in detail who is to be rebuked." Probably you forgot what you said previously.

You responded, "[Furthermore, you say,] 'Outside of a market and a kitchen, and so on.' Well, in offering to Heaven and Earth, calf's horns [are used]; in the state offering the three domestic animals, [cows, pigs, and sheep] are sacrificed; and the thick soup of beef or pork is served in a wooden vessel on a painted wooden stand to offer to guests of honor. An old man of seventy years is not satisfied until he eats meat. Why can you merely display herbs and medicines and reserve them as the best remedy? The reason I am worried that [your argument] does not stand up is not that it is difficult for me to support your great discussion, but I take a step back and suspect this matter; simply, [such dietary habits] cannot be suddenly removed from the world."

My explanation is this: Shen Nong laid down how to live and the people of the Zhou dynasty provided the instruction [for rites]. They already advocated a diet of grains. In addition, the best remedy was mentioned and sacrifice was already offered. Moreover, [plants to be used for offering in rites, such as] duckweed and white southernwood, were praised.[353] In the way to offer sacrifices [to Heaven and the ancestors] and the way to victuals, there is originally no fixed method. I previously adduced that outside of the market and the kitchen, there are other things that support and nourish us. I mean to remove the longstanding [foul habit of] cutting meat apart or boiling it in soup in order to clarify that there is more than one way to prolong one's life span, but I mean neither to manage the habits of the world nor [to insist] that everyone must obtain and prepare herbs and medicines. Even with the merit of eating the meat of domestic animals, however, it is rare to live a hundred years. As a good aspect of taking divine herbs, I often hear about a life span of a thousand years. For this reason I say, why is it necessary for an old man of seventy years to appreciate the great favor of eating meat? If, however, one who sequesters himself completely in a closed-in area gives up this [meat diet], he simply has no other means [for his sustenance]. I think that [your statement:] "[Such dietary habits] cannot be suddenly removed from the world" is similar to "They (i.e., emperors and sages) cannot suddenly take away [the habits that] remain entrenched [in the world]," which I expressed in my previous expatiation. We can agree on a point for the first time. Why don't you dare to attribute it to good? Since you understand that [these dietary habits] cannot be suddenly removed from the world, probably you do not think that the Way is complete in this [point].

You respond, "[Moreover, you say, 'If you say that even though there are spirits and they have no form,] could there be beings without form in the world? and so on.' I examined the intention [of this point] in your letter, as [I feel] it seems you do not reject that there are spiritual beings. Just on the point in which you say that spiritual beings should have some substance, isn't it possible you are confused, since Indian books state that spiritual beings become other living creatures? People of former days considered spiritual beings to be [the foundation of] the teaching. Moreover, they wrote it down in books and scriptures, and it is widely found in written materials. [Lord Sun] Qiao (i.e., Zichang) of Zheng state and [Ji]zha of Wu state considered this so, too. Therefore, when music is played six times [with the Chinese zithers made out of wood from] Mount Yunhe, the spirits of Heaven really descend from Heaven, and when it is played nine times [with the Chinese zithers made out of wood from] Mount Longmen, the manes of people all come and gather. You often adhere to the *Rites of Zhou,* but recently you disregard this meaning. Just now you berate beings without form. It is an incoherent argument!"

My explanation is this: It is not only that I do not reject that there are spiritual beings but also I think that if there are [spiritual beings], they must have a form. You do not think that they do not exist and I agree with you, but we have different views on whether or not [the spirits] have [forms]. Hence, you recently questioned closely and wanted to demand [answers] thoroughly. Please forget about the Indian theory, and strictly comply with the Chinese classics. Moreover, put aside the issue that [spiritual beings]
26a become other living creatures. Let us discuss the exquisite spirits that ascend far to [Heaven].

The appearance and the issue of existence or nonexistence should be assuredly reported and settled. Spiritual beings are very often mentioned in stories and writings. It is not that I do not understand their names and titles. Recently I received three discussions [from you]. Every time I received [a new discussion], the number of [spirits] increased. A myriad of spirits have all gathered together, but you have not answered even a part of the question [about the appearance and the issue of existence or nonexistence]. Even though your letter is thorough and erudite, it does not relieve my thirst to know. Regarding beings without form, you do not teach at all. You vainly said that it is an incoherent argument, and considered it a common opinion. If investigating honestly is considered to be incoherent, is being superficial and unsystematic considered to be fair and intelligent?

You respond, "[Again, you say: '[Zhuangzi's and Xunzi's] statements are set forth] to admonish us for our future life,' and so on. You have not made it clear about so-called merciful people. What are they? If you depend on the doctrine of reward and retribution [in accordance with] actions that is stated in books other than [Confucian texts], it is entirely the teaching of expedients to which I refer. In investigating the utmost doctrine, you have not analyzed with the sages' words and yet you have adopted many crafty and strange [words] in order to support [your argument]. Can it be to give the impression of rescuing by means of water from disasters caused by water?"

My explanation is this: Thinking about merciful people, I hear for a long time that there are such people. Since you demand who they are, I would say that they are Mañjuśrī and Śākyamuni. I know that you think the doctrine of reward and retribution is entirely the teaching of expedients. The way of expedients is mysterious and deep; only sages can accomplish it. Even though you are proficient in knowledge and understanding, you have not seen its culmination. I am exhausted from trying to ascertain it, yet you easily make your own judgment. It is very shameful. If what the doctrine of expedients states is all deceptive and delusive, there would be no reward and retribution in the [law of] Nature. I am reluctant to jump to a conclusion, while you vehemently make an arbitrary decision. Again, this is dreadful! The spirit [of the doctrine] is lofty, but the one who hears it is low. How can you bring a false accusation?

I think that the "sages' words" you mentioned must be the words of the Duke of Zhou and Confucius. What we talk about now is entirely the issue of "believing and following" [of which they speak]. Nevertheless, you say that I have not analyzed [the issue]. This again shows a lack of complete prudence. Since your discussion respects the Duke of Zhou and rejects Śākyamuni, I refer to Śākyamuni and equate him to the Duke of Zhou. My answers do not go beyond your questions. I do not feel that I have "adopted many [crafty and strange words]." [Great men such as] You Yu and [Jin] Ridi were not born in the Chinese region. How can we specify that there is no one who has mastered the principles outside of the nine regions away from the royal domain? It is also really difficult to distinguish Buddhism from non-Buddhist teaching (i.e., Confucianism). If you believe your own criteria, have only your ears and eyes to teach you, and consider that everything except what you have already learned and known is crafty and strange, then I will stop my argument!

You responded, "Furthermore, you say, 'I think that there are no absurd things. Each one is moved with good virtue, and so on.' If these words are certainly so, those who are moved with good virtue must be equal in degree of seriousness, and the force of a sundial must have a certain extent in length. As to decorations in building or construction, they are not initiated by a benevolent mind. Even though hunting is done according to the [appropriate] seasons, the extremely cruel nature [of human beings] has not been uprooted. For what is a person rewarded to ascend to Heaven, which is splendid and joyful? For what is one punished to fall into Hell, which is dark and full of suffering? Excellent words come to an end in differentiating high from low, and the law is made without a scale (i.e., measure or standard). All things have come to this point!"

26b My explanation is this: I spoke of [the force of] a sundial in order to give evidence [of perceiving reward or retribution]. The intention of your letter is to raise a doubt that it is not necessarily that [actions and the way of reward and retribution] correspond to each other and to suspect that there is no rule between them, and then you again try to remove a fortunate response. A fortunate response is nothing other than what is produced by fate. If a fortunate response is extinguished, there is no fate. You are accomplished in astronomy and proud of your knowledge. I think that one who keeps it in mind to believe in the Way must not come to this point. If you think that decorations in building or construction are not initiated by a benevolent mind and it is worse than taking another's life in accordance with [appropriate] seasons, wouldn't it be seriously ungrateful to the mind of that man (i.e., Śākyamuni)? The emperor's vehicle and seal are not necessarily the sentiments of Yao and Shun. Would respectful buildings and magnificent offerings be Śākyamuni's intention? To demand the reward [of rebirth] in Heaven and to ask for punishment in Hell are very similar to the stories that the ancient questioned [Zhou] Yafu (a general and minister of the Han dynasty who died of starvation, as had been foretold by an elderly woman physiognomist) about, and that Ying [Bu] asked a question [to a guest who had foretold his future misfortune].[354] How tasteful these words are! This is, however, what many *śramaṇa*s fully know. I will leave it out.

You responded, "Moreover, a guardian attendant who teaches and loves [his master] encourages [his master] to abstain from eating the intestines of dogs and hogs [which resemble those of human beings]. A good cook who wields a knife [to butcher cattle for meat] feels afraid whenever he comes to a complicated joint. The Sage is as bright as the sun and moon, and his edification can open the three powers. If [actions and the way of] reward and retribution inevitably tally, how is it hindered by the teaching? Why was it sealed in the ages of [Fu]xi and Tang [Yao]? Why was it buried in the time of the Duke of Zhou and Confucius? In the beginning, nets [to catch animals and fish] were made and this gave rise to a number of sins. [The practice of] offering animal sacrifices was established and opened the punishment of the long night [of spiritual darkness]. The heavenly kitchen (i.e., food naturally collected) is abandoned, and those animals [that are] fed grass and grain are considered delicious. There has been no benevolence to save people from drowning [in extreme misery]. The cruelty of putting people into a dry moat was carried out without restraint. In order that these acts not be repeated, you should sincerely consider the issues deeply. If you think that the intelligence of the exquisite spirit [of sages] is not yet complete in some points, even though you are thoughtful and love strange ideas, you have not come to disgrace sages."

My explanation is this: I know that you think the meaning of reward and retribution was sealed in the times of [Fu]xi and the Zhou dynasty. For this reason, you ascertain that it is testimony that [reward and retribution] do not correspond to [good and bad actions]. The time of [Fu]xi and Tang [Yao] was long ago, which no one knows fully. The record [of that time] in the *Book of History* comprises no more than a few sections. When the merits of virtue and punishment were just mentioned, they had no scope to record the origin of weal and woe. Now, in the writings on emperors and kings, the issue of a person's life is still not written, but taking the lack of a written record as evidence, you consider that indeed it did not exist in ancient times. This is again a fault caused by considering your mind as your teacher.

Moreover, it is all displayed in the works of the Duke of Zhou and Confucius to believe and follow [the view of] blessings [left to one's children] and misfortune [which makes itself felt long after the seed was sown]. You said, "[Why] was it buried [in the time of the Duke of Zhou and Confucius]?" Was it [buried] just like a narrow path? Since there are familiar and unfamiliar in language and shallow and deep in teaching, is it to have the wise give this and snatch away that?

While we live, we indeed have desires. When we have desires, we certainly ask for something. If desires are not satisfied, there is conflict. If desires are satisfied, the mind becomes peaceful. If we fight, we harm each other. If we are peaceful, we stabilize each other. The reason a net was made is to remove harmful things in order to have peace. Furthermore, hunting and fishing are no different from the sacrifice of livestock. In the previous reply you were already aware that sacrifices of livestock could not suddenly be removed from the world. [Now] you say, "Wasn't it possible to abandon at least hunting and fishing in ancient times?" This has not yet been a coherent discussion.

[The tendency] to cling to life becomes stronger the lower the social
26c class. Therefore, to try to dispense with death is [an action] of following one's feeling and to take away other [sentient beings'] lives is [an action] of going against one's nature. The perfect person (i.e., Śākyamuni) is esteemed. Why would he offend and go against the natural course? From this, we know that since we cannot suddenly remove longstanding customs, [Śākyamuni] simply set up a system to control them. Even though the spirits of sages are vigorous, they have nothing to make [people's] ignorant minds wise and clever. How could the people who left their homelands and wander in other lands (i.e., those who left the truth and who do not know the way to return to it) be better?[355] The reason sin and punishment visit is that people themselves invite them.

The heavenly kitchen was involuntarily abandoned since [heavenly] matters are far away and difficult for us to reach. Since substantial things are familiar and easy for us to indulge in, [we feel that the meat of] domestic animals is always delicious. [Good deeds such as] saving a man from drowning and taking a man out of a dry moat [in which he had fallen] are common to many wise people, but [the way] to teach people differs [for each person]. It is not that the Way itself differs. Your reprimand that [I think the intelligence of the exquisite spirit of the sages] is not yet complete in some points also seems inappropriate. Zichang (Sima Qian) loved strange ideas, but it is originally not similar to this.

You respond, "When you talk about benevolence and righteousness, you say 'Those who care about [benevolence and righteousness] are few and those who use them for their own benefit are many.' However, when you speak of doing kindness, you approve that men of virtue and talents who are left neglected forget a reward. Since those who care about [benevolence and righteousness] are few, who are able to be the men of virtue and talents yet who are left neglected? Since those who use [benevolence and righteousness] for their own benefit are many, how can you say to forget a reward? If you can encourage people who are willing to give [to the poor], expect companions who want to be benevolent, expound the meaning of forgetting reward and retribution, and lead the people toward a mind of righteousness, then righteousness is truly here and you are not far [from the goal] in seeking benevolence."

My explanation is this: "Those who care about benevolence and righteousness are few and those who use them for their own benefit are many." I learned this [expression] from Zhuangzi's book.[356] It is not my own statement. You hastily impeached me before you made a complete examination. Well, "Since those who care about [benevolence and righteousness] are few and those who use them for their own benefits are many, no one is able to be a man of virtue and talents. Yet who is left neglected, and how can you say to forget a reward?" [Your statement] is really what I have diligently and prudently considered from the beginning: simply, we cannot set [human beings] down for [the three powers] arranging with the two polarities [of Heaven and Earth]. It is not something on which you should depend in order to show that your great discussion is correct. If being willing to give [to the poor] and forgetting a reward are to master benevolence, and if forgetting a reward and giving [to the poor] tally with righteousness, we may leave behind the word "want" [in the phrase "in order to hope for companions who want to be benevolent"] and also remove the word "toward" [from the phrase "lead the people toward a mind of righteousness"]. If [righteousness is truly] here and you are not far [from the goal in seeking benevolence], who would not long for these?

You respond, "As to your statement, '[The Buddhist teaching] is to increase good qualities, prevent evils, return the people to the grand submission [to the natural course], deliver sentient beings [from evils], and so on,' the intention of this is nonsense, and it is not what I am concerned with in this discussion. Isn't this like the case when the Qin army was about to escape and their messenger talked nonsense?"

My explanation is this: Your discussion holds [the teachings of] the Duke of Zhou and Śākyamuni. I also respond to it taking [examples] from both the foreign land (India) and the land of Zhou (China). You repress [the teaching of] that land using [the teaching of] this land, and you say that the highest level of happiness is [achieved] in an illustrious family. I inculcate [the teaching of] that land, explain [the teaching of] this land, and say that [the Buddhist teaching] brings about widespread blessings for everyone. Based on the views of this land, you say that blessings rest with high-ranking officials. I believe in the information from that land and say that [the Buddha] is the highest in nobility among a hundred deities. These are controversial points in our discussion. Why do you say "It is not what I am concerned with [in this discussion]"? The foundation of the criticism of this discussion takes [presenting] by turns to be the essence. If every time it gets beyond your control you say that it is vast and preposterous, then the road to look for principles is nearly blocked up. The statement "When [the Qin] army was about to escape [and their messenger] talked nonsense" is probably not relevant to this case.

You respond, "How could I continue to press you? Please take a seat. I will explain it to you. Sages are [originally] placed above, and they do not
27a have to strive for supremacy against a hundred deities. If there is a beginning, there is an end. How can you be in the land of eternal life? And so on."

My explanation is this: "How could I continue to press you?" How wholeheartedly you strive after virtue! "Please take a seat, and I will explain it to you." What great expressions these are! In general, would being a leader of people be something to attain through fighting? [The one who becomes a leader] not only refrains from fighting but also certainly assumes a humble attitude. When you see the phrase "The highest in nobility among a hundred deities," you may not think to contend with a hundred deities for supremacy. Instead, you take it as Lord Teng and Lord Xue, [who fought each other for supremacy][357] and forget to master benevolence. I am aware that you think there is a beginning and an end in things, and that there is no land of eternal life. If we look for it within our realm [of existence], it is true, just as the purpose of your letter, and it is just as I said in my previous expatiation, "Various existing things are really suitable for this (i.e., in the great law of Nature life and death are the same in arising and falling)." As to illustrations in the

Book of Mountains and Seas and records in the *Biographies of Arrayed Transcendents,* these issues are concerned with this world, but they can no longer be traced back, not to mention the case where the Way separates from common practices and the principles separate from an ordinary pattern. Since something is not within your own [experience], you think that it must be entirely discarded. This is again hard to understand.

You respond, "Well, the other world and this world are distinguished clearly from each other. Various things are investigated completely," and so on.

My explanation is this: When I came to examine the section on this subject, [I realized that] you enthusiastically relate [historical events of] successive generations. Your writing is extensive, the content is complete, and you are very good at methods [taught by] your teacher. Your voice to sing for the world of sages is vigorous, but you simply have not made a key remark in studying to find the significance of the Way. Formerly, when I was young, I spent a little time randomly studying a large number of historical records. I have been vaguely informed of the outline of the ways of emperors and kings and the traces of the virtuous and the intelligent. I dare to thank you for your detailed explanation. You have given me a generous instruction. Truly you are diligent in the management of business.

You respond, "Why is it necessary to consider the future blessings of the family that has accumulated enough good deeds to be vile, and to hope for the blessings of the next existence of which there is no proof" and "[A Buddhist monk's] squatting or kneeling upright in worship and [the Chinese style of] bowing complaisantly are inconsistent with each other after all. I personally wish that you would give up practicing both [Buddhism and Confucianism] and abide by [Confucianism] alone," and so on.

My explanation is this: [The issue that the future] blessings [of the family] that has accumulated [enough good deeds] are not considered to be vile was already explicated in the section of "believing and following." The issue about hoping thoroughly for the next existence was also [presented] completely, when I spoke of perceiving reward or retribution. The five-colored strings of the emperor's ceremonial cap (*zao*) and the emperors' ceremonial gown [of dragon patterns] (*gun*) and the great robe of fur (*daqiu*) [worn by emperors for the rite of making sacrificial offerings to Heaven] are the same, and integral to the rites. Why wouldn't it be possible that [a Buddhist monk's] squatting or kneeling upright in worship and [the Chinese style of] bowing complaisantly are practiced together in the same world? In principle, it is possible to practice them concurrently. Do not presume that [one of them] should be rejected.

You respond, "Metaphors such as a single-plank bridge, the two men [Guan]shu and [Cai]shu, a person in the world [who keeps an unpolished gem and displays it in a market], and an officer in charge of translation, have nothing to do with the original discussion. Therefore, I say nothing about them."

My explanation is this: These several passages in my latest letter arose somewhat from a joke. It is similar to the incident in which the story of the people of Yue, [who were always naked,] asked about clothing was adopted in an old tale. When an arbitrary opinion has come to this point there is no help, but it is just very strange. The reason, however, that I questioned using the metaphor of two persons, [Guan]shu and [Cai]shu, is because I want to dispel your suspicion that [a diet without meat could not be recommended to] common people. Since you have never responded to this, it is really promising [for me]. You are powerful, as if allied nations follow you just like clouds, and your great discourse has become popular. I, [on the other hand], live apart from society, and every time I present my solitary opinion, it is commented on in whispers. There is no doubt of the fact that I am not equal to you in this way. I truly rely on a versatile scholar. We are common in principles. I abruptly forgot about the troublesomeness [of this] and have greedily written all to my heart's content.

27b End of Fascicle Four of *The Collection for the Propagation and Clarification* [*of Buddhism*]

Fascicle Five

The *Discourse on Regeneration* (*Gengshenglun*) by Luo Junzhang

It is good that the scholar Xiang [Xiu] said, "What is Heaven? It is the general name of all things. What is Man? It is one of the things in Heaven." From this, we may say that each thing has its own term of existence, while Heaven and Earth are everlasting. In that case, changes of the everlasting [Heaven and Earth] do not go beyond [the boundary of] all things from the beginning. If all things did not regenerate, Heaven and Earth would have an end. Heaven and Earth are not supposed to have an end. So we can conclude that [all things] regenerate.

I seek [this fact] in various ancient discussions. It is said that "Omens of all things were determined a long time ago. All living creatures repeat birth and death," "The sage composed the *Book of Changes,* in which the culmination was already provided," "To trace to the very source of the spirit is to know [the law of] transformation,"[358] and "To trace to the very source of the principles is [to know] completely the nature [of all things]."[359]

If it is possible to trace to the very source of the spirit, anything that has a form cannot have no term of existence [in this world]. In that case, human beings and things have their fixed terms. You and I have our own station [in existence]. It is impossible that existence extinguishes and becomes non-existence. It is impossible that you can transform to become me. Gathering, scattering, disappearing, appearing, we circle round and round on our eternal path. [Anyone]—the wise, the ignorant, one who lives long, or one who dies young—circles round and returns to one's [original] being. [The circle] spontaneously goes on consistently, and there is not an iota of difference. Together with their fate [all things] extinguish and then return. People of the world are absurdly not aware of this. How far and distant it is! Its way is profound. Even though Heaven and Earth are vast, they are harmonious, without disorder.

Although all things are numerous, they are sorted according to their classes. Each of them has its foundation. There is the sequence in successive

ancestors. In the direct line and the collateral branches for a hundred generations its longstanding [element] is never lost. Furthermore, the spirit and the physical substance are a natural couple. The natural couple's separation and reunion are the change in birth and death. There are gathering and scattering in the physical substance. It is the natural course of transmigration [of birth and death]. When people and things undergo change, each of them goes [from life to death]. Each is its own part in going [from life to death]. There-
27c fore, when each of them returns [from death to life], there is a principle. Even though things are confused and indistinguishable when they scatter, they are not out of order when they gather. The farther they go, the closer they return. In addition, the spirit and the physical substance profoundly meet each other, and spontaneously unite together exactly, just as two pieces of a tally fit together. People of the world all lament that uniting leads to separation without fail, yet no one consoles himself with [the thought] that separation leads to uniting without fail, as well. All people know that gathering leads to scattering without fail, but no one recognizes that scattering leads to gathering without fail, as well. They do not give much thought to this [matter]. How could there be distance [between uniting and separating, or gathering and scattering]?

Generally, since the present existence arises in conformity with the former existence, [present] affairs are in alignment with past affairs. In the essence there is nothing disordered. In the intention, we are not aware that [the one of the former life] profoundly unites with [the one of the present life]. Who would say "I realize this"? Now, a talker merely knows that the one of the former life is not [the one of] the present life, but he simply does not know that the one of the present life is the one of the former life. Those who have extensive views, therefore, see that life is equal to death, and say that life and death are just like wakefulness and sleep. How true this statement is!

Sun Changsha's Letter [to Luo Junzhang] by Anguo (Sun Sheng)

I have examined the *Discourse on Regeneration,* in which you sum up the issue of changes, and thoroughly analyze gathering and scattering. Your logic is distinguished. Moreover, your purpose and composition are also pleasant. This is a good discussion. Nevertheless, I still have a different opinion.

Since now there are innumerable cases that all things transform into other forms, you do not miss in complying with the law. However, it takes many years until what is hidden reveals itself. If this is so, the cases that all things transform [into other forms] should still be many, but there is no case that being obtains its [original] form again. When things exhaust the condition [to exist in this world], they must go far off to an unseen place where our ears and eyes cannot perceive them. Only at that point do they return to their foundations. Therefore, I think that since our physical bodies scatter all over, so do our sensory perceptions. They are disorderly, confused, and mixed, and they transform into other substances. Each of the other substances loses its former [state]. They are not what they used to be. This is the reason why all creatures that have feelings grieve. If this is so, you cannot console only yourself.

Response to Sun [Sheng]

I received your letter. Your composition is brief yet your purpose is expressed, and the logic upholds actual facts. Even though I am glad for your simple and easily understandable reply, I have not yet appreciated it. Moreover, I have in my mind small and unimportant things endlessly. Please examine my original [discourse again].

In the original [discourse] I did not say that things do not change at all. Each of those things that change, however, attains by itself what it transforms into. Those that decay do not lose their former essence. Who takes charge of molding them, namely, mixing [clay] and making [each form]? This statement is the most apt for the case. [Things] are separated and never thrown into disorder. If they are like this, would regeneration occur only once? [Things] arise endlessly and regenerate for a long time. When they come to an end, they return to the beginning. The truth is evident. While you are not able to know the present, how can you know about [the next life after] regeneration? Probably, since my grief had accumulated, I spoke in a rough way and consulted with you about what I came to understand. How could it be said that I console only myself? I simply have a little diversion under pretense of this.

The *Discourse on the Immortality of the Spirit* (*Shen bumielun*) by Zheng Daozi (364–427)

Many [people] think that body and spirit perish together and the function of the spirit (*zhao*) and consciousness are extinguished along with them.
28a Can it be explained why this is so? All people of the world already consider the Duke of Zhou and Confucius to be the culmination. Benevolence, righteousness, and ethical education were first formed in their minds. The foundation of the spiritual intelligence is never mentioned in even a single word. Therefore, [in their teachings] what is done with sensory perception is limited within the concrete [realm]. The Buddha speaks words of the utmost importance, but ordinary people do not believe in him. I fell into delusions when I was young, but I thought to get out of the delusions. I sought the profound purport and examined the essence of the spirit. I realized that the principle is more exquisite than a physical body and the spirit is more subtle than the principle. Entrusting what has appeared, I will transmit my mind and briefly adduce the testimony. I hope that this will shine upon all who will be awakened to [the truth] and consequently contribute to [removing] longstanding delusions.

Spirit and body are mixed and come together. Even though they exist together while one lives, with regard to the point that there is a difference between coarseness and subtlety in their origins, there is a distinction between corporeality and incorporeality. Why do I say this? A body consists of the five viscera (i.e., liver, lungs, heart, kidneys, and spleen), the six entrails (i.e., gall, stomach, bladder, the three parts of the abdominal cavity, small intestine, and lower intestine), the limbs and the seven apertures in the head (i.e., eyes, ears, nostrils, and mouth). All unite to become one [body]. Therefore, one is alive. At just the moment when people are born, each one receives the five primary elements in a different way [from others]. Hence, some people suffer from being crippled in a limb or some part of the body, or lack either ears or eyes, but this does not prove fatal. Even with the body it is like this, not to mention with the spirit whose essence mysteriously shines. It governs all bodies ingeniously. Body and breath move together, while the spirit and the wonderful realization flow in the same way. Although motion (i.e., the body) and inactivity (i.e., the spirit) support each other, exquisiteness and coarseness separate from each other in their origins. Wouldn't it be because each has its origin and they depend on each other to function? When you take a familiar example of this, the reason is clear. I hope you can comprehend this.

In what a body supports, muscles and bones have sensations of pain and itching, while nails and hair do not. Why is this so? Wouldn't it be because muscles and bones are the essence of life but nails and hair are not the foundation of life? When life is in the foundation, sensations exist. When life is in the periphery, there is no sensation. For the function of a body, it is still considered that the foundation and the periphery are concerned with rising and falling, not to mention the spirit that is the foundation of life, and whose origin is the most subtle. How could [the spirit] wither along with a seven *chi*-tall [body] and be exhausted together with [the sense organs that are like] doors and windows? If you infer from this truth, you can clearly understand that the spirit is immortal.

A guest criticizes, "Your argument on the body and spirit is complete. It is astute to speak of sensibility and insensibility in a body. Nevertheless, even though the body and spirit have different origins—[the body] is of coarse origin and [the spirit] is of subtle origin—both consider existence to be their status. The reason for being is that life is the foundation. Why, then, is it possible that the foundation of existence has become exhausted and that which has depended on the foundation alone exists? Beyond the outside of life, it is vast and completely obscure. Since it is completely obscure, it is not only that there is nothing to establish with words but also that there is nothing to extablish with consciousness. If it is not established by the consciousness, where does the spirit deposit itself? Since there is nothing [into which the spirit] can deposit itself, how can it be immortal?"

I respond, "Your criticism is good as an argument. It has not yet been based on the mind. Is this why a criticism such as this comes up? Now all changes are entirely existence. Prospering, declining, rising, falling, dying or being born, take the place of each other. A body becomes exhausted and 28b
another is born. This is the whole process of a living being. With regard to water and fire, they prevail over all sentient beings thoroughly and are abundant, without deficiency. Wouldn't it be because the essence of fire follows things, the law of water annihilates [water itself] and follows others, [both

fire and water] are not self-generated when they are generated, they are what all sentient beings depend on, they are useful in the light of [other things], and therefore things cannot use them up? Even [fire and water that] exist in the same sphere of life are clever in this way, not to mention the principle of the spirit that is singularly transcendent and unparalleled. It is not on the same level with ordinary things, but is it fixed that, since it is outside of life and is completely obscure, the spirit has nothing into which to deposit itself? If we carry out a discussion on this basis, the Grand Terminus (*taiji*) is the mother of the two elementary forms [*yin* and *yang*], and the two elementary forms are the foundation of all things.[360] The Grand Terminus, [however,] is simply the vapor of Heaven and Earth. It can still unite the roots of all these changes, and it does not change that it is the root. How much more can the spiritual intelligence—the apex of the numinous being that exhausts both existence and nonexistence—do? You can comprehend that [the spirit] is immortal."

The critic says, "You infer that the function of the spirit is beyond the body and you indicate that the Grand Terminus comes before things. This is really significant. It is, however, valuable that reason satisfies the minds [of people]. Then a discussion can [actually] be carried out. The spirit and the body have not been separate from each other even for a moment. If they were separate from each other, there would be no spirit. There is no spirit in trees and plants because they do not have consciousness. When the body is exhausted, to what does the spirit attach itself, being called immortal? If it is able to be immortal, it rides on the numinous being [of the dead] without availing itself of a body. Since it does not avail itself of a body, why does it exist with a body? It is not separate from [the body] at last. If [the spirit and the body] cannot be separated from each other, it can certainly be understood that the foundation of life [in both spirit and body] is the same."

I respond, "There is a criticism of this. The body and the spirit have their own origins. Let me explain it for you from the beginning, in orderly fashion. As to fire, there is fire on the basis of firewood. If there is no firewood, there is no fire. Even though firewood is a device to make fire, it is not the foundation of fire. The foundation of fire spontaneously exists, and simply comes to function complying with firewood. If firewood came before fire, would it be reasonable to say that there was no fire before Suiren (a legendary ruler who first discovered fire)? The foundation of fire is the utmost degree of *yang,* and *yang* is the culmination of fire. Therefore, firewood is what fire deposits itself into, but it is not the foundation [of fire]. That the spirit and the body avail of each other is also like this. Availing of and complying with each other are merely the cause of the path [of transmigration] of birth [and death]. Why could it be that if there is a body, the spirit exists; and if there is no body, the spirit is exhausted? Its foundation is entranced, unconscious, and indescribable.

"Let me extensively give an example in order to clarify this for you. When firewood is in water, fire is dead. When firewood is out of water, it makes fire.[361] The firewood remains the same, but fire is designated beforehand [to either burn or be extinguished in accordance with conditions]. That the spirit does not rely on a body is also like this. You can understand thoroughly that the spirit does not need a body."

The critic says, "It cannot be promptly concluded that the spirit does not need a body. If [the spirit] does not need a body, as you said, what avails itself of a body and what shines alone are usually the same in the principles. Even though [the spirit and the body] avail themselves of each other, this is 28c
not interdependence in the foundation. According to what the Buddhist doctrine clarifies, we must educate and mold this spirit in order to save that body. Why is this so?"

I respond, "Your question has some intention. This is what ordinary people are deluded by, because they have not reached the foundation. Although the spirit does not need a body, that body is surely produced. In the body that is surely produced, this spirit certainly dwells. If [the spirit] certainly dwells in [the body] that is surely produced, the function [of the spirit] and the perception [of the body] become one, and they are spontaneously beneficial to each other. If they are spontaneously beneficial to each other, it is the highest degree of educating and molding in the principles. If it is [the highest degree of] educating and molding, it is fruitful. If it is fruitful, the Way is practiced. This can be compared to [the relationship between the changes of] the four seasons and [the changes of] all things. How could it be intentional to be mutually beneficial? It is what the principles follow and what is naturally reached."

The critic says, "I have respectfully heard that although the body and the spirit are different from each other, they are mutually beneficial. You have already compared the spirit in the body to fire in firewood. Firewood has no intention to make fire and fire has no frame of mind to deposit itself into firewood. Therefore, they can collaborate endlessly. They spontaneously transform together for a long time. It is not that the fire of this firewood moves to that firewood and becomes fire. Nevertheless, in Buddhist doctrine, on the basis that after the body is exhausted [the spirit] further dwells in that body, the coming into and going out [of life] of the spirit and the body originate in evil acts and meritorious deeds. Let me ask you: If this body performs evil acts, are evil acts done by the physical body or by the spirit? If the body [commits evil acts], [the body] is merely one of all things created by the Great Founder.[362] If the spirit [commits evil acts], since the spirit does not act independently and is tied to something else, namely the body, your assertion that the body and spirit do not avail themselves of each other fails in this point."

I respond, "It is good to have this question so that I can explain the reason thoroughly. I said [previously] that body and spirit do not avail themselves of each other, by which I simply meant that they have different foundations. Once they come into life, in the endless transmigration of birth and death each of them pervades its function. If this life is used in order to commit evil acts and perform meritorious deeds, could it be possible that the spirit performs its function subtly by itself and does not do anything for the function of the body? If this is so, it would be intentional to be [either] wise or ignorant. It is not that [the spirit] neglects the function and mysteriously meets with [a body]. It is logical that [the spirit] meets mysteriously with [a body], and it is logical that the body is exhausted. The spirit that was educated dwells in a body. You do not doubt the original [assertion that spirit and body are interdependent]. That (i.e., the previous discussion) and this (i.e., the latter discussion) follow the same logic. Why do you doubt only the latter part?"[363]

The critic says, "The spirit functions in conformity with the body, and the body functions in accordance with the spirit. This is exactly so! Since realization derives from the spirit, delusion lies in the spirit as well. The spirit follows the body. Therefore, there are the wise and the ignorant. Being wise or ignorant is not [a function of] the spirit but [results from the fact that] the spirit does something in the functioning of the body. [The spirit] revolves in the three periods (past, present, and future) for a very long time, beyond calculation. Being wise or ignorant has no beginning, and the potency [of being wise or ignorant] becomes evident midway [through the course of the transmigration of birth and death]. The law of non-beginning is profound, while the potency [manifested] midway is immature. Could it be possible that what exists in the later potency rises far above the origin of non-beginning? If you have a good [explanation] for me to understand this thoroughly, please let me follow in your footsteps."

I respond, "Since you inquired into the origin [of being wise or ignorant], you made this statement. In the principles there is neither beginning nor end. The culmination of profundity is boundless. Once we have already been born 29a
or transformed, continuously committing evil acts or performing meritorious deeds simply takes place naturally. So-called sagacity truly derives from the ears and eyes, but the foundation of the ears and eyes is not sagacity. What is called being wise or ignorant really ought to have a beginning. If there is already being wise or ignorant, nothing about the beginning can be known. There is something, but it cannot control [other] things. There is only nothing [as the foundation] that is later able to become to what things return. If there is a beginning, it is impossible to have no end.[364] Only when there is non-beginning do beginning and end become inexhaustible. This is naturally a matter of course. It is impossible [to deny this]. Based on the assumption that things have a beginning, you cannot demand that the spirit is the same as things. The Way of the Spirit is abstruse and subtle. The ultimate principle is unspeakable. As the principle is indicated indistinctly, we come to understand it together. If we seek for the foundation from the end, we are apt to fail to catch its entirety. So I would like to abide by this viewpoint and hope that it offers steps to lead to the peak [of realization]. If you [were to continue to] indulge in arguing and competing in compositions, I know that you should cease.

"The *Hongfan* chapter [of the *Book of History*] speaks of the foundation of living. On this point it is the same as Buddhism. As to the matter that in what the Buddha expounds there are many [statements like] the Milky Way [that are too far-fetched to gain credulity],[365] this is simply because you indulge in daily matters. Shangchen (King Mu of Chu state) extremely transgressed against [ethics] (i.e., he killed his father, King Cheng), but his descendants made the state prosperous. Yan [Hui] and Ran [Boniu] were virtuous, but they were not well known because they died young. The teaching of the

Duke of Zhou and Confucius is for matters of this world (i.e., this existence). If this reason is inferred, it can be understood.

"Let me extend the testimony in order to examine it in more detail. If one receives a numinous being and embraces harmony, he can master the ultimate way and become pure. Yao begat Danzhu, who was stupid and evil, who had no sense of order, and who did not know benevolence and righteousness. Gusou begat Shun. When we trace the origin of [Shun's] birth, [we find that the father] was not a man who could raise [a virtuous son]. When we seek the principle [based on the teaching of the Duke of Zhou and Confucius, we know that] good qualities should be passed on, but the [real] matters are like this. You, however, said that the Buddhist doctrine is unrealistic. Shouldn't you realize [that this is not true]?"

The *New Discourse on Body and Spirit* by Huan Junshan

I, [Lu] Cheng (425–494), think that Junshan had never heard Śākyamuni's teaching, but he already excerpted the simile of firewood and fire when he discussed [the relationship of] body and spirit. In the later disputant's statement, there is a point that obscurely matches with [this simile]. Accordingly, I carry on [his discourse] here.

I once visited the former magistrate of Chen county, Du Fang, who [now resides] in Tong prefecture. I saw that he was reading Laozi's book. He said, "Laozi preserved his health by [living] a tranquil life without worldly desires and enjoyed his life for as long as several hundred years. Today if we practice the way he did, would we be able to prolong life and stay young?"

I responded, "Even though [human beings] are the same in form and name, each has a different degree in their temperament, nature, and ability. Some have strong air, some have weak air; some have determined air, and some have timid air. By loving, cultivating, and appropriately using [our natures and abilities], we can simply alleviate [the pain of] our aging. It is just like if we take good care of clothes, footwear, and utensils, they remain in good condition and last long."

Nearby I saw the embers of a flaxen torch that hung down one *chi*. On the basis of this, I then made the analogy, "[The condition] of the spirit dwelling

in a body is similar to that of a fire burning a [flaxen] torch. If we are good at holding it and shifting its position in accordance with the flame, it is possible that the fire will not go out until the torch fuel is entirely consumed. Without the torch, no fire can be produced by itself in emptiness. Moreover, it is impossible for the embers [of the torch] to burn after [the fire goes out]. The embers are like a person's aging and infirm [body]. When teeth fall out, hair turns grey, and muscles lose their vigor, the spirit cannot invigorate [the body]. When [the symptoms of aging] completely cover the inside and outside [of the body], the vapor is exhausted and we die. It is just as the flame and the torch come to an end together. [Suppose] a man encounters an evil thing and 29b
is injured or falls ill. If he does not receive [medical] treatment or meet a good doctor, he will probably die an unnatural death. If he dies [in this way], his muscles and bones are usually just like flames that are fanned by a strong wind, which are not protected from [being extinguished], and which die out. Namely, the body remains, [just as] the main part [of the torch] remains.

"Once while sitting and drinking in my inner chamber at night, I lit a flaxen torch. In the midst of burning, the torch was crushed and about to go out. I closely inspected it by myself and found that the bark [of the torch] covered [the top] like a scab. So I supported [the torch by my hand] and shifted its position. Consequently, the flame recovered [its strength]. This indicates that when a human body has a sickness or is severely injured, if it is taken care of and maintained well, it is possible to restore the body to [good] condition.

"Furthermore, no one can know the beginning of the time of his birth, and even when he gets old, he ought not to know when he will die, either. In ancient times, when it was a peaceful world, people were born under goodness and prosperity. All were strong and enjoyed longevity. They lived for about a hundred years and died. When they died, they looked like they were sleeping and suddenly [their spirits] left [their bodies]. It is just like fruits and grains that fully ripen and naturally fall [to the ground]. People of later ages are victimized by the vicious vapors of declining and waning. Moreover, they lose [their chance for] a timely marriage and work excessively and diligently despite hardships. Hence, even if they give birth, both [parents and children] are impaired, and their bones, muscles, blood, and breath are not strong enough. Therefore, many people die of misfortune that shortens their life, or while still young in midlife. When they fall ill, they may suffer from pain, sadness, and worry, and later they pass away. Therefore, we sigh, we hate death, and we consider it to be a great [occasion].

Formerly Lord Jing of Qi state praised his state, commended his happiness, and said, 'If from the earliest times there were no death, what would that be like?' Yanzi (i.e., Yan Ying), [prime minister of Qi state,] answered, 'The Supreme Thearch considers that human death is good, the virtuous consider it to be a rest, and those who are not virtuous consider [that death is simply] to go away.'[366] Today [people] do not think to make effort to broaden [their knowledge], to study every day, and to understand [the Way] thoroughly in order to quickly rise in the world and become famous. If they have a long life only coveting profit and still seek to prolong their life, they are deluded and do not understand [the truth]."

Someone criticized this, "When the body and spirit are compared to a torch and fire, it appears that there is a parallel point, but I am afraid that there is not. The reason human skin and flesh are healed spontaneously when they are flayed or injured is that the blood and breath circulate. When the flaxen torch is damaged, although it burns, it cannot completely recover [its original force]. Hence, [human beings] grow with the spiritual breath. If the torch is unable to recover by itself, this is probably what is considered different [from human beings]. Why do you assert that [human beings and a torch] are the same?"

I responded, "A fire begins from the edge [of a torch], but the spiritual vapor of a human being is within the body. It is gradually released from the interior and united at the exterior. Even if it moves from the exterior toward the interior, assuredly it is not necessary to go in from an edge. This is similar to a red-hot charcoal fire: if water is sprinkled on it, it may seem to be about to go out but it glows again. This is the same as the case where the human blood and breath stimulate the growth of skin and flesh. When we look at [the state of something after complete combustion, we find] that some parts become ashes, and other parts become embers. Why is it impossible to compare this to [the human body and spirit]?"

On another night I was talking with [Liu] Boshi, sitting face to face, burning the oil of a lamp. Since the oil in the lamp was exhausted and the

wick was bare, the light was going out. Then, showing this to Boshi, I said, "Human aging is also like the bare [wick of] the lamp." Furthermore, I spoke 29c
of the matter of the flaxen torch that I previously [mentioned to you]. Boshi said, "When the lamp [oil] and the torch burn out, we must add oil or switch to a [new] torch. When a man becomes old, he should quickly pour [blood and breath in his body in order to sustain his life]."

I responded, "A man has already received a body [from Heaven] and formed himself. This is just like holding that lamp or torch. When [the lamp and torch] are exhausted, how can they change themselves, since they have been exhausted? When they are exhausted, the one who changes them is a human being. That which quickly pours [blood and breath in a human body in order to sustain its life] is Heaven. If Heaven is able to do well for human beings and fill up their bodies with blood and breath and strengthen their muscles and bones, then their bodies and spirits become vigorous, even to the extremities, and they live for a long time. Otherwise, they get a fatal illness or are injured. It is just as a flame lasts a short or long time according to the quality of the oil or the length of the torch. If you want a lamp to add [oil to itself] or a torch to [replace] itself [with a new one], it is impossible. Just by collecting nearby oil in order to soak the tip of [the wick], or shifting the position of the main part of a torch in order to make the flame stable, their brightness can be recovered. [But] when the foundation [of the flame] is exhausted, there is no longer anything to burn.

"Now, regarding the preservation of our health, we may be able to replace a lost tooth, dye gray hair black, or regain lustrous skin and face, just as in the case of collecting [nearby] oil or shifting [the position of] a torch. When life comes to an end, [however,] one dies alone. Since intelligent people are aware that it is difficult to seek [a long life], they do not trouble themselves about that. Ignorant people are deluded and hope to gain the power to add oil or replace a torch. Therefore, they are anxious and restless. Moreover, trees, plants, and the five kinds of grains spring up on the earth by the vapor of *yin* and *yang,* and produce fruits and seeds when they mature. The fruits and seeds go back into the earth and are later reborn. This is compared to human beings, birds, beasts, and insects: all are born through the union of male and female. When they are born, they grow up; when they grow up, they become old; and when they are old, they die. It is similar to the changes of the four seasons. To attempt to change its nature and seek to practice a peculiar way are done only by those who are deluded and who do not understand [the truth]."

The *Discourse on Why Śramaṇas Do Not Bow to the Sovereign* (*Shamen bujing wangzhelun*) by Dharma Teacher [Hui]yuan

During the reign of Emperor Cheng (321–342; r. 337–342) and of Emperor Kang (322–344; r. 342–344) of the [Eastern] Jin dynasty, Chariot and Horse General Yu Bing (296–344) had doubts about why *śramaṇa*s treat the emperor as equal to themselves, without regard to formalities. [Yu Bing] clarified the reason, and Cavalry General He [Chong] (292–346) responded to this.[367] Later, in the Yuanxing era (402–404) [of Emperor An (382–418)], Defender-in-Chief Lord Huan [Xuan] agreed with [Yu Bing], but he thought that Yu's argument was not complete. He then gave a letter to the eight executives, in which he wrote:

"Even though the Buddha's edification is endlessly vast and infers the world beyond the visual and aural senses, respect is considered to be its foundation. On this point, there is no difference between the [Buddhist] clergy and laypeople. I assume that what they aspire for differ, but this does not mean that respect should be abolished.

"In the *Laozi* [*Daodejing*], princes are considered equal to the three great elements, [the Way, Heaven, and Earth].[368] When [we examine] why they are considered so important, [we find that the reason] entirely lies in that they support [all things] to grow and [the heavenly bodies] to move smoothly. [Otherwise,] how could they be referred to be equal to the two polarities, [Heaven and Earth,] only for the reason that sages are on the throne? [As the *Book of Changes* says,] 'The great virtue of Heaven and Earth is called life.'[369] [The virtue] to make life all over the country and arrange all things lies in sovereigns. Therefore, we respect the throne and we are gloriously courteous to it. How could we vainly revere and value them? The significance is simply
30a in the fact that sovereigns control [all things]. The reason *śramaṇa*s are born in succession and live with supports is also that they are every day under the government ordinance [made by sovereigns]. How could it be that [*śramaṇa*s]

enjoy the virtue [given by sovereigns] and abandon courtesy [toward them], or benefit from [sovereigns'] kindness but reject [the propriety of] paying respect to them?"

At that time, many people of distinction both in and out of the government responded [to Huan Xuan's inquiry]. Although their statements did not awaken [the people] of that time, they all made good points. [Nevertheless,] generally [their statements] consisted only of what these people expressed from their hearts, and [the objective] truth was hidden by [their subjective] feelings. Consequently, this caused the supreme monk's robes to be damaged by earthly affairs. The mind that brightly aspires [for the Buddhist teaching] gave way to human customs. It is sad! This is precisely a cause for the case that "[The world and the Way] were lost to each other"[370] or the bad luck that happens every thousand years.

I am deeply afraid that the Great Dharma is going to ruin, and I am impressed with [the old warning] that "Not to forget that previous lessons are [a teacher for later events]."[371] Hence, I wrote a discourse of five sections, in which I actually expressed my humble intention. How could it be said that [Buddhism], which is as deep as a gully, needs [my humble statement that is as powerless as] the morning dew? I, however, would like to set forth my boundless mind [for Buddhism]. I hope that among gentlemen of later generations those who hold Buddhism in esteem will read [my discourse] carefully.

Section One: Lay Buddhists

When we examine what Buddhism clarifies, we find that in general the idea of renouncing the world is considered different [from other teachings]. Generally there are four different classes for those who have renounced the world: [*bhikṣu*s, *bhikṣuṇī*s, *śrāmaṇera*s, and *śrāmaṇerikā*s]. In propagating the teaching and educating the people, their achievement is equivalent to that of sovereigns, and their edification concurrently takes the way of statecraft. Regarding the time to awaken people, there is no time not to do so (i.e., people may be awakened anytime), but according to the period [in which Buddhism] is encountered, [Buddhists may] go out [to edify others] or retreat [for self-cultivation]. Therefore, following the rise and fall [of the world, the teaching] simply becomes evident or not evident. Let me briefly mention here what among the issues can be discussed.

Those who remain householders and respectfully perform the Dharma are the people who obey the [sovereign's] edification, whose feelings are no different from those of people in general, and whose lifestyle is the same as that of non-Buddhists. Accordingly, they have attachment to their families and relatives and offer courtesy to their rulers. Courtesy and respect lie in the foundation [of the people's feelings]. Consequently, on the basis of [the foundation,] the teaching is established. When we [inquire into] the origin of [the foundation] we find that the accomplishment is derived from the world of antiquity. Therefore "By teaching love on the basis of the feeling of intimacy" we cause the people to become aware that there is spontaneous kindness. "By teaching respect on the basis of sternness"[372] we cause the people to become aware that there is a natural important one.

The two issues (i.e., relationships between parents and children and between sovereign and subjects) actually stem from the reward and retribution of the unseen world. Reward and retribution do not begin in the present life. One must inquire into their origins. Therefore, [in Buddhism] retribution for a sin is considered punishment, and [Buddhism] makes people fear [retribution] and exercise caution for their later [existences]. [Rebirth in] Heaven is considered to be a noble reward, and [Buddhism] makes the people happy and has them perform [good] acts for their later [existences]. These all clarify the teaching with the law of reward and retribution, just as the shadow [responds to the form] and the sound [follows the voice].

To submit causes is taken as proficiency, and [the teaching was established] without changing the nature. This is because if one treats oneself generously to maintain his life, he sticks to the confrontation [between himself and others] and has confusion, a nuisance roots deeply, and he assuredly never misses maintaining his life. He considers sensual desires to be a [pleasurable] garden, and music and women to be as joyful as sightseeing travel. He is addicted to worldly pleasures, from which he is unable to escape by his own effort. Accordingly, for the teaching to restrict [sensual desires, the law of reward and retribution is expounded] and taken as the limit [of the teaching for lay Buddhists], and nothing more than this is clarified. Since nothing more than this is clarified [for lay Buddhists], generally [they] are very much the same in obeying the law [established by the sovereign]. Therefore, it is impossible for them to receive the virtue [from their parents and the sovereign] and yet fail to show courtesy toward them, or to benefit from the favor [of their parents and sovereign] and yet reject paying respect to them. Consequently, [lay Buddhists] who are delighted with the teaching style of Śākyamuni always first admire their parents and respect their sovereign.

When one abandons secular [life] and takes the tonsure, he must await the orders [of his parents and sovereign] and take action following [their orders]. If the sovereign and the parents have doubts about [his determination 30b
to abandon secular life], he should retreat, ask their intentions, and wait for the time when they have the same state of mind as his. This is precisely the reason why Buddhism values supporting [people's] daily lives and helps the sovereign educate [the people] in the way of administration. The purpose of statements made by the advocates appears to be the same [as mine]. Therefore, I have posited the distinction between Buddhist clergy (*nei*) and laypeople (*wai*) in order to clarify the purpose regarding the three most revered people. I have briefly narrated the tenor of Buddhist scriptures and pronounced my thoughts.

Section Two: The Buddhist Clergy

The Buddhist clergy are visitors from beyond the mundane world. Their lifestyle is beyond that of people of the world. The teaching for them is to master [the fact] that affliction is caused by having a body and that affliction is ended through not preserving the body, to know that [the operation of] life after life is derived from receiving the principle of the mutation [of birth and death in the phenomenal world], and to seek the ultimate law of Nature through not following the principle of the mutation [of birth and death]. Since they seek the ultimate law of Nature through not following the principle of the mutation [of birth and death], they do not value the support of [a sovereign who] manages the movement of [Heaven and Earth]. Since they bring an end to affliction through not preserving the body, they do not esteem the advantage of [the sovereign's] welfare [toward the people]. This means that principles and forms go against each other and monks and secular people are contrary to each other.

This kind of person makes a vow for himself by taking the tonsure at the beginning, and shows [his determination] in changing his ordinary clothes [to monk's robes]. Accordingly, in general all members of the clergy renounce the world in order to pursue their aspiration, and they become different from secular people in order to realize their way. Since they become different from secular people, their clothing code must not be the same as the secular rule. Since they renounce the world, they ought to follow a lofty lifestyle. Well, [Buddhist] monks are like this. Therefore, they are able to save secular people who are drowning in the deep stream [of transmigration of birth and death], uproot their deep roots [of karma] for numerous *kalpa*s, profoundly lead [them] to the ferry of the three vehicles, and open widely the passes to the realms of heavenly beings and human beings.

If a person completes the virtue [of a monk], the Buddhist Way diffuses [virtuous influence] over his family members of the six relations, and the benefit spreads to all people. Even though [monks] are not placed in the rank of princes, [their way] is already compatible with the fundamental way the emperor rules over the world, and they can let the people be as they are. Consequently, while privately they oppose their family's valuable [attachment to him and become a monk], they do not go against filial piety. While they may lack the courtesy of paying respect to the ruler in public, they are not impolite [to him].

Judging from this point of view, you know that if you go outside beyond the principle of the mutation [of birth and death in the phenomenal world] in order to seek the ultimate law of Nature, [you will know that to investigate] the principles is profound and the significance is great. It is clear that [the Confucian] benevolence spoken of [by people], heaving a sigh, is insignificant in merit and of little benefit. If that is the case, [Buddhist monks] are still ashamed to hear the teaching of "those who are about to face toward Mount Ming"[373] (i.e., those who aspire to the way of Laozi and Zhuangzi beyond the Confucian ethics) and turn back. How could [monks] be compared with those who follow the [sovereign's] education and the wise men who receive a stipend without rendering any service, and be [considered] the same as them in regard to showing filial piety and respect [for their parents and the sovereign]?

Section Three: Those Who Pursue the Ultimate Law of Nature Do Not Follow the Principle of the Mutation [of Birth and Death in the Phenomenal World]

Question: "When we look to Laozi's thought, we find he means that Heaven and Earth are considered to be great because of their attainment of the One (i.e., the Way); princes and kings are considered to be noble since they master to follow [the One];[374] since [Heaven and Earth] attain the One, they are the foundation of myriad changes; and since [princes and kings] master to follow [the One], they have the function of leading the movement of Heaven and Earth. If this is so, to clarify the ultimate law of Nature must lie in mastering the root [of the Way]. To master the root [of the Way] must be due to following the principle of the mutation [of birth and death in the phenomenal world]. Therefore, wise people of former times thought that [Lao's statement of this] is good. It is impossible that many other theories differ from this. If a theory that differs from these many theories is established, it is unworthy of serious consideration. Nevertheless, you said not to follow the principle of the mutation [of birth and death in the phenomenal world in order to pursue the ultimate law of Nature]. Why is this so?"

Answer: "Every existence in the finite world equally receives a life in 30c
[the law of] the great change (i.e., the Way). Even though a large number of individuals are multifarious and there is a difference between the exquisite and the coarse, generally speaking, in the long run they are simply divided into [two kinds:] those who have a mental function and those who do not. Those who have [a mental function] give rise to a feeling for change, and those who have no feeling for change. Since they do not have a feeling for change, when the change ends, their life is completed. Since their life has nothing to do with feeling, when the form decays, the change ceases to exist. [On the other hand,] those who give rise to a feeling for change respond to things and are moved. Since this movement must be caused by the feeling, their life does not cease. Since their life does not cease, the change becomes broader, the form (i.e., the body) goes through [the transmigration of birth and death] more and more, the feeling is more pent-up, and the affliction gets deeper. How can this affliction be described?

"Therefore, a sutra states, 'Nirvana is the state of no change. Thereby the exhaustion of change is considered to be the realm [of nirvana]. The three realms of existence are the state of flowing motion. Thereby, they are places full of sin and suffering.' When the change comes to an end, causes and conditions cease eternally. When [the change] is in flowing motion, we receive suffering forever. How can this be clarified?

"Life is shackled by the body, and it continues to exist due to [the law of] the change. When [we human beings] give rise to a feeling for change, the spirit is tied to its foundation, and the intelligence becomes dull. When [the mind] is firmly blocked [by feelings], one tries to preserve only himself and gets involved only in the state of [flowing] motion. Then the reins of mental function lose control, the path to [the transmigration of] birth and death is daily opened, and one just follows greed and clinging in the long flow [of the transmigration of birth and death]. How would it be to receive a life only [in this world]?

"Consequently, those who turn back to the origin and seek the ultimate law of Nature do not toil their spirits with [the work of] life. Those who transcend the mundane world do not trouble their life with feelings. If we do not trouble our life with feelings, it is possible to sever [the transmigration of] birth and death. If we do not trouble our spirits with [the work of] life, it is possible that the spirit profoundly unites with [the transcendental world]. Since the spirit profoundly unites with the transcendental world, it is called nirvana. How could the term nirvana be named groundlessly?

"Let me infer and actualize it. Even though Heaven and Earth are great for producing and raising all things, they cannot make living creatures immortal. Although princes and kings consider causing all beings to survive to be their [major] achievement, they cannot cause them all to be free of affliction. Therefore, in the previous discussion I said, '[The teaching for Buddhist monks is] to master [the fact] that affliction is caused by having a body and that affliction is ended through not preserving the body, to know that [the operation of] life after life is derived from receiving the principle of the mutation [of birth and death in the phenomenal world], and to seek the ultimate law of Nature through not following the principle of the mutation [of birth and death].' The meaning lies in this. Since the meaning lies herein, this is why *śramaṇa*s treat sovereigns as equal, without regard to formalities; they exalt their tasks, they are not graced with a title of nobility from princes and kings, and yet they benefit from the kindness of [princes and kings]."

Section Four: Those Who Have Mastered the Ultimate Way Do Not Respond to the World by Serving Both [for Relief by Politics and Emancipation by Religion]

Question: "Looking at all previous histories, from the time of the earlier emperors on, those who occupy the throne and are united with the fundamental

ways [of the world] do not necessarily differ from each other in the original base. Since the original base cannot be dual, through all the generations ceremonial forms are the same and the system is consistent. It is 'Only Heaven is great and Yao solely modeled after it.'[375] If it is like this, it is not the case that the wisdom [of sages] has nothing to illuminate, and there is nothing else that can be illuminated. Since it is not the case that in the law of Nature there is something that is not completed, there is nothing the law of Nature can complete. Inferring from this, [the world] beyond what we see and hear is empty; there is nothing to ascertain about it. Since there is nothing to ascertain in reason [about the world beyond what we see and hear], it can be clear 31a
what are the ultimate law of Nature and the ultimate Way [mastered by sages]. Today, all *śramaṇa*s do not understand the meaning beyond writings, and they are puzzled about [the sages'] purpose that is beyond the teaching. Certainly they are terribly wrong. If there were an apparent sign for this (i.e., that the Chinese sages did not realize the truth of the transcendental world), it would be invaluable information."

Answer: "The mysterious ultimate law of Nature is vast and remote. The Way of the Spirit is profound. It can be sought with [philosophical] principles, but it is difficult to cross-examine with phenomenal facts. Once [the Way of the Spirit] is established as a teaching, the teaching aims at following the fashion of the day. The capacity according to [the fashion of the day] varies between superiority and inferiority, but regarding [the fact that the teaching] completes [the nature of] all things, it lies in using the function of human receptivity of mysterious responsive activity, conforming to people's minds, and leading their endowments. When their endowments reach the utmost limits, 'the knowledge stops at what it does not know'[376] and does not participate in more than that.

"If this is so, it is not that those who have mastered the ultimate Way do not comprehend both [worlds within and beyond human limits]; they comprehend both, but they simply cannot manage both simultaneously. Therefore, [the *Zhuangzi* says,] 'When the ancients spoke of the Great Way, [first Heaven was clarified], "objects and their names could be mentioned at the fifth from the beginning," and "rewards and penalties" could be stated at the ninth.'[77] This [indicates] only the steps [to rule] the secular world, but [a teaching, regardless of the steps,] still cannot be suddenly established, not to mention about [teachings] in the world beyond [the secular world]. Let me infer this more broadly [in order to explore] the purport more deeply.

"As for the statement [in the *Zhuangzi*], 'Outside the six conjunctions (i.e., the limits of the world of humans, literally, the four cardinal directions plus zenith and nadir), [the sage] keeps it in mind, but does not discuss [anything],'[378] this does not mean that it is impossible to discuss it but that if [the sage] dares to discuss it, he may be at variance [with the truth]. The statement 'Inside the limits of the world of humans, [the sage] discusses [in outline] but does not debate anything about it' does not mean that [the sage] cannot debate, but that if he dared to debate it he may [cause others] to have doubts. The statement 'The spring and autumn manages the affairs of the former kings' designs. [The sage] debates these but does not criticize them' does not mean that [the sage] cannot criticize them, but that if he criticizes he may [cause others] to be confused. These three manners (i.e., not discussing, not debating, and not criticizing) are all based on the fact that our visual-auditory senses are limited and place restrictions on our behaviors, and do not get involved in the world beyond our visual-auditory senses. If we seek the sage's purport on this basis, the ways inside and outside [the limits of the world of humans] can be united and clarified.

"I always think that the Buddhist and Confucian teachings, and that the Tathāgata and Yao and Confucius secretly have a close relationship with each other even though they differ from each other in establishing their teaching. [These two groups] actually make a distinction about renouncing [the world] or staying [in the secular world], but they are the same after all. Debating it in detail, we will be able to see a main theme [that the two ways are the same]. In reason, there may be those that are united at the beginning and separate [into more than one] later, and those that are separate at the beginning and become united later. Those that are first united and later separate are none other than all buddhas and tathāgatas, while those who are first separate and later united are successive sovereigns who have not mastered the ultimate Way; they are in the [latter] group.

"Why is this made clear? A sutra says, 'The Buddha mastered the spontaneous, marvelous Dharma. He edifies the people with expedients. Following the revealed world extensively, he becomes an immortal, the wheel-turning noble king, a high-ranking official, a minister, the most reverend priest, or a monk. As [one of] these, he transforms and manifests himself everywhere. No one among all the kings and virtuous men knows who he is.'[379] This case is that of the so-called one that is first united and later separate.

"On the other hand, there are [sovereigns] who began a great enterprise [of educating the people] but have not yet achieved the meritorious education. Since the form [of the teaching] varies, what [the people] receive is uneven. Some expect achievement after death, or some have the testimony that responds to [the education] revealed in their lifetimes. Among sage kings, those who have accomplished the teaching based on [the Buddhist Way] are countless. Even though [their method of teaching] is that of the stick and carrot and has no set rules, their goals must converge. This case is that of the 31b
so-called ones that are first separate and later united.

"If [things] are now separate and later united, those who intend to walk on a road leading everywhere will assuredly not limit themselves to only one passage. If [things] are united now and later separate, it can be certainly known that the conclusive point of Śākyamuni and that of Yao and Confucius are no different from each other. Hence, if we seek unification from separation, we will know that [Buddhism and Confucianism] must arrive at the same truth. If we seek separation from unification, we will realize that there are many methods to master the ultimate Way. Those who only look at [the surface of] phenomena, however, do not understand that both are one. Therefore, they are merely confused by the many ways and surprised by their differences.

"Observing on this basis, the merit of the way of Heaven and Earth is nothing more than operating [the universe] and producing and nourishing [all things]. The virtue of emperors and kings is nothing more than following the way [of Heaven and Earth] and helping it in nourishing and leading [the people]. If we compare them (i.e., the merit of the way of Heaven and Earth and the virtue of emperors and kings) with [Buddhism], the singularly transcendent teaching and the immutable religion, it is already clear that it is doubtlessly impossible to talk about its superiority and inferiority in the same breath."

Section Five: The Body is Mortal but the Spirit is Immortal

Question: "Your discussion takes the case that the mutation [of birth and death] comes to an end to be the utmost supremacy. Hence, those who want to reach the utmost supremacy must go against the mutation [of birth and death] and seek the ultimate law of Nature. Since in order to seek the ultimate law of Nature one does not go through following the mutation [of birth and death], you refer to successive sovereigns and equate [their teachings] with Buddhism, and take the one who has mastered the utmost supremacy to be a sovereign who rules with expedients. This is what your discussion entails. You must believe that it is the Great Pervader.[380] When I inquire whether or not this conforms to reality, it is not so in reason. Why? A person [is born] receiving the vapor [of *yin* and *yang*], which lasts only for his lifetime. When his life comes to an end, he will vanish and return to nothing. Even though 'the spirit is the most mysterious of a myriad of things,'[381] this is originally just what *yin* and *yang* transform into. 'By a transformation a person is born. By another transformation a person dies.'[382] Since [the vapor] is collected, there is a beginning; when it is dispersed, there is an end.

"Inferring from this basis, it is assuredly known that spirit and body altogether transform, they are originally not in different lines from each other, the exquisite [vapor of the spirit] and the coarse [vapor of the body] are the same, and [both spirit and body] are one unit from beginning to end. When the body is complete, the vapor is collected and the spirit comes to exist. When the body is destroyed, the vapor is dispersed and the function [of the spirit] extinguishes. When [the vapor] is dispersed, [life] returns to the original place of Heaven where it received [the vapor]. When the function [of the spirit] is extinguished, it returns and becomes nothing. It is simply the law of Nature that all [existence] repeats extinction. What else could do this?

If [spirit and body] are fundamentally different from each other, these two different kinds of vapor are united in the law [of Nature]. When they are united, [spirit and body] equally transform. In addition, the spirit that dwells in the body is compared to a fire that burns wood. When [the body] is produced, [the spirit] must exist. When [the body] is destroyed, [the spirit] must be extinguished. When the body is broken up, the spirit is dispersed, as it no longer has [the body] to rely on. When the [vigor of] the wood is lost, the fire goes out, as it no longer has [fuel] to rely on. It stands to reason.

"Even if it is difficult to distinguish and clarify whether or not [spirit and body] are homogeneous, it can be said that existence and nonexistence are certainly due to the collection and dispersion [of the vapor]. The phrase 'collection and dispersion' is the general term for the change of the vapor [of *yin* and *yang*], and for birth and death of myriad transformations. Accordingly, the *Zhuangzi* says: 'Human life is due to the collection of the vapor. When [the vapor] is collected, there is life. When it is dispersed, there is death. If death and life are in the same category, what is there to worry about?'[383] The ancients who were good at speaking of the Way must have the idea [that life and death are due to the collection and dispersion of the vapor]. If that is so, the highest truth (i.e., life) terminates in one's lifetime. I should ask you the meaning [of your statement] that the life [of the body] comes to an end, but [the life of the spirit] does not change."

Answer: "Whatever can the spirit be? It is a being that comes to have 31c
mysterious functions at the apex of exquisiteness [of the vapor of *yin* and *yang*]. Since it is the highest exquisiteness, it cannot be illustrated with the symbols [of the *Book of Changes*]. For that reason, sages call it 'the most subtle [of a myriad of things].' Even the most intelligent person cannot define its form and cannot trace the very source of its profound purpose. Nevertheless, you, the speaker, have doubts based on general knowledge, join many others [who accuse Buddhism], and make yourself confused. Your false accusation is already serious. You intend to talk about [the spirit]. This is to speak of an unspeakable matter. Here, within [the limit of] unspeakableness, I would like to draw an outline of it for you.

"The spirit perfectly complies with [every change], being free from anything, and it is extremely mysterious and indescribable. It is moved by [external] objects and acts on them, and it operates availing itself of the law [of the phenomenal world]. It is moved by [external] objects, but since it is not a thing, when the thing changes [the spirit] is not extinguished [along with the thing]. It avails itself of the law [of the phenomenal world], but since it is not the law, even if the law comes to an end [the spirit] is not exhausted. Since we [human beings] have feelings, we can be moved by [external] objects. Since we have consciousness, we can seek with the law. There are [both] exquisiteness and coarseness in the law [of the phenomenal world]. Hence, the nature [of the law] varies. In intelligence there are sharp and dull. Therefore, the function [of intelligence] varies.

"Carrying out the discussion inferring from this point of view (i.e., that feeling and consciousness form the phenomenal world), it is known that the mutation (i.e., transmigration) [of birth and death] is affected by feeling, and the spirit is transmitted by the mutation [of birth and death]. Feeling is the mother of the mutation [of birth and death]. Spirit is the root of feeling. For feeling there is the law of encountering [external] objects, while for spirit there is the function of moving into the unseen world. Those who have become awakened thoroughly simply return to the origin [of the mutation of birth and death], but those who are deluded merely chase after [external] objects. The ancients who discussed the Way did not come to agreement [on this matter]. Let me cite [instances from their discussions] and clarify the matter.

"Zhuangzi, in the chapter on the 'Great and Most Honored Master' (*Dazongshi*) [in the *Zhuangzi*], pronounces profoundly that 'the great mass [of Nature] gives us life so that we toil, and grants us death so that we can rest.'[384] Moreover, he says, 'Life is considered as being a human. Ah! Death is to return to the truth.'[385] This is, as they say, to know that life is a great calamity and non-life is considered as returning to the origin. Wenzi quotes the words of the Yellow Emperor, 'Although the body is dispersed, the spirit does not change itself. Based on the fact that it does not change itself, [the spirit] takes advantage of [every] change [of others]. Therefore, its change is boundless.'[386]

"Zhuangzi furthermore says, 'When we take only the body of a human being [from the infinite nature], we still have joy. This body undergoes myriad changes endlessly.'[387] These words are, as they say, to know that human life is not exhausted only in one mutation [of birth and death], but follows [the changes of various] things and never returns [to the origin]. Even though the discussions of these two gentlemen (i.e., Zhuangzi and Wenzi) do not investigate exhaustively the truth, they try to go along with the ultimate law of Nature, and it is worthy to listen to them.

"You, the disputant, have not examined [Zhuangzi's] theory that 'birth and death simultaneously exist side by side,'[388] and you are deluded by the idea that [the vapor of *yin* and *yang*] is collected and dispersed just in one mutation [of birth and death]. You do not think that in the Way of the Spirit there exist numinous beings that are more mysterious than anything else, and you say that the exquisite vapor (i.e., the spirit) and the coarse vapor (i.e., the body) are equally exhausted. How sad would this be?

"The metaphor of fire and wood [you cited as a quote from Zhuangzi] is originally derived from a sacred [Buddhist] scripture. Since its [correct] transmission was lost, the deep purport has not been investigated, and the subtle words thereupon sank into a secular teaching. It causes you to avail yourself of it, and yet to have doubt.

"If until now there was no chance for a leader who was awakened to the ultimate law of Nature, we would not know that there was a pioneer who had insight into this law, and the function that [the spirit] transmigrates in the unseen world would never reach [the people of the world] until the end of their lives. Why is this so? When feeling and consciousness move each other[389] [it gives rise to] the mutation [of birth and death], which is endless. [The relation between] cause and condition is firmly established, and it is transmitted imperceptibly. Other than those who thoroughly investigate, who could discern [the truth of] this change? Let me testify to it with facts for 32a
your sake.

"That a fire is passed on to firewood is similar to the spirit transmigrating to the body. The fire transferring to other firewood is just like the spirit moving to another body. The former firewood is not the same as the latter, and then we know the extremely skillful performance of a hand [in transmitting the fire from one piece of wood to another]. The former body is different from the latter, so we realize the profound response between feeling and consciousness. Deluded people, [however,] see the body decay in one existence and then they think that the spirit, feeling, [and consciousness] die together with [the body]. This is simply compared to the case that when one sees that the firewood is burned up he says [that the fire] is extinguished forever. This is to strain the passage from the chapter on 'Nourishing the Lord of Life' (*Yangshengzhu*) [in the *Zhuangzi*] and not to look deeply into the virtue [of the passage].

"Now, as you say in the discussion, if spirit and body altogether transform [and life returns to the original place of Heaven where it received the vapor], then [human life] begins from the original place of Heaven, and one's disposition of being dull or intelligent is the same as the natural endowments he receives [from Heaven]. Therefore I would like to ask you: Does a person receive his disposition [of being dull or intelligent] in the body, or in the spirit? If he receives it in the body, [since the disposition of being dull or intelligent is an attribute of the spirit,] everyone who has a body would all change and become spirit. If he receives it in the spirit, [since the spirit is not exhausted,] it would be passed on from spirit to spirit. [If this were the case,] then the [good-for-nothing] Danzhu would have been as holy as [his father,] Emperor Yao, and Zhonghua (i.e., Emperor Shun) would have had as [obstinate] a function of a spirit as [his father,] Gusou. Would this be possible? Could this be possible? If it is impossible, we assuredly know that the unseen [cause and] condition was apparently established in the long-distant past, and the distinction of being intelligent or dull is destined before the body [is produced]. Although the marvelous lathe (i.e., the movement of Nature) revolves well, it still cannot change the character of Nature, not to mention that of [human beings, who] are more humble than [Nature]. If we examine [the metaphor of fire and firewood] logically, [we find] it is sublime language and has a verification. If we follow it with the facts, it is possible that there is no delusion in the Great Pervader (i.e., the great truth)."[390]

After [the composition of] this discourse was completed, the guests who had retired from public life walked under a bright moon and visited me one evening. We all gathered at the Dharma hall. Thereupon, one of the guests asked me, "I respectfully read your discourse. The fundamental point of argument was perceivable and there was almost no flaw in it. One day, [however,] when I tried to study it again I found there is a certain point that I do not understand thoroughly. You think that the *śramaṇa*s' system of deportment (i.e., religious precepts) is a special regulation that differs from the secular system, and which is an excellent tool (i.e., the rule of deportment) for those who cultivate the [Buddhist] Way; therefore, they certainly should omit making perfunctory respect to their sovereigns and parents.

"My present question is this: [*Śramaṇa*s] devote themselves to begin the difficult enterprise [of delivering sentient beings] and they hope [to achieve] the merit of transcending the world of the mutation [of birth and death] in the far future, yet their kindness is still latent and there is no [immediate] revelation of the efficacy of the teaching. The reward and retribution for the next existence is profound and has not appeared responding to [what one does in this existence]. Nevertheless, they cause princes to offer [various things to them] and nobles who believe [in Buddhism] to kneel down [to worship them]. Shouldn't they be censured for receiving kindness from others for doing nothing and being too hasty? Should they not be chastised for benefiting from others' favors in vain, just like a parasite?"

I, the host, answered after awhile, "Let me take an example from familiar matters [and explain] for you, all wise people. [For instance,] suppose here is someone who, in order to announce an order he had received from the [government] of that time, is traveling to a remote place where the customs are different and where he needs nine different translators [to reach his destination]. The question is whether or not the king must provide him provisions and bestow upon him a carriage and clothes."

[The questioner] replied, "Yes, he must do so."

I said, "We can discover the case [of *śramaṇa*s] from this example. What kind of person is called a *śramaṇa*? They are those who uncover the obscurity and confusion that cover common people, who open the profound path to the world beyond the mutation [of birth and death], who together with the people of the world follow the way of 'forgetting both [others and myself],'[391] who cause those who wish for loftiness (i.e., enlightenment) to take the custom handed down [from the Buddha], and who have those who rinse their 32b
mouths in a stream taste its surplus drops. If they are so, even though the great achievement has not yet been accomplished, when we see the trace of their superb footsteps, what we realize will indeed be magnanimous.

"In that case, [the sovereign's] achievement in leading the operation [of Heaven and Earth] and advantage in supporting the existence [of all things] are still not as worthy as a *śramaṇa*'s initial vow [to save all sentient beings]. Needless to say, [the sovereign's favors] do not match [a *śramaṇa*'s] toil to practice the three kinds of acts (i.e., of body, speech, and mind). In addition, although these people (*śramaṇa*s) need [support from others to sustain] their bodies, they feel no inclination toward secular matters. They consider that to receive offerings of the four [requisite] things (clothing, food, shelter, and medicine) is just as if a horsefly or a mosquito were to fly in front of them. Why is a favor [as tiny as] a bubble sufficient to talk about?"

Thereafter, all the guests realized for the first time that on the unseen path, to open the wheel tracks is considered to be a [*śramaṇa*'s] achievement, and a *śramaṇa*'s guidance is considered to be the way [to enlightenment]. Then they were happy, their minds at peace, and they all left, exclaiming.

This was the third year of the Yuanxing era of the Jin dynasty (404), the year of *efeng*.[392] At that time, Emperor [An] fled from the capital and the people were all anxious [about the world]. All my comrades lamented the fact that the emperor was a puppet of his subjects. Consequently, based on [these facts], I set forth this discourse.

The *Discourse on the Śramaṇa's Robe Worn with a Bared Shoulder* (*Shamen tanfulun*) by Dharma Teacher [Hui]yuan

Someone asked, "The *śramaṇa*'s robe that shows a bared right shoulder is derived from the Buddha's teaching. Does it conform with [proper] decorum?"

I answered, "Yes, it does."

He asked [further], "The three dynasties (i.e., Xia, Yin, and Zhou) had different systems from each other and the decorum of each was not the same; [sometimes it was] simple and [sometimes it was] embellished. These changes are detailed in ancient books, but [the decorum of] Buddhism is excluded from those [of the three dynasties]. All the debaters have doubts about this. If there is a profound principle, I would be happy to receive your instruction for what I have not yet learned."

I responded [to his question], "Primitive people did not lose the great simplicity and their decorum was not embellished. Since the three kings (i.e., King Yu of Xia, King Tang of Yin, and King Wu of Zhou) appeared in the world [and established their system], [decorum] changed in accordance with the times. Seen from this basis, what you, the debaters, maintain is simply the word regulated in the secular world [of ethical education]. How do I know this is so? What we do not have in China might be obtained from the customs of other countries. Since the people there have been without changes, their way (i.e., traditional decorum) has not been ruined. Hence, in Indian decorum, when they completely pay respect to virtuous ones or when they show their sincerity to gods, they usually dress with part of the body bared, which [the *Book of Rites*] refers to as a high degree in removing decorations [from clothing].[393] Although the books that explain [this style of clothing] have not been circulated in this land, it appears that [the correct meaning of this style of clothing] was known at the beginning [when the style of clothing was established].

"The Buddha rose in the world and based on [Indian traditional customs] he established the teaching. He clarified that since [Buddhists' acts] are not evil they should bare the right shoulder. Why is this? It is because the noble and the humble must be distinguished in their ranking; if virtuous ones are promoted by [receiving] a high rank, the mind to uphold the virtuous ones will arise. Therefore, *śramaṇa*s go beyond fame and rank in order to cast away [the customs of] the times. They withdraw and never desire to take the initiative [in the world].

"Moreover, people are generally right-handed. If we do not follow [right-handedness] in doing something, we will have difficulties in everything. If we commit a blunder, although we may try to recover, it is not easy even for the middle level of wise people [to recover it], not to speak of those who are below this level. Let me try to explain this.

"The body consists of right and left, and the function of principles consists of right and wrong. To make up these two issues (i.e., right and left in the body and right and wrong in principles), each one avails itself of the foundation. If the foundation is blocked and [the blockage] is not uprooted, [each] 32c responds more and more to the demands of the phenomenal world. Accordingly, if the body and principles help each other, the way [of the foundation] will be subtle and clear. [Nevertheless,] if the customs of the world do not change, to respond to the subtle [way of the foundation] is difficult to manage. Once [the practice of wearing] a robe with one shoulder bared is made known, we will follow the practice in the body, be moved with the principles, and comprehend it in the mind. Thus, we control the vapor of following [the nature] and show the form of sincerity. Accordingly, the simultaneous practice of right and wrong is originally impossible.

"Hence, by wearing a robe with one shoulder bared, the World-honored One (Skt. Bhagavat) consolidated sincerity and shut off evil; he made the name and reality [of *śramaṇa*s] well matched, and he caused reverence and laxity to not mix with each other. Later he opened the path to seek [enlightenment]. He leads those who have been deluded for a long time to the true nature, he causes the wise who are stranded in the world to not despair by thinking that they have no hope [for salvation], and he causes those who hope to advance [in Buddhism] to not turn back by being deluded in the path.

"In this way, those who have in mind the sacred gate [of Buddhism] all walk on the right [path]; they think of following [the law of Nature]; they obey the same rules regardless of the time or location, recollecting the past, they think of the simple [life]style [of ancient times]; they go against the splendid [customs] of the secular world in order to cleanse the mind; they examine the foundation to understand [the law of] changes thoroughly; they realize the profound [philosophical principles] in conformity with familiar matters; they feel shame if [their actions] contradict their appearance and dress; and they become deeply aware of the principles.

"If we act in this way, our feeling is edified, we earnestly approach [the Buddhist Way], and we do not tire of practicing [Buddhism]. Our acts must follow [the law of Nature], and our appearance unconsciously becomes respectful. This is indeed the external cause that the Tathāgata invites [people to Buddhism] and his wonderful method to teach ordinary people and to lead [them to Buddhism]. Nevertheless, many debaters have not been instructed [in the meaning of wearing a robe with one shoulder bared], and some people want to eliminate [this style]. It goes against the method of antiquity. How serious this problem is!"

A Criticism by He [Wuji], Zhennan [General]

I received your response to my question regarding the monk's robe with one shoulder bared. Both the main point and the teaching are magnanimous. You connect the simplicity [of the robe] with [the customs of] primitive times, take [an example for the subsidiary relation between] the body and principles from familiar matters, distinguish respect from laxity, and completely explain both sincerity and clothing. There is almost no flaw. Regarding the reason you clarify, that [having the right shoulder bared] is to follow [the law of Nature], however, I still do not agree with you. This is because to establish the system of decorum and clothing may be in accordance with the needs of the times. Hence, there are inside (i.e., statecraft) and outside (i.e., religion) in the phenomenal world, and then [the system] can be established roughly or minutely according to them.

Regarding Li (i.e., Laozi), Śākyamuni, the Duke of Zhou, and Confucius, there are those who live in the secular world and those who leave the secular world behind. They are not the same in following their traditions, but it is clear that there is no difference between one who goes against [tradition] and one who follows it. Therefore, Laozi clarifies to make much use of the right side in military honors and unfortunate rites,[394] and in the *Book of Rites* it is instituted not to use the left in funeral rites.[395] Moreover, the four immeasurable minds (Skt. *catur-apramāṇa* or *catvāryapramāṇāni*) thoroughly refer to the most sincere mind to respect one's parents, and the method of hunting called *sanqu* (i.e., driving game from three directions, leaving one side open for some to escape) shows the benevolence of the king's acts.[396]

When we examine [events that happened] in later ages, the purpose [of those events] can be seen. Would we rather entrust the utmost way of following [the law of Nature] to inauspicious incidents, and show the auspicious sincerity in funeral rites? The reason that [Lord Xiang of] Zheng state stripped off the upper garment [and stood in front of the king of Chu state] is similar to the reason that [Lord] Xi of Xu loaded a coffin on his carriage [to meet the king of Chu state].[397] All these [incidents occured] because they thought that if what they availed themselves of went against [the law of Nature], they would assuredly receive an unexpected punishment. Testifying from this, where does following [the law of Nature] exist? [It exists in both China and India.] Therefore, I act in accordance with what I have in my mind, hoping you will explain more thoroughly and cause the inside (i.e., Buddhism) and the outside (i.e., Confucianism) to be united into one.

Dharma Teacher [Hui]yuan's Response [to He]

I respectfully inquired into the purpose of your question. [Your assertion] may open the lofty path, illuminate what I have not rendered, and cause the exquisite and the coarse to follow [the law of Nature] at the same time and Buddhism and Confucianism to be united into one. I read your instruction of this repeatedly and came to realize numerous things. I always think that 33a
in the teaching of the Way (i.e., Buddhism) and the teaching on social relationships (i.e., Confucianism), or in [the case of] Śākyamuni, the Duke of Zhou, and Confucius, although the method of establishing their teachings differs they secretly have a close relationship with each other. They actually differ in renouncing [the world] or staying [in the world], but they are the same after all. The trace of the wonderful [teaching of Chinese sages], however, is hidden in daily use. The purport is deep and profound, and it is difficult to seek. Consequently, [sages'] words of utmost [significance] were blocked

by scriptures of worldly teaching, and this caused those who speak [of Buddhism and Confucianism] to regard them as separate from each other.

The reason I know this is so is that [Chinese] sages teach based on the idea of "fishing [without a net] and shooting [at game excepting those in nests]."[398] [They teach people] to remove the extremities [of hunting], to lessen [the trouble caused by] taking excessive catches by hunting in accordance with the four seasons, to not be stingy by letting some animals escape through the politeness of the method of hunting called *sanqu,* and to be sure to wait until [fish and animals] have grown to maturity before [fishing for them and hunting] them with nets. [The Chinese sages' teaching] is thorough, [extending even] to benevolence for the grass at the roadside in remote ages. Its tenor is a match for Śākyamuni's compassion. If we think [everything that exists] in the world is equal to us and if we see ourselves as the same as others, [a large tree whose trunk] fills the arms and the fine hair of an animal are the same. Would there be a difference between superior and inferior, or would they not be all of a sort? Nevertheless, examining from the trace [of the Chinese sages' teaching], [the foundation of its tenor] is on the whole similar to universal love, but when we deeply seek reality, there are roles in social classes [in the Chinese sages' teaching], and what is well constructed with the roles is too detailed to describe [here]. Accordingly, [in the Chinese sages' teaching] we progress in virtue along with [our roles in social classes], and make our duties clear for our superiors and parents.

The teachings in Buddhism and Confucianism can be understood from this viewpoint. The Chinese sages' intention can be known. However, since the path that unites [Buddhism and Confucianism] into one has not been clarified, people of the world do not know it. If [my view] of this is approved, the reason why *śramaṇa*s wear a robe with the right shoulder bared is not open to question. In your letter, [however,] you wrote that I should explain it more thoroughly. Therefore, I would like to examine and express again my long-cherished thoughts.

When we seek how one takes a body that goes through changes, [we find that the body] is molded by *yin* and *yang* and we receive a body that consists of a right side and a left side. With the shift of day and night, [the change of] life and death is explained. In human feelings, everyone is delighted with living and afraid of dying, and everyone is fond of advancing but detests retreating. For this reason, former monarchs followed the people's nature. Comforming to the nature [of human feelings,] they distinguished the [ceremonial] system for auspicious [occasions] from that for inauspicious [occasions], and set up [two] different positions: the left and the right. Hence, on auspicious occasions the left is esteemed, one is promoted in the peerage, and he lives in comfort; while on inauspicious occasions the right is honored, and one expresses grief in order to dissolve the nature [of human life]. These are all based on what we receive [from Heaven]. We follow it in order to understand the teaching thoroughly, respond to the changes of the times, and recollect the virtue of our predecessors.

What people of the world value is nothing more than survival. When they live long, [according to the situation,] they stoop, stretch, advance, or retreat. This is entirely the way [of the secular world]. [The concept that "The system of decorum and clothing can be established] roughly or minutely according to [inside (i.e., statecraft) and outside (i.e., religion) in the phenomenal world," as you mentioned,] lies here.

*Śramaṇa*s are not like this. They put their own persons last, withdraw [from society], and yet do not detest being humble. If the time is not for them, they are resigned to the humble position. To govern oneself by being in the humble position is called modesty. To stay in the low place which many people dislike is called obedience. If we do not lose modesty and obedience as the base, it is easy to accumulate the merit of "reducing day by day [to attain *wuwei*],"[399] and it is possible to find joy on the path to escape from [delusions] and to attain [enlightenment]. Hence, [the *śramaṇa*] lives in seclusion, forgets glory, and conducts himself contrary to [the ways of] the secular world. Those who conduct themelves contrary to [the ways of] the secular world are different in reality from wise people who live in the world of ethical education, even though they may resemble each other in appearance.

How can I clarify this? Generally speaking, those who have renounced the world understand thoroughly that suffering is caused by having a physical body and it can be stopped by not keeping the body. They know that [the endless succession of] life after life is derived from receiving the mutation [of birth and death], and they can seek the ultimate law of Nature by not following that mutation. Inferring from this point, we certainly know that those 33b
who aspire to the ultimate stage do not trouble their spirit by living, and those

who are far beyond worldly affairs do not trouble their life by feelings. If we do not trouble our life by feelings, life can be cut off. If we do not trouble our spirit, it can profoundly unite with [the transcendental world].

In that case, regarding the establishment of ceremonies for auspicious and inauspicious occasions, admiring parents, and serving a monarch, as mentioned above, these are probably just statements for a limited world. They are what "have not been out from the closed world from the beginning."[400] If we do not go out of the closed world, we will just play with our writings and will not thoroughly understand [the law of] the change. If that is the case, [such people] just remain in [the world of] Confucianism and lose themselves in their lives; they avail themselves of myriad changes and go against the ultimate law of Nature. Seen from the position of utmost obedience, couldn't it be said that this is contrary to [the way of *śramaṇa*s]? [The difference] between those who remain in the secular world and those who abandon the secular world lies in this point.

The *Discourse on the Clarification of Reward and Retribution* (*Ming baoyinglun*) by Dharma Teacher [Hui]yuan, Responding to Huan [Xuan] of Nanjun

Question: "In Buddhist scriptures, the destruction of life is considered to be a grave offense; [the one who committed such an act] will be punished in Hell; retribution meted out by the officials of Hell according to the laws of Hell is just as a shadow [follows its original form] or a sound [responds to its voice]. I have a doubt about this. Why? The substances of the four great elements are merely earth, water, fire, and wind. They gather together and result in a physical body, in which the spirit dwells, life lodges, and the mental function settles. Then the clear consciousness begins to develop [based on this]. Although [the spirit] exists entrusting itself to [the physical body], the law [of the spirit] is very different from that [of the body]. How could there be only the difference between exquisite and coarse? Certainly [unlike the body] there is no situation in which [the spirit] gets injured. When [the body] is destroyed, there is no harm to the spirit at all. [That the body is destroyed] is simply as if the water and fire between Heaven and Earth were destroyed."

Second question: "In the mind of all people, affection and desire are luxuriant, there is just the self, and emotion and anxieties are deep. If a person's reward or retribution is brought about based on feelings, and if, based on affections of the mind, a response is produced, in what does the reason of following nature have its foundation?"

Answer: "I think these two issues are a key point of your questions and the pivot of your argument. If the pivot is cleared, myriad doubts will be dispelled in the same way. People who begin to practice [Buddhism] will probably awaken to [the teaching] in accordance with this. It can be said that you clarify [people's] stagnant feelings in the realm beyond common knowledge and offer unexplored wonderful advocacy. Nevertheless, Buddhism is deep and profound. It is hard to talk about its subtle language. If we do not [understand] the fundamental purport wholly, how can we speak of its profound purpose? Here, I would like to try to speak of what I have in my mind complying with the great ultimate law of Nature.

"If the fundamental reason why human beings receive a body is clarified through inferring from the nature of the four great elements, 'they borrow different substances, and pretend that the common form of the body is composed of them.'[401] Life is just like a particle of dust that is easily brushed away. Arising and extinguishing are just a change of [the vapor]. [In the temporary nature of life] like this, we should perceive truth through intelligence and insight and freely wield the sword of wisdom. So, if we take advantage of the movement, the coming and going, of nature, even though [the four great elements] gather together [to form the body] or scatter [to extinguish the body], this has nothing to do with the self. [When we see] a large number of bodies temporarily dwelling in a great dream,[402] they are actually in the realm of existence, but it is the same as if they were in the realm of nonexistence. How could it be the case that we are blocked by what we receive (i.e., the body) and bound by that for which we feel a persistent attachment (i.e., life)?

"If one comprehends this reason in one's mind and yet other people have not understood it, he feels sad about the fact that he alone has attained the truth without having achieved [saving others]; he is grateful to have become 33c
awakened before others and gives rise to the thought [of leading others to Buddhism]. Then, since he hopes to propagate the [Buddhist] Way and clarify the teaching, the virtue of benevolence comes into existence. If both others and

myself attain [the Buddhist Way] equally, there is no opposition in our minds. Then, when we freely wield a sword, we will unite ourselves [with the Buddhist Way] and observe [all things] with the tranquil mind; even when we engage in battle, all whom we encounter are friends [since we have no opposition in our minds]. If someone tries to injure us, it is not only that we will have no harm in the spirit; it is also possible that there is indeed no life to be destroyed [from the beginning].

"This is exactly [why] when Mañjuśrī placed his hand on a sword[403]—the action is wrong, but the principle [behind performing this action] is right—and although he brandished his weapon all day long, there was no place to catch the sword. If this is the case, it is brought to realization that the mysterious [works of the universe] are put to the best use by stimulating [diagrams and symbols as stated in the *Book of Changes*],[404] or the education [of the barbarian people] is accomplished through [performing a dance while] holding a shield and a battle ax, [just as was done by Yao and Shun].[405] Even though the achievement covers [all things, just as Heaven and Earth do], no [secular] reward is especially given. Why are sin and punishment brought into question? If we return to this point (i.e., that those who realize the Way go beyond reward or retribution), and look for the fundamental [law], then we will be able to clarify [the meaning of] reward and retribution [in the Buddhist sense]. If we analyze from the phenomenal world and seek the ultimate law of Nature, then we will be able to discuss sin and punishment [in the Buddhist sense]. I will try to explain this more.

"When cause and condition affect together and a change arises, wouldn't they be derived from the [fixed] law? Ignorance is an abyss of delusion. Greed and attachment is a mansion of numerous sufferings. When these two (i.e., ignorance and greed and attachment) work together, supernatural effects occur in the unseen world. Good fortune and ill, occasion for repentance or regret, all simply arise here.[406] Since the function of ignorance covers up that of intelligence, feelings and thoughts stick to external objects. Since greed and attachment wash away [human] nature, the four great elements unite and form a physical body. When the body is formed, there is discrimination between self and others. When feelings stick to [external objects], there is subjective [discrimination] between good and evil. When there is discrimination between self and others, we favor ourselves and are never unaware of self-existence. When there is subjective [discrimination] between good and evil, we feel a persistent attachment to life, and [the transmigration of] birth [and death] never ceases. Thereafter, we sleep soundly in a great dream, we are confused in the midst of delusions, we suffer doubts in the long night of spiritual darkness, and we cling to whatever exists. Therefore, loss and gain come alternately, and weal and woe visit us one after another. For accumulated evils, disasters spontaneously come from Heaven; for committed sins, punishments [are inflicted] in Hell. This is precisely an inevitable destiny, and it leaves no room for doubt.

"Why is this so? There is the foundation to understand it; that is to say, in the law [cause and effect] spontaneously cope with each other in the unseen world. Even though its [outward] sign is obscure, when its force reaches an extreme point it becomes evident. Consequently, good and evil in the mind are considered to be [like] a form and a voice, and happiness and suffering as reward and retribution are considered to be [like] the shadow [of the form] and the sound [of the voice]. The foundation (i.e., the mind) is moved by feelings, and then the response (i.e., reward and retribution) spontaneously arises. Would there be officials of Hell? It is because [people] mismanage [their minds] and lose the [proper] way. In that case, happiness and suffering as the response (i.e., reward and retribution) are merely due to [the mind], which is moved [by feelings]. Since [the mind] is moved and [a situation] becomes so, it is called Nature. Nature is simply nothing but the shadow and sound of the self. What achievement would even a Creator of the Universe have [in this matter]?

"Let me examine the essential points of your questions and analyze them with the realities. In the purpose of your criticism, you completely agree that earth, water, fire, and wind unite and form a physical body, which is taken as a dwelling of the spirit. This precisely means that there is a master in the house. I will ask you a question. While the master (i.e., the spirit) stays in the house (i.e., the body), does he have feelings or not? If your answer is no, he does not, the uniting of the four great elements [to form a body] is not due to the master of the house having been moved. If [the master] lives [in the house] without feelings, since [the uniting of the four great elements] is not derived from the result of the master [of the house] having been moved, even if the spirit dwells in a physical body he has no feeling and no perception, such as

pain or an itch. If the spirit has no perception and the house has no pain or
34a itchiness, either, when it makes contact with other things, [the situation] is like mowing grass or cutting trees. It does not make sense.

"If [the master (i.e., the spirit)] has feelings, the uniting of the four great elements [to form a physical body] is due to the fact that the master was moved [by feeling]. If [the master] stays [in the house] with feelings, since [the uniting of the four great elements] is due to the fact that he was moved, while the spirit dwells in the house it must have perception of pain or itchiness. The spirit has perception and the house feels pain and itchiness as well. When it makes contact with other things, it certainly cannot be the same as water and fire in the realm of nature.

"Speaking from this basis, spirit and body differ from each other, but they change together. They really differ from each other in the fact that [the spirit] is inside and [the body] is outside, but they are joined together. Except for those who reach the point of view [of the fundamental law], who could discern the relation between [spirit and body]? If one cannot discern this, simply the more time passes, the more deluded he will be. Generally, among those who receive a body and accept life, there is not one who is not like this. Since we receive [body and life] and we are like this, everyone is blocked by having a persistent attachment to the self. If the root of the blockage is not pulled out, [attachment to] the way to continue to exist will become firmer. If the origin of the persistent attachment [to the self] is not removed, [the desire] to maintain [life] will become deeper as well.

"In the case where a thing goes athwart [in our daily life], the mind becomes deranged; not to mention the case where the whole body is totally lost. Accordingly, when friends and foes mutually take advantage of a chance and are estranged from each other, unless the evil intention is removed, animosities arise and never cease. Even if one has exhausted happiness, receives annoyance, and has no regret in the mind, since a form and a voice (i.e., one's acts) are set forth, their shadow and sound (i.e., reward and retribution) spontaneously manifest. There is nothing fixed beforehand in reason, but the laws [of acts and reward and retribution] come together and make it so. Even though we want to escape from it, how can we do so? This is exactly to invite reward and retribution in accordance with feelings, or to produce responses by availing oneself of being moved. [You and I] fundamentally differ from each other in the purpose of our arguments. Therefore, we are simply not the same in understanding [the reason]."

Question: "If, since people's feelings cling to life and cannot cause death, then that feelings are brought into existence is simply derived from the delusion of egoistic attachment. [The Buddha] should clarify this by his transcendent view and let [people] understand it by the right path. Could it be possible, [without doing so,] to conform to [sentient beings'] delusion and consider [the delusion] as the object of retribution?"

Answer: "That phenomena arise is indeed derived from the mind. Retribution must be derived from the phenomena [that are derived from the mind]. Hence, if we observe phenomena through retribution, the phenomena can be changed. If we are strict with the mind through seeing phenomena, the mind can return [to the right path]. Inferring from this point of view, we know that the Sage (i.e., the Buddha) clarifies the object of retribution based on delusion and obstruction; it is not to conform to [sentient beings'] delusion and consider [the delusion] as the object of retribution, [as you said]. Why is this so? It is difficult for people to be awakened and [this fact] has indeed existed for a long time.[407] For this reason, in Buddhism, on the basis of what it is derived from, the teaching is certainly given little by little. Since [the Buddha] knows that longtime habits cannot be given up immediately, he first teaches that [retribution and reward are caused by] evil acts and meritorious deeds. [Retribution and reward caused by] evil acts and meritorious deeds cannot be totally forgotten. Therefore, he has [people] weigh the value [of retribution and reward]. If they assess which is valuable, [reward caused by] meritorious deeds or [retribution caused by] evil acts, they examine good and evil and [through this examination] place their mind [in good]. If [they know] good and evil are blocked by egoistic attachment, they [abandon the egoistic attachment], and advance the ego a step further in order to lead other people to [salvation]. If these two issues (i.e., examining good and evil and advancing the ego a step further in order to lead others to salvation) are concurrently developed, nothing binds the feelings. Accordingly, we will be able to 'honor the talented and virtuous, bear with all people,'[408] be benevolent to ourselves, give peace [to others], and ponder far ahead the reward and retribution that are like shadow and sound, in order to relieve ourselves from the delusive realm of transmigration of birth and death. Once delusive feelings

are dispelled, later words about the right path can be understood, and the
34b defilement to maintain life can be cut off. Since even wise people of the middle class cannot cut off the defilement to maintain life, how would people of ordinary intelligence be able to accomplish this?"

The *Discourse on Three Periods of Reward and Retribution* (*Sanbaolun*), Composed for Those Who Doubt That There is No Testimony [of Reward or Retribution] Corresponding to Good or Bad Conduct, by Dharma Teacher [Hui]yuan

It is stated in a Buddhist scripture that there are three different periods in which [good or evil] actions mature and bring about [their effects], reward or retribution: the first is reward or retribution of the present existence, the second is that of the next existence, and the last is that of an existence after the next. The reward or retribution of the present existence refers to that for a good or evil [act] begun in one's present life, [reward or retribution] is given to him in the present existence. The reward or retribution of the next existence refers to that [for a good or evil act begun in one's present life, reward or retribution] is given in one's next existence. The reward or retribution of an existence after the next refers to that [for a good or evil act begun in one's present life, reward or retribution] is given after the second, the third, the hundredth, or the thousandth existence from the present existence.

There is no subject that receives [reward or retribution other than the mind]; receiving [reward or retribution] must be due to [the good or evil of] the mind. The mind has no fixed task; it is moved by phenomena and responds to them. Since in its response there is [velocity], fast and slow, reward or retribution comes early or later. Even though there is variation in the time of its occurrence, following what the mind encounters, all reward and retribution respond to it. Since there is variation in the strength of response [of reward or retribution], [they] are not the same in relative gravity. This is exactly natural reward and punishment, and the outline of the three periods of reward or retribution. Unless people have the all-around talent, intelligence, and brightness to reach the essential point [of the Buddhist Way], it is rare to be able to enter the gate [of this doctrine]. Regarding those in the level below them, probably there are people who experience for the first time the right path, who awaken taking a precursor as a guidepost, who broadly take account of Buddhist scriptures, who [are sharp enough to] ask a question on the remaining three corners [when they are told about one corner],[409] who consider the virtuous to be their teachers and friends, and who improve their natures through learning. These people may be able to speak a little about [this doctrine]. Let me try to discuss it.

Good and evil arise through being gradually fostered [for a long time]. When they are gradually [fostered and eventually] reach an extreme, [they become evident]. There is [a traditional] theory [in China] on the nine grades of [good and evil]. Generally, what is included in [the classification of] the nine grades is not what reward or retribution of the present existence regulates. In that case, it can be known that reward or retribution of the present existence is beyond the ordinary classification, and the classifications other than the nine grades are not what the three periods of reward or retribution regulate. Why is this so? If advantages and disadvantages intersect in front of one's eyes and suddenly a dispute arises between them, the mechanics of the spirit spontaneously move and take action before thinking. If it takes action before thinking, reward or retribution responds to [the action] immediately. This is one example of reward or retribution of the present existence that is beyond the theory of the nine grades.

Moreover, the three kinds of acts (i.e., of body, speech, and mind) are different from each other in essence, but the same in regard to having fixed [reward or retribution]. Since [having] reward or retribution is fixed, people must receive them when the time comes. This is not something we can remove by prayer or avoid through intellectual power. When we infer and investigate this thoroughly, [we know that] the significance is deep and the law is extensive. Since it cannot be examined in detail, I briefly stated the characteristics. Through [my explanation of] this, those who participate in Buddhism will be able to understand [the issue of reward and retribution].

There are people in the world who encounter misfortunes even though they accumulate good deeds, and there are people who do evil deeds and yet are happy. These are all cases in which the reward or retribution of the present existence has not yet come and the response to actions one took in a previous existence has begun to manifest. Therefore, it is said that a person of a good

omen encounters a disaster, while someone of an unlucky omen meets happiness. A suspicion regarding the ambiguous issue [of reward or retribution] arises here. Why is this so? There are those who intend to lend a helping hand to the monarch, aid the conditions of the times, save other people, model themselves after the lofty traces [of the wise], and make up their minds to render a [great] achievement, and yet who collapse in the middle of a great enterprise and are suddenly visited by heavenly disasters; or there are those who live leisurely in [a humble house with] a gate made out of only one beam, who have no attachment to the secular world, who consider a peaceful walk to be [equal to traveling in] a carriage, who live in comfort, and yet who encounter an undesirable fate unexpectedly when the destined time comes, who come to associate with and fall into secular ways and secular customs, and who [eventually] become accustomed to [the secular life]; or
34c there are those whose names are known to be among the top of [the ten virtuous people of] the four subjects (i.e., virtuous principles and practice, ability of speech, administrative talents, and literary acquirements) [of Confucianism], who have mastered the heart of the Way, who have perfect love, who have realized benevolence, and who develop virtue through cherishing the highest wholesomeness. Among people like this, there are those who held [the vapor of] harmony and became ill, or who fulfilled [the way of] having faith and following it, and yet died young. These are all cases in which people encountered misfortune while they were achieving merit or virtue, and this causes [other people] to doubt [the mechanics of reward and retribution]. Since the fundamental reason is clear, we should examine the responses. Each response has its base (i.e., the mind), which moves by [external objects]. Although [the responses]—the favorable (i.e., happiness) and the unfavorable (i.e., misfortune)—differ from each other, the principle is simply the same.

The reason for this is that the situation in which [misfortune] stands close to [happiness, which] is lurking behind [misfortune], was settled a very long time ago, and the auspicious omen declared in the unseen world secretly keeps recurring. Therefore, the vapor of happiness and the vapor of misfortune alternately shift, while [the spirit transmigrates in] the six realms of existence. Reward and retribution for good or evil acts appear to be very disordered, but they work simultaneously. This causes both the ignorant and the wise to be equally confused when the response (i.e., reward or retribution) manifests as phenomena; to think that even though they accumulate good deeds there is no blessing, or if they accumulate evil deeds there is no misfortune; to be moved by the gods [of Heaven and Earth] and yet grieve at misfortune; and to lament that a heavenly disaster befalls a good person.

All [people] think that Confucianism covers everything completely and there is no ultimate law of Nature above it, and consequently this causes the Great Way to become obscured by the minor way. If we consider the correct words to be good guidance and seek the true [law] responding to the mind, we must arrive at [the fact] that there is no such case in the law of Nature. When we trace back to what causes it, [we find that] according to secular books [the issue of happiness and misfortune] is considered to be concerned with a single lifetime; anything beyond [a single lifetime] is not clarified. Since [the issue of happiness and misfortune] beyond [a single lifetime] has not been clarified, people who seek the law of Nature limit it to within [the sensual world] where they can see and hear. This is because monarchs of former times conformed to the people's minds, understood their temperaments, and took [the sensual world] [that can be experienced by] ears and eyes to be within a boundary, [leaving unclear the world beyond the boundary].

If we now combine the way for outside (i.e., Confucianism) and the way for inside (i.e., Buddhism) and seek the [sages'] intention to propagate their teachings, we will know that [both these teachings] must be the same in the ultimate law, and we will not be confused by many different paths and frightened at the differences between them. If we can look into the three periods of reward and retribution and view the distinction between those who are distressed and those who go smoothly, it will be entirely understandable why Confucius did not answer Zhong You's (i.e., Zilu's) [question about serving spirits] and Yan [Hui] and Ran [Boniu] were like ignorant people when they faced their sage teacher [Confucius].[410] It is also because there is the law of dependent arising from causation (Skt. *pratītyasamutpāda*) and the law of existence arising from causation (Skt. *pratītyasamutpanna*). Even though they were bright enough to be ready to enter the truth [of Buddhism], they still did not forget [the way of] benevolence bequeathed by [monarchs of former times], and they still considered the three periods of reward and retribution to be a beautiful garden; or they made rapid progress [to the lofty state of the mind] and yet did not leave behind the abyss (i.e., the realm of the three periods of reward and retribution).

From the viewpoint of inferring in this way, it is known that if the guests beyond the secular world (i.e., *śramaṇa*s) keep the wondrous Dharma in mind, cleanse their minds in the profound gate [of Buddhism], and obtain [the Buddhist doctrine] by inspiration at once, they can transcend to the uppermost state [of mind]. Although people like this may have accumulated misfortune in some previous life, even if they do not control their achievement, [the accumulated misfortune] will spontaneously be put to extinction, and they are not subject to the three periods of reward and retribution.

Speaking from this basis of why [the teaching expounded in] Buddhist scriptures surpasses Confucianism and is beyond [the teachings] of the nine philosophical schools [of China], would it not be because [Buddhism teaches] to reach the essence [of the Way] through governing the spirit, to train the mind, to trace completely the very source of the change, and to mirror myriad phenomena upon [the world of] no phenomena (i.e., the world of truth)?

End of Fascicle Five of *The Collection for the Propagation and Clarification* [*of Buddhism*]

Fascicle Six

The *Discourse to Elucidate the Refutation* (*Shibolun*) by Shi Daoheng (346–417)

During the Yixi era (405–418) of the Jin dynasty, according to what I have heard, the two wise men of the Jiangsu area, Yuan and He, got together to 35a
make a discourse on statecraft, and satirized the current administration. Even though I have not read this composition, its intention seems to be to ridicule the pitfalls of the world, modeling itself after the chapter on the "Five Kinds of Vermin" in the *Han Feizi,*[411] and they issued the *Discourse on the Five Kinds of Perversions. Śramaṇa*s, however, took no action [against this discourse] and it vulgarly lowers their case. I am afraid that [the discourse composed by Yuan and He] misleads people of the world and causes them to fall into vicious delusion eternally. I cannot stand the extremity of resentfulness and regret. Therefore, I would like to elucidate this through a discussion in the form of [questions and answers between] the guest and the host.

There was a gentleman who was controlled by Confucianism in a metropolis in the east, who cross-questioned an impudent rustic in an out-of-the-way place in the west.

He said, "I have heard that the Buddhist teaching is too deep to discuss on the basis of Confucianism; the style of the teaching is too profound to determine by physical methods; it is too refined, non-aggressive, simple, and distinctive to get involved in with common knowledge; it is too wondrous and beyond all existences; and it cannot be fathomed by ordinary thought. Consequently, [Buddhism] is often respectfully followed by sovereigns of the times and admired by the nobles, and then the common people crowd together, plight their faith, chime in, and quickly head [toward Buddhism]. All of them sigh together in admiration and praise the virtue [of the Buddha], saying 'If we are imbued with the refined taste [of Buddhism], we will reach the subtlety of its exquisite meaning. If we study the delicacy of its doctrine, we will be mysteriously harmonious in the function of the spirit, we will wash away the defilements of the mind, we will leave behind the shackles of the physical body, we will transcend the nuisances of mundane life of the place of confinement, and we will stay away from worldly duties and be aloof from the world. When we submerge in the true essence (i.e., awakening), even [Bo]yi and [Shu]qi would have no chance to surpass us in keeping integrity. When we abandon glorious favor, even Chao[fu, a recluse during the time of Emperor Yao,] and Xu [You, a philosopher during the time of Emperor Yao,] would have no chance to go beyond us in determination. When we taste the profound tenet [of Buddhism], even Yan [Hui] and Ran [Boniu] would have no chance to join us in the practice. When we leave behind disorder and impurity, even [Chi]song[zi] and [Wangzi]qiao, [immortals of ancient times,] could not compare with us in purity.' If things are truly just as have been spoken, there is no flaw in reason.

"Now, however, when I observe all *śramaṇa*s, [I feel that] they are all lacking in talent; they live gregariously and they are vulgar. I have not seen anyone outstanding [among them]. They are confused and indistinguishable, just like a river in which the [muddy] water of the Jing River and the [clear] water of the Wei River have merged. They are disordered, just as if perfume and *you* (i.e., *caryopteris divaricata*), [the foul-smelling water plant,] are put in the same box. If the source of the water is clean, the stream must [also] be clear. If the root [of a plant] is deep, its branches and leaves will certainly be luxuriant. Examining the speech and behavior [of *śramaṇa*s], they are not logical all the time. Examining their whole aspect, there is almost nothing to compare with [their disorderliness]. The reason I am surprised at them is precisely derived from these points. Just as the [Yellow] Emperor forgot that he is intelligent, and Ju Liang forgot that he has [great] physical strength,
35b [when they heard about the Way], they all became sages by being forged in a furnace and hammered or molded.[412] If 'the Way is not to be practiced in vain,' [as is stated in the *Book of Changes,*][413] the talent [for propagating Buddhism] must correspond to the capacity [of sages]. If so, since *śramaṇa*s have left their homes, renounced the world, and attend to their own ambitions in a lofty spirit,[414] they must go against their blood relations, abandon the secular value of glory, disfigure themselves, abide by the precepts, study the doctrines earnestly, take refuge in the Dharma wholeheartedly, sit easily stretching out their legs, and content themselves with a vegetarian diet. Even if their virtuous deeds are outstanding, they become esteemed by [the people

of] the time, their appearance and deportment are peaceful and majestic, and they serve as a good example to the people, even then they are in fact dark in everything and good for nothing.

"Why is their behavior contemptible and ignoble while they have such lofty [ambitions]? They never weary in seeking [fame and profit]; they are anxious, lacking even temporary peaceful relaxation. Some reclaim land and cultivate it in agriculture, living like farmers. Some peddle or engage in trade widely and compete with many others for profit. Some conduct medical practice and hastily treat illness with cold or heat.[415] Some devise tactics with heretics in order to benefit their occupation. Some practice divination by directions and time and speak recklessly about the auspicious and the inauspicious. Some go against the Way, avail themselves of authority, and skillfully curry favor of the time. Some hoard and save to nourish themselves excessively. Some talk idly pointing at their palms and consume [the fruit of] the common people's labors without moving from their own place. This is all because [*śramaṇa*s] are not equipped with virtue and their behavior is often against the Dharma. Even if they may temporarily have a good point, how much could it help to elevate their reputation? They should abolish these [behaviors] by themselves and standardize their customs. [Their present conduct] is futile for the political affairs of the time, and harmful to the study of the Way. This is what people who lead a virtuous life detest deeply, and what concerns greatly those who rule over the state.

"Moreover, there are five kinds of perversions in the world and *śramaṇa*s are included among them. The basis to clarify this is that *śramaṇa*s skillfully devise expedients and instigate ignorant secular people; one way [they do this] is to give parables to induce the people, and the other is to coerce them. [*Śramaṇa*s] say, 'If you do evil deeds, you will certainly have misfortune for successive *kalpa*s. [On the other hand,] if you cultivate good deeds, you will have eternal blessing.' They say that those who are sinful will be investigated in Hell, and those who have merit will be helped by deities. They earnestly encourage and lead the people, exhorting them to do what they ordinarily cannot do. They force people to improve themselves and urge them to do what they usually cannot do. [As a result,] in the worst case one will reduce [one's] support for one's parents, and the least bad case is that one will decrease the share [of living costs] for one's wife and children. At a gathering of [*śramaṇa*s] they have the best feast. Buddhist temples run the gamut of splendor.

"[*Śramaṇa*s] make off with people's valuable items; they waste more money on useless things; they use up others' personal annual savings; and they cause a deficiency of funds for the state and military. In vain they raise their voice for the future; they pursue the formless before it shows a sign of manifestation. When we listen to their statements, they sound great and fill our ears. When we look at their appearance, they look aloof and fill our eyes. [Yet] if I seek evidence [for their greatness] through examining actual facts, I have not seen any indication of it at all. It is truly as it is said: 'Even though one tries to keep his shadow tied up, he catches [only] the wind.'[416] I have no clue to [understanding them]. This is clearly what I have not been content with and what the learned are very confused about. If you have good information on [this matter], please let me humbly receive it. If I attain realization even for the time being, I will be able to leave behind this hindrance eternally."

The host was disappointed [with the guest's account]. After awhile he
35c lamented with a long sigh and said, "What a strange story! How vile your account is! The reason it is impossible for a vulgar [person] to talk about the Great Way is that he is hampered by the appearance of things, and the reason it is impossible to explain the ultimate way to obscure people is that they adhere to the letter. Here, I will briefly illustrate one corner [of a subject] for you,[417] so that you can think and return to the ultimate Way.

"Now, when the Sage teaches, he gives the Dharma according to the capacity [of the recipient]. Since there is a limit to people's capacity to accept [the Dharma], edification is given gradually. Conscience is recorded even if it is [as minor as] the tip of a hair. A mean and stingy frame [of mind] is omitted even if it is [as large as] a hill or a ravine. Even a very minor virtuous act becomes eternally one's own property. Even a momentary meritorious act results in [an object of] mysterious exertion in the end. When one begins turning over a bamboo basket of earth, we cannot blame him [because] he aims to achieve the making of a mountain.[418] When one is about to proceed to the ultimate state of mind (i.e., enlightenment), we cannot slander him [because of] the fact [that he is completely prudent just as] he ties up a sack.[419] On the other hand, the reason a sea is said to be great is because there is no clamor for excessive cleanliness. The reason the Way is said to be obscure in trace is because there is no astonishing appearance.

"Loving parents and being affectionate to a wife and children are attachments of the people who possess a mind, but *śramaṇas* abandon these, just as they take off their shoes. Fame, social status, wealth, and carnal pleasure are what people of the world value, but *śramaṇas* regard those things [as being as insubstantial as] rice bran. It can be said that they put up with what people cannot leave behind. This indicates the lofty and refined taste and the excellent task to propagate the [Buddhist] Way, yet you say that [*śramaṇas*] are dark [in everything]. Isn't this a statement of very good appreciation? Moreover, if your ambition and actions are not the same [as those of *śramaṇas*], your course to proceed differs from [that of *śramaṇas*]; wheel tracks separate at the fork in the road. Then [you and *śramaṇas*] do not mutually understand. Since you have not seen any outstanding points [of *śramaṇas*], [your unflattering account] is simply a natural consequence. It is quite natural that the ancients often lamented that it is difficult [to obtain] people of talent.[420]

"The Zhou dynasty is known for having many scholars; there were ten talented vassals who helped their monarch (i.e., King Wu) in administration. During the halcyon days of Emperor Yao and Emperor Shun, there were eight virtuous men [for Gaoxin] and eight gentlemen [for Gaoyang]. Confucius had three thousand [talented disciples]. They were all of outstanding ability in the country, but those who were selected to become proficient in the four subjects (i.e., virtuous deeds, speech, administration, and writing) were less than ten people. Among them, [Ran] Boniu had an incapacitating disease,[421] [Yan] Hui had [one of] the six extreme evils (i.e., an early death),[422] [Zi]shang (i.e., Zixia) was stingy,[423] [Zi]si (i.e., Zigong) was interested in [hoarding commodities] to make a profit,[424] [Zai] Yu was [compared to rotten wood that] cannot be carved,[425] [Zhong] You (i.e., Zilu) was fierce and obstinate,[426] [Ran] Qiu imposed heavy taxes [on the people] and was incompetent in his official post,[427] and although Zhong Gong was [as good as] a red[-horned] cow, he was born from [a man who was nothing more than] a brindled oxen.[428] Nevertheless, the whole world praises their virtues, which became the foundation for the principles of human relationships; and respects their lofty tracks, which became examples for the gentry. The people admire their footsteps for a hundred generations, and revere their great conduct for a thousand years.

"With regard to *śramaṇa*s, they torture themselves [until it is] as if their muscles were to drop off, and cruelly treat themselves like worthless things. Would this be the way widely practiced and a well-intentioned argument for gentlemen? This is compared to the case where a deluded man goes into the workshop of Gongshu Ban [of Lu state] and does not praise [Gongshu Ban's] skillful guidance, yet jeers that a worker of poor skill has injured his hand. It can truly be said that such a person stoops to vulgar thought and has a base frame of mind.

"Formerly a prime minister asked a guest, 'It is commonly said that an owl eats its mother. Could such a thing occur?' The guest replied, 'I have heard only that a benevolent crow repays [its parents for their kindness in] raising it.' The prime minister felt sorry and ashamed of his improper question. Isn't your present state of mind similar to that of the prime minister who asked the question? Gentlemen refrain from [talking about anothe person's] evildoing but [instead] cite his good points. On the contrary, what have you said?

"Furthermore, you said, '[*Śramaṇa*s] sit easily stretching out their legs.'
36a Since the forest and countryside are deserted, they often have to worry about insurgents. [But if they live near] a bustling city, they are often inflicted with the carping criticism of companionship [with secular people]. If they stay in an inappropriate place, they invite the nuisances of the secular world. If they hover around a rural community, they risk a [disparaging] comment from the people of the world. Anyway, there is nothing good [in this]. They are just driven to the wall. Even though the universe is vast, they do not know where to stay.

"Again, you said, '[*Śramaṇa*s must content themselves with] a vegetarian diet.' Well, there is deficiency of supply in this world; there are indeed no accumulated stores [of food] in hills and valleys. When they take just a necessary amount of food, they once again use it in accordance with the Dharma. What they face is complicated. On what basis can they support themselves?

"Even at the dignified time of sages, there were people (i.e., Boyi and Shuqi) who starved to death at [the foot of] Mount Shouyang. When the world was peaceful and brilliant people were promoted, there was a man (i.e., Lu Zhonglian) who went to the sea and died there.[429] What do you think [about these incidents]?

"Furthermore, since *śramaṇa*s have no feathers on their bodies, they cannot live being naked without clothes, and since their bellies are not gourds, they cannot let them hang down [like gourds], without eating. As long as [their desire for food and clothes] does not reach the extreme, they must have support. When the harvest is good, they can take enough [as offerings] from the common people. When it is bad, they do their best to support themselves [by secular ways]. This is really not proper, but it cannot be helped. Consequently, if a viper bites one's hand, [the hand] is cut off in order to save the body. This is because we ponder what is more important and maintain the more important thing.

"Even though one may make a living for himself, if he does not seek anything, he has nothing to obtain; and if he seeks something, it is not necessarily that he uses only one method [to seek]. When he gives relief to himself, if [his purpose] is reasonable, why does he have to reject many methods? [*Śramaṇa*s] consider that everything within the boundary of desires is troublesome and vile, and cause [their desires] to not move recklessly. Why [is it said that] they exceedingly attach [to things]?

"Long ago, Bocheng [Zigao] reclaimed land and cultivated it by himself,[430] [Chang] Ju and [Jie] Ni ploughed side by side and practiced agriculture,[431] Tao Zhu[gong] engaged in trade and made a living,[432] Yuling irrigated a vegetable garden in order to support himself,[433] Cui Wen[zi] sold medicines and led a life of poverty,[434] [Yan] Junping used to practice divination to augment his insufficent income,[435] Zhang Heng won fame for the art of divination,[436] and Ma Jun gave full display to his achievement (i.e., making a compass chariot, which shows the correct direction) of marvelous skills. These are simply people who went against the secular world and led the life of recluses. However, it has not been positively observed that they cut off all relationships to the secular world and stayed far away from people of the world, and yet [the people of the world] all sigh in admiration and do not stop praising them.

"Nevertheless, it often happens that among *śramaṇa*s, those whose conduct surpasses that of many people and who feel shame at associating with fellows of a sort are numerous. As for [*śramaṇa*s] who master the Way, who enter nirvana, or who transcend the secular domain, their numbers are incalculable.

You, however, have not mentioned anything [about these *śramaṇa*s]. Why do you have a partial view? You should view [*śramaṇa*s] based on inspecting the facts. You cannot make a discussion separating the present from the past, and you cannot make an expression dividing a small number from the larger number. The rare and the simple are noble, while the numerous and the lewd are humble. This is, I am afraid, not a discussion intended to seek the essence and examine a theorem.

"You said, '[*Śramaṇa*s] should abolish these [behaviors] by themselves and standardize their customs.' What do you mean by this? The sage (i.e., Confucius) did not deceive us [regarding the fact that there was one sincere person in a hamlet of] ten families.[437] If you do something with two others, they must serve you as your teachers.[438] When fragrant orchids are completely luxuriant, if you were to collect, pile up, and burn them, wouldn't this too be atrocious? Among [*śramaṇa*s], there are spontaneously those whose virtue is profound and whose capacity is expected by the times. Some are outstandingly pure and live uprightly; some contemplate, enter into subtlety, and pacify their spirits in the absolute state [of mind]; some expound subtle words, clarify obscurity, and explain problematic points; and some diligently devote
36b themselves to meritorious deeds, exhort for the edification [of others], and esteem wholesomeness.

"Generally, the foundation of the Buddhist monastic life lies in the day of tonsure, when they all individually make an oath, in mind and in words, with genuine feelings and the highest sincerity. Even though life and death are completely associated and the profound path is long and far, [the monks] must urge themselves [to proceed]. Then, they will certainly be on the way leading to [the goal]; the glory of the golden wheel-turning king [who rules the four continents of the world] will be disregarded as if it were dust and dirt; and the importance of Śakra-devendra, [lord god of Trāyastriṃśa Heaven,] will be slighted as if it were rice bran. Everyone is earnest and sincere at the beginning and has reasons of his own. Naturally [the Way] is, [however,] neither suddenly attained at a stroke nor perfectly mastered. How could there not be a minor fault in the course of time?

"Moreover, when you take up the true element and briefly mention [the reality of] the universe, why do you unite everything together without examining and distinguishng them? We cannot execute the entire Ji clan [of the Zhou dynasty] because of the fault made by Guan[shu] and Cai[shu],[439] and we cannot exile all the men of the court [of Emperor Shun] because of the four villains (i.e., Gonggong, Huandou, Sanmiao, and Gunyu) who committed cruel conduct.[440] This is no different from the case where a man who suffers from head lice wants to burn his own head along with the lice, or the case of a man who is troubled by irritation on his legs consequently wants to remove all the parts of his body below the hips. Isn't this also excessive?

"You said, '[Their present conduct] is futile for the political affairs of the times, and harmful to the study of the Way.' When those who propagate the Way benefit the world, common people act daily according to it, yet have no knowledge of it. Therefore, regarding the edification of *wuwei,* Laozi says, 'The people all said, "We are as we are, of ourselves!"'[441] This statement is appropriate. Hence, [Duan]gan Mu slept peacefully and yet Wei state was well governed.[442] Gengsang [Chu] was good at instructing and [the people in the area of] Mount Weilei [of Lu state] submitted themselves to his virtue.[443]

"Presently in their lifetimes *śramaṇa*s really have no achievements for which the government could assess value, but they do in fact confer an invisible benefit in the sphere beyond Confucianism. Taking a familiar [example], to instruct the people through the five precepts is not on the same [low] level of [giving instructions through] the Six Classics [of Confucianism]. Taking profound [examples], the hidden severity of the eight difficulties is not equal to [the sternness of] the criminal code; to engage in evaluating sins according to the Buddhist canon is not the same as [evaluating according to] the laws and regulations [of the secular world]; to speak of delusions with transcendental wisdom is not the same sense as do Laozi and Zhuangzi. Regarding the cause and condition of purity (Skt. *anāsrava*) and uprooting suffering in the [thirty-seven] elements to attain enlightenment (*daopin*), 'we occupy our thoughts, but do not discuss anything.'[444]

"In the teaching of the Duke of Zhou and Confucius, the doctrine is put to the best use in appearance, while in the highest level of the ultimate Dharma (i.e., Buddhism) the issue about the spirit is simultaneously managed in detail. Regarding quality and ranking, [these two teachings] cannot be spoken of in the same breath in terms of which is superior and which is inferior.

"In ancient times [in India,] Bei helped with the edification and assisted in governing the state by means of the [Buddhist] Way.[445] [Consequently,] the border regions of the state were peaceful, the people knew righteousness [that they had to follow], the harvest was rich and preserved, and there was no disaster. What do you mean by saying that [Buddhism] does not benefit [the world]?

"You said, 'There are five kinds of perversions in the world and *śramaṇa*s account for one of them.' Generally, what perversion means is to have no will to work, to be unspeakably self-indulgent; to gamble, dissipating one's fortune and ruining one's family property; to register one's name in the household register and yet wander around at all times of the year; to neglect the duties of office while receiving pay and not be willing to apply one's mind to anything; to hold the reins of government and be in power, and yet exploit the common people; to compete for promotion and incur both public and private losses; or to indulge in violence, vice, and cruelty and engage in conspiracy. All of these damage the teaching, disturb order, and greatly harm the customs of the world. As a result of this, Xun Yue wielded his pen and his discourse on the chivalrous (i.e., the *Shenjian*) came into existence. Han Fei took up a brush and the composition on the "Five Kinds of Vermin" was completed. It is, therefore, suitable to consider these to be perversions, but isn't it a false accusation to apply this to *śramaṇa*s?

"Our nation is just now competing with the times of Emperor Yao and
36c Emperor Shun for lofty virtue as the primary goal, and trying to equal the Yin and Zhou dynasties in elegant education as the secondary goal. They do not allow Mount Ji and the Ying River, [where Xu You and Chaofu lived in seclusion,] to be occupied exclusively by guests who look down upon the world (i.e., recluses), or for Mount Shang [where the four old men lived in seclusion] and the Luo River to be designated only for honored recluse-guests. [Our nation] intends to greatly encourage the style of hermits, and to honor and respect [all of] those who transcend the secular world.

"When I examine what you think, [I find that] as regards managing and operating the government of the time, you want to follow mean and crafty methods, like those of the tiger and the wolf, which were employed by the ruined Qin dynasty; and you want to inherit the cruel and harmful pattern that Shangjun (i.e., Shang Yang) carried out. They burned the books on the Chinese classics and buried Confucian scholars alive; they did not have the discipline to rule the country. By establishing very heavy taxation, each household had no unbudgeted extra money, and by setting up prohibitions for miscellaneous minor matters, they treated the people as if they were bandits. [Consequently,] the world became unhappy, and the people felt no interest in their lives. [This] caused the Ying family (i.e., the royal family of the Qin dynasty) to come to an end in three generations. The disaster caused by the two men (i.e., Shang Yang and Han Fei) was ended during their lifetimes. On the very day they were being punished, they repented for the first time that the law they had established was wrong. Originally they wanted to pacify the country and make the people harmonious. They did not expect that the bank they had built was too high and harsh, and did not hold living space for themselves, to the contrary of [their initial plan]. The incident had already happened. What did they attain by their grief?

"You said, 'The basis to clarify this is that *śramaṇa*s skillfully devise expedients and instigate ignorant secular people; one way [they do this] is to give parables to induce the people, and the other is to coerce them.' In sentient beings' relation to [the Buddha,] there are strength and weakness, and also in their abilities, there are sharpness and dullness. In understanding, there are difficulty and ease. In practices, there are shallowness and depth. Hence, the way to explain and teach varies. The causes to inspire beings to awaken differ. They melodiously try to cause them to follow wholesomeness. This is precisely a key phrase in the use of schemes and power, and a bridge for a marvelous salvation. It really does not mean to induce and coerce the people.

"You said, '[They (i.e., *śramaṇa*s) say that] those who are sinful will be investigated in Hell, and those who have merit will be helped by deities.' All wholesomeness belongs to those who possess virtue and who are the most sincere. The *Book of Changes* states, 'Those who tread [the path of] sincerity and admire docility will be given help from Heaven. There will be good fortune, advantage in every respect.'[446] Furthermore, it is said [in the *Zhuangzi*] that if those who do what is not good in darkness and secrecy, spirits will inflict the punishment.[447] Wouldn't this mean 'to be investigated in Hell and helped by deities'? Regarding reward or retribution for good or evil, there are indeed [many] testimonies [found] in Buddhist scriptures. I will not enumerate them here.

"You said, 'At a gathering of [*śramaṇa*s] they have the best feast. Buddhist temples run the gamut of splendor.' This is due to families who make good deeds [in order to win blessings]; they merely expend their wealth in order to prepare for future help, and they use up [their wealth] simply because they are making long-range plans for themselves. It does not seem that deities are delighted with the splendor [of temple buildings] and that all monks wish for delicious food. This is compared to when a farmer sows seed: he is keen in selecting [good] seeds in order to reap good-quality grain; or when a carpenter makes a building, he hopes to choose good timber when seeking the adornments of the building. Therefore, in agricultural operations it is necessary to plant in fertile soil, and in selecting a site for a residence it is important to choose high and dry ground. Hence, we know that the three revered ones are fields of merit for sentient beings,[448] and it is said that making offerings to them simply results in merit in the course of cultivating oneself.

"You said, '[*Śramaṇa*s] make off with people's valuable items; they waste more money on useless things.' To extensively confer benefits [to others] and love without distinction are great virtues of benevolent people. To respect and adorn the ancestral temple is [the manifestation of] the most sincere heart showing filial piety and respect [for one's ancestors]. Since in the worldly teaching (i.e., Confucianism) things are like this, in the [Buddhist] Way things are like this as well. 'Things are increased by being diminished.'[449] If we do something, we must obtain [a result]. Moreover, the wealth of this
37a transitory [world] is just like impure soil, but to give it graciously [to others] is a marvelous faculty. It is compared to the case that even a boat made of decayed wood is essential for ferrying people over [to the yonder shore]. Why is this seen as a waste of money? To intend to sit upright viewing nature [without doing anything], or to hope for comfort in silence with one's arms folded, is similar to wishing to cut wood without an ax or hoping to feel full without eating. How could this be possible?

"If one does not lead a virtuous life, that is his own problem. Why is it necessary to cover the common people's ears and eyes and conceal the great virtue of the world? You have already drunk poison and now you want to poison others. Why are you so cruel? It can be said that you ruin yourself, entrap others, and cause everyone to suffer from disasters. Therefore, for the blind, the deaf, and the dumb there is the disaster of being in a place without sight or sound for the completion of one whole *kalpa*, and as retribution to Devadatta, there is the experience of suffering in Avīci Hell.

"You said, 'They (i.e., *śramaṇas*) use up others' personal annual savings; and they cause a deficiency of funds for the state and military.' If a sage king manages the world, if simple and sincere customs spread far, if the whole wide world is united through shaking the rope of morality, and if many talented people are caught up by the spreading of a net of virtue, there will be no one who [laments] the striking waves of a river, there will be no scholar who grieves in a valley, all the four classes of people (i.e., scholars, farmers, artisans, and merchants) will be content with their occupations, each and every official of all ranks and descriptions will do his duty, [everyone in] the land within the [four] seas will be brought together and understood thoroughly, and the nine provinces (i.e., China) will be linked equally together. Then the war vehicles will cease to be dispatched, armed soldiers will run back [to their homes] and fertilize [the land], good grains will be piled up in the fields, food will be stored up even to the extent of some going rotten, the youth will improve in virtue day after day, the old will enjoy a long life, the people will all live together in peace and comfort and praise the great peace, and they will drum their bellies [signifying that they have had enough to eat,] and see the prosperous edification. Why are you unreasonably weak, worrying about the world even though you think deeply of various things? Isn't this also a gross fault? There is a saying that when a ranking official who is quite stingy and whose mouth is swollen faces the blue sea, [since he cannot drink the seawater because of his swollen mouth,] he just holds his stomach. This truly refers to you.

"You said, 'It is truly as it is said: "Even though one tries to keep his shadow tied up, he catches [only] the wind." I have no clue to [understanding them].' To disorder truth by using sophistry is something that the great sages lament. [When Bian He obtained unpolished jade in the mountains of Chu,] since the people did not recognize it is a precious stone [and thought that he was trying to deceive them], Bian He wept bitterly.[450] Nevertheless, the subtle purpose [of Buddhism] is delicate, and those who master it reach the Way. [The doctrine] is lofty and simple, and those who comprehend it attain [enlightenment. Buddhism] employs deep competence and functions as a bridge for ruined or drowned people to cross over to [the yonder shore]. It pulls [people] out from darkness and saves them from hindrance. The excellence of [the teaching] is always on a level to that of the time [when the Buddha resided in this world], and the edification has spread boundlessly. Therefore, when a mysterious light flashes once, it moves the trichiliocosm. When benevolence is sprinkled even for a short time, the whole land of China receives the favor. Hence, Śakra-devendra and the king of the Brahmā Heaven realized the deep purpose [of the teaching] and reverted to sincerity. Emperors and kings hope for the profound belief and consign themselves [to Buddhism]. The eight kinds of gods and demigods [who protect Buddhism] take the spiritual edification and reform themselves. The common people come in a hurry to observe the real deportment.

"Since [the Buddhist teaching] is lofty, it is not the same as Confucianism, the teaching for the secular world; and since it is so solemn, it is the profound path to transcend the secular world. Nevertheless, since the fence is steep and high, it is seldom that one can pass through the gate, and since the house is dark and deep, it is rare for people to enter its rooms. Therefore, the [Buddhist] Way saves those who are completely sunk in [delusion], but the doctrine is at variance with this. The virtue envelops all endlessly, but the fact is at a distance from this. Probably there is a reason why you obstinately hold on to wrong beliefs for your whole life and do not awaken until the end of your life.

"Even though the sun and moon ride in the sky, a blind man is not able
37b to see the brightness. Even if thunder shakes the earth, a deaf man is unable to hear the rumbling. Whose fault is this? To just now wish to comment on the notes *gong* and *shang* or to stain the appearance of a composition is really the worst fault.

"In ancient times, King Mucalinda recovered his eyesight as the [Buddha's] first disciple [at the Buddha's first sermon].[451] Subhadra listened to [the Buddha's sermon] as his last disciple.[452] What sin causes you to be so unfortunate as to harbor only suspicion throughout your life? Compared to what many people feel sad about, your case is the biggest problem."

Hereupon, [the guest] withdrew in a hesitant manner. He was in low spirits and disoriented. After a while he said, "I have just heard the doctrine of the Great Way, which completely follows in a continuous line from ancient times to the present, which greatly establishes the law of cause and condition, and which probes into the very point of principles and completely understands every nature. The establishment of the doctrine is not intended only for a specific period of time, nor is the propagation of the teaching expected [to occur] for only one generation. It can be said that one traces things to their beginning, understands them to their end, and returns to life. I have really been asleep, at a standstill, for the long night [of spiritual darkness]. Since I had not mastered the purpose [of Buddhism], I always cause hindrances. Now, fortunately, I have heard your discussion. My defilements have been dispersed and my doubts have been scattered. I have awakened all of a sudden, as if I had opened the layers of clouds and seen the bright sun, or as if I had taken off something that had covered me and realized true wisdom. I am truly not intelligent, but I will respectfully follow the excellent teaching."

The *Discourse to Rectify [the Argument on] the Two Teachings (Zheng erjiaolun)* by Ming Zhengjun

There is a Daoist monk who composed the *Discourse on the Non-Chinese and the Chinese*. Therefore, I composed this in order to correct [his argument].

Ming Zhengjun,
Sengshao

I came to know that this outstanding discourse of sharp words had an established reputation. Since I am afraid that the Sage (i.e., the Buddha) will be falsely accused and I would like to clarify the goals [of Buddhism and Daoism], I will first explain the phrases from two scriptures that [the Daoist monk] cited [in his discussion] and correct [his interpretation]. I earnestly hope that everyone can understand both [of these] profound teachings.

The *Discourse* states: "It is said in a Daoist scripture that Laozi arrived at Guanzhong (present-day Shensi province) and left for Kapilavastu in India, where the king's wife is called Māyā (Qingmiao). As [Māyā] was napping, Laozi availed of the essence of the sun and entered into Māyā's mouth. At midnight on the eighth day of the fourth month of the next year, he cut [Māyā's] right armpit open and was born. He landed on the earth and took seven steps forward. Then, he raised his [right] hand and pointed to the sky, saying, 'Holy am I alone throughout Heaven and Earth. The three realms of existence are full of suffering. How could we be happy?' Thereupon, the Buddhist Way arose. This event is found in the *Inner Section of the Mysterious and Sublime* (*Xuanmiao neipian*), which is an authentic scripture composed during the Han dynasty, not a far-fetched book."

I corrected this, saying, "The Daoist purpose of this is based on Laozi's scripture of two [chapters] (i.e., the *Laozi Daodejing*). The explanation about the mysterious and sublime is provided in seven chapters of [the *Inner Chapters* of the] *Zhuangzi,* and [the Daoist fundamental tenet is] to attain the One and master [the law of] the void thoroughly. There is nothing to hear regarding the wonders of the transformation of a body. [In the *Zhuangzi,*] Peng[zu] (a legendary official who was said to have lived eight hundred years) is equal in life span to a child who dies prematurely.[453] I have never seen that [this text] advocates immortality.

"Therefore, those who are in harmony with Heaven do not engage in changing normal ways, and they are content with their time and place themselves in order. Why would they seek a long life? If [Laozi] availed of the essence of the sun, entered into [Māyā's] mouth, cut [Māyā's] right armpit open, [and was born,] there is discrepancy between the time and the event. This is [a story] that combines various different tales under the pretense of a miracle. [The Daoist scripture composed during the Han dynasty] tells an imaginary story and preposterously speaks of deification. Absurd [statements made] during the Qin and Han dynasties extend to Wei and Jin times. The statement [of this Daoist scripture] does not follow [the law of] sages. How can you say that it is an authentic scripture?"

The *Discourse* states: "It is said in Buddhist scriptures that it has already been an immeasurably long time since the time the Buddha attained buddhahood, or that [the Buddha was] once the leader of the circle of Confucian scholars, the most reverend priest of the country, or a monk.[454] These are all derived from actual Buddhist scriptures, not expedient talks."

I corrected this, saying, "The foundation of Buddhism takes root in clarifying the ultimate teaching, and regarding the issue of three periods (past,
37c present, and future) there is nothing that can testify to it in secular ways. The way to enlightenment is not something that can manifest evidence. Nevertheless, at the point where the exquisite and the profound meet, there are internally signs of meditation and wisdom. When there is a reaction between condition

and sensation, the law of causation has nothing wrong externally. Śākyamuni gave the very fundamental cry of truth, and clarified the goal to which the Way of the Spirit leads. Consequently, to train one's essential [mind] and to examine the function of one's intelligence are not [equal to] the merit of preserving one's righteousness. In completing the way to the goal through minor virtue, [Buddhism] is different from [the teaching] that comes close to haughtiness. Salvation in the [Buddhist] Way lies in neglecting the physical body and what is valued is not to complete life. Since living life [for its own sake] is not valued, what merit is there in keeping existing things? In neglecting merit, merit manifests. In the tranquil state of complete extinction (i.e., nirvana), there is the regular course of the [Buddhist] Way. [Everything] comes out of non-beginning and enters into non-ending. All responses go to one [who has made causes]. Even an immeasurably long time is not that long. This is the teaching that [the Buddha] regards as [the Buddhist Way]."

The *Discourse* states: "The tenets of the two teachings (i.e., Buddhism and Daoism) are as if [two pieces of] a tally are matched."

I corrected this, saying, "Since the Buddha explains [the teaching for] the three periods, [the teaching] completely complies with all things boundlessly. Laozi only nourishes our physical body and his teaching dampens enthusiasm to the utmost. Therefore, in the teaching that is confined to issues about the physical body, [Laozi] does not discuss life in the other world. In the edification [of Buddhism] that completely complies with everything, it accordingly covers all things entirely. The Duke of Zhou, Confucius, Laozi, and Zhuangzi are truly teachers of emperors and kings, but they cannot provide testimony for the opinion we formerly read. [Buddhism and Daoism] are teachings that have different [strategic positions]. In addition, the testimony [that the tenets of the two teachings are as if two pieces of] a tally are matched is disregarded."

The *Discourse* states: "Daoism is precisely Buddhism; Buddhism is none other than Daoism."

I corrected this, saying, "Since there is a difference between the [two] teachings, just as there is between a square and a circle, how could we see them as the same? Those who follow Buddhism can firmly weigh [the teaching of] Laozi, but how can those who learn [the teaching of] Laozi take it to be the same as [that of] the Buddha? If [the compiler of the *Discourse*] presumes to compete with [Buddhism], trying to cling to the supremacy [of the teaching of Daoism], recklessly mixing up [the two teachings] through selecting and collecting [materials], and intends to establish the unorthodox and remove the orthodox based on the similarity [of the two teachings], then this is precisely that what should be learned is not what he has learned. He reveals himself to be a vermin of the Way. He seriously fails to know himself. He must be ashamed to face those who maintain their proper province."

The *Discourse* states: "[Since the Way is helpful to all in the world, it penetrates all areas, and since its knowledge embraces all things,[455] it governs all things. Since the areas] penetrated vary, the ways to govern [the areas] must differ. [The Way] causes each [of all things] to accomplish its nature and does not change its task."

Moreover, it states: "Some [sages] clarify the Five Classics and some spread [the teaching of] the three vehicles" and "They teach Chinese people in the Chinese language and edify non-Chinese in their native languages."

In addition, it states: "Buddhism and Daoism are equal in universally edifying, but there is a difference between the Chinese and the non-Chinese [in their objects of edification]."

I corrected these, saying, "He who is quietly inspired and attains thorough understanding must do everything smoothly. By a single voice, the Buddha lets [sentient beings] receive awakening, complying with each of their species. Would the teaching of the three vehicles be necessary to edify [only] the non-Chinese? Why does the Chinese way require strict adherence to the teaching of the Five Classics? In emptying one's mind and exerting oneself in accordance with affections of his mind, there is no difference between Chinese people and non-Chinese. How could differences in customs contradict [the teaching of] the Sage (i.e., the Buddha)? Although the areas penetrated [by the teachings] are not the same, the teachings are naturally equal."

The *Discourse* states: "[The full formal dress of] the black garment called *xuanduan* together with the cap called *weimao* and the formal dress for government officials are the garb of many Chinese people; while the trimmed hair and black garment [of a Buddhist monk] are the manner of dress of many non-Chinese people."

I corrected this, saying, "When we seek the valuable point of a principle, we should first base it on the manners and customs of the people. There are differences in the way to follow a tradition. It is simply an issue of the times. Therefore, the gentleman makes achievements beautifully, just as the leopard's spots become more beautiful [in autumn],[456] and the people's culture is first reformed. Zhuan Sun (i.e., Zichang) received an instruction [from Confucius], and lost his determination to learn about the Yin dynasty.[457] Regarding the 38a virtue of Emperor Shun and Emperor Wu [of the Zhou dynasty], Yao abdicated the throne [for Shun], and [Wu] expelled [Emperor Yang] from the throne by force of arms and made a different statute. Sages of later generations had achievements. Could there be a boundary between Chinese people and the non-Chinese?

"Moreover, is it necessary to adhere to the national dress in thinking through the ultimate teaching? Therefore, when we link [the manner of dress] to unchangeable sorts of things, our delusion becomes deep and our actions are stymied. Since water and land differ from each other, there are [different] methods of sending things to a distant place. The example of the boat and the carriage [found in the *Discourse*] cannot be considered well done. Moreover, [*śramaṇa*s, like] the one who carved a mark on the side of his boat [to indicate the place where he dropped his sword into water],[458] and [Daoist monks, like] the one who waited by the stump [where he previously had caught a hare], in the hope that other hares would come by that spot,[459] assuredly show two points to which we are led."

The *Discourse* says, "[Buddhist monks] abandon their wives and children in token of a minor degree and discontinue their ancestor worship in token of a major degree. They fulfill all things they desire with the politeness [of Confucianism], but they completely warp the rule of showing filial piety and respect for one's parents with the [Buddhist] Dharma. [Buddhists] go against virtue and offend the [right] order, and yet they have been unaware of this."

Moreover, it states: "To maintain completely one's body and to abide by ancestor worship are in the teaching to continue wholesomeness. To damage one's physical form and change one's family name are in the learning to cut off evil. What should be valued in the ultimate principle of the universe is the Way, and what should be despised in phenomena is secularity."

I corrected this, saying, "Now [the *Discourse*] takes rejecting ancestor worship as offending [the social] order. [In Confucianism, however,] they retain desires and expand politeness. This means exactly that the rule of showing filial piety and respect for one's parents exists for one's own benefit. Secularity is not necessarily despised. To damage one's physical form [and change one's family name] to cut off evil are despicable [acts] from [the Confucian] viewpoint, but their way is not necessarily noble. [The compiler of the *Discourse*] is fond of the secular [world], adheres to former times, honors China, and esteems politeness. He turns the noble and the humble upside down and falsely makes self-satisfied talk. He vainly wishes to be a vermin and drowns in ordinary views. How could he expect the fundamental principle in the words of the Sage (i.e., the Buddha)?"

The *Discourse* states: "Either nirvana or the transformation of becoming a Transcendent is a method [to unite with the Way]. In Buddhism it is called right and true (*zhengzhen*), while in Daoism it is called right and One (*zhengyi*). The term 'One' means to return to non-death and the term 'true' means to meet nonarising."

I corrected this, "[Laozi says:] 'Princes and kings attain the One and become the head of the world.'[460] He does not talk about the transformation of becoming a Transcendent. Since [Laozi says] 'The one who does not lose [even a part of his body] when he dies is of longevity,'[461] he does not discuss the issue of non-death. [The compiler of the *Discourse*] makes a personal assumption and a false accusation. His words are smooth, but they are wrong. The Great Way has already been obscured and small comprehensions [of the mind] have risen one after another.[462] How true this saying is! All those who make false accusations and deceptions and who are too arrogant intend to look for sages' words in order to illicitly make up for their faults. We indeed do not tolerate to examine it. The Daoist teaching today merely takes long life to be a belief and immortality to be the main goal. Alchemy, golden elixir, eating clouds, taking jade as food, mysteriously flying up, sprouting wings or exuviating to ascend to Heaven, deliverance through the corpse, and transformation are the methods with which they entrust themselves. [Yet] when we try to verify these things, [we find that] no such things can be seen after all.

"Furthermore, [the Daoist teaching] claims that if one does not ascend to [the realm of] immortals he will become a ghost after he dies, or he will be summoned and appointed an officer of Heaven, according to his original merit. Even though these [notions] are greatly against the worthy writings left by Laozi and Zhuangzi, in the fundamental principles they still have nothing wrong in the worldly teaching. If one loses desires, directs his course to wholesomeness, avails himself of edification, goes at will, and forgets the purpose of multiplying endlessly, [the search for] truth results in absurdity, but does not throw a normal [condition] into disorder.

"Regarding [Daoists] like Zhang [Ling] and Ge [Xuan], all of them additionally concocted supernatural transformation to educate the common people; they concocted weird accounts and misled the people of the world. By means of talismans and spells, they appeal to [the Heavenly Thearch] in written and verbal form, and as a pretext they say that these are all what Laozi transmitted to them. Moreover, they have gradually expanded [their teaching]. Then they quote Buddhism, which is far away [from their teaching], and try to testify that [Buddhism] consists of forgeries. Their argument is confused, and there 38b
is no model of scholarship on which they base [their argument]. When we examine [their teaching] against the meanings of [orthodox] texts, we cannot find anything similar. They cause the true and the absurd to be mixed up, people who wish for awakening to be deluded eternally, and no one to be able to dispute it. It is a serious false accusation and severe disorder.

"You are already fully aware that [the teachings of] the Buddha and Laozi are right, but you have not yet encountered a ferry [to the teachings]. Now I would like to briefly explain a corner [of the teachings] and cause you to have self-introspection.

"The two teachings (i.e., Buddhism and Daoism) possess both the study of the truth and the examination of the mind. Therefore, [the teachings] can avail themselves of all states of things whenever they encounter them.

"The teaching of Laozi consists of moral training, statecraft, cutting off and abandoning the honor of high rank, and things to rectify their nature. It takes the absolute vacancy as the foundation and softness and meekness as the function. It encourages self-examination without blaming others, striking one's root deeply in oneself and being perfectly still,[463] regarding the movement of the primordial vapor of Heaven as an integral whole, going peacefully beyond the human world, cultivating harmoniously the great primordial vapor,[464] having equanimity toward loss and gain, not scheming to go with obstruction even when one is driven to the wall, waiting [for good fortune and] submitting to fate, not planning [to profit oneself] even though one rises in the world, and taking public opinion as a measure of his worth. This is why scholars truly admire even the branch stream [of the original teaching] and why the teaching exists. Why do they take up the issues that deification has no set pattern, of benefiting the world, and of immortality?

"As for collecting clouds, sprouting wings or exuviating [to ascend as a Transcendent], changing the spirit, and tracing to the very source of the numinous being, these are [practices] from a teaching of a different vapor which was created through mending and accumulating [teachings] that were formerly completed. Therefore, although there are records of strange matters, what are called the principles do not follow them. When we investigate supernatural accomplishments we reach all things accordingly; the large are extraordinary auspicious cases, such as a female *kylin* or a male phoenix; and the small is the transformation of sparrows or pheasants. Once we have received a physical body, we wish for learning. Can we achieve it?

"So Yan [Hui] and Confucius are contiguous to each other in their ways, and they are close to the apex of natural endowments and learnedness. If we indeed admire the mysterious trace and yet stop it, or if we desire to follow and yet there is nothing to follow, to be contented with our fate is not reckless defilement. When we infer from this, [everything] can be clear. Therefore, Confucius esteemed to know the decrees [of Heaven] and he certainly had something he did not say. Boyang (i.e., Laozi) left behind strangeness and honor, and he firmly abided by *wuwei*. All these are attempts to restrain the causes of deception. Then, in tracing to the very source of the spirit and devoting oneself to the teaching, there is assuredly the ultimate law of Nature that we follow. In accomplishing the Way and attaining things, there is the origin that we realize in each of them.

"Actions manifest in one's previous existence, but you seek merit through forcing yourself to learn. A deep-rooted practice is accomplished habitually, but you perversely long for absurd desires and change them to the highest priority. If [one faces toward] Yan state [in the north] yet desires [to go to] Yue state [in the south], what could make his desire come true? Therefore, in learning we first find what [should be] learned and then learn it in order to accomplish it. To do what can be done is to do what can be achieved. In order to study and clarify about the people, the teaching was established in the middle of Heaven. Regarding the observation of phenomena and the survey of changes, [the sages] occupy their thoughts with them but do not discuss them. This is the profundity in managing the affairs of the secular world, and the ultimate [teaching] of Confucius and Laozi.

"To do what has not happened, to complete the function of intelligence, to trace to the very source of causality, to share reason among living creatures who are different from each other, to have a thorough [knowledge] of falsehood and return to truth, and the authentic supernatural accomplishments all [indicate] the greatness of Buddhism. Hereupon, the Buddha precisely clarifies the ultimate law of Nature. Laozi [teaches] how to complete one's life. Those who stick to life are blocked [from the way to truth] and those who clarify the ultimate law of Nature reach it. Nevertheless, if one quietly rests in the right path, even if he is blocked, he is not deluded. If he actively follows the ultimate law of Nature, he will reach reason and illuminate the ultimate Way.

"Therefore, people of virtue certainly esteem to complete the pure nature
given by Heaven and seek the Way by themselves. They respect the foun- 38c
dation, help [people] understand [the teaching] thoroughly, and return the merit to the four great elements. If one does not try to do things that are not so, abides by the teaching, and maintains the constant Way, he can learn the purity of the teachings of Confucius and Laozi. He goes beyond the ultimate law of Nature and sees as far as the horizon. He searches the stream [of the teaching], looks into the origin, and considers life to be dust and poison. Therefore, he stops extending respect to monarchs and parents, he does not talk about changes and extraordinary things with surprise, he does not hold stubbornly to one side, he is not frightened by mysterious things, and he develops his thoughts through pacifying his mind and contemplation.

"When accumulated merits are revealed and the important [time] comes, the essence of Buddhism is clear in our actions. Consequently, if in learning we find what [should be] learned, it is possible to support all the people and the teaching is revered in the world. If actions become clear in the doing [of them], we will exterminate defilements, return to the stream [of the teaching], and go far away from heavenly and human beings. Anything beyond this point has probably not been known. What we attain through clearing our thoughts lies just in this."

Family Law (*Menlü*) by Zhang Rong (444–497) and the Criticism by Zhou [Yong, Director of] Shan

Generation after generation, my family has revered Buddhism and the family on my mother's side respects Daoism. Daoism and Buddhism are not dual in the final consequence; [both teachings] aim toward tranquility and stability and they are the same at the foundation. When one is inspired, he is successful in understanding [the teaching] thoroughly. When we come across traces [of the teachings, we may find that] they become different from each other. This is comparable to the case where although the music was not handed down, we are not far from the mystery of the Five Thearchs; or the case where although the ceremony was not transmitted, the holiness of the Three Augusts is not suspended.[465] The times of the Three Augusts and the Five Thearchs were different. Therefore their customs were not the same. They belonged to different ages. Hence their righteousness varied. Why can we arbitrarily exercise common or dull [intelligence] and falsely accuse the ultimate Way of the Spirit?

I see that Daoist monks fight Buddhist monks [just as] Confucianists [fight] Mohists, and that Buddhist monks judge the rights or wrongs of Daoist monks, and vice versa. Once upon a time there was a wild goose that flew in the Way of Heaven. Since it was far [from the earth] it was difficult to see [the goose] clearly. The people of Yue thought the goose was a wild duck, while the people of Chu thought it was a swallow. [The difference] is simply due to [the fact that] people lived in either Yue or Chu. The wild goose was always just a wild goose, wasn't it? [In the same way,] only the pure foundation is one, and we all believe in the foundation. The traces of the wild goose have already dissipated. I will soar in the essence gathered [from all the traces]. You may wholeheartedly follow in the footprints of the Buddha without disgracing the foundation of Daoism.

A Letter Given to He [Dian], He [Yin], Kong [Zhigui], Kong [Zhongzhi], and Zhou [Yong, Director of] Shan, Shanci[466]

I, Shaozi, will send a letter and make a statement to all those who roam about in life. I, Zhang Rong, state:

A bird cries mournfully when it is going to die. A man speaks good words when he is approaching the end of his life.[467] Recently my disease has worsened and my vitality has weakened. In this condition, I [wonder] how many times I can breathe while my spirit stays [in this world]. Moreover, I am afraid that my boat lost the rudder in a deserted narrow ravine, and there is nothing to fasten a hill to a marsh.[468] Therefore, the time I can view the moon (i.e., his remaining lifetime) is very short. Every moment I am busy. If I do not stitch [everything together], it drifts away. I would like to make my lingering intention of the afterlife the rules of conduct for my brothers and nieces. Therefore, I created the *Family Law,* and I recite this writing often. I try to reach the origin of the two teachings (i.e., Buddhism and Daoism). Now I am reporting this to you, gentlemen. What do you think about this?

Response to Zhang's Letter Together with Questions to Zhang

I, Zhou [Yong, Director of] Shan, Shanci, wrote back to you, Shaozi, and stated:

I, Zhou Yong, bow to you with my head to the ground. A great composition came to me. I read that you are making your family code more severe. We, 39a
those who visit your family, have nothing with which to involve ourselves in this, and you really do not expect any help from us. When I respectfully examine the same foundation, [I find that] there is something to measure your lofty mind. Even though I know the primary to which the Way of the Spirit returns, in addition to Buddhism, the principle of Confucianism is magnanimous. Beside these, as to what can equal [the teaching of] Confucius, [the teaching of] the Yellow Emperor and Laozi is truly majestic. This teaching has gradually spread [as time goes by]. It is not that there is not anything perverse [in the teaching]. In its basic principle, simplicity, there is something respectable. I select traditional thoughts, briefly differentiate the pure from the murky, and do not mix them up in the process of selection. I just have held these thoughts in mind and have not yet expressed them. In any system there is order and disorder, and we cannot make a mistake in distinguishing the similarities from the differences. We should make a conclusion in written form.

Discerning the intention of your writing, you said that [the three teachings] are fundamentally the same. It appears that [your intended meaning of "same"] is not [the same as what] I think. [Your idea of "difference,"] as you mentioned that customs differ according to the time, is not [the same as what] I think, either. It has been my long-cherished desire to put in order some of my thoughts on this point. Fortunately, in the light of your opinion, I would like to try to articulate my view together with you. It is brief, as you see below. I look forward to hearing your profound instruction.

In the *Discourse on the Way to Reach the Origin* [*of the Two Teachings*] you say, "Daoism and Buddhism are not dual in the final consequence; [both teachings] aim toward tranquility and stability and they are the same in their foundation. When one is inspired, he is successful in understanding [the teaching] thoroughly. When we come across traces [of the teachings, we may find that] they become different from each other."

Zhou says, "You mention in your discussion that they are the same in their foundation. Please let me ask you: What is the meaning of the foundation to which you refer here? Wouldn't it be that those who speak of Daoism consider the two-chapter text (i.e., the *Daodejing*) to be primary, and those who speak of Buddhism should take *prajñā* to be the ultimate law of Nature? The reason why the two-chapter text is esteemed is that the significance reaches the absolute vacancy at the extreme point. With *prajñā* one observes that the extremity of the spiritual function is the Dharma-nature. Even though the absolute vacancy and the Dharma-nature are the same in respect to tranquility, they differ from each other in the purport of the way to position tranquility. As for your statement in the discussion, '[Daoism and Buddhism] are not dual in the final consequence,' do you mean that [the two teachings] settle in the absolute vacancy or that they are not dual in the Dharma-nature? Is there another foundation in addition to those of the two paths, or are the absolute vacancy and the Dharma-nature not different from each other in purport? If there is another foundation, please tell me about it in detail. If [the absolute vacancy and the Dharma-nature] are not different from each other, I wish to hear your explanation of why they are not."

In the *Discourse on the Way to Reach the Origin* [*of the Two Teachings*] you say that "The times [of the Three Augusts and the Five Thearchs] were different. Therefore their customs were not the same. They belonged to different ages. Hence their righteousness varied." [And you say,] "I see that Daoist monks fight Buddhist monks [just as] Confucianists [fight] Mohists, and that Buddhist monks judge the rights or wrongs of Daoist monks and vice versa. Once upon a time there was a wild goose that flew in the Way of Heaven. Since it was far [from the earth] it was difficult to see [the goose] clearly. The people of Yue thought the goose was a wild duck, while the people of Chu thought it was a swallow. [The difference] is simply due to [the fact that] people lived in either Yue or Chu. The wild goose was always just a wild goose, wasn't it? [In the same way,] only the pure foundation is one, and we all believe in the foundation. The traces of the wild goose have already dissipated. I will soar in the essence gathered [from all the traces]."

Zhou says, "You say in the discussion, 'The times [of the Three Augusts and the Five Thearchs] were different. Therefore their customs were not the same.' This means that Buddhism is different from Daoism. Your statement, 'They belonged to different ages. Hence their righteousness varied,' refers to the Daoist teaching being separate from the Buddhist [teaching]. Daoism 39b
and Buddhism are different from each other. If it is not a wild duck, it is a swallow. This means only that the foundation in which you believe is just one: a wild goose. If you run about busily [advocating both] Buddhism and Daoism, you will have neither of them. In your lofty examination, you have not been aware of what you are following in order to discern the foundation. You easily revere [both teachings]. Is there any purpose in doing so?

"If you still take hold of the two teachings and position their foundations, I am afraid that fighting and judging [between the two different teachings] will just begin and you will not be able to pass good judgment on anything. If we survey equally the origin of teaching on the basis of the two teachings, the origin of each teaching always reveals itself along with the teaching itself. We should put on a deerskin cap and hold a staff with rings [just as a hermit does], and see [the world] in a leisurely manner. Then, Confucianists and Mohists will calmly discuss. [They may wonder] why they formerly competed. If the origin in which [the two teachings] are well matched is correct and the traces that separated [from the origin] are wrong, the functions of the two traces should be all removed. Why do you go in the direction to soar in the essence [gathered from many sources], while diligently engaged only in Buddhism, concentrate your vapor, hold the One fast in your embrace, and yet have no respect for Daoism? Your words are deep and your purpose is profound. I hope to hear your later account."

In the *Discourse on the Way to Reach the Origin* [*of the Two Teachings*] you say, "You may wholeheartedly follow in the footprints of the Buddha without disgracing the foundation of Daoism."

Zhou says, "You wholeheartedly follow in the footprints of the Buddha without disgracing the foundation of Daoism. I hold Śākyamuni's instruction in my mind and am attached to the Confucian statements in my daily conduct. I have not yet understood your intention. How are Buddhism and Confucianism positioned? Do you think that they are one in the foundation and differ in their later development, or are they different both in the foundation and in later development? Since I wish to thoroughly inquire about this or that and investigate exhaustively issues related to the principles, I cannot help but to ask you [these questions]."

The Second Letter Given to Zhou with Answers to His Questions

I, Zhang Rong, say, "Since I have still been unable to forget myself, I have attachment to my family. My body has already weakened and my gray-haired head has come to an extreme point. I stay in this world for my young dependents. I do not want to cause my mind to be deserted day and night, like the former capitol, and what I have troubled with throughout my life to run wild. For that reason, I created this *Family Law* in order to regulate the family. If Buddhism and Daoism are not employed, by what means would my family be regulated? Therefore, I try to postpone my last day depending on my vital breath and to extend my life span relying on animation. I am often moved and wish for divine response. I [hope to] reach the origin [of Buddhism and Daoism] and to settle the foundation. I truly wanted you to give me a wonderful opinion. Sure enough, you wrote back in this way and gave me your thoughts, clever views, and correct analysis. Since you have given me your thoughts, I now speak for you."

Zhou says, "You mention in your discussion that they are the same in their foundation. Please let me ask you: What is the meaning of the foundation to which you refer here?"

I respond to Zhou, "The nature of the mind is the capability to know. The way of morality is what can be known. If one has the capability to know and yet he does not know what can be known, this does not mean that he has the capability to know. If there is what can be known and yet it is not known by one who has the capability to know, it is not what can be known. Hence, we see that one who has the capability to know must go to the way [of morality] and what can be known must know what it goes to.

"Nevertheless, an ordinary person trembles with feeling, disturbs the function of intelligence, stirs up desires, agitates the spirit, drives his sharpness out, and clouds the function of recognition. Therefore, the mind goes in the 39c
wrong direction and flows downward, and the function of intelligence separates from the way [of morality]. As to [the teaching of] Boyang (i.e., Laozi), giving undivided attention to the [vital] breath and bringing it to the utmost degree of pliancy, staying in the void to let the animation act at will, putting the restless at ease, and holding all together in one embrace,[469] one stays put as if frozen and understands tranquility thoroughly. When one is solely proficient in tranquility, the function of intelligence has no chance to disappear and the animation halts in the void. Hence, he directs himself joyfully. If you want to have Boyang not be tranquil, how could this be possible? If you would have him be tranquil and not anchored in the Way, how could this be possible, either? Now that it is tranquil and has two spirits, the spirits are tranquil and there are two ways. I have never heard this.

"Consequently, at the final point it is one. [Nevertheless, an ordinary person whose] nature is restless and too hasty and whose appearance is wild is unable to widely practice further. [This is comparable to the case where] a man thinks to assume hegemony in the world in the next battle and yet just exhorts the people to respect his determination. I hope you may become free from all thoughts and hold the [dark-colored] pearl (i.e., the foundation).[470] Hence, although there are five people who are categorized as a 'Thearch,' the spirit is always one. There are three people who have the title 'August,' but the Way is not more than one. Even though a wild duck and a swallow are mistaken for one another, in the end it is a wild goose, isn't it? This is why I straighten [your] rope."

Zhou says, "Wouldn't it be that those who speak of Daoism consider the two-chapter text (i.e., the *Daodejing*) to be primary, and those who speak of Buddhism should take *prajñā* to be the ultimate law of Nature? The reason why the two-chapter text is esteemed is that the significance reaches the absolute vacancy at the extreme point. With *prajñā* one observes that the extremity of the spiritual function is the Dharma-nature. Even though the absolute vacancy and the Dharma-nature are the same in respect to tranquility, they differ from each other in the purport of the way to position tranquility."

I respond to Zhou, "Even though the Dharma-nature seeks emptiness by means of [the doctrine that emptiness] is precisely form [in the phenomenal world], the absolute vacancy [in Daoism] actually extends the meaning beyond the phenomenal world. As to the point that they (i.e., Dharma-nature and absolute vacancy) are linked together, however, you must think about this more closely. In regard to roaming around without distraction in the mind, brushing off the dust of the mind by oneself, thinking without disturbance, and being antecedent to the material form by one's effort, in respect to forgetting existence, Lao's [teaching] appears to go against Śākyamuni's, but from the viewpoint that [the concept of] forgetting is included [in Lao's teaching], Śākyamuni's [teaching] does not take the place of Lao's [teaching]. One has a leisurely state of mind, he is pure and peaceful, he sits and abandons [all things], he is quiet in order to calm the spirit, and he successfully understands [everything] thoroughly in order to empty the functions of them. When I ascend to this state [of mind], I do not see [any difference between] a Buddhist and a Daoist. When I give rise to this inclination, how do I know what is Buddhist or Daoist? There is only one in the final consequence. The real state of things is originally subtle and we realize [that the two teachings derive from] the One. Since what people sense varies, it is hard to come to an agreement in responding to things.

"All things in the universe and visual and auditory senses interlock; visual and auditory senses mutually cross all things in the universe. When they adhere to each other, they are already profound. When they separate from each other, certainly they are superficial. Hence the old man in Ku [county in Chu] (i.e., Laozi) concealed [the doctrine of 'emptiness is] precisely form' for the time being; he followed what exists without agitating the feeling, and he respected what does not exist and imbued the mind with what it follows. Things having been hidden away, the people then wish for nonexistence. Since it is possible that the wind from the west (i.e., Śākyamuni) rose in the daytime and reached the essence of the south (i.e., Laozi), wouldn't it be possible to dream of the spirit of China (i.e., Confucius) while asleep at night?[471]

"If you think that Laozi did not accomplish anything about nonexistence, I do not expect you to grasp the meaning. If you think that [Laozi] accomplished something about nonexistence and yet did not accomplish anything about existence, what you understand differs from what I expect. If you have 40a doubt because Laozi accomplished something about existence and yet did not clarify it in his teaching, why do Buddhists who accomplished something [about existence] make the traces high? At such a time, if you think that Buddhists had better make the traces high sometimes, this is comparable to the case where Laozi made the traces high occasionally. [The two teachings are] the same in the final consequence. This is my intention."

Zhou says, "You say in the discussion, 'The times [of the Three Augusts and the Five Thearchs] were different. Therefore their customs were not the same.' This means that Buddhism is different from Daoism. Your statement 'They belonged to different ages. Hence their righteousness varied' refers to the Daoist teaching being separate from the Buddhist [teaching]. Daoism and Buddhism are different from each other. If it is not a wild duck, it is a swallow."

I respond to Zhou, "If it is not a wild duck, it is a swallow. The trace is assuredly so. About the trace that is assuredly so, I will not give an answer. However, even though it is possible that there are differences in time and age, we should not create a difference just for the sake of making differences."

Zhou says, "In your lofty examination, you have not been aware of what you are following in order to discern the foundation."

I respond to Zhou, "I have already explained about recognizing overall the foundation in my previous letter. My recognition about [the teachings of] Laozi and Śākyamuni is exactly like this. This is precisely 'When I see with my own eyes, the Way exists there.'[472] If you want to make unjustifiable investigation into the words, I do not know how I can discuss the issue."

Zhou says, "If you still take hold of the two teachings and position their foundations, I am afraid that fighting and judging [between the two different teachings] will just begin and you will not be able to pass good judgment on anything."

I respond to Zhou, "In grasping the meaning, there is the foundation. Why do you extend your effort to take the teaching [if you have attained the foundation]?"

Zhou says, "If we survey equally the origin of teaching on the basis of the two teachings, the origin of each teaching always reveals itself along with the teaching itself."

I respond to Zhou, "You are correct, indeed. This is why I see the derivation of Daoism as the same as that of Buddhism, but for the reason why I agree with these words, there is just separately a wonderful base."

Zhou says, "We should put on a deerskin cap and hold a staff with rings [just as a hermit does], and see [the world] in a leisurely manner. Then, Confucianists and Mohists will calm down. [They may wonder] why they formerly competed."

I respond to Zhou, "The two states of Yu and Rui had legal struggles over farmland, but this is something with which King Wen did not have to be concerned.[473] Even if the natural jade is broken into pieces in order to put an end to a fight over the jade, is this particularly respectful? Moreover, we are fighting for a wild goose at night, but you recklessly have a wild duck and swallow fight each other. This means to put a deerskin cap on the head in vain and to hold a staff with rings in the hand to fabricate oneself. How could I understand this?"

Zhou says, "If the origin in which [the two teachings] are well matched is correct and the traces that separated [from the origin] are wrong, the functions of the two traces should be equally removed. Why do you go in the direction to soar in the essence [gathered from many sources], while diligently engaged only in Buddhism, concentrate your vapor, hold the One fast in your embrace, and yet have no respect for Daoism?"

40b I respond to Zhou, "The movements of the mind responding to eternal objects are diverse and one's feelings are various. Although I do not fly with a flap of the wings up to the four fruits [of sainthood in the Hinayana], you have no doubt that I abide in Buddhism. Even though I do not fly with a flap of the wings up to the five supernatural powers [of the immortals], what regret would I have in abiding in Daoism? Moreover, the honorable sacredness should be the foundation; I do not worry about the traces. Furthermore, I already have what I have abided in. Would I now change [the destination] to which I am flying? Since you can understand that there is only one [foundation] in the two parallel pillars, I will not rigorously press you to remove [the wrong view]."

Zhou says, "I hold Śākyamuni's instruction in my mind and am attached to the Confucian statements in my daily conduct. I have not yet understood your intention. How are Buddhism and Confucianism positioned? Do you think that they are one in the foundation and differ in their later development, or are they different both in the foundation and in later development?"

I respond to Zhou, "I originally blend a hundred sages together and throw them equally into the One, the ultimate. Recently I discussed this in the *Discourse on the Way to Reach the Origin* [*of the Two Teachings*], but Confucianism was not included in the discussion. Now you carry Confucianism to an extreme, and you precisely want to arrange Confucianism in a line and encircle Daoism. Therefore, you act as if you first prick up your ears, think of causing a war, and then plan to mount a surprise attack on the heavenly city at night, but I am afraid that it is difficult to ascend there; it is too precipitous for you to ascend there. Even if I see the troops going out, I will not see them return. I have already said that a hundred sages are thrown into the same place. Why would I allow that [Buddhism and Confucianism] differ both in the foundation and in later development? Moreover, you oppose me with all your force displaying your intelligence and bravery willfully. My bravery and intelligence spontaneously come together and flow out with great ease."

The Second Response and Further Questions by Zhou Yong

I, Zhou Yong, bow to you with my head to the ground. As for what can move the mind and to what we consign our mind, what other than truth can be our teacher? Edifications in China and foreign countries are what the practitioners dedicate, but if we distinguish between these (i.e., edifications in China and foreign countries) and make our choice clear, this causes me to become discontented and lost. Why would it be difficult for me? You virtuously wish to say it, and I have not stopped speaking, either. That is to say, I will send [this letter] to examine [the issue] furthermore. I will await your explanation to me.

You say in the *Discourse on the Way to Reach the Origin* [*of the Two Teachings*], "Even though the Dharma-nature seeks emptiness by means of [the doctrine that emptiness] is precisely form [in the phenomenal world], the absolute vacancy [in Daoism] actually extends the meaning beyond the phenomenal world" and "Hence the old man in Ku [county in Chu] concealed [the doctrine of 'emptiness is] precisely form' for the time being; he followed what exists without agitating the feeling; and he respected what does not exist and imbued the mind with what it follows."

Zhou says, "It is true that [the old man] in Ku [county in Chu] concealed [the doctrine of 'emptiness is] precisely form,' but I am afraid that in this statement you have not reached [the doctrine of 'emptiness is] precisely form.' If you make a pretext of being able to conceal [the doctrine], those who can conceal it are many, and probably there is not only the man from Li village (i.e., Laozi) [who can do so].

"When existence is existence, people perceive existence. When nonexistence is nonexistence, people recognize nonexistence. Laozi dealt with existence and wrote on nonexistence, but he did not go beyond this boundary. This is what I stated in my shallow discussion, the *Discourse on Three Sects* (*Sanzonglun*): 'If we select and run about busily, no one has been able to go beyond that level.' In Buddhism, the reason why worldly-mindedness is left behind in theory and why the rules governing the rhythm of words go against
40c the norm is probably because ['emptiness is] precisely form' means [that form in the phenomenal world] is not existence. Therefore, [Buddhism] is absolutely outstanding among many schools. What merits are there in Laozi, who did not clarify this point?

"Being confused, perverse, or unrestful is entirely due to attachment to existence. In going against the Way or being drowned in secular [customs], here is the trouble. Since the trouble is due to adhering to existence and the nature of existence has not been clarified, the school that rectifies existence follows and respects the art of nonexistence. If the nature of existence is not clear, even though this is a big problem, whom do we go against in esteeming tranquility? Those who experience nuisances are really few. This is why the Daoist teaching is added to the propagation of the [Buddhist] teaching and why I said in my previous letter that 'the teaching of] the Yellow Emperor and Laozi is truly majestic.'

"All the former opinions by Wang [Bi] and He [Yan] indicate that Laozi is no match for the sage (i.e., Confucius). If [Laozi] was just as he is presented in this view, [his teaching] could not influence Śākyamuni's teaching. When I position Laozi, I do not think this. When a bodhisattva manifests in the world, the manifestation has no fixed form; he manifests at times as the leader of the circle of Confucian scholars, the most reverent priest of the country, or a monk. This is the established dogma found in Buddhist scripture.[474] Sometimes he appears even in the guise of a prime minister or a wealthy man. Why wouldn't Laozi's life be only one track [of his]? It is only because we have not known the depth of observation and the level of nobility. This is all because the great brightness has not been opened and for the time being we have received only one side [of the truth].

"When the sun or moon comes out, the torch should be put out.[475] Since [the teaching of] no remaining is expounded, many interim [teachings] will spontaneously cease. You still want to resist in order to save the brightness [of the torch] even under the [light of the] sun and moon, and to clarify that this [torchlight] and [the light of] the sun and moon are of common origin.

"You already worship the sun and moon in your mind and you have no intention of disgracing the foundation of the torch, but you have not been aware of what the foundation of this torch is. Is it a name, or reality? If it is only a name, where does the fundamental Way exist? If you say you want it to be reality, the sun and moon are reality. This means that the issue comes to an end with a buddha, and you do not understand the [Buddhist] Way. In the purport of the *Discourse on the Way to Reach the Origin* [*of the Two Teachings*], whom does the origin reach?

"You say in the *Discourse on the Way to Reach the Origin* [*of the Two Teachings*], 'One has a leisurely state of mind; he is pure and peaceful; he sits and abandons [all things]' and 'When I ascend to this state [of mind], I do not see [any difference between] a Buddhist and a Daoist. When I give rise to this inclination, how do I know what is Buddhism or Daoism?'

"Again, you say, 'Now that it is tranquil and has two spirits, the spirits are tranquil and there are two ways. I have never heard this.'

"Furthermore, you say, 'As to [the teaching of] Boyang, giving undivided attention to the [vital] breath and bringing it to the utmost degree of pliancy, staying in the void to let the animation act at will . . . the animation halts in the void. Hence, he directs himself joyfully.'

In addition, you say, '[In regard to] brushing off the dust of the mind by oneself, . . . and being antecedent to the material form by one's effort, . . .'

Zhou says, "You state that 'Even though the Dharma-nature seeks emptiness by means of [the doctrine that emptiness] is precisely form [in the phenomenal world], the absolute vacancy [in Daoism] actually extends the meaning beyond the phenomenal world.' I think personally that Laozi and Śākyamuni came [to the world] about the same time and took charge of their own fields, and about their spheres there is nothing better than [your] statement of this. In that case, that the state of Laozi's mind was leisurely indicates spontaneously that it was leisurely [in the world] outside existence, and that Buddhists are pure and peaceful and sit and abandon [all things] means that they sit and abandon [all things in the world where] form is precisely empty. If we ascend to the state of Laozi's mind, [we will know that] Laozi differs
41a from Śākyamuni; if we experience Śākyamuni's intentions, [we will know that] Śākyamuni differs from Laozi. Since the spirits are in tranquility, they are two,[476] and there are two ways. Even though you had not heard this before, I have previously heard it. If this is so, the animation that halts in the void is spontaneously void; it is in the void that you mentioned, and to direct oneself joyfully is not the way I mean, either. Regarding the statement, '[In regard to] brushing off the dust of the mind by oneself, . . . and being antecedent to the material form by one's effort,' you have not entirely gotten involved in the grand law, so I do not dare agree with your *Discourse on the Way to Reach the Origin* [*of the Two Teachings*].

"You say in the *Discourse on the Way to Reach the Origin* [*of the Two Teachings*], 'If you want to have Boyang not be tranquil, how could this be possible? If you would have him be tranquil and not anchored in the Way, how could this be possible, either?'"

Zhou says, "Your statement is very apt, but I am still worried that [you] have not yet reached the utmost mastery. In what you say here, you hit the mark in regard to the tranquility of the spirit, but you miss the point as to the void of things. If you think that tranquility is [temporary] tranquility and you do not mean that it is the ultimate tranquility, and if you think that the animation is [temporary] animation and you do not say it is the complete animation, I approve of this. It is faultless.

"You say in the *Discourse on the Way to Reach the Origin* [*of the Two Teachings*], 'If you think that Laozi did not accomplish anything about nonexistence, I do not expect you to grasp the meaning. If you think that [Laozi] accomplished something about nonexistence and yet did not accomplish anything about existence, what you understand differs from what I expect.'

Zhou says, "As for the accomplishments about existence and nonexistence, if we do not [understand] the apex, we are not ready [to know them]. In knowing nonexistence and knowing existence, I approve of the Daoist [standpoint]. Daoist words, however, simply do not reach the state of neither existence nor nonexistence. Neither existence nor nonexistence is what [the *Discourse on*] *Three Sects* has in store. If you reverence additional thought, you may just take a look at [this discourse]. I only think that in order not to cause your understanding to be erroneous, I remove mistakes and settle the issue.

"You say in the *Discourse on the Way to Reach the Origin* [*of the Two Teachings*], 'If it is not a wild duck, it is a swallow. The trace is assuredly so. About the trace that is assuredly so, I will not give an answer.'

"Moreover, you say, 'My recognition about [the teachings of] Laozi and Śākyamuni is exactly like this. This is precisely 'When I see with my own eyes, the Way exists there.'

"In addition you say, 'In grasping the meaning, there is the foundation. Why do you extend your effort to take the teaching [if you have attained the foundation]?'

"Again, you say, 'You are correct, indeed. This is why I see the derivation of Daoism as the same as that of Buddhism.'"

Zhou says, "Regarding your statement: 'When I see with my own eyes, the Way exists there' and 'In grasping the meaning, there is the foundation,' I think that the true meaning of the Dharma-nature is precisely this state [of mind]. Buddhism has it, but what you obtained does not have the reason. Why do you extend your effort to take the teaching? The foundation of what you see with your own eyes exists in the traces of the teaching. If we think [these traces are] a wild duck and a swallow, where has the wild goose gone?

"As for the true nature of all *dharma*s, Laozi's [teaching] does not have the purpose. Even if you try to see the lofty nature (i.e., the Way) with your own eyes, there is no such thing in Laozi's traces. Since both the purpose and the traces are missing, there is no means by which to search for the ultimate law of Nature.

"Your discussion says, '[You may wholeheartedly follow in the footprints of the Buddha] without disgracing the foundation of Daoism.' On what point [in the foundation of Daoism] must we bring no disgrace? If when you search the traces of Daoists you think you find that its derivation is the same as that
41b of Buddhism, the real meaning of the ultimate truth can be found in writings. Do we ascertain [the real meaning of the ultimate truth] in the *Dao* chapter [in the *Daodejing*] or do we encounter it in the *De* chapter? If both chapters [of the *Daodejing*] are not what you follow and you attain the profound [meaning of the ultimate truth] in your mind, this is naturally your subjective point of view and it is simply the third [standpoint], following [those of] Laozi and Śākyamuni. Probably you can establish another school independently. This is not what I dare to bring up here."

"You say in the *Discourse on the Way to Reach the Origin* [*of the Two Teachings*], 'The two states of Yu and Rui had legal struggles over farmland, but this is something with which King Wen did not have to be concerned. . . . This means to put a deerskin cap on the head in vain and to hold a staff with rings in the hand to fabricate oneself. How could I understand this?'"

Zhou says, "You said that '[the old man] in Ku [county in Chu] concealed [the doctrine of "emptiness is] precisely form" for the time being.' If that is the case, the nothingness (*xukong*) [advocated by Laozi] is insufficient. You said that 'The Dharma-nature seeks emptiness by means of [the doctrine that emptiness] is precisely form.' If this is so, the Dharma-nature is perfect. Now here is a man who talks about the Dharma-nature holding a staff with rings. A scholar wearing a deerskin cap arrives, and grasping the absolute vacancy, says with censure, 'Your [view] is not the same as mine. I will fight against you.' You serenely lean against a thorny tree (in ancient times, a place where lawsuits would be heard) and pass judgment after hearing the argument between them. You say that neither of them is good, and you comment that one of them wears a deerskin cap on his head in vain and the other holds a staff with rings in his hand in order to fabricate himself. If you, a sharp and outstanding person, cast such judgments, the people of Yu and Rui will be very sad.

"You say in the *Discourse on the Way to Reach the Origin* [*of the Two Teachings*], 'Although I do not fly with a flap of the wings up to the four fruits [of sainthood in the Hinayana], you have no doubt that I abide in Buddhism. Even though I do not fly with a flap of the wings up to the five supernatural powers, what regret would I have in abiding in Daoism?'"

Zhou says, "You said, 'I do not fly with a flap of the wings up to the four fruits' but still you diligently abide in Buddhism. You said, 'I do not fly with a flap of the wings up to the five supernatural powers.' Why do you cast aside only the Daoist trace?

"Since this is illogical, I have just made such a complaint.

"You say in the *Discourse on the Way to Reach the Origin* [*of the Two Teachings*], 'You precisely want to arrange Confucianism in a line and encircle Daoism. Therefore, you act as if you first prick up your ears.'"

Zhou says, "Your *Discourse on the Way to Reach the Origin* [*of the Two Teachings* consists of] only the origin of Daoism and does not refer to that of Confucianism. Since I have doubts about this lack, I inquired about it to you. I have not known about directing oneself joyfully. Can one [direct himself] joyfully only by Daoism? Is it possible that he directs himself joyfully while cultivating in Confucianism? Even though this is not the main point of our discussion, if I speak freely, I must come to [this point]. I will be fortunate if you give me extra instruction in your spare time, apart from explaining about the foundation."

I (i.e., Sengyou) have researched the criticisms and questions between Zhou and Zhang. Although the correspondence between them is numerous, the standpoints, intentions, and grounds of their arguments can be found in their earliest correspondence. Therefore I omitted their later writings. My purpose is to keep to the main point of the discussion.

Letter to the Daoist Gu [Huan] (420–483) by Xie Zhenzhi

I, Xie Zhenzhi, say, I respectfully read the *Discourse on the Non-Chinese and the Chinese*. You argue and discuss the origin [of Buddhism and Daoism] in detail on the basis of the scriptures of these two teachings. The expression 41c
[of the *Discourse*] is clear; it is a brilliant composition. [The writing style] is as sonorous as the harmony of the notes *gong* and *shang*. It is full of strenuous endeavors in the profound principle. It is enjoyable!

Regardless of my narrow view and ignorance, I put forth my efforts to steal a glance at the profound ultimate law of Nature. I painstakingly explore what is profound, but I have nothing at all on which to rely. I, however, have tried to take a lesson [from the *Discourse on the Non-Chinese and the Chinese*] and read it more than three times, but my humble doubts have not yet been resolved. I would like to slightly express my doubts, hoping to hear your explanations later.

At the beginning of the *Discourse* you state that the Buddha is precisely Laozi and Laozi is none other than the Buddha.[477] Moreover, you compare the transformation of becoming a Transcendent [in Daoism] with nirvana [in Buddhism] and see that longevity [in Daoism] is equal to no death [in Buddhism]. Accordingly, you refer to the worldly instructions in order to tally them with the profound teaching (i.e., Buddhism). When I collect examples of these words, they probably appear equal to [those of Buddhism]. In the last [section of the *Discourse*, however], you ridicule [Buddhism] and say that [Buddhist monks] annihilate Chinese [traditional customs] and reject [ancestor] worship. In addition, you say that [the foreign language used by Buddhists] is similar to the noisy chirps of insects or birds, and that it is not something we should follow. Please let me try to speak about these issues.

The Duke of Zhou and Confucius took Confucianism and Mozi's teaching as a model to be followed. Laozi and Zhuangzi spoke about the teaching and clarified a method to lead to [the Way]. These [efforts] all open [the Way] little by little and cause [people] to approach the Way, [but the people] have not yet been ready for the great development [to the Way] with these. Moreover, insects and birds are different species [from human beings]. The edification originally separates from the Way. When we want to say something about this, we must first investigate the reasons.

Originally, when a person participates in the two polarities (i.e., Heaven and Earth), this is called the three powers (*sancai*). How could the foreign country (i.e., India) and China be divided in a place governed by the three powers? Then, we know that a person must be part of the human species and an animal must belong to groups of animals. Let us seek [an example of this] in familiar matters. The seven treasures are what people love. Consequently, Chinese and non-Chinese people equally value them. Since being respectful is what people honor, people of the world are sincerely concerned with this.

Hence, perfect marital relations were practiced in the four states,[478] not to mention the influences of the great edification. Wouldn't it then be diffused throughout the trichiliocosm?

Speaking on the basis of Buddhist scriptures, you perhaps have heard that the Buddha appeared in the world. He united all traditional teachings into one; the world was placed in one orbit. At the time Śākyamuni was first cultivating as a bodhisattva, he extensively edified people. Those who lived in that land when he attained buddhahood were granted special benevolences and favors; and they were all reborn in our domain. Our [domain] means Jambudvīpa (i.e., the continent situated to the south of Mount Sumeru). [People,] however, have been deluded for a long time in [the transmigration of] birth and death; they have followed and been imbued with secular customs; they temporarily lose the right path; and they simply have not been aware of the present enlightenment.

I think that the Sage looks down upon all with the wisdom of the three transcendental knowledges, observes the faculties of each person, and understands that [faculties] vary from person to person. Therefore, he expounded [the teaching of] the three vehicles and spread it.

First of all, the true Way is only one and the Dharma is nondual, too. Now, for the time being [the teaching of] the three vehicles is expounded and there are different ways to guide [people], but the place to which all return is one. Hence, when [the Buddha] traveled about, gathered people, and expounded the teaching, those who attained awakening were as numerous as grains of sand. In saving [people] from drowning [in extreme misery] and delivering them from delusions, there is nothing to surpass this teaching. Therefore, the boundless world, including the present, the future, and the past, is collectively here. We know that the ninety-five [non-Buddhist] schools are clearly not branches [of Buddhism]. At the beginning they said that their teaching is the same [as Buddhism], but in the end they said that it is different [from Buddhism]. Consequently, we know that what [they thought] is the same at the beginning is [in fact] not the same, and what [they thought] is different is, in the end, no different either. Isn't this like absurdly beating an earthen pot and recklessly trying to harmonize with the basic sound *huang-zhong*?[479] Wouldn't this be a deception?

As for matters such as that [Chinese people] keep their bodies complete [at death], maintain sacrifices, wear a crown and a big sash tied behind with the ends hanging, while [non-Chinese people] throw on a felt garment, put on adornments made of shells, bury themselves in dust and dirt, and cremate the body [at death]; or, as for things such as the sound of the Zhengshi era [of the Wei kingdom] (i.e., the authentic Chinese sound) and the barbarian sound, these [indicate] only minor differences in secular manners and customs [between Chinese and non-Chinese people]. Now we see that a bird sings in
42a the world of birds, and an animal roars in the world of beasts. If we truly hold one of many sounds and feel that it is different from all other sounds, we respond to it in a different manner. In this case, if the foreign country differs from China in the way to edify [the people], why do you mix everything up? [Your statement in the *Discourse* that] if a boat [moves on land] it will be dried out, and if a carriage [sails in a river] it will be submerged, can be compared to this case.

Propriety of the secular customs is the attenuated form of loyalty and good faith;[480] it is not the purity of the Way. Those who cultivate the purity of the Way strive to go against secular customs. When secular customs can be defied, the Way can be pure. It is difficult to defy secular customs. Hence, we ought to leave behind extremes. In order to leave behind extremes, you must first take off the crown, shave your head, put on a Buddhist monk's robe, and abstain from a [meat] diet. If we take off the crown, we need no expense for worldly ornamentation. When we shave the head, we need not trouble with hairpins and combs. When we put on a Buddhist monk's robe, we do not bother tailors to make our clothes. When we abstain from a [meat] diet, we stop thinking about our favorite foods. This is precisely [Laozi's saying] "Those who devote themselves to the Way [seek] from day to day to diminish [their doings]."[481] How could this be what the secular customs of the foreign country established? Regarding [Buddhist] writings and subtle books such as the Tripiṭaka and the four Āgama sutras, they are exactly [what Laozi said:] "Those who devote themselves to learning [seek] from day to day to increase [their knowledge]."[482] How could this be what Chinese customs could create?

Moreover, you say, "Buddhist scriptures are complicated and illustrious, while Daoist scriptures are concise and profound." Inferring from this, this means that if [the scriptures] are profound, it is difficult to hope to study them intensively and to rely on them; if they are illustrious, it is easy to hope to seek them carefully; if they are concise, they must be insufficient in indicating the reasons; and if they are complicated, they are a collection of interesting points and there are many keys to the way [to awakening]. In the Buddhist teaching, anything that has a form is considered to be illusory. Therefore [Buddhists] forget themselves in order to save sentient beings. In the Daoist teaching, [on the contrary,] one's self is considered to be true. Hence [Daoists] take medicine and food in order to preserve their lives. Furthermore, if life can be preserved, could a rose of Sharon (or an althea) compete with a thousand-year-old pine tree for longevity, or could an ephemeral organism be equal to a ten thousand-year-old *chun* tree in life span? This is certainly impossible.

If we deeply realize that the three realms of existence are abodes for the long night of spiritual darkness, and life is a master of the great dream,[483] we long for the Way to awakening. Why would we treasure our body? Even if our body could be refined and we could live without death, this originally differs from Laozi's fundamental way, and it is not the same as the Buddhist principle. Why do you make such a statement?

The spirit dwells in a body, similar to [how one stays] at an inn. If we go to an inn, why should we feel a persistent attachment to the eaves? The perception of the sensory perception and the form of what can be formed are not the substance of sacredness. Even the life spans of Yao and Confucius were less than a hundred years. [The period between Śākyamuni's attainment of buddhahood and] his entering nirvana is as long as the time it took [Confucius] to recognize the ordinances of Heaven (i.e., fifty years). Hence, from an eternal *kalpa* ago, the spiritual intelligence has been purified and refined. As the spiritual intelligence has been purified [and refined], its function severs [the confrontation between] existence and nonexistence; it brilliantly transcends [the boundary between existence and nonexistence] with the wisdom of the four phrases (i.e., existence, emptiness, existence and emptiness, and neither existence nor emptiness). This is exactly genuine and the unalterable Way from beginning to end.

Furthermore, those who "carve a mark on the side of a boat" (i.e., Buddhist monks) pray to a golden [buddha image], while those who "wait by the stump" (i.e., Daoist monks) harbor the hope to ascend to Heaven as a Transcendent sprouting wings.[484] Consequently [Buddhist monks] practice the six *pāramitās* in the phenomenal world, while [Daoist monks] are hindered by delusion and eat numinous mushrooms [that are believed to possess supernatural powers]. Even though being stuck in the phenomenal world is theoretically against the six *pāramitās*, practicing them can probably save people; but if one is hindered by delusion, he assuredly does not ascend to Heaven as a Transcendent sprouting wings. How then can he have more energy than his own share [to help others] in close touch with the realities [of life]?

When we seek some traces of the origins of two teachings (i.e., Buddhism and Daoism), there are different views, the broad and the narrow, and there is an apparent difference between superior and inferior. You cannot question closely fellows like these. They have entirely an intimate feeling of self; it is not the universal great knowledge. Then, it is known that they can discern differences in the secular customs [of China and the foreign country] by the
42b teachings. It is sad! The profound Sage (i.e., the Buddha) is already far away. [Various schools] brilliantly have arisen competing with each other. It can be said that [to respect such teachings is like] pointing to the trails made by an insect and considering them to be the Chinese written language invented by Cang [Jie], or like drinking the milk of a poisonous insect and thinking that it is clarified butter. This is very sad!

The Buddhist Way is vast and extensive. The capacity of wisdom cannot be completely expressed. It is difficult to survey the traces of responses by form. While we argue about existence, myriad aspects are luxuriantly displayed as if a thousand mountains stand in a row. When we analyze nonexistence, even Mount Tai is exhausted in vain; it scatters along with an autumn down.[485] We make use of the ten powers [attributed to a buddha] in order to destroy devils (Skt. *māras*), and promote the four immeasurable minds in order to deliver secular people. When we raise the Dharma torch of *prajñā,* what dark place would we be unable to illuminate? If we concentrate with the Dharma might of *samādhi,* what distant place would we be unable to subdue? Why should we doubt that [the Buddhist teaching] is not effective in both the foreign country and in China?

The Second Letter Given to the Daoist Gu

I, Xie Zhenzhi, address myself to you. Thank you very much for your response and explanation! I exhaustively examined the profound situation. You already have harmonized smoothly Daoism and Buddhism and yet [separated] Śākyamuni from Li (i.e., Laozi) just as separating [the muddy water of] the Jing River from [the clear water of] the Wei River. "If we prolonged each by the addition of the proper lines, [then all events possible under the sky might have their representation.]"[486] They will accordingly become games or gambles, [which are better than doing nothing].[487] The more you explain about the Buddha, the more obscure the exquisite purpose becomes. When we decorate a shop counter in order to trade valuables, we do not sell them on a bright night. [What you do] is like, as [the *Zhuangzi*] says, trying to erase your footprints by running around, or trying to stop casting a shadow by jumping.[488] How could you avoid [such criticism]? According to on what your discourse is grounded, you think that insects and birds are different species [from human beings] and that the non-Chinese and the Chinese differ from each other in manners and customs. I think that the three powers equally unite, the human reason is one, there are [only] minor differences in secular teachings, and the teaching of the Dharma is almost the same [for non-Chinese and Chinese]. You respond, "It is found in the *Book of Changes;* it is not what foreign books imitate." Then you say "A white flag has already been hoisted, but you do not inspect it closely and take a black flag to be white. [Your case] is different from [the historical fact in which] Cao [Gui] saw a flag [and became aware of enemy troops].[489] You arbitrarily omit all familiar essential points in order to indicate the great conclusion." If so, even though a pearl is hidden in the topknot [of the wheel-turning noble king],[490] the deception of the inconsistency is easily discovered.[491] I speak somewhat in jest, but I do not intend to defy you at all.

The Grand Terminus is divided into the two polarities (i.e., *yin* and *yang*),[492] which are intertwined in vain. When the five *skandhas* get together, the body and consciousness unreasonably manifest. Consciousness is formed on the basis of defilements, while the body arises from the condition of attachment and hindrance. Before the time of Fuxi, many people were basically foolish. Since they were basically foolish, they lived in trees or dwelled in caves, and [ate the flesh of birds and beasts,] drinking their blood, and swallowing [also] the hair and feathers.[493] Sovereign and subject, father and son, saw each other just as people of the northern tribes and those of Yue state [of the south] saw each other. They were still like beasts. Moreover, they could be compared with ignorant children. It was not the world into which Daoism was introduced and where [the teaching of] love and justice had influenced the people. When the people became bogged down in desires and lost themselves in waves, they thought to deliver themselves by clinging to a precipice. When we deliver ourselves, we pray for wholesomeness. When we pray for wholesomeness, sacredness responds to us.

What is sacredness? It is what we communicate with through our receptivity to things. Communicating is not self-communication and receptivity is not self-receptivity, either. Receptivity is constantly on this side, while communication comes always from that side. Speaking from that side, [it is like] a mirror hung in a lofty hall. Speaking of this side, [it is like] all images coming back to this side. Therefore, we know that India is located in the central region of this world (Skt. *sahā*); since it is placed in the excellent assemblage of purity and wholesomeness, it is possible to communicate through receptivity with the ultimate sacredness, and the land is situated in the center of the trichiliocosm. Since the sacredness responded to that land (India), the voice [of the teaching] spreads in this land (China). When we see the brightness of the sun and moon, why do we have to borrow the observation of Li Zhu, [who has the excellent faculty of sight]? When we hear wrathful thunder, why do we have to have Ziye (i.e., music master Kuang,
42c a blind musician of the Spring and Autumn period) hear it?

Consequently, it does not matter that different things, such as the humble and the noble, go with each other in the same way, and in the difference between the two polarities of left and right there is no harm in natural relations. Since there is no harm in natural relations, [the people gather like] clouds and practice the Dharma teaching. Since it does not matter that [different things] go with each other, [the Dharma teaching] bestows [mercy], just like the rain falls on both the foreign country and China.

The Way is one, while form is dual. The Way is truth, and form is worldliness. Since truth is still one, worldliness is still dual. We make a thorough investigation of duality to attain unity; we ought to unify the law. If we eliminate worldliness and return to truth, we will certainly go against worldliness. For this reason, the Tathāgata established the model and made various teachings the same in the eternal past. If Confucius and Laozi were the Buddha, they would dim the light, secretly lead [the people], rectify their prejudice to deliver them, establish benevolence, create righteousness, and conform to secular people's feelings. Hence, [people] maintain their bodies [at death] to be complete, continue [ancestor] worship, extend their kindness to their family members of the six relations, attend to their health, nourish their natures, [establish] themselves, and [do not adhere to] other things. However while these are considered to be very good, they are not considered to be perfect. Probably this is for a limited system; [neither of them] "whip up their lagging [sheep] (i.e., neglecting one of two aspects)."[494] How is it possible to compare the Way with supreme enlightenment (Skt. *bodhi*), and to compare the sages (i.e., Confucius and Laozi) with Śākyamuni?

When Buddhism is expounded clearly, it has essential points and it is competent and extensive. Since it has essential points and is competent and extensive, [people of] exquisite [faculties] and those of coarse [faculties] fathom it. Since [people of] exquisite [faculties] and those of coarse [faculties] fathom it, strongness and weakness agree with each other. Therefore, the pure ferry [to truth] reaches profound points; it is really a pair of accurate compasses. It is easy to draw a circle by using a pair of compasses, but difficult to do this only by hand. Why wouldn't we follow the easy way and abandon the difficult way?

Daoist scriptures are simple and crude. Many are composed in a far-fetched manner. Regarding scriptures such as the *Wonderful Scripture of the Truth of the Numinous Jewel* (*Lingbao miaozhenjing*), [the Daoists] adopted the *Lotus Sutra* (*Fahuajing*) for it. Their manner of composition is particularly poor. As for scriptures such as the *Scripture of the Yellow Court* (*Huangtingjing*) of the Shangqing (Supreme Purity) school, what it upholds is ingesting drugs: to chew rocks and eat clouds. It is not simply that their law cannot be followed, it is also difficult to consider that their way is the same [as that of Buddhists]. Among [such texts], the good point is found only in the teaching of the *Five Thousand Words* (i.e., *Daodejing*), which completely employs *wuwei*. Yet to completely employ *wuwei* has not been able to remove existence. If to remove existence is their purpose, what then do they nourish with numinous mushrooms?

The nine philosophical schools [of China] are even closer to what [the teaching of] the three vehicles of the Buddhist school leads to. Since the nine philosophical schools are even closer to [what the Buddhist teaching of the three vehicles leads to], we attain [the movements of] motion and rest here. The noumenal principle of meditative power is merely part of [the teaching of] the three [vehicles]; it is not the culmination. Meditation sutras are subtle. The characteristics of the objective world are exquisite and profound. Even if we try to become united in truth with these, it is still impossible to accomplish it.

Now you say, "The Way lies in *wuwei* and is simply to attain the One." "It lies in *wuwei* and is simply to attain the One" means to commune with what is profound for a thousand years. If you would like to commune with what is profound for a thousand years,[495] I need not wait for your lofty talk.

[Buddhism] is the brilliant ultimate law that leads people to reach the refined state. If one were to reject studying and refining his thought, would this not be negligence? How could it be a tentative method to lead to Daoism? Examining respectfully what you said, [I come to know that] not only do you not understand Buddhism, you do not understand Daoism either. I send a poem to you to offer a little laugh.

The poem says:

> [Heaven and Earth] go on. The light becomes dim.
> The profound Sage (i.e., the Buddha) concealed himself
> (i.e., entered nirvana).
> The long night drifts slowly. Many stars shine brightly.
> When the sun luminously rises and shines, the lunar mansions
> rapidly disappear.
> Round and square [pieces of wood] should be uniform for use
> as construction materials,
> Even though they are different from each other as raw materials.
> If one is solely deluded, he is not awakened.
> 43a The big-headed fellows are surprised that [the Buddha] departs
> [and goes] far away.

Bian He [of Chu state] wept bitterly at the foot of Mount Jing.[496]
How could we onesidedly blame King Li of Chu state?
Even if a good grasscutter slights *prajñā,*
How could we censure transcendental wisdom?

End of Fascicle Six of *The Collection for the Propagation and Clarification* [*of Buddhism*]

Fascicle Seven

Critique of the Daoist Gu's *Discourse on the Non-Chinese and the Chinese* by Zhu Zhaozhi, Attendant-in-Ordinary

I read your lofty talk on the non-Chinese and the Chinese. You discuss the two teachings (i.e., Buddhism and Daoism) and present the purposes of each of the scriptures. [Your opinion] deeply accords with what is profound, and your wonderful words are virtuous and pleasant. It is not a meaningless statement. Formerly Ying Jifu (i.e., Ying Zheng of the Jin dynasty, ?–269) saw that [the teachings of] Confucius and Laozi are equal, and now in a later generation you, our wise man, consider that [the teachings of] Li (i.e., Laozi) and Śākyamuni are also equal. The distinct paths for all ages are united into one path in the present dynasty. Questions and disputes for successive generations are happily [satisfied] today. You appreciate [the teachings] deeply and understand them profoundly. There are many people who are cleansed and comforted. There is no discussion more beneficial to the world than this.

Regarding statements of the favorable aspects of each (i.e., Buddhism and Daoism), however, there are points as close together as the liver and the gall bladder, and points as far apart as Chu state and Yue state. This is because it is not understood that although there are two different tastes, sweet and bitter, they must be the same in nature in order to make a body. Therefore, [Buddhists and Daoists] attack each other and then strange doctrines arise. [Disputes] are repeated and become complicated. This causes quite a lot of harm. It is pitiful! [Your discourse] is at the beginning, just as [when the sun] rises in the sky and the light covers the outside of this world; and yet in the end, just as [the sun] sets in an abyss, the light is obscured and the brightness is lost.

If a spiritual guide loses himself, many others are also lost. Therefore, I forget that I am shallow and ignorant, and then lead and deliver [others]. Now, I will first express my thoughts [about your *Discourse*] and later I will speak of what I find regrettable. I think that since "it is right to follow the good [way smoothly,] as on the course of a stream,"[497] it is not regrettable merely to go against traditional [notions]. I live far away from you, [beyond] the mountain and rivers where you live, and I cannot expect to have a good conversation [with you in person]. So, I send this to you for the time being in order to temporarily substitute it for a [face-to-face] meeting. Once the flags of our feelings meet each other, what we have explained is not shallow.

I, Zhu Zhaozhi, speak.

Since the sacred Way is void and tranquil, it perfectly responds to anything with no set pattern; because of its response with no set pattern, it responds to everything. Therefore, if we inspect the mind from the point of sacredness, originally there is no name in a myriad of understandings. When things are spontaneously understood and named, with the names they are considered to be evident. Hence, those who have complete intelligence are called ones
43b of right, perfect enlightenment (Skt. *samyaksaṃbodhi*); those who smoothly and thoroughly understand are called sages; and what opens up [the knowledge of the issues of] things and accomplishes the undertakings [of men] is called the Way.[498] In this case, a sage is merely the one of right, perfect enlightenment and the one of right, perfect enlightenment is nothing other than the Way. You should understand this. Why is it necessary to seek it in a distant place?

The Chinese and the non-Chinese differ from each other in manners and customs, and also, in terms of their affections, they are different. Since sages usually take action in accordance with [all things], there is probably a difference in the establishment of each teaching. Nevertheless, [Chinese] rules of propriety and the [Buddhist] pure precepts have three hundred rules, they are equal in number, and there are equally three thousand [rules of] deportment or formal manners [in both China and the non-Chinese country]. What may differ between [China and the non-Chinese country] lies only in the names "Buddhism" and "Daoism" and in their appearances. A mastermind still considers the physical body to be like an inn (i.e., a temporary abode). How would it be worthwhile for him to discuss the Chinese formal dress called *gunmian*?[499] What may be questioned lies only in the beginning of establishing teachings, in which China and the non-Chinese country differ from each other in their function. It is proper to argue the point that present manners and customs are managed concurrently and will change according to the current of the times. Now I will speak about this point.

In a sage's instruction, action is certainly based on the right order. In the eastern country (i.e., China), where splendor is valued, there is the Chinese formal dress called *gunmian;* the formal manners of ceremonies and music; rules for deportment; and decorations such as full court dress, a formal gown, a crown, and hairpins, in order to propagate the [sages'] way; it is probably [intended] to lead [the people] to become close to [the sages' way]. Since simplicity is valued in non-Chinese manners and customs, the people are instructed with extreme plainness; a shaved head is [considered] a beautiful appearance; clothing is made without cutting to shape; emotions are calmed; the intellectual function is opened; and the spirit is expected to be free [from anxiety and agitation] for *kalpa*s, in order to develop the minds; it is [intended] to recommend [people] to keep away from [extravagance].

The Daoist teaching is to take transcendent elixirs called *zhiying,* to eat clouds, to take [golden] elixir, to breathe in the Grand One (*taiyi*), to exhale the old, and to inhale the new. The great [achievement] is that the spirit flies [out of the body], sprouting wings [as a Transcendent]. The minor [achievement] is that the body becomes light and strong and has no illness; that is to say, maintaining the body, one can expect the efficacies.

All three teachings (i.e., Buddhism, Daoism, and Confucianism) have one function of being moved by something and responding to it, but this is not what I think is the culmination [of the Way].

The culmination of the Way is neither splendid nor simple, neither following nor leaving, neither close nor distant, neither abandoned nor sustained by anyone, neither partisan nor nonpartisan, and neither slandered nor praised; it completely flows without obstruction and it is tranquil and vast. This is tentatively called nonexistence. The subtle state [of the mind] is like this. How is it different from this?

Nevertheless, since the time of the [Three] Augusts and [Fu]xi, each [of the sages] propagated his own way, which has been transmitted in a lineage, and there was no interaction [between different lineages]. This is really due to the fact that they were all satisfied with [their own way] and never sought [any teaching] other than their own. Therefore, from the time of the Han dynasty on, simple customs have degenerated, benevolence and righteousness have gradually declined, the rules of the Great Way have not been transmitted, studies of the Five Classics have declined even more, great justice has already become perversely bad, and sublime and profound words have vanished as well. No one roams at "the gate of many wonders" [that Laozi asserts];[500]

deportment based on the golden mean is not observed, the art of courtesy is already ruined, Chinese ceremonial music falls as well, [Chinese traditional] manners and customs come to an end, there is no division between sovereign and subject, the authentic teaching has deteriorated, and human ethics have become disordered.

Thereupon, the sacred way (i.e., Buddhism) completely governs [all things] and reaches distant lands as time goes by. The profound edification was transmitted to the eastern land (i.e., China) and granted benevolence to this world and kindness to sentient beings. The people despise what they learned previously and were delighted with what they newly heard. They showed their obedience and followed [the teaching] harmoniously. The essential significance has been revived. Consequently, houses of sublime and profound words (i.e., Buddhist temples) were built here and there, and there are guests (i.e., Buddhist monks) who chant the profound words all around. This
43c can be observed in reality; it is not merely empty talk, a series of vain words. Isn't this just that everything cannot end with the *pi* hexagram (i.e., Confucianism), which is received by the *tongren* hexagram (i.e., Buddhism) [in the *Book of Changes*]?[501]

I think that the sages nurturing common people is like an affectionate mother raising a baby. When [the baby] begins to eat, she feeds the baby tasty meat; when [the baby] becomes bored of the tasty meat, she changes [his food] to tallow and honey; and when [the baby] is tired of tallow and honey, she lets the [baby's] whole body rest peacefully. It is extremely beneficial to the baby to be peaceful and comfortable both on the inside and on the outside, isn't it? Reason is just like this. Nevertheless, if one unrestrainedly slanders [Buddhism] and recklessly separates it from [Confucianism and Daoism], he has not realized the center of the ring [of thought] (i.e., the absolute state beyond the judgment of right or wrong).[502] I cannot discuss [with such a person]. Correspondence exchanged between you two wise men (i.e., Gu Huan and Xie Zhenzhi) pushes and swings me; it is as powerful as breaking timber. Even if it could break timber, it is not a reasonable labor. If we analyze it with reason, would it be necessary to push and swing [people with such powerful correspondence]?

You began [the *Discourse*] with the clear [statement] that Confucius and Laozi are the Buddha, but at the conclusion of the writing, your discussion is desultory. Why [do you say that] Chinese government officials' ceremonial robes and the manner of raising [a ceremonial tablet] and kneeling on the ground are all types of Chinese deportment, and slanderingly say that the worship of putting one's head on the Buddha's feet is just like when a fox squats down? Why [do you say that] Chinese ceremonial dress and bowing by completely bending the [upper] body are respectful manners in the region near the imperial capital, and increase humiliation by saying that the practice of kneeling with one's right knee on the ground is just like a crouching dog?

Let me ask you a question. If [you say that] Confucius is one of right, perfect enlightenment and Śākyamuni is one of wrong views, I cannot tolerate to hear this talk. If you approve of [Śākyamuni] as one of rightness and truth, for what reason do you despise and reproach him? You have already lost the intention to stand in awe of the admonitions of sages. Moreover, you have forgotten the courtesy of not having one's own way. This is the first thing I find regrettable.

Futhermore, you say, "To maintain completely one's body and to abide by ancestor worship are in the teaching to continue wholesomeness. To damage one's physical form and change one's family name are in the learning to cut off evil." This means that [King Zhuang,] son of Shangchen (King Mu of Chu state, who killed his father and usurped the throne)[503] would have had the achievement of carrying on wholesomeness [from his murderous father], and that [Śākyamuni's son] Rāhula, who became a Buddhist monk, would have had the determination to cut off evils. Analyzing your discourse together with reality, I consider this to be the second point I find regrettable.

Again, you say, "[Buddhist monks] abandon their wives and children in token of a minor degree, and discontinue their ancestor worship in token of a major degree." The law of spiritall beings is obscure and vast; it is difficult to clarify. Therefore, when Zilu asked a question [about spirits], Confucius did not explain.[504] It must be because life and death belong to different paths, and the condition of spirits are hard to understand. Would it be because the sage was unable to explain it? In fact, [Confucius] was afraid that the wise (i.e., Zilu) would not be able to understand this. If we reflect with the mirror of the three transcendental knowledges, we will know that [spirits] exist. You already accept that the spiritual edification (i.e., Buddhism) was transmitted to the east, and yet you also say that [Buddhism] took the tide with funeral services. This is incoherent. This is the third point I find regrettable.

Moreover, you say, "The direct teaching (i.e., Daoism) can promote modesty and suppleness [of human nature], while the indirect teaching (i.e., Buddhism) can restrain arrogance and toughness." I read this statement three times, and [I am afraid that] it is egregiously disordered. Since modesty and suppleness are easily contravened, we should promote them harmoniously with the indirect [teaching]. Since arrogance and toughness are difficult to edify, we need to restrain them diligently with the direct [teaching]. When we examine the mind and inspect these matters, isn't this indeed the case? If rice bran gets in your eye, you cannot tell east from west. If you are attached to your biased view, you are confused about the meaning of an expression. Your statement misses the mark. This is the fourth point I find regrettable.

In addition, you say, "Since [the words of the Daoist teaching cause people to] humble themselves, only the intelligent advance; and since [the words of the Buddhist teaching] promote [people to feel better], the ignorant vie with each other in moving forward." Your statement about the words of the Daoist teaching is true. I respectfully agree with you and sing it loudly. It covers and carries all things. It raises and educates all things that have a form. Your statement, "Only the intelligent advance," however, seems to be your own discretion.

Once the Buddha's voice sounds, those who practice the four immeasurable minds are equally in line, the three vehicles equally follow him obe-
44a diently, and heavenly beings and dragons altogether submit themselves to him. Your statement "The ignorant vie with each other in moving forward" appears to be a false accusation as well. This is a discussion to explore what is complex and profound, but you recklessly form a boil and a papule (i.e., create problems) and freely make unfounded remarks. This is the fifth point I find regrettable.

Furthermore, you say, "Buddhism is the way to destroy evils, while Daoism is the way to give rise to wholesomeness." Regarding the way to destroy evils, I can find no fault. Stopping evils and performing good deeds are the reasons why [all] teachings arise. I have not understood about the way to give rise to wholesomeness. Who has the way [to give rise to wholesomeness]?

If wholesomeness is already wholesomeness, why is it necessary to give rise to it? If wholesomeness is not wholesomeness, it does not mean to give rise to wholesomeness. Then the outward reason for giving rise to wholesomeness has no entrustment. The Way is wholesomeness. If you take to give rise to wholesomeness as the outward reason, this is to excessively add to the wealth of the rich (i.e., it is too wasteful). If it cannot shake off evils, it is distorted as a teaching. The Great Way is equally broad for all, but you want to limit it [to Daoism]. This is the sixth point I find regrettable.

Moreover you say, "For those who are brutal and stubborn, it is the best to be taught by the Buddha. For those who are kind and gentle and who keep their minds free from preoccupation and open to receive [others' influences], it is the utmost to follow the [Daoist] way."[505] To beat and bring a man who is brave and fierce to submission and to have a man who is brutal and tyrannical become peaceful are really Śākyamuni's great achievements. I am not against your bright purpose [in this point]. Nevertheless, the power of the Way is strong and brilliant and the merit of its edification reaches far-distant places.

[The Way] "makes the nature [of humans] complete and preserves what exists continually."[506] There is nothing that is not placed under its favor. Even owls and the venomous birds called *zhen* reform themselves. There is nothing that is not controlled by the might [of the Way]. Your saying that only those who keep their minds free from preoccupation and open to receive [others' influences] are all right is too shallow and harsh. You unconsciously fall into a persistent biased view. Don't you realize that being narrow-minded and inferior impedes the Way? When I open and examine the heading [of your *Discourse,* I see that] you first admonish one's personal assumption, but while making a statement and presenting a discussion you unconsciously change your mind, and you have difficulty in maintaining both your claim and nominal definition. This is the seventh point I find regrettable.

You say, furthermore, "The eight [diagrams] represent all foreign scriptures of the western region and describe both extensive things and small things." The *Diamond Sutra* (Skt. *Vajracchedikāprajñāpāramitā-sūtra; Jingang borejing*) consists of less than a thousand sentences. Even the teachings propagated by four-line verses (Skt. *catuṣpādikā gāthā*) encompass all existing things. [Scriptures of Buddhism and Daoism] explain both coarse and sublime [things], and contain both complicated and simple [matters]. There are minute teachings and detailed precepts [in Buddhism], and ritual codes go into particulars [in Daoism] as well. [Nevertheless,] you say that exquisite and coarse [things] arise in total disregard of law [in Buddhism]. This statement goes against reality. This is the eighth point I find regrettable.

Moreover, you say, "Observing [the nature of] each country, the non-Chinese country is of a cruel nature, while China is of a mild nature." Let me ask you a question. Would the torture called *paoluo* (forcing a person to walk on a slippery metal beam placed above fire) be a punishment carried out in Samarkand or India?[507] The sad [son who was whipped by his parents and who] shed blood was a boy in China.[508] The miserable destruction of scraping [a fetus from a pregnant woman] was not in the minds of the non-Chinese.[509] [To moisten all things] with dew in fall and [to grant favors] enduring disgrace are not done by a person who lives on the seacoast [and who enjoys himself in forgetting the world].[510] Examining the natures [of the non-Chinese country and of China], the Chinese and the non-Chinese have the same principles. You unfoundedly think that [the nature of the Chinese] is mild while [the nature of the non-Chinese] is harsh. This is the ninth point I find regrettable.

Moreover, you say, "One who plays the *go* game is wiser than one who travels around. One who expounds and chants [Buddhist scriptures] is better than one who makes quips and jokes." Thinking this over, the reasons why the refined taste [of Buddhism] could be transmitted and why the scriptures and writings were not abandoned are really due to [efforts] to make people understand by expounding and chanting [Buddhist scriptures] and to attain enlightenment through inquiring and seeking. Therefore, [Confucius] said, "Not thoroughly discussing what is learned is the thing that occasions me solicitude."[511] You, however, compare [expounding and chanting Buddhist scriptures] with making quips and jokes. You are very rude in treating the virtue [of the Sage]. Let me ask you a question. Where do you place a fish trap (i.e., the tool) to lead [people] to wholesomeness? First of all, you want to forget the words [of Buddhist scriptures] before you apprehend the ideas. This is the tenth point I find regrettable.

[Your *Discourse*] has these ten points that I find regrettable. I cannot resolve them myself. I hope that you, a gentleman, will explain them further for me. Mr. Xie [Zhenzhi] had a criticism and a different view [on your *Discourse*] as well. You refuted [his criticism] with detailed explanations. I focus here only on what I want to ask, and will not take further risks.[512] 44b

Doubts about the *Discourse on the Non-Chinese and the Chinese* and Inquiries to the Daoist Gu by Zhu Guangzhi

I, Zhu Guangzhi, bow with my head to the ground.

I have had a look at the correspondence between you and Xie [Zhenzhi], Attendant-in-Ordinary, regarding the *Discourse on the Non-Chinese and the Chinese,* in which you clarify the meaning that [Buddhism and Daoism] are united into one. It can be said that they are concise, detailed, and refine discussions. With regard to deeply honoring the decorations of Chinese ceremonial robes and crowns, rejecting the simplicity of taking the tonsure, stating that the manner of raising [a ceremonial tablet] and kneeling on the ground is respectful, and disgracing the manner of sitting like a squatting fox, they confine the Chinese people and cut off their adoption of foreign methods. Even though the metaphor of a boat and a carriage is skillful, the feeling of impartiality and benevolence is not enough. You already leveled the origin [that Buddhism and Daoism] reach and meet, but the way with which the tool entrusts itself [in order to lead people to the origin] is blocked. In this case, we only get a distant view of the awakening of the three vehicles in this land, and the ferry of the six *pāramita*s is a long way off from us at the present point. Those who open Buddhist scriptures and play with the doctrines are greatly disappointed and discontented.

Mr. Xie looks down on the Way of [Divine] Transcendents (i.e., Daoism) and praises Buddhism; he considers the art of sprouting wings [and ascending to Heaven as a Transcendent] to be a groundless doctrine and takes the assertion of becoming a Buddhist monk as following the authentic text. It is as if one knows his fingers are fingers and does not know there is no difference from other people's fingers. Is this the reason to reach all aspects to grasp the meaning, or the thought that [Buddhism and Daoism] are virtuously the same?

I was gradually educated in the Dharma early in my life and later enjoyed the taste of Daoism. I always think that respecting the emptiness [of Buddhism] and valuing the nothingness [of Daoism] are the same in the ultimate purport. Both a snare and a net are laid; in principle there is no prejudice. Each person should follow whichever teaching he can best understand and enter that way. It is [important] that it be the place where the mind can be peaceful. Why is it necessary to be able to inherit the emperor's upper robe with the dragon figures and yet be unable to ride on [a carriage decorated with] precious stones?

I have to work a lot because of my poverty. I am behind in my studies. It has been more than ten years since I covered the boxes of my books and writings. What I learned in my childhood and what I heard previously are now all forgotten. I have spent years in idleness, having a willful mind. [Even though] I wish to start studying, I have no means [to do so]. Every day I lament by myself through the long night. Then I try to prompt myself until daybreak, without sparing myself, but even though I try to purify my mind, I am still far away from faith and increasingly suffer from defilements. If faith does not go along with the doctrine, it will be fickle and have no subjectivity. Because of this, it causes guests who censure me to arise. Hence, I am writing down my humble opinion, exhausting my poor ability. I hope you will again give instruction for me and give guidance on the points about which I am doubtful. I, Guangzhi, bow with my head to the ground.

The *Discourse* [*on the Non-Chinese and the Chinese*] says, "Raising [a ceremonial tablet], kneeling on the ground, and bowing by completely bending the [upper] body are respectful manners in the region near the imperial capital, while squatting like a fox and crouching like a dog are reverential manners in uncivilized places."

My question is this: Each country has its own manners. Since it has been this way for a long time, it is difficult to equalize them. Regarding the point that each person attains what he is content with, there is originally nothing with which to argue [on this point]. As for the deportment in the regions near the imperial capital, your statement is correct. Regarding the expression of [squatting like] a fox and [crouching like] a dog, isn't this said merely to hurt [people's feelings]?

The *Discourse* says, "Even if it is said that since the united point of the teachings is equal, and that the teachings are interchangeable, is it possible to wade across the river by carriage or travel on land by boat? It is certainly impossible."

My question is this: Teaching is intended to follow human feelings, but human feelings are not a teaching. Teaching has no fixed pattern because human feelings are not unified. What human feelings, which are not unified, proceed to varies. They become strong as well as soft. If [strong and soft feelings] are exercised together, the Chinese and the non-Chinese are assuredly the same. Therefore, in [crossing over] a large river that flows grandly, it is 44c
not appropriate to use this (i.e., a carriage). In [traveling over] a prairie to a remote land, why would we take that (i.e., a boat)? Why is it impossible to use both forms of transportation, both boat and carriage?

The *Discourse* says, "[Everything] is neither completely the same nor completely different. [Buddhist monks] abandon their wives and children in token of a minor degree and discontinue their ancestor worship in token of a major degree."

My question is this: If one discontinues [ancestor] worship in token of a major degree and yet is not able to abandon his family in token of a minor degree, this means to intend the difference and yet enter the same. It is not a fault of being the same. Would an ox used to plough a field rather be forever released from sacrificial use since it is useless for an ancestral temple?

The *Discourse* says, "They fulfill all things they desire with the politeness [of Confucianism], but they completely warp the rule of showing filial piety and respect for one's parents with the [Buddhist] Dharma. [Buddhists] go against virtue and offend the [right] order and yet they have been unaware of it."

My question is this: If [Buddhists] go against virtue and offend the [right] order, they should make no action. Being benevolent, devoted, gentle, and harmonious is the mind to keep one's feet on the ground and holds true. Therefore, having a simple meal and practicing the [Buddhist] Way are not unfortunate signs, and being in full [ceremonial] dress and eating the bread of idleness are not the ways to cultivate the right [mind]. Your opinion that "They fulfill [all things they desire with the politeness of Confucianism, but they completely] warp [the rule of showing filial piety and respect for one's parents with the Buddhist] Dharma" can be cut off here.

The *Discourse* says, "What should be valued in the ultimate principle of the universe is the Way, and what should be despised in phenomena is secularity. Now if we reject Chinese [teachings] and devote ourselves to the foreign [teaching], what does this mean? If it is because of the Way, the Way is originally one. If it is because of secular [customs], the secular [customs of Chinese and non-Chinese] are completely different [from each other]."

My question is this: Since the ultimate Way is void and comprehended, it is honorable even without having a rank of nobility. Since secular [customs] have nothing that is not stagnant, they are humble even if they are not rejected. The humble is unable to have no trouble. The honored is naturally content with itself. The state of being content with itself is already one. The sphere of secular troubles is also equal. If the Way is one and [the sphere of secular] troubles is equal, what is good and what is bad? (I.e., there is no distinction between good and bad.) Therefore, they are all [the subject of] edification by sages. Only in the mental functions is there delusion. When delusion is exhausted and intelligence arises, [the distinction between] oneself and others is spontaneously forgotten. What are you worried about? Why do you hesitantly stay on the border between rejection of [the Chinese teachings] and devotion to [the foreign teaching], and the righteousness of China and the foreign [country]?

The *Discourse* says, "The teaching of nonarising (i.e., Buddhism) is indirect, while the teaching of immortality (i.e., Daoism) is direct. The direct teaching can promote modesty and suppleness [of human nature], while the indirect teaching can restrain arrogance and toughness."

My question is this: Nonarising is precisely immortality, and immortality is nothing other than nonarising. The names differ but the contents are the same. Is it possible to hold the distinction between the direct and the indirect? If we separate the superior from the inferior because of the difference of their later development, we should restrain toughness by the direct [teaching] and promote suppleness by the indirect [teaching]. Therefore, Confucius said, "Since [Ran] Qiu withdraws, I urge him forward. [Zhong] You (i.e., Zilu) is busy with other people's affairs. Therefore, I keep You back."[513] As for the way to instruct people, isn't this right?

The *Discourse* says, "Buddhism is elegant and extensive, while Daoism is simple and exquisite. What is exquisite is not something in which clumsy people believe, and what is extensive is not something that exquisite people can handle."

My question is this: One who acquires extensive information and a retentive memory must go along with the mental function that is profound and broad. If he sincerely cultivates good conduct, he must follow the principles and reach the subtle [state of mind]. If his mental function is clear, he has nothing that is not exquisite in principle. If his principles are exquisite, he has nothing that is not exhausted in intelligence. In that case, what is exquisite and what is extensive are equally meritorious and mutually make use of each other. If the extensive means the exquisite, would [the extensive] still be 45a
believed by clumsy people? If the exquisite means the extensive, would [the exquisite] be wanted only by those who are broadly proficient in [Buddhism]?

The *Discourse* says, "The words of the Buddhist teaching are splendid and they promote [people to feel better], while the words of the Daoist teaching are sincere and cause [people] to humble themselves. Since [the words of the Daoist teaching] cause [people] to humble themselves, only the intelligent advance; and since [the words of the Buddhist teaching promote people to feel better,] the ignorant vie with each other in moving forward."

My question is this: [The words of the Buddhist teaching] are splendid, but they are not apart from the principles. They were molded by the One of Transcendent Wisdom. [The words of the Daoist teaching] are sincere, but they have not reached the void. Therefore, they were crafted by one who had gained a good reputation. There is order in the relation between being molded and crafted. Is it because [the teachings] are aimed at those whose natural disposition is ignorant, or those who possess intelligence? If the teachings are aimed at those whose natural disposition is ignorant, then not only the intelligent advance. If [the teachings are] certainly aimed at those who possess intelligence, the ignorant are unable to go forward. If both the intelligent and the ignorant can [advance], why is it necessary to promote them [to feel better] or [to cause them] to humble themselves? Your wonderful comparison is not in a position to make clear the point. This is something about which you ought to make a further argument.

The *Discourse* says, "Buddhist scriptures are complicated and illustrious, while Daoist scriptures are concise and profound. Since [Daoist scriptures] are profound, it is hard to discern the gate to the subtle [Way]. Since [Buddhist scriptures] are apparent, it is easy to follow the road to true [awakening]. If we follow [the road to] true [awakening], we will not get lost on our way home (i.e., the ultimate state of mind). If we discern [the gate to] the subtle [Way], we will completely attain all thoughts."

My question is this: Since [Daoist scriptures] are concise, it is easy to follow them. Why do you say it is hard to discern [the gate to the subtle Way]? If [Buddhist scriptures] are complicated, it would be difficult to follow them logically. How [then] could you easily follow [the road to true awakening]? If we follow [the road to] true [awakening], we will not get lost on our way home. We will be able to be led to the culmination of the [Buddhist] Way. Even though [the Buddhist scriptures] are not profound and concise, we will spontaneously reach there deeply. Why do you borrow a method that is difficult to clarify and replace it with this path that is easy to understand?

The *Discourse* says, "For those who are brutal and stubborn, it is the best to be taught by the Buddha. For those who are kind and gentle and who keep their minds free from preoccupation and open to receive [others' influences], it is the utmost to follow Daoism."

My question is this: Wrong views and the distortion of truth are what the Dharma does not allow. Giving pleasure and happiness, relieving pain and suffering, making other people happy, and giving up all attachments (i.e., the four immeasurable minds) are little by little recorded [in Buddhist scriptures]. Making other people happy means to be able to accept anything. Giving up all attachments means that one must efface oneself. The meaning of [the Daoist assertion] to keep one's mind free from preoccupation and open to receive [the influences of others] mysteriously matches [the meaning of the Buddhist tenet to make other people happy and give up all attachments]. I do not know on what teaching brutal and stubborn people rely. If you say that [the teaching that people] receive varies, you are rather like the one who carved a mark on the side of his boat [to indicate the place where he dropped his sword into the water]. How could there be a case in which [Buddhism and Daoism] tally with each other?

The *Discourse* says, "Buddhism is the way to destroy evils, while Daoism is the way to give rise to wholesomeness. Moreover, we should not imitate the teaching of the western tribes with the nature of the Chinese people."

My question is this: Your saying that [Daoism] is the way to give rise to wholesomeness is very good, but your statement "We should not imitate [the teaching of the western tribes with the nature of the Chinese people]" is disgraceful [to Buddhism]. I am unconvinced. Let me ask you a question about the nature of the Chinese people and the nature of the western tribesmen. You consider the nature of the Chinese people to be purely good, and that of the western tribesmen to be fundamentally evil. If [the nature of the western tribesmen] was fundamentally evil, how could it be broken by reason? If [the nature of the Chinese people] was purely good, what significance would there be in giving rise to wholesomeness? Therefore, we know that if [people] have evil, which can be broken, they have not left behind wholesomeness; and if [people] have wholesomeness, which can arise, they have not escaped from evil. In that case, wholesomeness and evil go together and mutually align as deep or shallow.

Accordingly, the fact that Rāhula was benevolent and gentle is not the influence of the light from the east (i.e., Chinese influence). King Jie and [the robber] Zhi were fierce and cruel; was this caused by a concentration of the vapors of the west? Why do you evaluate highly only the Chinese tradition and despise the teaching of the western tribes? If the wholesomeness of this [land of China] is different from the wholesomeness of that [land of the western tribes], and if the evil of that [land of the western tribes] differs from the evil of this [land of China], in wholesomeness and evil [the Chinese people and the western tribesmen] would be essentially against each other. [If this is so,] could there then be a case where they reach the same point?

The *Discourse* says, "Regarding the manner of squatting and the incom- 45b
prehensible foreign language that can be compared to the noisy chirping of insects and birds, why is it worthy to imitate them?"

My question is this: Rites are to develop respect [in the mind], and music is to perceive [the world of] harmony. Even though the respectful mind is developed through rites, rites are not the same as the respectful mind. Although the harmony [of sounds] is perceived through music, music is not the same as harmony. Consequently, when a ruler sets[the people] at ease and the people obey him, the gems and silk [used for rites] are kept in a bamboo chest [because the rites are no longer necessary]. When manners and customs are simple, sincere, and peaceful, bells and drums [for music] are no longer sounded. Moreover, the use of bells and drums is not on the same level of that of the two polarities (i.e., Heaven and Earth), probably because [bells and drums] are used as tentative expedients from necessity in order to rescue [the disordered world]. In that case, as long as moral principles exist, [superficial] form does not matter. If we return [to the foundation], we do not mind whether [Chinese manners and customs] are the same as or different from [those of the western tribes].

Now, as for squatting like a fox and crouching like a dog, who says [these behaviors] are not respectful? With respect one straightens his mind. Who says [such behaviors] are impolite? Politeness and respect profoundly tally. Why do you reject [the manners and customs of the western tribes] in vain? Among groups of those who bear consciousness, [only] human beings show their nobility. The nobility [of human beings] does not consist in language. [The value of] language lies in treasuring principles. Therefore, since the *kylin* and the male phoenix harbor benevolence in mind, they are valued in sages' books. The chimpanzee (*xingxing*) can speak [but he does not know principles]. [Therefore,] he is laughed at in the *Book of Rites*.[514] I do not understand on what you rely for the meaning in your discourse. If one sticks to language and removes principles, this is not what the wise depend on. He who relies upon principles and goes beyond language breaks superficial phenomena and clarifies the ultimate law of Nature. Accordingly even the unchanging [way advocated by] the elder Li (i.e., Laozi) is beyond the desire for fame.[515] Vimalakīrti's silence is not superceded by [all bodhisattvas'] skillful speeches.[516] If we inspect the words [of Buddhist and Daoist scriptures], both his (i.e., Daoism) and mine (i.e., Buddhism) have aspects to be driven away. If we examine their purposes, there is no boundary between those of Laozi and those of Śākyamuni. When the aspects of both [Buddhism and Daoism] are driven away, [struggling in vain, like] trying to moisten something with tiny bubbles, should be rejected. If there is no boundary [between Laozi's purpose and that of Śākyamuni], neither goes against nobility. Why do you view *prajñā* from a distance and say that it is not wisdom? Why do you humiliate [the foreigners] and rigorously compare them to insects and birds? I carefully examined your discussion repeatedly, day after day. I have not yet been satisfied.

Moreover, according to regional custom there are different languages. How then would [such a difference] be exclusively between the foreign country and China? Taking only China as a familiar example, Qi state and Lu state are not the same [in terms of dialect]. The use of the terms that mean "to begin," *quanyu* and *chuluo,* has also changed from ancient times to the present. Since there is no harm in recording, both terms have been transmitted in the world in practice. If that (i.e., Buddhism) is wrong, this (i.e., Daoism) is not right either. If this is right, that alone cannot be wrong. Since both cannot be right, they are equally wrong.

Imagine a case in which our Chinese spoken language flows into that [foreign] country. It will incur blame and be reproached [as "the] noisy chirping of insects and birds." It can be seen that [the people of that country will say that Chinese] is an incomprehensible foreign language. When we solely clarify this point, beams and pillars become equal [in value].[517] If [the biased views of] both sides are concurrently removed, wouldn't they then understand each other? Principles are inmost, deep, and subtle; they are not what we ought to take part in. I sincerely wish to discern the right profound teaching, and for the time being I simply express [my thoughts] in a straightforward manner. Standing far from you, I admire you wholeheartedly. I will await your further instructions.

The Disputation on the Daoist Gu's *Discourse on the Non-Chinese and the Chinese* by Huitong at Yecheng [Temple]

I was at leisure at the beginning of the summer, with nothing particular to do, and I forgot the time passing by, when I opened Mr. Gu's discourse, which is so bright to inspire the ignorant. I saw that it discusses the origin of the differences and similarities [between the non-Chinese and the Chinese] and clarifies the purport of right and wrong. The expressions are rich, the principles are evident, the writing is splendid, and [the content] is truly profound. Every time I closely read it, I forget my fatigue. It comforts me just as the daylily does. It is really the so-called refined work by a distinguished literary person. 45c

Nevertheless, when I examine the ultimate purpose, there are many points that make me doubt and laugh. It is like the story of the blind man who went to collect pearls and returned home with red beans, thinking that he had obtained treasures, or the story of the deaf man who wanted to listen to music—he hears a donkey braying, is delighted by it, and thinks that he understands music. Here, it is probably a major fallacy that you have discussed the non-Chinese and the Chinese and consider that you have attained the principles.

When I saw that you refer to Daoist scriptures in your discussion, I became more confused. What Laozi composed in ancient times is only the *Five Thousand Words.* Everything else is miscellaneous and they are dissolutely fallacious doctrines, yet you distinguish and call them Daoist scriptures. On what basis does this happen? Since they are not what Laozi composed, how can they be authentic statute books? I hope you will examine this point thrice and remove the delusion soon.

The *Discourse* says, "If Confucius and Laozi were not the Buddha, who else would this be applicable to? Daoism is precisely Buddhism; Buddhism is none other than Daoism."

Speaking about this statement, I am afraid that you are completely confused. [Buddhist] scriptures state, "Mahākāśyapa is called Laozi and Kumāra Guangjing is called Confucius over there."[518] We know that Laozi is not the Buddha. That is clear. In fact, your views about principles have not yet been great. Therefore, you have an opinionated viewpoint—in this case, that Laozi and Confucius were sent [to China] by the Buddha. They, moreover, propagated the virtue [of the Buddha], and showed [the law of] merit and demerit of beings. Later Buddhism was transmitted.

Nevertheless, it is difficult to observe the Great Way, while it is easy to follow small comprehensions [of the mind]. This is a lamentation from ancient times and not a lamentation with signs originated today. Laozi composed the *Five Thousand Words,* but many people offer dubious explanations. Some people set forth fallacies to confuse people's minds, and some pass on licentious and cruel stories to arouse people's nature. Hence those who perform good deeds are few, while those who are steeped in vice are many. I think that the decorative adornments of the official class, the respectful manner of bowing by completely bending the [upper] body, the funeral rite—these were probably [established] when the Great Way declined. Benevolence and righteousness consequently arose, and filial piety and showing respect for one's parents emerged. Knowledge and desires arose and dishonest practices increased day after day. Sages accordingly prohibited these by ethical education and controlled them through laws and institutions. Therefore, "propriety was established when faith and honesty became weak; it was the commencement of disorder."[519]

We have already lost *wuwei* and esteem phenomena (*youwei;* Skt. *saṃskṛta*). Could there be more to add to this? Regarding the appearance of shaving one's head, bowing down to squat like a fox, and the custom of [water] burial, I think that these are insufficient in splendor; they are parsimonious. [But] it is already true that wealth cannot be maintained. Laozi said that the five colors (i.e., blue, yellow, red, white, and black) consequently cause people to become blind,[520] and that even if one amasses a lot of wealth he will certainly lose it later.[521] Accordingly, it is the highest degree of modesty to take the tonsure, put on a black robe, abandon one's wealth, and leave behind the secular world. For this reason, Confucius praised Taibo, whose virtue the people did not [praise].[522] This is but one of many examples.

The tribal custom of kneeling down with one's right knee on the ground began in India and people of the four regions followed it. India is the center of the world where Buddhism originated. This [custom] indicates the good order and solemnity of the Great Dharma and the gravity and reverence of the highest teaching. You, [however,] compare it to a fox's squatting. How do you justify this? Hence, evil spirits assist vice and violent devils destroy what is right. This refers to you. [Your action] is similar to using a ladle to attempt to reduce [the volume of water in] a large river or the sea, or raising a hand to block the light of the sun and moon. [Although you may do these 46a
things,] you can neither reduce the water in a large river or the sea, nor shield [your eyes from] the brightness of the sun and moon.

In early antiquity the nature of the people was still pure. People could be bright without availing themselves of ethical education, and they were spontaneously well governed, without being inflicted with punishment. When a man died [his body] was laid in an open field. No mound was raised over it, nor were trees planted around it, nor was there any fixed period of mourning;[523] whenever the people grieved, they cried. This is the pure practice of ancient times. It is good enough to follow, yet you wish to deny it. What do you mean [by this]?

Furthermore, you compare the two teachings of Daoism and Buddhism to a boat and carriage. If knowledgeable people hear this, there is no one [among them] who would not smile [ironically]. I think that the Way of

Heaven keeps silent and sages have no attachment. Therefore, the Way is enlarged by people; it is not that the Way enlarges people.[524] In that case, the Sage's spiritual mirror (i.e., the mind) is proficient in everything. How could there be a case where their intellectual function does not embrace anything? Nevertheless, referring exclusively to one [teaching], you say that it is impossible to practice both [teachings] for salvation.

It is just as when the wonderful sunshine appears in the morning it offers illumination according to each thing, and when timely wind blows unceasingly in the evening, things produce various sounds according to their shapes. Accordingly, just as there are differences in shapes, the sounds are not the same, and since things differ from each other, the way [the sun] illuminates them also varies. The sun does not illuminate differently in accordance with each thing. The wind does not cause things of various shapes to produce sound differently in accordance with each shape. It is simply known that the sun is one and the wind is one, but the things that receive them vary. You take up the metaphor of a boat and carriage. How appropriate is your connotation?

The great teaching is impartial and the highest virtue is unbiased. There is a common purport in educating sentient beings and the same destination toward which to lead people. [Sages] make the sound [of teaching] equally in the land of the western tribes as well as that of the northern tribes. They have the same voice in the foreign land and in China. How could there be a case where sages give a different teaching in each of the different lands and a different edification in each of the different regions? Would there be [a teaching and an edification] only for the non-Chinese? Could there be [a teaching and an edification] only for the Chinese?

In the past, when Gongming Yi [of Lu state] played the musical piece *Cao* in the note *qingjue* for a cow, [the cow] just lowered her head and ate [grass] as before. This does not mean that she did not listen to [the music], but [the music] did not meet her ears. On the other hand, if there were the buzz of a mosquito or gadfly or the lowing of an orphaned calf, she would promptly prick up her ears, swish her tail, and stamp on the ground, listening [intently] to it. What you hear now is probably something like the buzz of a mosquito or a gadfly. What is your intention regarding the difference between the foreign country and China?

Furthermore, you say, "[Buddhist monks] abandon their wives and children in token of a minor degree and discontinue their ancestor worship in token of a major degree. They fulfill all things they desire with the politeness [of Confucianism], but they completely warp the rule of showing filial piety and respect for one's parents with the [Buddhist] Dharma."

There is as much difference between the [Buddhist] Way and the secular [way] as there is between night and day. The inner [way] is different from the outer [way], just as speech differs from silence.

As for offering worship at the ancestral temple, one's deceased father is jointly worshiped [with all his ancestors].[525] In that case, it is the highest degree of showing filial piety and respect to one's parent. People of the world have nothing to add to this. If one burns incense at the altar in the evening, intones a Buddhist scripture at the temple in the morning, worships, repents, and entreats unceasingly, [the merit] will reach his relatives in successive *kalpa*s as a token of the great degree, and [will reach] all people of the world as a token of the minor degree. The immensity of filial piety and benevolence like this cannot be surmised by the ignorant. The nation avails of the people and takes them as the foundation, and the ruler establishes [his power] depending on the people. The reason why the nation is peaceful is due to the power of the people. I infer that your discussion seems to be an empty scheme.

In addition, you say that *śramaṇa*s, [just like the one who] carved [a mark on the side of] the boat [to indicate the place where he dropped his sword into the water], and Daoists, [like the one who] waited by the stump [hoping that other hares would come to the place where he had previously caught a hare], fight each other in vain for supremacy; they impeach each other. I opened and read your discourse, which deeply relieved the hindrances 46b
I had had for a long time. I pondered the sentences and looked for the meanings. What is your sincere conclusion?

People of the heretical way have been wanton for a very long time. They have been submerged in darkness and do not move from there. They have been engulfed in delusion. How could they return [from delusion]? They roam around small villages and insincerely go beyond the border villages. In public they follow the sacred practice but in private they conduct debauchery. If attainment of the Way is like this, how shameful it would be!

In former times a man of Qi state was fond of hunting, but he did not have a dog or a deer at home. Even though he rushed around for many years, he could not catch even a single animal. Thereafter he withdrew [from hunting] and returned to tilling the land. Now that you are intelligent, if you go back to tilling the land, you will attain good wisdom.

Moreover, you say, "The Great Way has already been obscured and small comprehensions [of the mind] have risen one after another. Both eloquent and awkward speakers exert themselves mutually in debate. Who can correct them?"

The right path is difficult to destroy, while wrong principles are easy to reject. For instance, it is just as when light feathers meet with wind high above, they are blown away; or when fine stones enter the flow of water from a mountain stream, they roll down [the stream]; yet Mount Tai remains unmoved in a whirlwind and massive rocks are not swept away even by a rapid current. Hence, it is true that when plum trees are nipped by the frost they become leafless, but pines and cypresses are hardly withered even in the coldest season of the year. When a wicked method contacts a right [method], it is defeated. If you have the Great Way, then who would have small comprehensions [of the mind]? I think I will talk about this more and later I will make a judgment.

A fellow like Yan Hui observed Dongye Bi's way of handling the horses and he predicted [that the horses] would break down.[526] Zigong witnessed the manners of [Prince Yin of] Zhu state and [Prince Ding of] Lu state, and discerned that [the two men] would certainly die.[527] Why are you as ignorant as this? Therefore, I will indicate the difference between the ignorant and the intelligent, make clear that the wise differs from the mean, and show you by presenting one corner of the subject for the time being. I hope you will be able to reply to me about the other three [corners].[528]

Moreover, you say, "Either nirvana or the transformation of becoming a Transcendent is a method [to unite with the Way]. In Buddhism it is called right and true (*zhengzhen*), while in Daoism it is called right and one (*zhengyi*). The term 'one' means to return to non-death and the term 'true' means to meet nonarising" and "The teaching of nonarising (i.e., Buddhism) is indirect, while the teaching of immortality (i.e., Daoism) is direct." These [statements] were probably made because you are astute, skillful in debate, and eloquent. That a mean man is disdained is just like this. In that case, the doctrine of nirvana, extinguishing and crossing over [to the yonder shore], is written in authentic Buddhist scriptures. As for the assertion of the transformation of becoming a Transcendent and entering the [Daoist] way, however, on what doctrine is it based?

Laozi said that those who endeavor excessively to perpetuate life must nonetheless enter the jaws of death.[529] He also said, "The reason why Heaven and Earth endure and continue thus long is because they do not live of, or for, themselves."[530] Those who forget life survive, while those who try to sustain life must die. Since you are approaching death, you think that [the teaching of non-death] is urgent.[531] It is indeed urgent. As the saying goes, "Pointing to the south which is in fact the north, one says to himself that he is not confused. Pointing to the west which is in fact east, he says to himself that he is not stupid." You take mortality as going to be [re]born. Why do you have such contrary thoughts? Therefore, you live in seclusion and abstain from food in order to cultivate the art of the [Divine] Transcendents. I have heard that Laozi has the admonition against the five flavors (i.e., sweet, sour, bitter, pungent, and salty),[532] but gives no instruction about abstaining from grain. For this reason, even though a cicada and a moth do not eat, who among gentlemen values them? Although a frog and a python live in burrows, why would sages attach importance to them?

Moreover, since ancient times, there is no one among the sages and wise people who has not died in the end. Only you speak of "immortality." Why are you so reckless? Consequently, Emperor Shun's tomb is in Cangwu;[533] Emperor Yu's mausoleum is in Guiji;[534] there is a chapter in the record regarding the reburial of the Duke of Zhou;[535] Confucius had a dream [before his death, in which he sat between] two pillars;[536] there is the expression "Uncover 46c
my feet!" for Zeng Shen;[537] and there are the records for Yan Yuan that [Confucius] said, "Unfortunately, he was short-lived."[538] Haven't you heard of these? Do they sound absurd to you?

Formerly a person who had not seen a *kylin* asked a person who had seen one, "What kind [of animal] is a *kylin*?" The one [who had seen it] answered, "A *kylin* is just like a *kylin*." The man who had asked then said, "If I had seen a *kylin*, then I would not have asked you the question. Nevertheless, you said that a *kylin* is just like a *kylin*. How can I understand this?" [The one who had seen a *kylin* said,] "A *kylin* has a body like a roe deer, a tail like a cow, hooves like a deer, and a back like a horse." The man who had asked the question then clearly understood. Now, do you want to see a *kylin*? Are you telling me [about a *kylin*] without ever having seen one?

In addition, you say, "Daoist scriptures are concise and profound. Since [Daoist scriptures] are profound, it is hard to discern the gate to the subtle [Way]."

I think Laozi's teaching is contained in the *Five Thousand Words* and anything other than this is not an authentic scripture. The more Daoist scriptures appear, the deeper my suspicions. Most [of these so-called Daoist scriptures] falsely consign beautiful expressions and vainly marshal [all sorts of] flowery words. This is similar to the story that a man of Zhou held out a [dried-up] mouse in order to sell it as uncarved jade, but a man of Zheng saw it and just withdrew.[539] This is what it means. Speaking from this viewpoint, how can [your statement] be appropriate?

Again, you say, "For those who are brutal and stubborn, it is the best to be taught by the Buddha. For those who are kind and gentle and who keep their minds free from preoccupation and open to receive [others' influences], it is the utmost to follow the [Daoist] way."

Formerly, Laozi said, "Violent and strong men do not die a natural death. I will make this the basis of my teaching."[540] Therefore, the reason people widely circulate books of admonitions and make culture and education known is for the sake of the ignorant; they do not do such things for those of outstanding virtue and learning. When people go against [these statutes] there must be misfortune, and when they follow them there must be [good] fortune. People who are violent, strong, and stubborn are a group of the low and the stupid. The great teaching (i.e., Buddhism) shows benevolence and compassion and saves such people with expedients. Isn't this the selfless learning? Regarding [the statement] "Those who are kind and gentle and who keep their minds free from preoccupation and open to receive [others' influences]," I think that this should be considered empty talk. People who learn Daoism today are against [the teaching]. [Daoists] make the *Yellow Books* (*Huangshu*), which they consider to be authentic, public;[541] they carry a purple talisman, which they take as an efficacious means; there is no distinction of sex [among them]; and there is discord in the family. Some Daoists pray for longevity by ingesting drugs; some try to cure diseases by licentious means. How does your statement "Those who are kind and gentle [and who keep their minds free from preoccupation and open to receive others' influences]" hold water?

Moreover, [you say,] "The trace of Daoist teaching is esoteric and sublime. The proper implements for use of [the Daoist teaching] lies in oneself." Formerly Laozi said, "What makes me liable to great calamity is my having the body [that I call myself]; if I did not have a body, what great calamity could come to me?"[542] Laozi took [having] a body as great calamity, but you consider the body as something to maintain for a long time. What a major contradiction this is! "[The sage] places himself behind everyone, and yet he is always in the foremost position; he treats his body as if it were foreign to him, and yet it is preserved."[543] You merely say, "[The proper implements for use of the Daoist teaching] lie in oneself." I do not know on what basis you make this statement.

Furthermore, you say, "The incomprehensible foreign language entirely derives from their customs. They understand it, but [to the Chinese people] it sounds similar to the noisy chirping of insects and birds. Why is it worthy of imitation?"

I think that those who eat bitter food do not know that bitter is bitter, and they do not covet sweet and fragrant food; those who are delighted with malodorous things are not aware that [such things are] stinky and they are not addicted to [the fragrance of] pepper and orchids. It is as if you were to indulge yourself in failing to follow the right path. How could you have a thought about the Great Dharma?

The sacred teaching is subtle and unobstructed, and the ultimate Way is profound and extensive. It can be said that they are neither existence nor 47a
nonexistence. [In the sacred teaching of the ultimate Way] there is neither the meaning of a confrontation between self and other, nor a view between dissimilarity and similarity.

Speaking is similar to shooting. Once an arrow leaves the bow, even if you feel sorry about [having shot it], it is too late. Why don't you use prudence in your speech? You say that "[the incomprehensible foreign language sounds similar to] the noisy chirping of insects and birds." What do you mean?

Recently Sun [En (?–402) of the Way of the Five Pecks of Grain] went mad and openly acted outrageously. [His teaching] is weird and licentious and destroys proprieties. His cruel and disordered [behavior] rejects righteousness. Only when people of high moral standing are united in common determination will ignorant people stop [producing] falsehoods and reform themselves. Vicious fellows filled a room and evil people overran the gates. There were grievous sorrows in the towns and grudges about disastrous sufferings on the streets. The Way of Heaven brings disaster to those who are arrrogant, and spiritual beings bless those who are humble. Later [Sun En] brought ruin down upon himself.

The *Discourse on the Western Tribe and China* (*Rong hualun*), Breaking the Daoist Gu's *Discourse on the Non-Chinese and the Chinese,* by Shi Sengmin at Guangling

Formerly Vimalakīrti availed himself of the lofty path in this world and displayed his merits outside of the phenomenal world. He lived in the secular world, hiding his great talent; he exposed his aspiration only in the deep sea (i.e., the Buddhist world); he sprinkled spiritual intelligence over the ten directions; and he regulated and corrected the world. Therefore his trace appeared in the western land (i.e., India) where he joined others in the profound teaching. If we speak of his mysterious supernatural powers, he was able to make Heaven and Earth turn upside down or expand or contract things as he pleased. If we speak of his natural disposition, beyond discretion, he profoundly concentrated on the state of maintaining silence. People like this person can be called a Buddhist layperson (*jushi;* Skt. *gṛhapati*). I have not understood the intention behind your calling yourself a Buddhist layman.

You have not destroyed the high mountain of the seven kinds of self-conceit, you have not filled in the gorge of the five desires, the sunlight of wisdom has not shone [within you], you have not cleared up the clouds of ignorance, you have not stopped the winds of eternal darkness, and you have not returned from the delusion of nocturnal roaming. Your understanding [of Buddhism] is still on the ordinary level. Yet you still put on airs and call yourself a Buddhist layman? I, one who has poor [knowledge of the Buddhist] Way and who appreciates your ability from afar, have come to know that you are not yet qualified to take possession of [the title of *jushi*]. Even though this is the entry level in the Great Dharma, it cannot be easily assumed.

I examined the intention of your *Discourse on the Non-Chinese and the Chinese,* which completely illuminated your mind. I tried to fulfill my learning at the altar to Heaven, hoping you would instruct on this issue. Regarding your discussion, however, there is no natural ability to enjoy the elegance of the writing, there is no knowledge to examine the efficacy of profound issues, there is not even a very small light in intellectual function, and the amount of benefit is less than the moisture in a dewdrop. It is deficient in myriads of ways. What significance would there be?

Moreover, holding vague ideas within [the discussion] and an obscure plot in mind, you play lightly with brush and ink and rely on and surmise the sages' purposes, or you mix up Daoism and Buddhism and say they are the same; you discuss the depth of the teachings and say there are differences between them; you speak of the spiritual lands and put one above the other; and you slander in saying that there is falsehood in the clean, honest, and just state (i.e., enlightenment).

A bitter plum tree is overburdened with fruit and its branches break. Luan Da [of the Han dynasty] talked wildly and was decapitated. These are entirely the established system of the prehistoric times and the beacon of the Yin dynasty for the wise of later generations. I will now tell you the differences between Daoism and Buddhism in both names and meanings.

The Buddha is the other name for the numinous being of right, perfect enlightenment; the Way is a general term for a hundred paths. Laozi is a sage who expounded one aspect [of phenomena], while the Buddha depended on the foundation of myriad deities. In Daoism [the transformation of becoming] a Transcendent is considered to be noble, but in Buddhism the exhaustion of 47b
defilement is taken as good. In the Way of [Divine] Transcendents there is a thousand-year life span. In the exhaustion of defilement, on the other hand, there is a numinous eternal being. Because a numinous being is eternal, it is outstanding and profound. Because [a Transcendent] has a thousand-year life span, he rides on a dragon and controls the clouds. To control the clouds and to ride on a dragon is the way of [those who undertake] birth and death.

The profound numinous being is permanently happy and eternally pure. Now that it is like this, the movement of Heaven completely responded and the trace [of the profound numinous being] (i.e., Śākyamuni) descended to the imperial capital. He quietly disliked the palace, surrounded by watchtowers, and completely abandoned the palace. Therefore, he let go of his worldly nations and made a vow to go beyond to the three kinds of emptiness. He flew like a dragon to the splendid house [of the Dharma] and readied a vehicle [to go to] the place where he attained enlightenment.

Thereupon, he first expounded at the Deer Park (Skt. Mṛgadāva), then he had an assembly at the palace of the [Trāyastriṃśa] Heaven, then he propagated [his teaching] at Vulture Peak (Skt. Gṛdhrakūṭa), and later glorified it near the Hiraṇyavatī (or Ajitavatī) River. Consequently, the great light [of Dharma] illuminated even distant areas; the sun [seemed to] rest from shining; the splendid carriages [of those who heard the teaching] covered the four directions; a vehicle of the king of the Brahmā Heaven descended from heaven; beings of the nine heavens together sang [of the Buddha's virtue]; many hermits had an opportunity for realization; among those who made bold to have a relationship [with the Buddhist Way], there was none who did not gather together like clouds and take refuge in it.

Nevertheless, the emperor of the Zhou dynasty, a supreme ruler of an outlying region, had not given rise to the aspiration for [the Buddhist] Way. Therefore, the Tathāgata caused Samantabhadra to practice [the Buddha's] authority at the western road (i.e., India) and all of the three sages (i.e., Confucius, Yan Hui, and Laozi) to lead the people in the eastern metropolis (i.e., China). Therefore, a Buddhist scripture states, "Great being [Mahā]kāśyapa is none other than Laozi."[544] Hence [Laozi] assisted and supported the world of the Zhou period by means of the sophisticated teaching of the *Five Thousand Words,* and then returned to India, since his relationship to the edification [in China] had been used up. This is why there is [a legend that Laozi] left Guan for the faraway west. Based on [this legend], the Chinese composed the *Scripture on Laozi who Edified the Barbarians* (*Laozi huahujing*), which makes those of little knowledge sigh in admiration for China.

You have not yet known the details of the profound purport. Why then do you insist that Laozi and the Buddha are the same? When people hear that the Great Sage (i.e., the Buddha) has manifested as the leader of the circle of Confucian scholars, they take Zhuangzi, Confucius, the Duke of Zhou, and Laozi to all be the Buddha. If this were the case, is it possible that you are none other than Laozi as well?

[You then say that] among sentient beings who transmigrate in the five realms of existence there is no one who is not the Buddha. What do you mean by this? [Your statement] is really [as reckless as] when Kuafu chased after the sun and surely died from thirst. You say in the *Discourse on the Non-Chinese and the Chinese* that there are abominable people of Koguryo and Paekche to the east, tribal people of Qiang and Rong to the west, unkempt people to the north, and people who cut their hair and have tattoos on their bodies to the south; on the other hand, since the Duke of Zhou and Confucius created rules of decorum in China, there is a distinction between the non-Chinese and the Chinese.

[My *Discourse on*] *the Western Tribe and China* advocates that the east ends at a place where no one lives, the west ends at a solitary village, the north goes beyond the sea, and the south comes to an end at the gate of a village with no inhabitants. Since the Tathāgata enhanced the edification in China, there is a difference between the western tribespeople and [the people of] China. You condemn those who have the nature of the Chinese for learning the teaching of the western tribes. This is because you have come out of the deep pit of a well and have not yet seen a view of rivers and lakes. As a Buddhist scripture says, "The Buddha occupies the center of the world and leads the people of the ten directions to purity";[545] therefore, we know that the land of India is the central kingdom.

The Duke of Zhou and Confucius have the graceful and upright system [of propriety], while the Tathāgata has the law to transcend the secular world. Since [the Chinese have] the graceful and upright system [of propriety], they are different from the tribal people of the four directions. Since [the Tathāgata has] the law to transcend the secular world, he is not the same as the Duke of Zhou and Confucius. Since the [graceful and upright] system [of propriety] diffuses to the tribal people of the four directions, the tribal people of every direction praise the virtue [of the Duke of Zhou and Confucius]. Since the 47c
law [to transcend the secular world] was appended to [the system of] the Duke of Zhou and Confucius, Laozi returned to the west (i.e., India). Since Laozi returned to the west, a large number of tribal people have arisen. Since the tribal people of the four directions praise the virtue [of the Duke of Zhou and Confucius], they (i.e., the Chinese) excessively increase confusion.

The upright decorum is unable to be changed, and the true Dharma does not change. Since the upright decorum cannot be changed, Taibo straightened his clothes even in [the uncivilized land of] Wu and Yue. Since the true Dharma does not change, Buddhism was transmitted to the east without alteration. Since [Taibo] straightened his clothes, he caused the people in the land where they barely clothed themselves to follow the custom of appreciating clothing. Since the Dharma does not change, it causes Chinese people of talent and virtue to take the tonsure. Since [the people of Wu and Yue] had the custom of appreciating clothing, it made their appearance closer to that of the people of the Zhou dynasty. Since [talented and virtuous Chinese people] take the tonsure, it makes them respectfully equal to the western tribal people in customs. Since the appearance [of the people of Wu and Yue] became close to that of the people of the Zhou dynasty, it made them feel that their uncivilized customs were useless and poor. Since [talented and virtuous Chinese people who took tonsure] are equal to the faraway western tribal people in customs, it makes all those who see them at close range believe [in Buddhism].

If you think that there is no fixed rule in the Sage's path and his response varies according to each locale, then Taibo should have walked naked in the lower reaches of the Yangzi River (i.e., the land of the Wu and Yue), and it is possible that even today you do not wear clothes, either. Hence, even though locality and race differ, the sacred Dharma does not. From where do you take the basis of the meaning of your statement? You might say that you rely on the right way.

Thus, [I would say that] Daoism depends on attaining the mystery (*dong-xuan*) to be foremost, and Buddhism takes the emptiness of emptiness (Skt. *śūnyatā-śūnyatā*) to be the ultimate law of Nature. Laozi considers the Grand Void to be the essence, while the Buddha thinks that conforming to present affairs is profound. Laozi thinks that nature gives rise to [all things], while the Buddha considers that the unity of [cause and] condition gives rise to [all things]. Daoism takes talismans to be effective, while Buddhism takes leading [sentient beings] through explaining [Buddhist scriptures] to be exquisite. Since [in Daoism] the Grand Void is considered to be the essence, there are things to produce all things [in the Grand Void]. Since [in Buddhism] conforming to the present affairs is profound, all things are essential. Since [in Laozi's teaching] Nature gives rise to [all things], there is no heavenly hall to which to ascend. Since [in Buddhism] the unity of [cause and] condition gives rise to [all things], there are noble stages to which one can ascend. Since talismans are considered to be effective, there is no efficacious god in Daoism. Since [in Buddhism] leading [sentient beings] through explaining [Buddhist scriptures] is considered to be exquisite, people study the mind of the Sage. Since there are things to produce all things [in the Grand Void], Daoism is not great. Since all things are essential [in Buddhism], the path of the Sage is lofty and vast. Since there is no heavenly hall to which to ascend, it is said that it is fruitless [to practice Laozi's teaching]. Since [in Buddhism] there are noble stages to which one may ascend, intelligent people throw themselves into [the Buddhist Way]. There is no efficacious god [in Daoism]. Therefore, what are you fascinated by and what do you seek? Ever since people began to study the mind of the Sage [in Buddhism], *śramaṇa*s have arisen like clouds.

Things are like this. Therefore, we know that the Daoist scriptures are minor and shallow, while the Buddhist scriptures are extensive and deep; the Daoist scriptures are few and vile, while the Buddhist scriptures are magnanimous and clean; the Daoist scriptures are disordered and lacking, while the Buddhist scriptures are simple and pure; and the Daoist scriptures are approachable and yet obscure, while the Buddhist scriptures are profound and yet clear.

You should change your polluted robe (i.e., the Daoist robe) to a simple one (i.e., the Buddhist robe) and faithfully take part in the lofty teaching [of Buddhism]. Those who wear a yellow turban on the head look depraved. Wearing a cap made of leather is really not a Chinese style. Selling [Daoist] talismans and registers is an evil custom that deceives people of the world. Patting the cheeks with both hands and grinding the teeth are the extremity of confusion. Binding one's hands behind one's back and rolling on the ground is a manner of hell. Talismans and the union of [*yin* and *yang*] vapors (i.e., the "art of the inner chamber," sexual practices) are the most cunning craft.

In this way, [regarding Buddhism and Daoism,] light and darkness are already evident and truth and falsehood are already obvious. You should lead your friends in an orderly manner and walk across to the pure path (i.e.,

48a Buddhism). I look after the graceful virtue in my mind, and at the same time I receive with respect the truth of the Sage. Would this be bad? I think that this must truly not be adverse to the distinguished instruction.

End of Fascicle Seven of *The Collection for the Propagation and Clarification* [*of Buddhism*]

Notes

1 Two interpretations for the "six masters" are suggested in Kyōto Daigaku Jinbun Kagaku Kenkyūjo Chūsei Shisōshi Kenkyū han, ed., *Gumyōshū kenkyū* (Kyoto: Kyōto Daigaku Jinbun Kagaku Kenkyūjo, 1973–1975), vol. 2, p. 3, n. 10. First, the six non-Buddhist masters who were influential during the same time period as Śākyamuni: Pūraṇa-kāśyapa, Maskarī-gośālīputra, Sañjayī-vairaṭīputra, Ajitakeśakambala, Kabuda-kātyāyana, and Nirgrantha-jñātiputra. Second, the group of six evil *bhikṣus* among the Buddha's disciples: Nanda, Upananda, Kālodāyin Udāyin, Chanda, Aśvaka, and Punarvasu.

2 The original source of this phrase is found in the *Lunyu, Yang Huo:* "[The master] hates for the color purple to overpower vermilion." Vermilion (or deep red) is a primary color, while purple is a secondary color. Therefore, vermilion represents wholesomeness and purple represents unwholesomeness. For an English translation of the phrase, see James Legge, *The Chinese Classics with a Translation, Critical and Exegetical Notes, Prolegomena, and Copious Indexes* (Taipei: Wen shih che ch'u pan she, 1972, second revised ed.), vol. 1, p. 326.

3 The bird called *jingwei* is a legendary small bird that was believed to have the habit of dropping bits of wood and stone into the ocean, in the vain hope of filling it. This story is found in the *Beishanjing* of the *Shanhaijing.* See Hsiao-Chieh Ching, Hui-Chen Pai Cheng, and Kenneth Lawrence Thern, trans., *Shan hai ching: Legendary Geography and Wonders of Ancient China* (Taibei, Taiwan: Committee for Compilation and Examination of the Series of Chinese Classics, National Institute for Compilation and Translation, 1985), p. 60.

4 Cangwu is one of seven prefectures that belonged to Jiaozhou (present-day Guangdong province, a southern part of Guangxi province, and Vietnam). The prefectural office of Cangwu was in present-day Guangxi province.

5 Mencius' accusation against Yang Zhu and Mo Di is found in the *Mengzi, Teng Wen Gong, xia.* Legge, *The Chinese Classics,* vol. 2, pp. 282–284, n. 9–14.

6 See the *Laozi,* chapter 19. English translation in James Legge, *Dao de jing ji Zhuangzi quan ji* (Taibei: Wen xing shu ju, 1963), p. 110, n. 1.

7 The term *zhonglü,* one of the twelve classical Chinese musical notes, is associated with the fourth month of the year. The twelve classical Chinese musical notes consist of six *yang lü* notes (*huangzhong, dacu, guxi, ruibin, yize,* and *wuyi*) and six *yin lü* notes (*dalü, jiazhong, zhonglü, linzhong, nanlü,* and *yingzhong*). Each note corresponds to one of the twelve months of the year: *dacu* to the first month, *jiazhong* to the second

month, *guxi* to the third month, *zhonglü* to the fourth month, *ruibin* to the fifth month, *linzhong* to the sixth month, *yize* to the seventh month, *nanlü* to the eighth month, *wuyi* to the ninth month, *yingzhong* to the tenth month, *huangzhong* to the eleventh month, and *dalü* to the twelfth month.

8 The Chinese term *wuwei* is usually translated as "non-action," "inactivity," or "spontaneity." In Buddhism *wuwei* is used, in addition to these meanings, as the Chinese rendering of the Sanskrit term *asaṃskṛta* ("unconditioned") and as another term for nirvana. In this instance, the meaning intended here seems to be closest to "nirvana." However, I did not translate this term consistently as "nirvana" throughout the text, since it is not always clear what the various authors intended.

9 See the *Laozi,* chapter 21. Legge, *Dao de jing ji Zhuangzi quan ji,* p. 112, translates this phrase as "The grandest forms of active force from [Dao] come, their only source"; this interpretation differs from this context.

10 *Gong* and *shang* are the first two of the five fundamental notes (*gong, shang, jue, zhi,* and *yu*) that correspond to *huangzhong, dacu, guxi, linzhong, and nanlü,* respectively, of the twelve classical Chinese musical notes. See note 7.

11 See the *Laozi,* chapter 25. Legge, *Dao de jing ji Zhuangzi quan ji,* p. 115, n. 1–2.

12 According to the *Liezi,* the "primordial substance" (*tianrui*) is the stage where "things have not only assumed definite shapes and forms but have taken on qualities," and "in the Primal Beginning, *yin* and *yang* divide, and their interaction produces limited but identifiable shapes and forms." English translation in Eva Wong, *Liezi: A Taoist Guide to Practical Living* (Boston: Shambhala Publications, 1995), p. 28.

13 See *Lunyu, Zizhang.* Legge, *The Chinese Classics,* vol. 1, chapter 22, p. 346, n. 2.

14 Lü Shang is a man for whom Taigong, King Wen's grandfather, had waited (*wang*). Therefore he is called Taigong Wang Lü Shang.

15 The meanings of the terms *shiwen* (the Chinese character for the number 10) and *erwu* (2 and 5) are not clear. I refer to Sawada Mizuho's Japanese translation in *Ressenden Shinsenden* (Tokyo: Heibonsha, 1993), p. 142, n. 23, 24. The "Ten Celestial Stems" are combinations of the five primary elements (i.e., metal, wood, water, fire, and earth) and either one of the two elements the former and the latter: *jia* (the former wood), *yi* (the latter wood), *bing* (the former fire), *ding* (the latter fire), *wu* (the former earth), *ji* (the latter earth), *geng* (the former metal), *xin* (the latter metal), *ren* (the former water), *gui* (the latter wood). Furthermore, combinations of the ten celestial stems and the twelve animals of the zodiac are used for the Chinese calendar and directions.

16 See the *Xiaojing.* English translation in Henry Rosemont, *The Chinese Classic of Family Reverence: A Philosophical Translation of the Xiaojing* (Honolulu: University of Hawai'i Press, 2009), p. 105.

17 See the *Lunyu, Taibo.* Legge, *The Chinese Classics,* vol. 1, p. 208.

[18] See the *Lunyu, Zi han.* Legge, *The Chinese Classics,* vol. 1, p. 226.

[19] See the *Lunyu, Taibo.* Legge, *The Chinese Classics,* vol. 1, p. 207.

[20] See the *Lunyu, Xian wen.* Legge, *The Chinese Classics,* vol. 1, p. 279.

[21] See the *Laozi,* chapter 44. Legge, *Dao de jing ji Zhuangzi quan ji,* p. 135, n. 1.

[22] The Marquis of Sui's pearl (*suihou zhi zhu* or *suizhu*) is a pearl presented to the state of the Marquis of Sui by a large serpent that had been cured of a grave injury by him. The reference implies the greatest treasure of the world.

[23] See the *Lunyu, Shuer.* Legge, *The Chinese Classics,* vol. 1, chapter 14, p. 199, n. 2.

[24] The phrase "with his garments hanging down (*chui yichang*)" derives from the passage, "[Huangdi] (i.e., the Yellow Emperor), Yao, and Shun [simply] wore their upper and lower garments [as patterns to the people], and good order was secured all under heaven," found in the *Yijing, Xici, xia.* English translation in James Legge, *I ching: Book of Changes* (New Hyde Park, NY: University Books, 1964), pp. 383–384, n. 15.

[25] See the *Shangshu, Hongfan.* Legge, *The Chinese Classics,* vol. 3, p. 326, n. 6.

[26] See the *Lunyu, Yao yue.* Legge, *The Chinese Classics,* vol. 1, p. 353, n. 2.

[27] See the *Laozi,* chapter 38. Legge, *Dao de jing ji Zhuangzi quan ji,* p. 128, n. 1.

[28] The *zhangfu* was originally a formal cap during the Shang (Yin) dynasty. Confucius later wore the cap, and since that time it was considered the Confucian cap.

[29] See the *Laozi,* chapter 13. Legge, *Dao de jing ji Zhuangzi quan ji,* p. 104, n. 2.

[30] See the *Laozi,* chapter 9. Legge, *Dao de jing ji Zhuangzi quan ji,* p. 101, n. 2.

[31] See the *Lunyu, Xianjin.* Legge, *The Chinese Classics,* vol. 1, pp. 240–241.

[32] See the *Xiaojing* for both quotations. Rosemont, *The Chinese Classic of Family Reverence,* p. 116.

[33] See the *Shangshu, Jinteng.* Legge, *The Chinese Classics,* vol. 3, p. 354, n. 6.

[34] See the *Laozi,* chapter 52. Legge, *Dao de jing ji Zhuangzi quan ji,* p. 143, n. 2.

[35] See the *Laozi,* chapter 52. Legge, *Dao de jing ji Zhuangzi quan ji,* p. 143, n. 5.

[36] See the *Lunyu, Bayi.* Legge, *The Chinese Classics,* vol. 1, p. 156.

[37] See the *Mengzi, Teng Wen Gong, shang.* Legge, *The Chinese Classics,* vol. 2, pp. 253–254, n. 12.

[38] See the *Lunyu, Zi han.* Legge, *The Chinese Classics,* vol. 1, p. 221, n. 1–2.

[39] See the *Taizi Xudanajing* (Skt. *Jinapatra-arthasiddhi-sūtra*), T.171.3:418c17–424a22.

[40] See the *Xiaojing.* Rosemont, *The Chinese Classic of Family Reverence,* p. 110.

[41] The phrase "a great hypocrisy" (*dawei*) derives from the *Laozi,* chapter 18. Legge, *Dao de jing ji Zhuangzi quan ji,* p. 109, n. 1.

[42] See the *Lunyu, Shuer.* Legge, *The Chinese Classics,* vol. 1, p. 207.

[43] See the *Zuozhuan,* Zhuanggong's twenty-fourth year. James Legge, *The Chinese Classics* (Hong Kong: Hong Kong University Press, 1960), vol. 5, p. 107.

[44] This expression derives from the *Mengzi, Gongsun Wu, xia.* Legge, *The Chinese Classics,* vol. 2, p. 232, n. 2.

[45] The text has only *taigong* ("grandfather"). Based on the exposition of the *Shiji* (thirty-second fascicle, *Qi taigong shijia*), Kagaku Kenkyūjo Chūsei Shisōshi Kenkyū han, ed., *Gumyōshū kenkyū,* vol. 2, p. 35, n. 5, interprets it to be Taigong Wang Lü Shang. I follow this.

[46] See the *Zuozhuan,* Xigong's twenty-third and twenty-eighth years. Legge, *The Chinese Classics,* vol. 5, p. 187 (left column) and p. 208 (right column).

[47] See the *Zuozhuan,* Xuangong's second year. Legge, *The Chinese Classics,* vol. 5, p. 290 (right column).

[48] See *Lunyu, Xueer.* Legge, *The Chinese Classics,* vol. 1, p. 137, n. 3.

[49] See the *Laozi,* chapter 5. Legge, *Dao de jing ji Zhuangzi quan ji,* p. 98, n. 2.

[50] See the *Laozi,* chapter 32. Legge, *Dao de jing ji Zhuangzi quan ji,* p. 123, n. 5.

[51] See the *Lunyu, Weizheng.* Legge, *The Chinese Classics,* vol. 1, p. 145.

[52] See the *Lunyu, Zizhang.* Legge, *The Chinese Classics,* vol. 1, p. 343, n. 2.

[53] See the *Lunyu, Xiangdang.* Legge, *The Chinese Classics,* vol. 1, p. 232, n. 1.

[54] See the *Lunyu, Liren.* Legge, *The Chinese Classics*, vol. 1, p. 166, n. 1.

[55] See the *Laozi,* chapter 12. Legge, *Dao de jing ji Zhuangzi quan ji,* p. 103, n. 1–2. See note 10 for the five notes of traditional Chinese music.

[56] See the *Mengzi, Jinxin, xia.* Legge, *The Chinese Classics,* vol. 2, p. 466.

[57] See the *Mengzi, Teng Wen Gong, xia.* Legge, *The Chinese Classics,* vol. 2, chapter 7, p. 276, n. 2.

[58] This sentence presents a series of things done contrary to established practice: the sacrificial stand and pot should be placed in a palace hall, while military flags and banners are supposed to be hoisted at a camp gate; wearing a fur robe in hot weather and light linen clothing in cold weather are also contrary actions. So these are all examples of "actions that are perverse in the orientation of time and place."

[59] See the *Laozi,* chapter 41. Legge, *Dao de jing ji Zhuangzi quan ji,* p. 132, n. 1.

60 See the *Laozi,* chapter 51. Legge, *Dao de jing ji Zhuangzi quan ji,* p. 148, n. 1.

61 See the *Laozi,* chapter 45. Legge, *Dao de jing ji Zhuangzi quan ji,* p. 136, n. 1.

62 See the *Lunyu, Xian wen.* Legge, *The Chinese Classics,* vol. 1, p. 286.

63 See the *Laozi,* chapter 9. Legge, *Dao de jing ji Zhuangzi quan ji,* p. 101, n. 2.

64 See the *Lunyu, Wei Linggong.* Legge, *The Chinese Classics,* vol. 1, p. 296, n. 2, translates the name as Qu Boyu.

65 See the *Lunyu, Gongzhi Chang.* Legge, *The Chinese Classics,* vol. 1, p. 180.

66 See the *Lunyu, Wei Linggong.* Legge, *The Chinese Classics,* vol. 1, p. 297.

67 See the *Wenxuan* (compiled by Prince Zhaoming of the Liang dynasty), fascicle 45, *dui Chu wang wen.*

68 See the *Lunyu, Weizi.* Legge, *The Chinese Classics,* vol. 1, pp. 332–333, n. 1–2.

69 Bian He, a man of Chu, obtained a jade on Mount Chu and presented it to King Li and King Wu, but both kings thought that it was only a stone and He's legs were amputated as punishment. Later, King Wen realized that it was a real jade. This story is found in the *Han Feizi, Heshi.* See Burton Watson, trans., *Han Feizi: Basic Writings* (New York: Columbia University Press, 2003), pp. 81–82.

70 This story implies that even a divine turtle cannot change his fate. See the *Zhuangzi, Waiwu.* Legge, *Dao de jing ji Zhuangzi quan ji,* pp. 576–577.

71 The term *tianjing* refers to a celestial body. I translate the term here as "high above the earth."

72 This is not a precise quotation. Kyōto Daigaku Jinbun Kagaku Kenkyūjo Chūsei Shisōshi Kenkyū han, ed., *Gumyōshū kenkyū,* vol. 1. p. 48, n. 4, suggests that a similar expression is found in the *Laozi,* chapter 44. Legge, *Dao de jing ji Zhuangzi quan ji,* pp. 135–136, n. 1–3.

73 This passage is not found in the *Laozi.*

74 See the *Kongzi Jiayu,* fascicle 6, *Zhipei.*

75 See the *Laozi,* chapter 48. Legge, *Dao de jing ji Zhuangzi quan ji,* p. 138, n. 2.

76 See *Lunyu, Weizheng.* Legge, *The Chinese Classics,* vol. 1, p. 146, n. 4.

77 See the *Laozi,* chapter 30. Legge, *Dao de jing ji Zhuangzi quan ji,* p. 121, n. 4.

78 Laozi's view of this is found in the *Laozi,* chapter 13. Legge, *Dao de jing ji Zhuangzi quan ji,* p. 104, n. 2.

79 See the *Shangshu, Jintengpian.* Legge, *The Chinese Classics,* vol. 3, pp. 351–356.

80 See the *Lunyu, Shuer.* Legge, *The Chinese Classics,* vol. 1, p. 206.

[81] See the *Huainanzi, Xiuwu xun.* See Evan Morgan, *Tao, The Great Luminant: Essays from Huai nan tzu* (Shanghai: Kelly & Walsh Ltd., 1934), pp. 220–221.

[82] This is based on the description found in the *Mengzi, Teng Wen Gong.* Legge, *The Chinese Classics,* vol. 2, pp. 282–284, n. 9–14.

[83] This expression derives from a story found in the *Huainanzi, Xiuwu xun.* Lord Ping of Jin state made a large bell, but the music master Kuang asked the lord to recast the bell because it had a poor tone and it might disgrace his name in later generations. See Morgan, *Tao, The Great Luminant,* p. 241.

[84] This expression also derives from the description found in the *Huainanzi, Fanlun xun:* "The diamond-cutter may mistake a piece of jade, thinking it to be an imitation stone, the Pi. But I, Tun (Dun), alone, would never miss the luster"; Morgan, *Tao, The Great Luminant,* p. 170.

[85] See the *Lunyu, Yang Huo.* Legge, *The Chinese Classics,* vol. 1, p. 326.

[86] In the *Lunyu, Gongzhi Chang,* Confucius criticizes Zang Wen Zhong and Weisheng Gao. See Legge, *The Chinese Classics,* vol. 1, p. 179 and pp. 181–182, respectively.

[87] See the *Lunyu, Weizheng.* Legge, *The Chinese Classics,* vol. 1, p. 149.

[88] See the *Huainanzi, Qisu xun.*

[89] See the *Zhuangzi, Dasheng.* In the *Zhuangzi* Dongye Bi is called Dongye Ji. See Legge, *Dao de jing ji Zhuangzi quan ji,* p. 463, n. 11.

[90] See the *Zuozhuan,* Dinggong's fifteenth year. Legge, *The Chinese Classics,* vol. 5, p. 791 (left column).

[91] See the *Shiji,* fascicle 47, *Kongzi shijia.* Hsien-yi Yang and Gladys Yang, trans., *Selections from Records of the Historian* (Peking: Foreign Languages Press, 1979), pp. 13–14.

[92] See the *Zuozhuan,* Xianggong's twenty-ninth year. Legge, *The Chinese Classics,* vol. 5, p. 549, right column, to p. 550, left column.

[93] See the *Xiaojing.* Rosemont, *The Chinese Classic of Family Reverence,* p. 110.

[94] When Confucius was the Minister of Justice in Lu state, Qi officials gave girls, music, and horses to the Duke of Lu (i.e., Ji), who, after receiving them, neglected state affairs. Consequently, Confucius left Lu state. See the *Shiji,* fascicle 47, *Kongzi shijia.* Yang and Yang, *Selections from Records of the Historian,* pp. 8–11.

[95] The king of Wu took Pi's advice and rejected Wuzi Xu's advice. See the *Shiji,* fascicle 66, *Wuzi Xu liezhuan.* Yang and Yang, *Selections from Records of the Historian,* pp. 41–42.

[96] See the *Laozi,* chapter 23. Legge, *Dao de jing ji Zhuangzi quan ji,* pp. 113–114, n. 1.

[97] See the *Lunyu, Xian wen.* Legge, *The Chinese Classics,* vol. 1, p. 290, n. 1.

98 See the *Lunyu, Yong ye*. Legge, *The Chinese Classics*, vol. 1, p. 188.

99 See the *Lunyu, Taibo*. Legge, *The Chinese Classics*, vol. 1, p. 208.

100 See the *Lunyu, Yong ye* and *Xianjin*. Legge, *The Chinese Classics*, vol. 1, p. 185, and p. 239, respectively.

101 See the *Lunyu, Zi han*. Legge, *The Chinese Classics*, vol. 1, p. 223.

102 The *Huainanzi, Shuoshan xun*, states, "Observing floating driftwood, boats were devised, looking at rolling mugwort, wheels were invented, and seeing bird tracks, [the Chinese] written language was created."

103 The Sanskrit term for the thirty-seven elements of enlightenment is *sapta-triṃśad-bodhi-pakṣa*, which was translated into Chinese as *sanshiqi daopin*, *sanshiqi juefen*, or *sanshiqi puti fenfa*. It refers to the practices that lead to the attainment of nirvana: the four bases of mindfulness, the four bases of transcendental knowledge, the four right efforts, the five roots of wholesomeness, the five powers obtained through practicing the five roots of wholesomeness, the seven factors of wisdom, and the eightfold holy path.

104 The *Daodejing* consists of the *Daojing*, the first thirty-seven chapters, and the *Dejing*, the remaining forty-four chapters.

105 The same quotation is found in the *Bianwei lu* (T.2116.52:760b3–4) compiled by Xiangmai in 1291, and the *Fozu lidai tongzai* (T.2036.49:717c20–22) compliled in 1341. According to these two sources, the title of this sutra is *Laozi xishengjing*, which appears to be an indigenous Chinese scripture.

106 The sentence "to use the road [of the other state] in order to carry out an atrocity [against its own enemy]" refers to the story of the Marquis of Jin who dug a tunnel through Yu to attack Guo. See the *Zuozhuan*, Xigong's fifth year. Legge, *The Chinese Classics*, vol. 5, p. 145, par. 9.

107 This story is found in the *Zuozhuan*, Xianggong's twenty-seventh year. Legge, *The Chinese Classics*, vol. 5, p. 532 (right column) to p. 533 (left column).

108 Bai Qi's biography is found in the *Shiji*, fascicle 73, *Bai Qi Wang Jian liezhuan*. See William H. Nienhauser, ed., *The Grand Scribe's Records* (Bloomington, IN: Indiana University Press, 1994–2011), vol. VII, pp. 167–173.

109 Dong Zhuo's biography is found in the *Hou Hanshu*, fascicle 102, *Dong Zhuo liezhuan*.

110 The phrase "displace violence with violence" (*yi bao yi bao*) derives from the *Shiji*, fascicle 61, *Boyi liezhuan*. See Nienhauser, ed., *The Grand Scribe's Records*, vol. VII, p. 3: "He replaces tyranny with tyranny."

111 See the *Loutanjing*, T.23.1:293b14, for the first half of the quotation; the latter half is not found in the Taishō canon.

112 The Chinese term *shide* ("ten virtuous acts") is interpreted as the ten wholesome acts (*shishan*).

[113] See the *Xiaojing*. See note 93.

[114] In *Liezi, Tianrui,* Confucius asked Rong Qiqi why he looked so happy and Rong Qiqi replied, "Among living creatures I have secured the lot of a human being; among human beings I am a man; and I have reached the age of ninety years old." Wong, *Liezi: A Taoist Guide to Practical Living,* p. 37.

[115] The *Wuling xiajing* is a Daoist scripture that is no longer extant.

[116] See the *Zuozhuan,* Huangong's second year. Legge, *The Chinese Classics,* vol. 5, p. 40 (left column).

[117] The Chinese zither *qin* is smaller than the *se;* usually the *qin* has one, five, or seven strings, while the *se* has fifteen, twenty-five, or fifty strings. The expressions in this sentence and the sentence before this derive from the *Liji, Yueji:* "When the ruler hears the sound of the lute and [zither], he thinks of his officers who are bent on righteousness. . . . When the ruler hears the sounds of his drums and tambours, he thinks of his leaders and commanders." See Max Müller, ed., *The Sacred Books of the East* (Oxford: Clarendon Press, 1879–1910), vol. 28, pp. 120–121.

[118] See *Shiji,* fascicle 105, *Bian Que Canggong liezhuan.*

[119] The phrase "an insane person who runs toward the east" is found in the *Huainanzi, Shuoshan xun:* "An insane person runs toward the east. A pursuer runs toward the east, too. Even though the action, running toward the east, is the same, [each person's] reason for the action is different from the other's."

[120] See the *Zhuangzi, Dasheng.* Legge, *Dao de jing ji Zhuangzi quan ji,* p. 451.

[121] See the *Lunyu, Xianjin.* Legge, *The Chinese Classics,* vol. 1, p. 239.

[122] See the *Shangshu, Yaodian.* Legge, *The Chinese Classics,* vol. 3, p. 24.

[123] See the *Zhuangzi, Dao Shi.* Legge, *Dao de jing ji Zhuangzi quan ji,* p. 611.

[124] The Yellow Emperor fought against Yandi in the wilds of Banquan. See the *Shiji,* fascicle 1, *Wudi benji.* Nienhauser, ed., *The Grand Scribe's Records,* vol. I, p. 2.

[125] The phrase "there was still something for which he had to wait" (*youdai*) derives from the *Zhuangzi, Xioayao you.* Legge, *Dao de jing ji Zhuangzi quan ji,* p. 217, n. 3.

[126] This expression is based on the phrase "[The master] hates for the color purple to overpower vermilion" found in the *Lunyu.* See note 2.

[127] See the *Laozi,* chapter 31. Legge, *Dao de jing ji Zhuangzi quan ji,* p. 121, n. 1.

[128] See the *Laozi,* chapters 10 and 28. Legge, *Dao de jing ji Zhuangzi quan ji,* pp. 101–102, n. 1 and p. 119, n. 1, respectively.

[129] See the *Shiji,* fascicle 3, *Yin benji.* Nienhauser, ed., *The Grand Scribe's Records,* vol. I, p. 51.

[130] See the *Lunyu, Yong ye.* Legge, *The Chinese Classics,* vol. 1, p. 192.

[131] This idea is found in the *Zhuangzi, Yangshengzhu.* Legge, *Dao de jing ji Zhuangzi quan ji,* p. 249.

[132] See the *Zhuangzi, Dianzifang.* Legge, *Dao de jing ji Zhuangzi quan ji,* p. 483, n. 2.

[133] See the *Shiji,* fascicle 117, *Sima Xiangru liezhuan,* for the quotation.

[134] The fight between Chu state and Man state is described in the *Zhuangzi, Zeyang.* Legge, *Dao de jing ji Zhuangzi quan ji,* p. 559.

[135] See the *Mengzi, Jinxin, shang.* Legge, *The Chinese Classics,* vol. 2, p. 463, n. 1.

[136] See the *Yijing, Xici, shang.* Legge, *I ching: Book of Changes,* p. 355, n. 24; p. 357, n. 32.

[137] See the *Daode zhengjing zhigui,* fascicle 8. The phrase "One produces two" is found in the *Laozi,* chapter 42. Legge, *Dao de jing ji Zhuangzi quan ji,* p. 133, n. 1.

[138] This passage is probably the summary of the section in the *Taizi ruiying benqi jing,* T.185.3:472c4–6.

[139] This episode is found in the *Lunyu, Yong ye.* Legge, *The Chinese Classics,* vol. 1, p. 188.

[140] See the *Yijing, Xici, xia.* Legge, *I ching: Book of Changes,* p. 382.

[141] The phrase "the spirit that attained the One" is found in the *Laozi,* chapter 39. Legge, *Dao de jing ji Zhuangzi quan ji,* p. 130, n. 1.

[142] See the *Yijing, Shuogua.* Legge, *I ching: Book of Changes,* p. 427.

[143] See the *Zhuangzi, Geyi.* Legge, *Dao de jing ji Zhuangzi quan ji,* p. 415.

[144] The expressions quoted here derive from the *Yijing, Xici, shang.* Legge, *I ching: Book of Changes,* p. 370, n. 63.

[145] The phrase *buji buxing* ("not to hurry, not to go") derives from the phrase *buji er su buxing er zhi* ("one goes fast although he does not hurry and arrives although he does not go") found in the *Yijing, Xici, shang.* Legge, *I ching: Book of Changes,* p. 370, n. 64, translates the phrase as "make speed without hurry, and reached their destination without traveling."

[146] See the *Liji, Jiaotesheng.* Müller, ed., *The Sacred Books of the East,* vol. 27, p. 448.

[147] See the *Liji, Tangong, xia.* Müller, ed., *The Sacred Books of the East,* vol. 27, p. 193.

[148] The phrase "to reach the Way by one change" (*yibian zhi yu dao*) derives from the *Lunyu, Yong ye.* Legge, *The Chinese Classics,* vol. 1, p. 192.

[149] Using the Chinese term *qing* ("feeling"), Zong Bing probably intends to explain mental functions such as sense, perception, and impression, which arise out of contact with

external objects, known as the Chinese *shou* and the Sanskrit *vedanā.* There is, however, no example of the Chinese *qing* being used to refer to *vedanā,* "feeling," one of the five *skandhas* in Buddhist scriptures. The term *qing* encompasses this meaning. Taking into consideration the fact that this text written in the early fifth century reflects contemporary Chinese Buddhists' understanding of Buddhism, I would like to be faithful to the original text and so translate *qing* as "feeling."

150 The expression "when a male and a female unite their essences, all creatures are incarnated" (*nannü goujing wanwu huasheng*) derives from the *Yijing, Xici, xia.* Legge, *I ching: Book of Changes,* p. 393, n. 43.

151 See the *Laozi,* chapter 48. Legge, *Dao de jing ji Zhuangzi quan ji,* p. 138, n. 2.

152 See the *Yijing, Xici, shang.* Legge, *I ching: Book of Changes,* p. 374, n. 73.

153 In the *Shiji,* fascicle 2, *Xia benji,* Emperor Shun bestowed on Yu a jade tablet. Nienhauser, ed., *The Grand Scribe's Records,* vol. I, p. 32, n. 77.

154 See the *Shiji,* fascicle 3, *Yin benji.* Nienhauser, ed., *The Grand Scribe's Records,* vol. I, p. 46.

155 See the *Shiji,* fascicle 4, *Zhou benji.* Nienhauser, ed., *The Grand Scribe's Records,* vol. I, p. 60, n. 120.

156 See the *Zuozhuan,* Xuangong's third year. See Legge, *The Chinese Classics,* vol. 5, p. 293, from the bottom of the left column to the upper right column.

157 In sutras there are a number of instances of the transformed body separate from a buddha or bodhisattva and an auspicious object that springs out from the earth. For instance, in the *Lotus Sutra,* Śākyamuni Buddha created a myriad of buddhas from his body (T.262.9:41a4), an immeasurable number of bodhisattvas spring out from the earth (T.262.9: 39c29–40a1 and 51c9-10), and a seven-treasure stupa springs out from the earth in front of the Buddha (T.262.9:32b17–18). Kyōto Daigaku Jinbun Kagaku Kenkyūjo Chūsei Shisōshi Kenkyū han, ed., *Gumyōshū kenkyū,* vol. 2, p. 95, interprets *fenshen yongchu* as "[The Buddha] has an immeasurable number of bodhisattvas, the transformed bodies from his own body, spring out from the earth" but there is no such phrase in the sutra.

158 Kyōto Daigaku Jinbun Kagaku Kenkyūjo Chūsei Shisōshi Kenkyū han, ed., *Gumyōshū kenkyū,* vol. 2, p. 95, interprets this phrase as "moving Merupradīparāja Buddha's great world in a moment into Vimalakīrti's ten-foot-square room." In the *Vimalakīrtinirdeśa-sūtra* (*Foshuo Weimojiejing,* T.474.14:527a25–26, and *Weimojie suoshuojing,* T.475.14:546b5–6, respectively), there is a passage describing that Merupradīparāja Tathāgata sent Vimalakīrti thirty-two thousand buddha seats. In addition, the *Vimalakīrtinirdeśa-sūtra,* T.474.14:529a10–11 and 548b18–19, indicate that one of the eight unprecedented matters is that all the decorated heavenly palaces and all the buddhas' pure lands are revealed and miraculously contained in Vimalakīrti's ten-foot-square room.

159 See the *Vimalakīrtinirdeśa-sūtra,* T.474.14:527b18–19, 546b29–c1.

160 This expression is found in the *Lunyu, Xianjin.* Legge, *The Chinese Classics,* vol. 1, p. 243, n. 1.

161 See the *Zhuangzi, Yangshengzhu,* for the good cook. Legge, *Dao de jing ji Zhuangzi quan ji,* pp. 246–247.

162 This expression is based on the passage found in the *Lunyu, Taibo:* "Possessed of much, and yet putting questions to those possessed of little; having, as though he had not; full, and yet counting himself as empty; offended against, and yet entering into no altercation." Legge, *The Chinese Classics,* vol. 1, p. 210.

163 This expression, based on the *Huainanzi, Shuoshan xun,* means that while each person runs toward the east in the same manner, each has his own reason for doing so. See note 119.

164 See the *Zhuangzi, Dazongshi.* Legge, *Dao de jing ji Zhuangzi quan ji,* p. 290, n. 6.

165 The expression "the deepest profundity" (*xuan zhi you xuan*) derives from the *Laozi,* chapter 1. Legge, *Dao de jing ji Zhuangzi quan ji,* p. 95, n. 4.

166 See the *Zhuangzi, Zhibeiyou.* Legge, *Dao de jing ji Zhuangzi quan ji,* p. 511, n. 10.

167 This expression derives from Confucius's answer to Ran Qiu when Ran Qiu asked for the second time how it was before Heaven and Earth. See note 166.

168 The phrase "[a sage] is simply moved and later responds" (*gan er hou ying*) is found in the *Zhuangzi, Keyi.* Legge translates it as "He responds to the influence acting on him, and moves as he feels the pressure" (*Dao de jing ji Zhuangzi quan ji,* p. 413, n. 2).

169 See note 168.

170 Legge, *Dao de jing ji Zhuangzi quan ji,* pp. 64–65.

171 See the *Lunyu, Wei Linggong.* Legge, *The Chinese Classics,* vol. 1, p. 297.

172 See the *Laozi,* chapter 37. Legge, *Dao de jing ji Zhuangzi quan ji,* p. 127, n. 1.

173 See the *Foshuo Chaoriming sanmei jing,* T.638.15:543b1.

174 The two quotations regarding the Yellow Emperor are found in the *Shiji,* fascicle 1, *Wudi benji.* Nienhauser, ed., *The Grand Scribe's Records,* vol. I, p. 1.

175 See the *Shiji,* fascicle 1, *Wudi benji.* Nienhauser, ed., *The Grand Scribe's Records,* vol. I, p. 5, n. 13.

176 See the *Shiji,* fascicle 1, *Wudi benji.* Nienhauser, ed., *The Grand Scribe's Records,* vol. I, p. 5, n. 11.

177 See the *Shiji,* fascicle 1, *Wudi benji.* Nienhauser, ed., *The Grand Scribe's Records,* vol. I, p. 6, n. 15.

[178] See the *Shiji,* fascicle 1, *Wudi benji.* Nienhauser, ed., *The Grand Scribe's Records,* vol. I, pp. 3–4.

[179] See the *Shiji,* fascicle 1, *Wudi benji.* Nienhauser, ed., *The Grand Scribe's Records,* vol. I, p. 5, n. 11.

[180] See the *Shiji,* fascicle 1, *Wudi benji.* Nienhauser, ed., *The Grand Scribe's Records,* vol. I, p. 17, n. 46.

[181] See the *Zhuangzi, Xuwugui.* Legge, *Dao de jing ji Zhuangzi quan ji,* p. 536, n. 3.

[182] See the *Zhuangzi, Xiaoyaoyou.* Legge, *Dao de jing ji Zhuangzi quan ji,* pp. 218–219, n. 5.

[183] See the *Zhuangzi, Zaiyou,* for Guang Chen's statements. Legge, *Dao de jing ji Zhuangzi quan ji,* p. 346.

[184] See the *Zhuangzi, Zaiyou.* Legge, *Dao de jing ji Zhuangzi quan ji,* pp. 347–348.

[185] See the *Zhuangzi, Xuwugui.* Legge, *Dao de jing ji Zhuangzi quan ji,* pp. 536–537, n. 3.

[186] See the *Shanhaijing, Haineijing.* Ching, Cheng, and Thern, *Shan hai ching,* p. 255.

[187] See the *Shiji,* fascicle 63, *Laozi Han Fei liezhuan.* Nienhauser, ed., *The Grand Scribe's Records,* vol. VII, p. 22, n. 2141.

[188] See the *Gaosengzhuan,* T.2059.50:323a19–23.

[189] See the *Gaosengzhuan,* T.2059.50:385b23–24.

[190] Bai Qi buried four hundred thousand people and Xiang Ji buried two hundred thousand people. See the *Shiji,* fascicle 73, *Bo Qi Wang Jian liezhuan* (Nienhauser, ed., *The Grand Scribe's Records,* vol. VII, p. 171), and the *Hanshu,* fascicle 3, *Xiang Ji zhuan,* respectively.

[191] See the *Huainanzi, Lanming xun.* English translation in Charles Le Blanc, *Huai-nan tzu. Philosophical Synthesis in Early Han Thought: The Idea of Resonance (kan-ying) with a Translation and Analysis of Chapter Six* (Hong Kong: Hong Kong University Press, 1985), pp. 105–106, 2a.6.

[192] See the *Hou Hanshu,* fascicle 49.

[193] See the *Hou Hanshu,* fascicle 71.

[194] See the *Vimalakīrtinirdeśa-sūtra,* T.474.14:527b17, 546b25–26, for the phrase "to put Mount Sumeru into a poppy seed"; the *Liudujijing,* T.152.3:2b8–26, 1b12–c25, for the stories of the tiger and the dove, respectively.

[195] There is no sutra that has this expression in the Taishō canon. The phrase "As [the Buddha's] toes touch the earth, a trichiliocosm quakes" is found in several sutras, including the *Vimalakīrtinirdeśa-sūtra,* T.474.14:520c7–8, 538c20–21, but the following passage is not found in any sutra.

[196] See the *Laozi,* chapter 37. Legge, *Dao de jing ji Zhuangzi quan ji,* p. 127, n. 1.

[197] See the *Lunheng, Dingxian.*

[198] See the *Miaofa lianhuajing,* T.262.9:32c12–20.

[199] See note 158.

[200] The phrase "The gentleman among men is, in fact, the small man of Heaven" derives from the *Zhuangzi, Dazongshi:* "The small man of Heaven is the superior man among men; the superior man among men is the small man of Heaven!" Legge, *Dao de jing ji Zhuangzi quan ji,* p. 301.

[201] See the *Yijing, Qian, Xiangzhuan.* Legge, *Dao de jing ji Zhuangzi quan ji,* p. 213, n. 4.

[202] See the *Hanshu,* fascicle 71: Through Lord Yu's virtue, his son Yu Dingguo became the prime minister; and fascicle 74: Emperor Xuan later appointed Bing Ji the Marquis of Boyang.

[203] See the *Zuozhuan,* Xigong's twenty-ninth year. Legge, *The Chinese Classics,* vol. 5, pp. 214, par. 5.

[204] See the *Han Feizi, Shuolin, shang.*

[205] This expression derives from an episode about King Hui of Liang found in the *Mengzi, Liang Huiwang, shang.* Legge, *The Chinese Classics,* vol. 2, pp. 140–141, n. 8.

[206] See the *Mengzi, Liang Huiwang, shang.* Legge, *The Chinese Classics,* vol. 2, p. 138, n. 4 to p. 141, n. 8.

[207] See the *Zengyi Ahanjing,* T.125.2:693b11–c9.

[208] See the *Shiji,* fascicle 73, *Bai Qi Wang Jian liezhuan.* Nienhauser, ed., *The Grand Scribe's Records,* vol. VII, pp. 170–171.

[209] This expression is based on a passage in the *Zhuangzi, Qiwu lun.* Legge translates it as "When [the wind] blows, [the sounds from] the myriad apertures are different, and [its cessation] makes them stop of themselves" (*Dao de jing ji Zhuangzi quan ji,* p. 226, n. 1).

[210] In the *Lunyu, Shuer,* Confucius lamented that his aging caused him to not dream of the Duke of Zhou as frequently as he had previously. Legge, *The Chinese Classics,* vol. 1, p. 196.

[211] See the *Shiji,* fascicle 3, *Yin benji.* Nienhauser, ed., *The Grand Scribe's Records,* vol. I, p. 48.

[212] The phrase "robbers and boasters" derives from the *Laozi,* chapter 53. Legge, *Dao de jing ji Zhuangzi quan ji,* p. 145.

[213] This expression derives from the *Zhuangzi, Dachongfu.* Legge, *Dao de jing ji Zhuangzi quan ji,* p. 275.

[214] The quoted passages are not found in any sutra in the *Taishō shinshū daizōkyō.*

[215] In the *Lunyu, Zilu,* Confucius said that Fan Xu is a mean man. Legge, *The Chinese Classics,* vol. 1, p. 265, n. 2.

[216] The Sanskrit name of Jiantuole is unknown. His biography is found in the *Gaoseng-zhuan,* T.2059.50:388c20–389a2.

[217] See the *Shiji,* fascicle 61, *Boyi liezhuan.* Nienhauser, ed., *The Grand Scribe's Records,* vol. VII, p. 4.

[218] See the *Yijing, Kun, Wenyan.* Legge, *I ching: Book of Changes,* p. 419, n. 5.

[219] See the *Mengzi, Jinxin, shang.* Legge, *The Chinese Classics,* vol. 2, p. 463, n. 1.

[220] The *Shiji,* fascicle 3, *Yin benji,* states that when Jiandi, the second wife of Emperor Ku, went out to bathe, she saw a black bird lay an egg; Jiandi swallowed it, became pregnant, and gave birth to Xie. Nienhauser, ed., *The Grand Scribe's Records,* vol. I, p. 41.

[221] The *Shiji,* fascicle 4, *Zhou benji,* states that Jiang Yuan, the primary wife of Emperor Ku, saw a giant footprint in the wilderness field, stepped in it, became pregnant, and gave birth to Houji. Nienhauser, ed., *The Grand Scribe's Records,* vol. I, p. 55.

[222] The phrase "he who is marvelous since he has gotten the One" is found in the *Laozi,* chapter 39. Legge, *Dao de jing ji Zhuangzi quan ji,* p. 130, n. 1.

[223] See the *Shangshu, Shundian.* Legge, *The Chinese Classics,* vol. 3, p. 49, n. 24.

[224] See the *Yijing, Shuogua zhuan.* Legge, *I ching: Book of Changes,* p. 422, n. 1.

[225] See the *Lunyu, Xianjin.* Legge, *The Chinese Classics,* vol. 1, p. 241.

[226] See the *Lunyu, Xianjin.* The original passage is "While you are not able to serve men, how can you serve their spirits?" Legge, *The Chinese Classics,* vol. 1, p. 240.

[227] See the *Lunyu, Gongzhi Chang.* Legge, *The Chinese Classics,* vol. 1, p. 177.

[228] See the *Dazhidulun,* T.1509.25:74c8–75a3.

[229] The two passages derive from the *Yijing, Jiaren.* Legge, *I ching: Book of Changes,* p. 137, n. 3.

[230] The phrase "a white colt's passing a crevice" derives from the *Zhuangzi, Zhi bei you.* Legge, *Dao de jing ji Zhuangzi quan ji,* p. 505.

[231] This probably refers to Marquis Wen of Jin state who heard the soldiers singing to themselves. See the *Zuozhuan,* Xigong's twenty-eighth year. Legge, *The Chinese Classics,* vol. 5, p. 209, right column.

[232] This episode is found in the *Shiji,* fascicle 10, *Xiaowen benji.* When a director of the Imperial of Granaries of the Han dynasty was punished, his daughter Tiying petitioned

the emperor to try to expiate her father's crime; the emperor, impressed by her filial piety, thereafter abolished corporal punishment. Nienhauser, ed., *The Grand Scribe's Records,* vol. II, pp. 170–171.

233 This expression is often found in the *Laozi Daodejing* and the *Zhuangzi.* For example, see Legge, *Dao de jing ji Zhuangzi quan ji,* p. 127, n. 1; p. 138, n. 2; p. 528.

234 There are several different kinds of the five different types of penalties, according to each dynasty. The example shown here is from the Zhou dynasty.

235 See the *Shiji,* fascicle 56, *Chen chengxiang shijia.*

236 See the *Shiji,* fascicle 73, *Bai Qi Wang Jian liezhuan.* Nienhauser, ed., *The Grand Scribe's Records,* vol. VII, p. 176.

237 Wei Ke's father had a beloved concubine. First Ke's father told him to have the concubine remarry after his death, but when his illness became serious he asked Ke to have her immolated to follow him into the grave. Ke, however, followed his father's initial request and did not have the concubine immolated. Later, when Ke fought the Qin army, an old man (the ghost of father of the concubine), helped Ke out of diffculty by making a trap to capture the general of Qin state, and consequently Ke could capture the general. See the *Zuozhuan,* Xuangong's fifteenth year. Legge, *The Chinese Classics,* vol. 5, p. 328, right column.

238 This story of Bao Zidu is found in the *Lieyizhuan* (a collection of extraordinary stories), authorship of which was attributed to Cao Pi (187–226). Zidu comforted a man who was dying on a street; after his death the man became a horse and led Zidu to the capital where Zidu was summoned as an official.

239 This story is found in the *Shiji, Qi Taigong shijia.* Nienhauser, ed., *The Grand Scribe's Records,* vol. I, pp. 52–54.

240 Prince Mu of Qin state gave grain to Jin state when the Jin people were suffering from a famine. Two years later, when the Qin people were starving, Prince Hui of Jin state took advantage of the situation and invaded Qin state. See *Zuozhuan,* Xigong's thirteenth and fifteenth years. Legge, *The Chinese Classics,* vol. 5, p. 161; p. 169, left column.

241 See the *Zuozhuan,* Xuangong's second year. Legge, *The Chinese Classics,* vol. 5, p. 290, right column.

242 See the *Shiji,* fascicle 92, *Huaiyin hou liezhuan.* Nienhauser, ed., *The Grand Scribe's Records,* vol. VIII, pp. 70, 95.

243 See the *Shiji,* fascicle 47, *Kongzi shijia.* Yang and Yang, *Selections from Records of the Historian,* p. 8.

244 See the *Shiji,* fascicle 33, *Lu Zhougong shijia.* Nienhauser, ed., *The Grand Scribe's Records,* vol. V, pt. 1, p. 135.

[245] The term "the politeness of providing a way of escape" (*sanqu zhi li*) derives from the *Yijing, Bi,* "The king urging his pursuit of the game [only] in three directions, and allowing the escape of all the animals before him." Legge, *I ching: Book of Changes,* p. 75.

[246] This expression derives from the *Lunyu, Shuer.* Legge, *The Chinese Classics,* vol. 1, p. 203.

[247] See the *Laozi,* chapter 10. Legge, *Dao de jing ji Zhuangzi quan ji,* p. 102, n. 3.

[248] A similar passage, "The common people, acting daily according to it, yet have no knowledge of it," is found in *Yijing, Xici, shang.* Legge, *I ching: Book of Changes,* p. 356, n. 26.

[249] See the *Mengzi, Wangzhang, xia.* Legge, *The Chinese Classics,* vol. 2, p. 363, n. 5.

[250] This expression derives from the *Lunyu, Xueer.* Legge, *The Chinese Classics,* vol. 1, p. 139.

[251] See the *Xiaojing.* Rosemont's translation differs slightly from this context; see *The Chinese Classic of Family Reverence,* p. 115.

[252] See both the *Xiaojing* and the *Mengzi, Lilou, shang.* Rosemont, *The Chinese Classic of Family Reverence,* chapter 11, p. 112; Legge, *The Chinese Classics,* vol. 2, chapter 26, p. 313, n. 1.

[253] See the *Xiaojing.* Rosemont, *The Chinese Classic of Family Reverence,* p. 105.

[254] See the *Liji, Jiyi.* Müller, ed., *The Sacred Books of the East,* vol. 28, p. 228, n. 14.

[255] See the *Xiaojing.* Rosemont, *The Chinese Classic of Family Reverence,* p. 105.

[256] This expression derives from the *Zhuangzi, Yangshengzhu.* The original reads: "To be in accordance with the central element [of our nature] is the regular path to save the body, to complete the life, to nourish our parents, and to complete our term of years." Legge, *Dao de jing ji Zhuangzi quan ji,* p. 246, n. 1.

[257] This expression derives from the *Laozi,* chapter 52. The original is: "The perception of what is small is [the secret of] clear-sightedness; the guarding of what is soft and tender is [the secret of] strength. Who uses well his light/Reverting to its [source so] bright/Will from his body ward all blight/And hides the unchanging from men's sight." Legge, *Dao de jing ji Zhuangzi quan ji,* p. 143, n. 4.

[258] See the *Zuozhuan,* Yingong's first year. Legge, *The Chinese Classics,* vol. 5, p. 5, right column, to p. 6, right column.

[259] See the *Zuozhuan,* Yingong's fourth year. Legge, *The Chinese Classics,* vol. 5, p. 16, right column, to p. 17, right column.

[260] See the *Zuozhuan,* Xigong's twenty-third year. Legge, *The Chinese Classics,* vol. 5, p. 186, left column.

[261] See the *Hou Hanshu,* fascicle 56, *Wei Biao Zhuan.*

[262] See the *Shiji,* fascicle 2, *Xia benji.* Nienhauser, ed., *The Grand Scribe's Records,* vol. I, p. 21.

[263] See the *Shiji,* fascicle 31, *Wu Taibo shijia.* Nienhauser, ed., *The Grand Scribe's Records,* vol. V, pt. 1, pp. 1–2.

[264] See the *Lunyu, Taibo.* See Legge, *The Chinese Classics,* vol. 1, p. 207.

[265] See the *Lunyu, Gongzhi Chang.* Legge, *The Chinese Classics,* vol. 1, p. 181.

[266] This expression derives from the *Yijing, Kun, Tuanzhuan.* Legge, *Dao de jing ji Zhuangzi quan ji,* p. 214, n. 2.

[267] The Chinese term *datong* is originally found in the *Zhuangzi, Dazongshi,* and *Qiushui.* According to Ogawa Tamaki, in *Rōshi Sōshi* (Tokyo: Chūō Kōronsha, 1998), pp. 278, 396, it refers to the great way beyond all discriminations. Legge says that it is another denomination of the Dao, and "is also explained as meaning, 'the great void in which there is no obstruction'" (*Dao de jing ji Zhuangzi quanji,* p. 305, n. 2). Following Legge, I translate *datong* as "Great Pervader."

[268] See the *Yijing, Jiqi, xiangci.* Legge, *I ching: Book of Changes,* p. 346, n. 5.

[269] The expressions "to be disrespectful to great men" and "to disgrace the ordinances of Heaven" derive from passages found in the *Lunyu, Jishi.* Legge, *The Chinese Classics,* vol. 1, p. 313, n. 2.

[270] The *Zhuangzi, Xiaoyaoyou,* has: "In the south of Chu there is the [tree] called Mingling, whose spring is 500 years, and its autumn the same." Legge, *Dao de jing ji Zhuangzi quan ji,* p. 214.

[271] The Chinese term *youdi* is known as *jiadi* ("truth of temporariness"), which is one of the triple truths, namely: all existences are temporary manifestations produced by causes and conditions.

[272] The term *wudi,* one of the triple truths, is also called *kongdi* ("truth of emptiness"), since all existences are empty and nonsubstantial in essence.

[273] See the *Zhuangzi, Tianxia,* in which the two sentences are in reverse order. Legge, *Dao de jing ji Zhuangzi quan ji,* p. 669.

[274] See the *Zuozhuan,* Zhaogong's twentieth year; Legge, *The Chinese Classics,* vol. 5, p. 684, right column. When the Marquis of Qi state said how happy he would be if there was no death, Yan Ying, the prime minister, told him that if there was no death, he could not enjoy his present life and the Shuangjiu family that had occupied the Marquis' territory would enjoy it instead.

[275] See the *Zhuangzi, Dazongshi,* for the story of a man who hid a boat in a ravine for safekeeping, but during the night the boat was carried away by a strong man. Legge, *Dao de jing ji Zhuangzi quan ji,* p. 290, n. 6. See also note 164.

[276] See the *Zhuangzi, Tian Zifang.* Legge, *Dao de jing ji Zhuangzi quan ji,* p. 486, n. 3.

[277] Yu Gong, father of Yu Dingguo, was a just and fair warden. His virtue led his family to prosperity. See the *Hanshu,* chapter 71, *Yu Dingguo zhuan.*

[278] See the *Hanshu,* chapter 90, *Kuli zhuan.*

[279] Chunyu Sheng (Chunyu Kun) was a man of Qi state in the Warring States period. He loved joking and talking. He once satirized King Wei of Qi state in secret language. See the *Shiji,* fascicle 126, *Huaji liezhuan.* Yang and Yang, *Selections from Records of the Historian,* pp. 403–409.

[280] The Chinese character *shi* ("true") is added between the characters *ke* ("possible") and the final particle *zai,* according to the original sentence found in T.2102.52:18a22.

[281] The allegory of the sword called Moye derives from the *Zhuangzi, Dazongshi.* See Legge, *Dao de jing ji Zhuangzi quan ji,* pp. 297–298.

[282] The allegory of those who retreated fifty steps (in a battlefield) who laughed at those who retreated a hundred steps derives from the *Mengzi, Liang Huiwang, shang.* Legge, *The Chinese Classics,* vol. 2, pp. 129–130, n. 2.

[283] See the *Zhuangzi, Dazongshi.* Here is a difference in interpretation from the original passage; Legge's translation of this section reads: "Mang-sun presented in his body the appearance of being agitated, but in his mind he was conscious of no loss. The death was to him like the issuing from one's dwelling at dawn, and no [more terrible] reality" (*Dao de jing ji Zhuangzi quanji,* p. 302).

[284] See the *Hanshu,* fascicle 48, *Jia Yi zhuan.*

[285] The sounds of metal and stone are two of the eight kinds of musical sounds produced from musical instruments made out of calabash gourd, earthenware, stretched hides, wood, stone, metal, silk strings, and bamboo, respectively.

[286] He Chengtian cites Zong Bing: "The sage has no invariable mind of his own; he simply accommodates himself to other people's minds," but changes the word "mind" to the word "nature." Zong Bing's original statement is at T.2102.52:18c19.

[287] See the *Shangshu, Zhoushu, Jiugao.* Legge, *The Chinese Classics,* vol. 3, pp. 399–412.

[288] The phrase, "[The ruler of a state,] during the spring hunting, will not surround a marshy thicket," derives from the *Liji, Qu li, xia.* See Müller, ed., *The Sacred Books of the East,* vol. 27, p. 106.

[289] The laws of the five offenses in hunting are not to hunt fawns, not to take eggs, not to kill pregnant animals, not to kill young animals, and not to destroy nests.

[290] There are several different interpretations for the three numinous beings. For instance, it may refer to Heaven, Earth, and human beings, or the sun, moon, and stars.

[291] Zilu asked Confucius about spirits and death in the *Lunyu, Xianjin.* Legge, *The Chinese Classics,* vol. 1, pp. 240–241.

[292] In the *Liji, Jiyi,* Confucius says that the energy of all living creatures becomes the fumes that rise as the vapor after death. Müller, ed., *The Sacred Books of the East,* vol. 28, p. 220, translates the phrase "the fume rising as the vapor" as "the vapours and odours which produce a feeling of sadness (and arise from the decay of their substance)."

[293] See the *Lunyu, Gongzhi Chang.* Legge, *The Chinese Classics,* vol. 1, p. 178.

[294] The phrase "to make an exhaustive discrimination of what is right, and effect the complete development of every nature, till they arrive at what is appointed for it [by Heaven]" derives from the *Yijing, Shuogua.* Legge, *I ching: Book of Changes,* p. 422, n. 3.

[295] See the *Gaosengzhuan,* T.2059.50:350b26–27.

[296] See note 186.

[297] See the *Shijing, Xiaoya, xiaowan.* Legge, *The Chinese Classics,* vol. 4, p. 334, n. 3.

[298] See the *Zuozhuan,* Zhuanggong's the fourth month of the seventh year. Legge, *The Chinese Classics*, vol. 5, p. 80, VII, 2.

[299] See the *Sanguozhi,* fascicle 11.

[300] Both Wang Xiang and Guo Ju are known as filial sons. See the *Jinshu,* fascicle 33, *Wang Xiang zhuan,* for Wang Xiang, and the *Soushenji* for Guo Ju.

[301] The *Shangshu, Jinteng,* states that when the Duke of Zhou (the uncle) assisted King Cheng (the nephew) after the death of King Wu, three of the Duke of Zhou's brothers spread a false rumor to cause difficulties for the duke. Legge, *The Chinese Classics,* vol. 3, p. 357, n. 12.

[302] The expressions "to ascend to the hall" and "to pass into the inner apartments" derive from the *Lunyu, Xianjin.* Legge, *The Chinese Classics,* vol. 1, p. 242, n. 2.

[303] See the *Lunyu, Zi han,* for the difficulties faced by Confucius in Kuang and the *Wei Linggong* for his difficulties in Chen. Legge, *The Chinese Classics,* vol. 1, pp. 217–218 and p. 294, respectively.

[304] This statement is not found in the *Shanhaijing.* In the *Nanshanjing* ("Southern Mountains") section of the *Shanhaijing,* however, it is recorded that there is the *lu* fish that dies in winter and lives in summer. Ching, Cheng, and Thern, *Shan hai ching,* p. 2.

[305] See the *Zuozhuan,* Zhaogong's seventh year. Legge, *The Chinese Classics,* vol. 5, p. 617, right column.

[306] See the *Zuozhuan,* Xigong's tenth year. Legge, *The Chinese Classics,* vol. 5, p. 157, left column.

[307] See the *Zuozhuan,* Zhaogong's seventh year. Legge, *The Chinese Classics,* vol. 5, p. 618, left column.

[308] The authorship of the *Zuozhuan* is attributed to Zuo Qiuming, a former disciple of Confucius.

[309] Kyōto Daigaku Jinbun Kagaku Kenkyūjo Chūsei Shisōshi Kenkyū han, ed., *Gumyōshū kenkyū,* vol. 2, p. 192, n. 29, suggests that "a daring soldier of the city of Pu" refers to Zilu, who was the chief magistrate of Pu.

[310] This statement is made on the basis of the description found in the *Liji, Wangji,* "When the otter sacrificed its fish, the foresters entered the meres and dams. When the wolf sacrificed its prey, the hunting commenced." See Müller, ed., *The Sacred Books of the East,* vol. 27, p. 221, n. 25.

[311] The song "Rushes" is found in the *Shijing, Daya.* Legge, *The Chinese Classics,* vol. 4, pp. 472–475.

[312] See note 289.

[313] Emperor Tang stopped the people from praying to be able to catch game by setting a net in all directions, and changed it to praying for the ability to catch game by leaving one side of the net open so that some animals could escape. See the *Shiji,* fascicle 3, *Yin benji.* Nienhauser, ed., *The Grand Scribe's Records,* vol. I, p. 43, n. 95.

[314] See the *Shijing, Daya, Hanlu.* Legge, *The Chinese Classics,* vol. 4, p. 446, n. 6.

[315] See the *Shijing, Daya, Wen Wang.* Legge, *The Chinese Classics,* vol. 4, p. 458, n. 1.

[316] The notes of *beilü* refer to *ruibin, linzhong, yize, nanlü, wuyi,* and *yingzhong.* The note of *gong* is the first of the five notes (*gong, shang, jue, zhi,* and *yu*) of traditional Chinese music. It is equivalant to *huangzhong* of the six *yang lü* notes. See note 7.

[317] See note 7 for the *lü* of *yin* notes and the *lü* of *yang* notes.

[318] See the *Yijing, Xici, xia.* Legge, *I ching: Book of Changes,* p. 381, n. 10.

[319] This expression is based on a statement by Mencius, "The trees of the Niu mountain were once beautiful. Being situated, however, in the borders of a large state, they were hewn down with axes and bills, and could they retain their beauty?" Legge, *The Chinese Classics,* vol. 2, p. 407, n. 1.

[320] See the *Lunyu, Xianjin.* Legge, *The Chinese Classics,* vol. 1, pp. 240–241.

[321] See the *Lunyu, Gongzhi Chang.* Legge, *The Chinese Classics,* vol. 1, p. 177.

[322] See the *Hanshu,* fascicle 71, *Yu Dingguo zhuan.*

[323] See the *Hanshu,* fascicle 74, *Bing Ji zhuan.*

[324] Qu Boyu is a wise man of Wei state, whom Confucius respected. In the *Lunyu, Xianwen,* there is a conversation between Qu Boyu's messenger and Confucius. Legge, *The Chinese Classics,* vol. 1, pp. 285–286.

[325] See the *Yijing, Qian, jiuer.* Legge, *I ching: Book of Changes,* p. 57, n. 2.

[326] The phrase "transformation and shaping" (*hua er caizhi*) derives from the *Yijing, Xici shang,* "Transformation and shaping is what we call change." Legge, *I ching: Book of Changes,* p. 377.

[327] See the *Hou Hanshu,* fascicle 79, *Zhong Changtong zhuan,* and fascicle 113, *Jiao Shen zhuan,* respectively. The practice of guiding the breath (*daoyin*) is one of the Daoist practices to preserve one's health by controlling the breath.

[328] See the *Zhuangzi, Zeyang.* Legge, *Dao de jing ji Zhuangzi quan ji,* p. 561, n. 6.

[329] See the *Hanshu, Jingfazhi.*

[330] The expression "grand submission [to the natural course] (*dashun*)" is found in the *Zhuangzi, Tiandi,* and the *Laozi,* chapter 65. Legge, *Dao de jing ji Zhuangzi quan ji,* p. 157, p. 365, n. 8.

[331] This expression is based on the phrase "Zuo Qiuming was ashamed of them. I also am ashamed of them" found in the *Lunyu, Gongzhi Chang.* Legge, *The Chinese Classics,* vol. 1, p. 182.

[332] See the *Yijing, Qian, Wenyan chujiu.* Legge, *I ching: Book of Changes,* p. 409, n. 4.

[333] See the *Yijing, Qian, Wenyan jiusan.* Legge, *I ching: Book of Changes,* p. 410, n. 6.

[334] As for the Chinese term *huncheng zhi wu* ("something undefined and complete"), the *Laozi,* chapter 25, explains that "There was something undefined and complete, coming into existence before Heaven and Earth. How still it was and formless, standing alone, and undergoing no change, reaching everywhere and in no danger [of being exhausted]! It may be regarded as the Mother of all things." Legge, *Dao de jing ji Zhuangzi quan ji,* p. 115, n. 1.

[335] See the *Zhouli, Chunguan Zong Bo.*

[336] See *Zhuangzi, Yangshengzhu.* See Legge, *Dao de jing ji Zhuangzi quan ji,* p. 248.

[337] The Chinese term *santong* ("three foundations") refers to the first month of the year in the calendar systems used in the Xia, Yin (Shang), and Zhou dynasties. The first month of the year in the Xia dynasty is called *rentong* ("the foundation of men"); that of the Yin dynasty (equivalent to the twelfth month of the Xia calendar) is called *ditong* ("the foundation of Earth"); and that of the Zhou dynasty (the eleventh month of the Xia calendar) is called *tiantong* ("the foundation of Heaven"). Here, this term is used to refer to the three powers instead of the term *sancai.*

[338] See the *Zuozhuan,* Wengong's twelfth year. Legge, *The Chinese Classics,* vol. 5, p. 261, right column.

[339] The Chinese term *sanpin zhi huo* ("the threefold use of game in hunting") derives from the *Yijing, Xun.* Legge, *I ching: Book of Changes,* p. 190, n. 4.

[340] See the *Ji Kang ji,* fascicle 8.

[341] See the *Baopuzi, Lunxian.*

[342] Teng Xiu did not believe that some shrimp have barbels longer than ten feet, but later it was reported to him that a shrimp with barbels over twenty feet long was caught in the eastern sea. See the *Taiping yulan,* fascicle 943.

[343] The Chinese *fangshu* ("square documents") refers to local gazettes, texts of divination, texts of medical practice, or texts of prescriptions. Here it probably means scriptures of doctrines and policies.

[344] The term *yao* consists of the *yang yao* (solid single line) and the *yin yao* (divided line).

[345] See the *Yijing, Qian.* Legge, *I ching: Book of Changes,* pp. 57–58, n. 1, 2, 4, 5, 6, 7.

[346] See *Yijing, Wenyan.* Legge, *I ching: Book of Changes,* p. 409, n. 6; p. 410, n. 4; and p. 414, n. 19.

[347] The phrase "a new thought of spring and autumn," found in the preface of the *Chunqiu Zuoshizhuan* by Du Yu, simply means the new thought of a later generation.

[348] See the *Laozi,* chapter 25. Legge, *Dao de jing ji Zhuangzi quan ji,* p. 116, n. 3.

[349] See the *Lunyu, Liren.* Legge, *The Chinese Classics,* vol. 1, p. 165.

[350] See the *Liji, Zhongyong.* Müller, ed., *The Sacred Books of the East,* vol. 28, p. 314, n. 12.

[351] See the *Liji, Biaoji.* Müller, ed., *The Sacred Books of the East,* vol. 28, p. 333, n. 14, translates the passage as "those who fear the guilt of transgression practice it by constraint."

[352] See the *Zhuangzi, Quqie.* Legge, *Dao de jing ji Zhuangzi quan ji,* p. 332.

[353] See the *Shijing, Zhaonan.* Legge, *The Chinese Classics,* vol. 4, pp. 22, 25.

[354] See the *Shiji,* fascicle 57, *Jiang hou Zhou Bo shijia,* for Zhou Yafu, and fascicle 91, *Qingbu liezhuan* for Ying Bu. Nienhauser, ed., *The Grand Scribe's Records,* vol. VIII, pp. 45–46.

[355] The Chinese term *ruosang,* which means to leave one's native place or homeland when young, is originally found in the *Zhuangzi, Qiwulun.* In the *Zhuangzi,* "homeland" refers to death, while the author here refers it to as the truth. Legge, *Dao de jing ji Zhuangzi quan ji,* p. 242.

[356] See the *Zhuangzi, Xuwugui.* Legge, *Dao de jing ji Zhuangzi quan ji,* p. 548.

[357] See the *Zuozhuan,* Yingong's eleventh year. Legge, *The Chinese Classics,* vol. 5, p. 32, right column.

358 See the *Yijing, Xici, xia*. Legge, *I ching: Book of Changes,* p. 390, n. 34.

359 See the *Yijing, Shuogua zhuan*. Legge, *I ching: Book of Changes,* p. 422, n. 3.

360 The *Yijing, Xici, shang,* states, "Therefore in (the system of) the Yi there is the Grand Terminus, which produced the two elementary Forms." Legge, *I ching: Book of Changes,* p. 373, n. 70.

361 These two sentences in all versions of the *Hongmingji* have three Chinese characters for *huo* ("fire"), but this does not make sense. Kyōto Daigaku Jinbun Kagaku Kenkyūjo Chūsei Shisōshi Kenkyū han, ed., *Gumyōshū kenkyū,* vol. 2, p. 256, n. 9) suggests the first of two instances of *huo* should be *shui* ("water"). I follow this.

362 This expression is based on a passage found in the *Zhuangzi, Dazongshi:* "When we once understand that Heaven and Earth are a great melting pot, and the Creator a great founder, where can we have to go to that shall not be right for us?" Legge, *Dao de jing ji Zhuangzi quan ji,* pp. 297–298.

363 The Chinese character *xing* ("nature") here does not make sense. Following Kyōto Daigaku Jinbun Kagaku Kenkyūjo Chūsei Shisōshi Kenkyū han, ed., *Gumyōshū kenkyū,* vol. 2, p. 259, n. 3), I read it as *guai,* "strange."

364 The Chinese character *wei* ("to do") is read as *wu* ("nothing").

365 This statement is based on a passage found in the *Zhuangzi, Xiaoyaoyou:* "I was frightened by them; they were like the Milky Way that cannot be traced to its beginning or end." Legge, *Dao de jing ji Zhuangzi quan ji,* p. 218, n. 5.

366 See the *Anshi Chunqiu, Neipian, Jianpian,* in which the last sentence, "those who are not virtuous consider [that death is simply] to go away," is given as "those who are not virtuous consider [that death is simply] to lie down."

367 Both discussions appear in Fascicle 12 in the *Collection for the Clarification and Propagation of Buddhism,* Volume II (forthcoming).

368 The *Daodejing* states, "Therefore the Dao is great; Heaven is great; Earth is great; and the [sage] king is also great. In the universe there are four that are great, and the [sage] king is one of them." See also note 348.

369 See the *Yijing, Xici, xia*. Legge translates this passage as "The great attribute of heaven and earth is the giving and maintaining [of] life" (*I ching: Book of Changes,* p. 381, n. 10).

370 See the *Zhuangzi, Shanxing*. Legge, *Dao de jing ji Zhuangzi quan ji,* p. 419, n. 3.

371 See the *Zhanguoce, Zhao ce.*

372 The expressions "By teaching love on the basis of the feeling of intimacy" and "By teaching respect on the basis of sternness" derive from the *Xiaojing*. Rosemont's translation differs slightly from this context; see *The Chinese Classic of Family Reverence,* p. 110.

[373] This expression is based on the *Zhuangzi, Tianyun:* "One, traveling to the south, comes [at last] to Ying, and there, standing with his face to the north, he does not see Mount Ming. Why does he not see it? Because he is so far from it." Legge, *Dao de jing ji Zhuangzi quan ji,* p. 395.

[374] See the *Laozi,* chapter 39. Legge, *Dao de jing ji Zhuangzi quan ji,* p. 130, n. 1.

[375] See the *Lunyu, Taibo.* Legge, *The Chinese Classics,* vol. 1, p. 214, n. 1.

[376] This expression derives from the *Zhuangzi, Qiwulun:* "Therefore the knowledge that stops at what it does not know is the greatest." Legge, *Dao de jing ji Zhuangzi quan ji,* p. 238.

[377] See the *Zhuangzi, Tiandao.* Legge, *Dao de jing ji Zhuangzi quan ji,* p. 385.

[378] See the *Zhuangzi, Qiwulun,* for this quotation and the following two quotations. Legge, *Dao de jing ji Zhuangzi quan ji,* p. 237.

[379] This is a summary of the passage found in the *Taizi ruiying benqi jing* (T.185.3: 473b1–11).

[380] See note 267 for the Great Pervader.

[381] The expression "the spirit is the most mysterious of a myriad of things" is based on a passage found in the *Yijing, Shuogua zhuan.* Legge translates this as "When we speak of Spirit we mean the subtle [presence and operation of God] with all things" (*I ching: Book of Changes,* chapter 6, p. 427, n. 10).

[382] The expression "By a transformation a person is born. By another transformation a person dies" derives from the *Zhuangzi, Zhibeiyou.* Legge, *Dao de jing ji Zhuangzi quan ji,* p. 505.

[383] Here, the translation of the phrase *ruo si sheng wei bi tu ku* should be "if death and life are vainly suffering for them (i.e., collection and dispersion)." This does not make sense. It should be *ruo si sheng wei tu* ("if death and life are the same category"), as found in the *Zhuangzi, Zhibeiyou.* Legge, *Dao de jing ji Zhuangzi quan ji,* p. 499.

[384] Legge, *Dao de jing ji Zhuangzi quan ji,* p. 290, n. 6.

[385] In the *Zhuangzi, Dazongshi,* when Sang Hu died, two men sang, "Ah! Come, Sang Hu! Ah! Come, Sang Hu! You already returned to the truth, but we are still in the human [world]. Ah!" Legge, *Dao de jing ji Zhuangzi quan ji,* p. 299.

[386] See the *Wenzi, Shoupu pian.*

[387] See the *Zhuangzi, Dazongshi.* Legge, *Dao de jing ji Zhuangzi quan ji,* p. 291, n. 6.

[388] See the *Zhuangzi, Qiwulun.* Legge translates it as "now life and now death." Legge, *Dao de jing ji Zhuangzi quan ji,* p. 230.

[389] Kimura Eiichi refers to Liu Shao's *Renwuzhi* and concludes that the Chinese character *shu* ("number" or "fate") is used as an equivalent to the character *shi* ("consciousness"

or "intelligence") here. See Kimura, *Eon kenkyū, ibun-hen* (Kyoto: Kyōto Daigaku Jinbun Kagaku Kenkyūjo, 1960), p. 396, n. 49.

[390] See note 267 for the "great truth."

[391] The expression "the way of 'forgetting both'" derives from passages found in the *Zhuangzi, Tianyun:* "If it were easy to make my parents forget me, it is difficult for me to forget all the people of the world. If it were easy to forget the people of the world, it is difficult to make the people of the world forget me." Legge, *Dao de jing ji Zhuangzi quan ji,* p. 395.

[392] The year of *efeng* is the year of *jia* of Taisui (Jupitor), considered to be a powerful time. The third year of Yuanxing is the year of *jia-chen* in the Chinese calendar.

[393] See the *Liji, Tangong, xia.* Müller, ed., *The Sacred Books of the East,* vol. 27, p. 169, n. 29.

[394] See the *Laozi,* chapter 31. Legge, *Dao de jing ji Zhuangzi quan ji,* pp. 121–122.

[395] Confucius had his right hand uppermost at a mourning rite. See the *Liji, Tangong,* shang. Müller, ed., *The Sacred Books of the East,* vol. 27, pp. 137–138, n. 19.

[396] See the *Yijing, Bi.* Legge, *I ching: Book of Changes,* p. 75, n. 5.

[397] To strip off the upper garment is a token of sincere apology. To load a coffin on one's carriage means to show one's determination to succeed on an undertaking or die. See the *Zuozhuan,* Xigong's sixth year and Xuangong's twelfth year. Legge, *The Chinese Classics,* vol. 5, p. 316, left column, and p. 147, right column, respectively.

[398] See the *Lunyu, Shuer.* Legge, *The Chinese Classics,* vol. 1, p. 203.

[399] The expression "reducing day by day to attain *wuwei*" derives from the *Laozi,* chapter 48. Legge, *Dao de jing ji Zhuangzi quan ji,* p. 138, n. 2.

[400] The expression "have not been out from the closed world from the beginning" (*wei shi chu yu youfeng*) is based on the expression "Things exist, but they have no boundary with others from the beginning" (*youwuyi er wei shi youfeng*) found in the *Zhuangzi, Qiwulun.* Legge translates this as "There was something, but without any responsive recognition of it [on the part of men]" (*Dao de jing ji Zhuangzi quan ji,* p. 233, n. 5). I translate the Chinese term *youfeng* as "the closed world."

[401] See the *Zhuangzi, Dazongshi.* Legge, *Dao de jing ji Zhuangzi quan ji,* p. 300.

[402] This phrase is based on a statement found in the *Zhuangzi, Qiwulun:* "There is further the great awakening. Later we will know that this [life] is a great dream." Legge, *Dao de jing ji Zhuangzi quan ji,* p. 243, n. 9.

[403] See the *Ruhuan sanmei jing,* T.342.12:150c12–15.

[404] This expression is based on a statement found in the *Yijing, Xici, shang.* Legge translates it as "They (i.e., sages) [thus] stimulated [the people] as by drums and

dances, thereby completely developing the spirit-like [character of the Yi]" (*I ching: Book of Changes,* p. 377, n. 76).

405 See the *Shangshu, Dayumo.* Legge, *The Chinese Classics,* vol. 3, p. 66.

406 This expression is also based on a statement found in the *Yijing, Xici, xia:* "Good fortune and ill, occasion for repentance or regret, all arise from these movements." Legge, *I ching: Book of Changes,* p. 380, n. 3.

407 This statement is based on a passage found in the *Laozi,* chapter 58: "The delusion of the people (on this point) has indeed subsisted for a long time." Legge, *Dao de jing ji Zhuangzi quan ji,* p. 150, n. 2.

408 The expression "to honor the talented and virtuous, bear with all people" derives from the *Lunyu, Zi Zhang:* "The superior man honors the talented and virtuous, and bears with all." Legge, *The Chinese Classics,* vol. 1, p. 340.

409 This statement is based on a passage found in the *Lunyu, Shuer:* "When I have presented one corner of a subject to any one, and he cannot from it learn the other three, I do not repeat my lesson." Legge, *The Chinese Classics,* vol. 1, p. 197.

410 See the *Lunyu, Xianjin* and *Weizheng,* respectively; the source for the phrase "Ran Boniu looks like the ignorant" is unknown. Legge, *The Chinese Classics,* vol. 1, pp. 240–241, and p. 149, respectively.

411 The "Five Kinds of Vermin" in the *Han Feizi* (fascicle 49) reads: "These are the customs of a disordered state: Its scholars praise the ways of the former kings and imitate their benevolence and righteousness, put on a fair appearance and speak in elegant phrases, thus casting doubt upon the laws of the time and causing the ruler to be of two minds. Its speechmakers propound false schemes and borrow influence from abroad, furthering their private interests and forgetting the welfare of the state's altars of soil and grain. Its swordsmen gather bands of followers about them and perform deeds of honor, making a fine name for themselves and violating the prohibitions of the five government bureaus. Those of its people who are worried about military service flock to the gates of private individuals and pour out their wealth in bribes to influential men who will plead for them, in this way escaping the hardship of battle. Its merchants and artisans spend their time making articles of no practical use and gathering stores of luxury goods, accumulating riches, waiting for the best time to sell, and exploiting the farmers." Watson, *Han Feizi: Basic Writings,* pp. 117–118.

412 This expression is based on a phrase found in the *Zhuangzi, Dazongshi:* "When [Wuzhuang] lost his beauty, [Ju Liang] his strength, and [Huangdi] (the Yellow Emperor) his wisdom, they all [recovered them] under the molding [of your system]." Legge, *Dao de jing ji Zhuangzi quan ji,* p. 304, n. 13.

413 See the *Yijing, Xici, xia.* Legge translates it as "The course cannot be pursued [without them (i.e., proper men)]" (*I ching: Book of Changes,* p. 399, n. 56).

[414] The expression "attend to their own ambition in a lofty spirit" derives from the *Yijing, Gu,* "in a lofty spirit prefers [to attend to] his own affairs." Legge, *I ching: Book of Changes,* p. 96, n. 6.

[415] This is the medical treatment for controlling the vapor of the body: treating with cold for illness caused by cold and with heat for illness caused by heat. It is also found in the third fascicle of this text. Zong Bing responded to He's letter, "[Furthermore,] when a doctor [practicing the medical science] of admonishing the vapor makes water or fire in the mind, [the patient's body] always responds to it by becoming cold or warm."

[416] The expression "Even though one tries to keep his shadow tied up, he catches [only] the wind" may derive from the expression "Even though one tries to keep the wind tied up, he catches his shadow" found in the *Qian Han ji, Xiaocheng huangdi ji* 3.

[417] This expression is based on the passage "When I have presented one corner of a subject to any one, and he cannot from it learn the other three, I do not repeat my lesson" found in the *Lunyu, Shuer.* See note 409.

[418] This expression is based on Confucius's statement in the *Lunyu, Zi han:* "The prosecution of learning may be compared to what may happen in raising a mound. If there want but one basket of earth to complete the work, and I stop, the stopping is my own work. It may be compared to throwing down the earth on the level ground. Though but one basketful is thrown at a time, the advancing with it is my own going forward." Legge, *The Chinese Classics,* vol. 1, pp. 222–223.

[419] This expression is based on the passage found in the *Yijing, Xiangzhuan:* "A sack tied up— there will be no error; this shows how, through carefulness, no injury will be received." Legge, *I ching: Book of Changes,* p. 269, n. 4.

[420] In the *Lunyu, Taibo,* Confucius says, "Is not the saying that talents are difficult to find, true?" Legge, *The Chinese Classics*, vol. 1, p. 214, n. 3.

[421] See the *Lunyu, Yong ye.* Legge, *The Chinese Classics,* vol. 1, p. 188.

[422] The six extreme sufferings refer to disease, anxiety, poverty, evil, weakness, and misfortune, including premature death. Yan Hui died young. See the *Lunyu, Xianjin.* Legge, *The Chinese Classics*, vol. 1, p. 239.

[423] Confucius's advice to Zixia is found in the *Lunyu, Zilu.* Legge, *The Chinese Classics,* vol. 1, p. 270.

[424] See the *Lunyu, Xianjin.* Legge, *The Chinese Classics,* vol. 1, p. 243.

[425] See the *Lunyu, Gongzhi Chang.* Legge, *The Chinese Classics,* vol. 1, p. 176, n. 1.

[426] See the *Lunyu, Gongzhi Chang.* Legge, *The Chinese Classics,* vol. 1, pp. 174–175.

[427] See the *Lunyu, Xianjin.* Legge, *The Chinese Classics,* vol. 1, pp. 242–243.

[428] See the *Lunyu, Yong ye.* Legge, *The Chinese Classics,* vol. 1, p. 186.

[429] See the *Shiji,* fascicle 83, *Lu Zhong Lian Zou Yang liezhuan.* Nienhauser, ed., *The Grand Scribe's Records,* vol. VII, p. 286.

[430] See the *Zhuangzi, Tiandi.* Legge, *Dao de jing ji Zhuangzi quan ji,* p. 363, n. 7.

[431] See the *Lunyu, Weizi.* Legge, *The Chinese Classics,* vol. 1, pp. 333–334.

[432] See the *Shiji,* fascicle 129, *Huozhi liezhuan.* Yang and Yang, *Selections from Records of the Historian,* pp. 413–414.

[433] See the *Lienuzhuan, Xianming, Chu Yuling qizhuan.*

[434] See the *Liexianzhuan* (*Biographies of Arrayed Transcendants*).

[435] See the *Hanshu,* fascicle 72 (*xu*).

[436] See the *Hou Hanshu, Zhang Hengzhuan.*

[437] See the *Lunyu, Gongzhi Chang.* Legge, *The Chinese Classics,* vol. 1, p. 183.

[438] See the *Lunyu, Shuer.* Legge, *The Chinese Classics*, vol. 1, p. 202.

[439] This refers to an incident in which Guanshu and Caishu made a false accusation against the Duke of Zhou. See the *Shujing, Jinteng.* Legge, *The Chinese Classics,* vol. 3, pp. 357–358, n. 12.

[440] See the *Shujing, Shundian.* Legge, *The Chinese Classics,* vol. 3, pp. 39–40, n. 12.

[441] See the *Laozi,* chapter 17. Legge, *Dao de jing ji Zhuangzi quan ji,* p. 109, n. 2.

[442] Duangan Mu, a man of Wei state, leaped over the wall of his house to avoid a prince who had come to invite him to court. Legge, *The Chinese Classics,* vol. 2, p. 270, n. 2.

[443] See the *Zhuangzi, Gengsang Chu.* Legge, *Dao de jing ji Zhuangzi quan ji,* pp. 514–515.

[444] The expression "we occupy our thoughts, but do not discuss anything" is based on a passage found in the *Zhuangzi, Qiwulun:* "Outside the limits of the world of men, the sage occupies his thoughts, but does not discuss about anything." Legge, *Dao de jing ji Zhuangzi quan ji,* p. 237.

[445] See the *Beijing chao,* translated by Zhi Jian (T.790.17:729a3–736b1).

[446] See the *Yijing, Xici, shang.* Legge, *I ching: Book of Changes,* pp. 375–376, n. 75.

[447] See the *Zhuangzi, Gengsang Chu.* Legge, *Dao de jing ji Zhuangzi quan ji,* p. 523, n. 8.

[448] The term "three revered ones" (*sanzun*) refers to: (1) the primary revered one (often, a buddha) and his two attendant bodhisattvas; (2) a buddha, a *pratyekabuddha,* and an arhat; or (3) Buddha, Dharma, and Sangha, i.e., the Three Treasures. From the context, the third interpretation is most appropriate here.

[449] See the *Laozi,* chapter 42. Legge, *Dao de jing ji Zhuangzi quan ji,* p. 133, n. 2.

450 See the *Han Feizi, Heshi.* See note 69.

451 See the *Taizi ruiying benqi jing,* T.185.3:479b26–28.

452 This story is found in several different sutras. For example, see the *Chang Ahanjing,* T.1.1:25a2–25b25.

453 See the *Zhuangzi, Qiwulun.* Legge, *Dao de jing ji Zhuangzi quan ji,* p. 236, n. 6.

454 See the *Taizi ruiying benqi jing,* T.185.3:473b10.

455 The phrases "the Way is helpful to all in the world" and "its knowledge embraces all things" derive from the *Yijing, Xici shang.* Legge, *I ching: Book of Changes,* p. 354, n. 22.

456 See the *Yijing, Ge.* Legge, *I ching: Book of Changes,* p. 168, n. 6.

457 This statement is based on Confucius's answer to Zhuan Sun's question. See the *Lunyu, Weizheng.* Legge, *The Chinese Classics,* vol. 1, p. 153.

458 In the *Lüoan* (*Lüshi chunqiu*), *Chajin,* there is a story that a man of Chu, when crossing a river aboard a boat, dropped his sword into water; he then marked the side of the boat at the point where the sword fell in order to be able to find it, not considering that the boat was moving. This fable describes a person who lacks adaptability.

459 This is a story of another man lacking adaptability, found in the *Han Feizi, Wudu.* Watson, *Han Feizi: Basic Writings,* p. 98.

460 See the *Laozi,* chapter 39. Legge, *Dao de jing ji Zhuangzi quan ji,* p. 130, n. 1.

461 See the *Laozi,* chapter 33. Legge, *Dao de jing ji Zhuangzi quan ji,* p. 123, n. 2.

462 This statement is based on the phrase "Dao becomes obscured through the small comprehension [of the mind]" found in the *Zhuangzi, Qiwulun.* Legge, *Dao de jing ji Zhuangzi quan ji,* p. 230.

463 The expression "striking one's root deeply in oneself and being perfectly still" derives from the *Zhuangzi, Shanxing.* Legge, *Dao de jing ji Zhuangzi quan ji,* p. 419, n. 3.

464 The Chinese term *haoran zhi qi* ("the great primordial vapor") is found in the *Mengzi, Gongsun Chou.* Legge translates this term as "flowing passion-nature" (*The Chinese Classics,* vol. 2, pp. 189–190, n. 11–14).

465 This statement is based on a passage found in the *Liji, Yueji:* "When the [ancient] kings had accomplished their undertakings, they made their music [to commemorate them]; when they had established their government, they framed their ceremonies. The excellence of their music was according to the greatness of their undertakings; and the completeness of their ceremonies was according to the comprehensiveness of their government. The dances with shields and axes did not belong to the most excellent music, nor did the sacrifices with cooked flesh mark the highest ceremonies. The times of the five Dis were different, and therefore they did not each adopt the

music of his predecessor. The three kings belonged to different ages, and so they did not each follow the ceremonies of his predecessor." See Müller, ed., *The Sacred Books of the East,* vol. 28, pp. 101–102, n. 26–27.

466 Shanci is Zhou Yong's pseudonym.

467 This statement is based on the the *Lunyu, Taibo:* "When a bird is about to die, its notes are mournful; when a man is about to die, his words are good." Legge, *The Chinese Classics,* vol. 1, p. 209, n. 3.

468 This expression is based on a phrase found in the *Zhuangzi, Dazongshi,* "to hide a boat in a narrow ravine and to hide a hill in a marsh." See notes 164, 275.

469 All these expressions except "staying in the void to let the animation act at will" derive from the *Laozi,* chapter 10. Legge, *Dao de jing ji Zhuangzi quan ji,* p. 101.

470 This statement is based on a story found in the *Zhuangzi, Tiandi,* about the Yellow Emperor who lost his dark-colored pearl. Legge, *Dao de jing ji Zhuangzi quan ji,* pp. 359–360, n. 4

471 I follow the interpretation for this sentence in Kyōto Daigaku Jinbun Kagaku Kenkyūjo Chūsei Shisōshi Kenkyū han, ed., *Gumyōshū kenkyū,* vol. 3, p. 369, n. 11.

472 This expression derives from the *Zhuangzi, Tian Zifang.* Legge translates it "As soon as my eyes lighted on that man, the [D]ao in him was apparent" (*Dao de jing ji Zhuangzi quan ji,* p. 484, n. 2).

473 The *Shiji, Zhou benji.* See Nienhauser, ed., *The Grand Scribe's Records,* vol. I, p. 58, in which King Wen is referred to as the Lord of the West.

474 See the *Taizi ruiying benqi jing,* T.185.3:473b10.

475 This expression is based on a passage found in the *Zhuangzi, Xiaoyao you:* "When the sun and moon have come forth, if the torches have not been put out, would it not be difficult for them to give light?" Legge, *Dao de jing ji Zhuangzi quan ji,* p. 217, n. 4.

476 The Chinese character *bu* ("not") is deleted according to the previous discussion (T.2101.52:39c5, 40c21).

477 In the *Discourse on the Non-Chinese and the Chinese* Gu Huan says, "Daoism is precisely Buddhism; Buddhism is none other than Daoism."

478 The Chinese term *guan ju* derives from a poem found in the *Shijing, Guan ju:* "*Guanguan* go the ospreys, /On the islet in the river./The modest, retiring, virtuous, young lady:/For our prince a good mate [is] she." Legge, *The Chinese Classics,* vol. 4, p. 1. The four states are found in *Shijing, Binfeng.* According to Kyōto Daigaku Jinbun Kagaku Kenkyūjo Chūsei Shisōshi Kenkyū han, ed., *Gumyōshū kenkyū,* vol. 3, p. 377, the four states refer to Guan, Cai, Shang, and Yan.

479 This expression is based on a phrase found in the *Chuci, Buju:* "The sound *huangzhong* is abrogated and an earthen pot sounds very loud" (a metaphor for the case where a

gentleman is rejected and a petty man becomes dominant). The term *huangzhong* refers to the first note of the twelve classical Chinese musical notes; see note 7.

480 This expression derives from the *Laozi,* chapter 38. Legge, *Dao de jing ji Zhuangzi quan ji,* p. 128, n. 6.

481 This expression is based on a passage found in the *Laozi,* chapter 48: "He who devotes himself to the Dao [seeks] from day to day to diminish [his doing]." Legge, *Dao de jing ji Zhuangzi quan ji,* p. 138, n. 2.

482 This expression is based on another passage found in the *Laozi,* chapter 48: "He who devotes himself to learning [seeks] from day to day to increase [his knowledge]." Legge, *Dao de jing ji Zhuangzi quan ji,* p. 138, n. 1.

483 This expression is based on a passage found in the *Zhuangzi, Qiwulun:* "When they were dreaming they did not know it was a dream; in their dream they may even have tried to interpret it; but when they awoke they knew that it was a dream. And there is the great [awakening], after which we shall know that this life was a great dream." Legge, *Dao de jing ji Zhuangzi quan ji,* pp. 242–243.

484 The expressions "carve a mark on a boat" and "wait by the stump" are used to indicate a person who lacks adaptability. See notes 458, 459.

485 This expression is based on a phrase found in the *Zhuangzi, Qiwulun:* "Under Heaven there is nothing greater than the tip of an autumn down, and the Tai mountain is small." Legge, *Dao de jing ji Zhuangzi quan ji,* p. 236.

486 See the *Yijing, Xici shang.* Legge, *I ching: Book of Changes,* p. 366, n. 56.

487 The interpretation of this sentence is based on a passage found in the *Lunyu, Yang Huo:* "Are there not gamesters and chess players? To be one of these would still be better than doing nothing at all." Legge, *The Chinese Classics,* vol. 1, p. 329.

488 See the *Zhuangzi, Yufu.* Legge, *Dao de jing ji Zhuangzi quan ji,* p. 637.

489 See the *Zuozhuan,* Zhuanggong's tenth year. Legge, *The Chinese Classics,* vol. 5, p. 86, left column.

490 See the *Miaofa lianhuajing,* T.262.9:38c22–29.

491 The Chinese term *chaosan* ("the deception of the inconsistency") derives from the *Zhuangzi, Qiwulun.* Legge, *Dao de jing ji Zhuangzi quan ji,* p. 233.

492 This expression is based on the *Yijing, Xici, shang.* See note 360.

493 The phrase "the flesh of birds and beasts, drinking their blood, and swallowing [also] the hair and feathers" derives from the *Liji, Liyun.* Müller, ed., *The Sacred Books of the East,* vol. 28, p. 369, n. 8.

494 This expression is based on a conversation between Duke Wei of the Zhou dynasty and Tian Kaizhi, found in the *Zhuangzi, Dasheng.* Responding to Duke Wei's question

about the subject of life, Kaizhi said, "I have heard my master say that they who skillfully nourish their life are like shepherds who whip up the sheep that they see lagging behind" and "Bao nourished his inner man, and a tiger ate his outer; while Yi nourished his outer man, and disease attacked his inner. Both of them neglected whipping up their lagging sheep." Legge, *Dao de jing ji Zhuangzi quan ji,* pp. 456–457.

495 The Chinese character *bu* ("not") is read as the character *qian* ("thousand"), since this sentence appears to be a repetition of the previous sentence.

496 See note 69.

497 See the *Zuozhuan,* Chenggong's eighth year. Legge translates it as "He followed the wise and good, as in the course of a stream, and right it was [that he should be so successful]" (*The Chinese Classics,* vol. 5, p. 367, left column).

498 The phrase "to open up [knowledge of the issues of] things and accomplish the undertakings [of men]" derives from the *Yijing, Xici shang.* Legge, *I ching: Book of Changes,* p. 371.

499 The emperor's formal robe with dragon patterns is called *gun* and a crown with a square-shaped top is called *mian.*

500 The Chinese term *zhongmiao zhi men* ("gate of many wonders") derives from the *Laozi,* chapter 1. Legge translates it as "the gate of all that is subtle and wonderful" (*Dao de jing ji Zhuangzi quan ji,* p. 95, n. 4).

501 The *tongren* hexagram comes after the *pi* hexagram. See *Yijing, shangjing.* Legge, *I ching: Book of Changes,* p. xii.

502 The term "the center of the ring [of thought]" derives from the *Zhuangzi, Qiwulun.* Legge, *Dao de jing ji Zhuangzi quan ji,* p. 231.

503 Shangchen forced his father King Cheng to strangle himself. See the *Shiji,* fascicle 40, *Chu shijia.* For an English translation, see Nienhauser, ed., *The Grand Scribe's Records,* vol. I, pp. 392–393.

504 See the *Lunyu, Xianjin.* See note 31.

505 If the term *dao* is taken to mean Daoism here, the following statement does not make sense. It is possible that Gu Huan originally meant *dao* to indicate Daoism and the author took its meaning as "the Way."

506 This expression derives from the *Yijing, Xici shang.* Legge translates it as "The nature [of man] having been completed, and being continually preserved" (*I ching: Book of Changes,* p. 360, n. 37).

507 The punishment called *paoluo* was invented by King Zhou of the Yin dynasty.

508 See the *Liji, Neize.* Müller, ed., *The Sacred Books of the East,* vol. 27, pp. 456–457, n. 15.

[509] This evil act was carried out by King Zhou of the Yin dynasty. See *Shujing, Zhoushu, Taishi.* Legge, *The Chinese Classics,* vol. 3, p. 285, n. 5.

[510] The expression "a person who lives on the seacoast and who enjoys himself in forgetting the world" is based on a passage found in the *Mengzi, Jinxin, shang:* ". . . living somewhere along the seacoast. There he would have been all his life, cheerful and happy, forgetting the kingdom." Legge, *The Chinese Classics,* vol. 2, p. 470.

[511] See the *Lunyu, Shuer.* Legge, *The Chinese Classics,* vol. 1, p. 195.

[512] The Chinese term *daijiang* ("instead of a carpenter") derives from a passage found in the *Laozi,* chapter 74: "Seldom is it that he who undertakes the hewing, instead of the great carpenter, does not cut his own hands!" Legge, *Dao de jing ji Zhuangzi quan ji,* p. 165. Hence I translate it as "taking risks."

[513] See the *Lunyu, Xianjin.* Legge, *The Chinese Classics,* vol. 1, pp. 244–245.

[514] See the *Liji, Quli, shang.* Muller, ed., *The Sacred Books of the East,* vol. 27, p. 64, n. 21.

[515] See the *Laozi,* chapter 1. Legge, *Dao de jing ji Zhuangzi quan ji,* p. 95, n. 1.

[516] See the *Weimojie suoshuojing,* T.475.14:550b29–551c26.

[517] This expression is based on a statement found in the *Zhuangzi, Qiwulun:* "Therefore, this being so, if we take a stalk of grain ("beams" in my translation) and a [large] pillar, a loathsome [leper] and [a beauty like] Xi Shi, things large and things insecure, things crafty and things strange; they may in the light of the Dao all be reduced to the same category (of opinion about them)." Legge, *Dao de jing ji Zhuangzi quan ji,* p. 232.

[518] This is found in indigenous Chinese texts such as the *Qingjing faxingjing* (*Sutra of Pure Dharma Acts*) and the *Laozi daquan pusajing.* See the *Weimojing xuanshu,* T.1777.38:523a15–18, the *Guang Hongmingji* (*Extensive Collection for the Propagation and Clarification of Buddhism*), T.2103.52:162b17, and the *Poyelun,* T.2109.52:477c22–23.

[519] See the *Laozi,* chapter 38. Legge, *Dao de jing ji Zhuangzi quan ji,* p. 128, n. 6.

[520] See the *Laozi,* chapter 12. Legge, *Dao de jing ji Zhuangzi quan ji,* p. 103, n. 1.

[521] See the *Laozi,* chapter 44. Legge, *Dao de jing ji Zhuangzi quan ji,* p. 135, n. 1–2.

[522] See the *Lunyu, Taibo.* Legge, *The Chinese Classics,* vol. 1, p. 207.

[523] See the *Yijing, Xici xia.* Legge, *I ching: Book of Changes,* p. 385, n. 22.

[524] See the *Lunyu, Wei Linggong.* Legge, *The Chinese Classics,* vol. 1, p. 302.

[525] In the ancestral sacrifices the father is called "'the sovereign father" (*huangkao*). See the *Liji, Quli, xia.* Müller, ed., *The Sacred Books of the East,* vol. 27, pp. 117–118.

[526] See note 89.

[527] See note 90.

[528] This expression is based on Confucius's statement in the *Lunyu, Shuer.* Legge translates it as: "When I have presented one corner of a subject to any one, and he cannot from it learn the other three, I do not repeat my lesson" (*The Chinese Classics,* vol. 1, p. 197).

[529] See the *Laozi,* chapter 50. Legge, *Dao de jing ji Zhuangzi quan ji,* pp. 140–141.

[530] See the *Laozi,* chapter 7. For Legge's translation, see *Dao de jing ji Zhuangzi quan ji,* p. 100, n. 1.

[531] The Chinese character *qie* has several different meanings. The Daoist Gu uses it in his discourse as "direct," but Huitong takes it to mean "urgent."

[532] See the *Laozi,* chapter 12. Legge, *Dao de jing ji Zhuangzi quan ji,* p. 103, n. 1.

[533] See the *Liji, Tangong, shang.* Müller, ed., *The Sacred Books of the East,* vol. 27, p. 132, n. 29.

[534] See the *Shiji, Xia benji.* Nienhauser, ed., *The Grand Scribe's Records,* vol. I, p. 36.

[535] The record is found in the last section of the *Shujing, Zhouguan.* Legge's translation in *The Chinese Classics,* vol. 3, pp. 523–534, does not include it.

[536] See the *Liji, Tangong, shang.* Müller, ed., *The Sacred Books of the East,* vol. 27, p. 139, n. 20.

[537] See note 99.

[538] See note 100.

[539] See the *Zhanguoce, Qin Zhaoxiangwang, xia.*

[540] See the *Laozi,* chapter 42. Legge, *Dao de jing ji Zhuangzi quan ji,* p. 133, n. 3.

[541] The *Yellow Books* are generally known as instruction books for the arts of the bedchamber. Presently, only four texts called *Huangshu* are extant in the *Daozang.*

[542] See the *Laozi,* chapter 13. Legge, *Dao de jing ji Zhuangzi quan ji,* p. 104, n. 2.

[543] See the *Laozi,* chapter 7. Legge, *Dao de jing ji Zhuangzi quan ji,* p. 100, n. 2.

[544] This passage is found in the Nanatsudera manuscript of the *Qingjing faxingjing* (*Sutra of Pure Dharma Acts*): "Mahākāśyapa is called Laozi over there." See Makita Tairyō and Ochiai Toshinori, ed., *Nanatsudera koitsu kyōten kenkyū sōsho,* vol. 2. *Chūgoku senjutsu kyōten (sono 2)* (Tokyo: Daitō Shuppansha, 1996), p. 13.

[545] See the *Taizi ruiying benqi jing,* T.185.3:473b12–20, for an example of this.

Glossary

bhikṣu (*biqiu*): A mendicant monk; a Buddhist monk. *See also* four kinds of Buddhist disciples.

bhikṣuṇī (*biqiuni*): A Buddhist nun. *See also* four kinds of Buddhist disciples.

dharmakāya (*fashen*): The Dharma body. There are various interpretations for this term. In the Sarvāstivādin school, it refers to the true Dharma expounded by the Buddha or the collection of the auspicious qualities of the Buddha, including his wisdom, compassion, and various powers. In the Mahāyāna the term evolved into a kind of cosmic principle that was regarded as the true nature of the Buddha or the body of ultimate reality and the source from which his other forms derived. For instance, the *dharmakāya* is one of the two kinds of buddha bodies along with the physical form (*rūpakāya*), or of the three kinds of buddha bodies along with the enjoyment or reward body (*saṃbhogakāya*) and the accommodative body (*nirmāṇakāya*), or of the four kinds of buddha bodies along with the enjoyment or reward body, the accommodative body, and the transformed body, or of the ten kinds of buddha bodies, two versions of which are presented in the *Huayanjing* (*Garlana Sutra*)..

Daodejing (*Scripture of the Way and Its Virtue*): The foundational Daoist scripture authored by Laozi.

eight kinds of gods and demigods who protect Buddhism (*babuzhong*): gods (*deva*s), demigods (*asura*s), dragons (*nāga*s), demons (*yakṣa*s), divine musicians (*gandharva*s), mythical birds (*garuḍa*s), half-horse, half-human beings (*kiṃnara*s), and great serpents (*mahoraga*s).

eight difficulties (*ba'nan*): The eight conditions in which one is unable to encounter a buddha or hear the Dharma: being in hell; being in the state of an animal; being in the state of a hungry ghost; being in the heaven of long life or in Uttarakuru, the continent to the north of Mount Sumeru where people always enjoy great happiness (people in these worlds would not therefore be motivated to seek truth); being deaf, blind, and mute; being knowledgeable about worldly affairs and eloquent (which may defer people from following the true path); and living during the period before or after the Buddha's appearance in the world.

eight kinds of suffering (*baku*): The suffering brought about by birth, aging, illness, death, separation from what one loves, encountering what one despises, not finding what one seeks; and the five *skandha*s. *See also* five *skandha*s.

eight precepts: (*bajiezhai*): Not to kill, not to steal, not to commit sexual conduct, not to use false speech, not to ingest intoxicants, not to perform such acts as wearing bodily decoration, using perfume, singing and dancing, and going to see dances or plays, sleeping in a raised bed, and eating after noon. *See also* five precepts; six purification days.

five cardinal duties (*wudian*): A father's righteousness, a mother's benevolence, an elder brother's love, a younger brother's respect, and a son's filial piety.

five cardinal virtues (*wuchang*): Benevolence, justice, politeness, wisdom, and fidelity.

Five Classics: The Confucian canon comprising the *Book of Changes* (*Yijing* or *Zhouyi*), which looks into the law between Heaven, Earth, and human beings by asserting that all phenomena of the universe come from changes caused by the union and separation of *yin* and *yang;* the *Book of History* (*Shujing* or *Shangshu*), a record of two ideal rulers, Yao and Shun, and the three dynasties of Xia, Yin (Shang), and Zhou; the *Book of Odes* (*Shijing* or *Maoshi*), a collection of three hundred odes composed prior to Confucius's time; the *Spring and Autumn Annals* (*Chunqiu*), which discerns virtue and vice in various historic events that happened in all states for a period of two hundred and forty-two years, from the first year of Lord Yin up to Lord Ai of Lu state; and the *Book of Rites* (*Liji*), a compilation of records of theory and practice regarding rites.

five desires (*wuyu* or *wuqing*): Desires that arise in connection with the five senses of sight, sound, smell, taste, and touch; or desires for wealth, sex, food and drink, fame, and sleep.

five penalties (*wuxing*): Branding, cutting off the nose, cutting off the feet, castration, and death. The earliest record that describes *wuxing* is the Canon of Shun in the *Book of History,* in which Gao Yao carried out these penalties at Shun's command.

five precepts (*wujie;* Skt. *pañcaśīla*): Not to kill, not to steal, not to use false speech, not to commit sexual misconduct, and not to ingest intoxicants. These are the five basic precepts taken by laypeople on entering the Buddhist path.

five primary elements (*wuchang*): Fire, wood, earth, metal, and water. *See also* four great elements.

five realms of existence (*wudao, wutu,* or *wuqu*): The realms of hell, hungry ghosts, animals, human beings, and heavenly beings. *See also* six realms of existence.

five roots of wholesomeness (*wugen*): 1) Belief in the Three Treasures, 2) making efforts to practice good, 3) being mindful of the true Dharma, 4) concentration, and 5) the investigation of the true nature of things. (Volume II)

Five Sacred Mountains (*wuyue*): The Eastern Mountain (Mount Tai), the Southern Mountain (Mount Heng or Huo), the Western Mountain (Mount Hua), the Northern Mountain (Mount Heng), and the Central Mountain (Mount Song).

five *skandha*s (Skt. *pañcaskandha; wuyin* or *wuyun*): The five constituent elements of existence that produce various kinds of suffering: matter or form (*rūpa*), perception (*vedanā*), conception (*samjñā*), volition (*samskāra*), and consciousness (*vijñāna*).

Five Thearchs (*wudi*): Five legendary emperors: Yellow Emperor (Huangdi), Emperor Gaoyang (Zhuanxu), Emperor Gaoxin (Diku), Emperor Yao, and Emperor Shun.

four devils (Skt. *māra*s; *simo*): Defilements (Skt. *kleśa*s), the five *skandha*s, death (Skt. *maraṇa*), and the king of devils, Māra, in the Paranirmitavaśavartin Heaven, who tries to thwart one's attempts to carry out good acts.

four fruits (*siguo*): The four stages of spiritual attainment in the Hinayana: the fruit of entering the stream of the sacred Dharma (Skt. *srota-āpanna*), the fruit of only one more rebirth (Skt. *sakṛdāgāmin*), the fruit of not returning (Skt. *anāgāmin*); and the fruit of arhatship.

four gravest offenses (Skt. *pārājika*; *boluoyi*): Engaging in sexual intercourse, stealing, taking life, and lying about one's spiritual attainment. Monks who commit even one of these offences is permanently expelled from the sangha.

four great elements (*sida*): Earth, water, fire and wind. *See also* five primary elements.

Four Holy Rivers (*sidu*): The Yangzi River, the Yellow River, the Huai River, and the Ji River.

four immeasurable minds (Skt. *catur-apramāṇa* or *catvāry apramāṇāni; sidengxin* or *siwuliangxin*): Benevolence (*ci*), or giving pleasure and happiness to others; compassion (*bei*), or removing others' pain and suffering; taking joy in making other people happy (*xi*); and giving up all attachments (*she* or *hu*).

four kinds of Buddhist disciples (*sizhong*): Monks (*bhikṣu*s), nuns (*bhikṣuṇī*s), laymen (*upāsaka*s), and laywomen (*upāsikā*s).

Grand Terminus (*taiji*): In Daosim, the origin of all things in the universe.

icchantika (*yichanti*): One who has no good roots and has no possibility of becoming a buddha.

kalpa (*jie*): An eon, an immeasurably long period of time.

Mount Sumeru (Xumishan): In Buddhist cosmology, the highest mountain that rises from the center of the world.

nine kinds of Buddhist scriptures (*jiubujing*): The first nine of the twelve kinds of Buddhist scriptures. *See* twelve kinds of Buddhist scriptures.

nine realms of the transmigration of birth and death (*jiudi*): Subdivisions of the three realms of samsaric existence, consisting of the realm of desire, the four meditation heavens of the realm of form, and the four domains of the realm of nonform. *See also* three realms of existence.

nine schools (*jiuliu*): Confucianism, Daoism, the school of *Yin-Yang,* Legalism, the Nominalist school, the school of Mo Di (i.e., Mohism), the school of the Political Strategists, the school of Miscellaneous Thoughts, and the school of the Farming Life.

nirvana (*niepan*): The ultimate goal of Buddhism, where delusions are extinguished and the highest wisdom is attained.

pure speech (*qingtan*): Discourse following doctrines or theories found in the *Laozi Daodejing* and the *Zhuangzi* without regard to its practicality. The earliest example is that carried out by Fu Gu and Xun Can in the first year of the Taihe era (227). It was popular during the period from the Wei kingdom (220–265) through the Jin dynasty (265–420).

Seven Classics: The Five Classics plus the *Book of Music* (*Yuejing*), no longer extant, and the *Analects* (*Lunyu*) of Confucius. *See also* Five Classics.

seven kinds of self-conceit (*qiman*): The feeling of superiority toward those who are inferior; the feeling of superiority toward those who are one's equals; the feeling of superiority toward those who are superior to oneself; being proud of oneself and despising others; considering oneself to be more worthy or virtuous than one actually is; false humility, i.e., feeling pride at one's humility; and proudly thinking that one is virtuous although, in fact, one is a person of little virtue.

six arts (*liuyi*): Six areas in which a refined person must be skilled: rites, music, archery, driving a chariot, learning, and mathematics.

Six Classics: The Five Classics plus the *Book of Music. See also* Five Classics.

six domestic animals: Horse, cattle, sheep, chickens, dogs, and pigs.

six extreme evils (*liuji*): Misfortune that results in shortening one's life, sickness, mental distress, poverty, wickedness, and weakness. Also called the six feelings (*liuqing*).

six *pāramitā*s (*liuboluomi* or *liudu*): The six qualities or "perfections" a bodhisattva practices in order to attain nirvana: (1) generosity (Skt. *dāna*), giving property, the Dharma, and peace; (2) morality (Skt. *śīla*), observing precepts; (3) forbearance or patience (Skt. *kṣānti*); 4) diligence or effort (Skt. *vīrya*); (5) meditation (Skt. *dhyāna*); and (5) wisdom (Skt. *prajñā*).

six purification days (*liuzhai*): The eighth, fourteenth, fifteenth, twenty-third, twenty-ninth, and thirtieth days of the month, during which laypeople observe eight precepts (the five basic precepts along with additional proscriptions against indulging in adornment or perfume, entertainment, sleeping in a raised bed, or eating after midday) in order to purify themselves. *See also* five precepts.

six realms of existence (*liudao* or *liuqu*): The six realms into which sentient beings are reborn in the course of samsaric existence: the realms of hell, hungry ghosts, animals, humans, *asura*s, and heavenly beings.

six relations (*liuqin*): Father, mother, elder and younger brothers, wife, and children.

six sense organs (*liugen*): Eyes, ears, nose, tongue, the tactile body, and mind.

six supernatural powers (*liutong* or *liushentong*): (1) The ability to go anywhere at will and to transform oneself or objects at will; (2) the capability of seeing anything at any distance; (3) the capability of hearing any sound at any distance: (4) the ability to know others' thoughts; (5) the ability to know one's own and others' former lives; and (6) the ability to destroy all evil passions.

śramaṇa (*shamen*): A Buddhist monk.

śrāmaṇera (*shami*): A male novice.

śrāmaṇerikā (*shamini*): A female novice.

tathāgata (*rulai*): One of ten epithets for a buddha, construed as "one who comes from thusness."

ten epithets for the Buddha (*shihao*): Thus-come One, One Worthy of Alms, Fully Enlightened, One Having Wisdom and Practice, One who Has Attained Emancipation, Knower of the World, Unsurpassed, Tamer of Humans, Teacher of Gods and Humans, and Enlightened and World-honored One.

ten powers (*shili*): Ten powers attributed to a buddha: (1) distinguishing right and wrong; (2) knowing the karma of all sentient beings of the past, present, and future, and its outcome; (3) knowing all forms of meditation; (4) knowing the greater and lesser capacities of sentient beings; (5) knowing the thoughts and desires of sentient beings; (6) knowing the different levels of existence of sentient beings; (7) knowing the results of various methods of practice; (8) knowing the transmigratory states of all sentient beings and the courses of karma they follow; (9) knowing the past lives of all sentient beings and the nirvanic state of nondefilement; and (10) knowing how to destroy all evil passions.

ten wholesome acts (*shishan*): Not killing living beings, not stealing, not committing adultery, not telling lies, not uttering harsh words, not uttering words that cause enmity between people, not engaging in idle talk, not being greedy, not being angry, and not holding wrong views.

Three Augusts (*sanhuang*): Three legendary monarchs of ancient China. There are several different theories about the identity of these figures. For instance, Sima Qian's *Shiji* lists Tianhuang (Emperor of Heaven), Dihuang (Emperor of Earth), and Renhuang (Emperor of People) in the *Sanhuangji* (*Chronicles of the Three Augusts*), and Tianhuang, Dihuang, and Qinhuang (the first emperor of the Qin dynasty) in the *Qin Shihuangji* (*Chronicles of the First Emperor of the Qin Dynasty*). The *Chunqiu wei* (a book about charms and omens circulated in the Han dynasty as appendices to the *Spring and Autumn Annals*) lists Fuxi, Shen Nong, and Nüwa as the Three Augusts.

three kinds of emptiness (*sankong*): The three gates of emancipation: emptiness (*kong*), devoid of characteristics (*wuxiang*), and absence of aspiration (*wuyuan*).

three lowest realms of existence (*santu, sanqu,* or *san'e*): The realms of hell, hungry ghosts, and animals. *See also* six realms of existence.

three most revered people (*zaisan*): The sovereign, one's parents, and one's teacher.

three periods of existence (*sanshi*): Past, present, and future.

three periods of the Dharma: The period of the True Dharma (*zhengfa*), when the Buddha's teaching is properly practiced and enlightenment can be attained; the period of the Semblance Dharma (*xiangfa*), when the teaching is practiced but enlightenment is no longer attainable; and the last period of the Decadent Dharma (*mofa*), when only the teaching still exists but practice and attainment are no longer possible.

three poisons (*sandu*): Greed, anger, and stupidity.

three powers (*sancai*): Heaven, human beings, and Earth.

three realms of existence (*sanjie*): The realm of desire (Skt. *kāmadhatu*), which comprises the realms of hell, hungry ghosts, animals, *asura*s, and human beings, and a part of heaven; the realm of form (Skt. *rūpadhātu*), which includes part of a lower heaven and in which there are only refined types of form without sexual desire and other appetitites; and the realm of nonform (Skt. *arūpyadhātu*), in which there is no material form, only meditative states.

three transcendental knowledges (*sanda* or *sanming*): The ability to know one's former lives and those of others, the ability to know one's future destiny and that of others, and the ability to know about all the suffering of the present life and to remove its root cause.

three vehicles (*sansheng*): The three kinds of teaching and paths of practice for *śrāvaka*s, *pratyekabuddha*s, and bodhisattvas.

trichiliocosm (Skt. *tri-sāhasra-mahāsāhasra*): In ancient Indian cosmology, the entire universe in which a thousand worlds make a small one-thousand world; a thousand of these make a medium one-thousand world; and a thousand of these make a great one-thousand world.

Tripiṭaka (*sanzang*): The three "baskets," or collections, of the Buddhist teachings; Sutra (discourses of the Buddha), Vinaya (monastic rules), and Abhidharma (treatises).

twelve causations (Skt. *pratītyasamupāda; shieryinyuan*): A foundational Buddhist teaching on the twelvefold links of cyclic existence: (1) ignorance (*avidyā*), (2) volition (*saṃskāra*), (3) consciousness (*vijñāna*), (4) mental functions and the formation of physical elements (*nāmarūpa*), (5) six senses (*āyatana*), (6) contact with sense objects (*sparśa*), (7) sensation or feeling (*vedanā*), (8) craving (*tṛṣṇā*), (9) grasping what one desires (*upādāna*), (10) existence (*bhava*), (11) birth (*jāti*), and (12) old age and death (*jāramaraṇa*).

twelve gates of meditation (*shiermen*): Three groups of the four stages of meditation: the four stages of meditation in the realm of form, the four immeasurable virtues attained through meditation, and the four stages of meditation in the realm of non-form.

twelve kinds of Buddhist scriptures (*shierbujing*): (1) *sūtra,* the Buddha's exposition of the Dharma in prose; (2) *geya,* verses that repeat the ideas already expressed in prose; 3) *gāthā,* verses containing ideas not expressed in the prose section of a *sūtra;* (4) *nidāna,* narratives of past occurrences that explain a person's present state; (5) *itivṛttaka,* narratives of past lives of the Buddha's disciples; (6) *jātaka,* narratives of the Buddha's past lives; (7) *adbhuta-dharma,* accounts of miracles performed by the Buddha or other deities; (8) *avadāna,* exposition of the Dharma through allegories; (9) *upadeśa,* discussions of doctrine, often in question-and-answer form; (10) *udāna,* exposition of the Dharma by the Buddha without awaiting questions or requests from his disciples; (11) *vaipulya,* full-length, in-depth exposition of principles of truth; and (12) *vyākaraṇa,* the Buddha's predictions of his disciples' attainment of buddhahood.

upāsaka: A layman. *See also* four kinds of Buddhist disciples.

upāsikā: A laywoman. *See also* four kinds of Buddhist disciples.

Way of the Spirit (*shendao*): In Daoism, the unfathomed mysterious way, the transcendental religious world, or a synonym for a supreme spiritual being.

Bibliography

Chūgoku Shūkyō Bunka Kenkyūkai, trans., and Shōjirō Abe, ed. "Kōkan hotei yakuchū Sō Hei 'Myōbutsuron' (4)," *Tōyō Daigaku Daigakuin kiyō* 28 (1992): 219–240.

—. "Kōkan hotei yakuchū Sō Hei 'Myōbutsuron' (5)," *Tōyō Daigaku Daigakuin kiyō* 29 (1992): 247–269.

—. "Kōkan hotei yakuchū Sō Hei 'Myōbutsuron' (6)," *Tōyō Daigaku Daigakuin kiyō* 31 (1994): 423–452.

—. "Kōkan hotei yakuchū Sō Hei 'Myōbutsuron' (7)," *Tōyō Daigaku Daigakuin kiyō* 32 (1995): 233–256.

—. "Kōkan hotei yakuchū Sō Hei 'Myōbutsuron' (8)," *Tōyō Daigaku Daigakuin kiyō* 33 (1996): 253–279.

Chūgoku Shūkyō Bunka Kenkyūkai, trans., and Shōkō Kanaoka, ed. "Kōkan hotei yakuchū Sō Hei 'Myōbutsuron' (1)," *Tōyō Daigaku Bungakubu kiyō* 37 (1984): 23–40.

—. "Kōkan hotei yakuchū Sō Hei 'Myōbutsuron' (2)." *Tōyō Daigaku Daigakuin kiyō* 26 (1989): 345–369.

—. "Kōkan hotei yakuchū Sō Hei 'Myōbutsuron' (3)," *Tōyō Daigaku Daigakuin kiyō* 27 (1990): 259–279.

The above eight issues of *Tōyō Daigaku Bungakubu kiyō* and *Tōyō Daigaku Daigakuin kiyō* comprise the Japanese translation of Zong Bing's *Mingfolu,* T.2102.52:9b5–16a24.

Hsiao-Chieh Cheng, Hui-Chen Pai Cheng, and Kenneth Lawrence Thern, trans. *Shan hai ching: Legendary Geography and Wonders of Ancient China.* Taibei: Committee for Compilation and Examination of the Series of Chinese Classics, National Institute for Compilation and Translation, 1985.

Inagaki, Hisao. *A Dictionary of Japanese Buddhist Terms.* Berkeley: Stone Bridge Press, 1992.

Keenan, John P. *How Master Mou Removes Our Doubts: A Reader-response Study and Translation of the Mou-tzu Li-huo lun.* Albany, NY: State University of New York Press, 1994. T.2102.52:1a29–7a22.

Kimura, Eiichi. *Eon kenkyū, ibun-hen.* Kyoto: Kyōto Daigaku Jinbun Kagaku Kenkyūjo, 1960.

Kopecki, Andrew Joseph. *Cultural Adaptation in the Chinese Acceptance of Buddhism: Selections from the "Hongmingji": A Thesis.* Ph.D. dissertation, Harvard University, Cambridge, 1981. Pp. 65–131: T.2102.52:35a9–11; pp. 185–197: 48a12–23; pp. 294–327: 95a2–96b2.

Kyōto Daigaku Jinbun Kagaku Kenkyūjo Chūsei Shisōshi Kenkyū han, ed. *Gumyōshū kenkyū,* 3 vols. Kyoto: Kyōto Daigaku Jinbun Kagaku Kenkyūjo, 1973–1975. Japanese translation of the entire text of the *Hongmingji.*

Le Blanc, Charles. *Huai-nan tzu. Philosophical Synthesis in Early Han Thought: The Idea of Resonance (kan-ying) with a Translation and Analysis of Chapter Six.* Hong Kong: Hong Kong University Press, 1985.

Legge, James, trans. *Dao de jing ji Zhuangzi quan ji.* Taibei: Wen xing shu ju, 1963.

—. *I ching: Book of Changes.* Ch'u Chai with Winberg Chai, ed. with introduction and study guide. New Hyde Park, NY: University Books, 1964.

—. *The Chinese Classics: With a Translation, Critical and Exegetical Notes, Prolegomena, and Copious Indexes,* vols. 1–4. Taipei: Wen shih che ch'u pan she, 1972, second revised ed.

—. *The Chinese Classics: With a Translation, Critical and Exegetical notes, Prolegomena, and Copious Indexes,* vol. 5. Hong Kong: Hong Kong University Press, 1960.

Liebenthal, Walter. "The Immortality of the Soul in Chinese Thought," *Monumenta Nipponica* 8 (1/2) (1952): 341–395. Pages 341–342: T.2102.52:3b10–23, 6b27–28, 6c29–7a2; pp. 343–353: 27b14–29a16; pp. 354–365: 30c1–17, 31b15–32a6, 33b9–34c25; pp. 376–395: 54b1–c19, without Shen Ji's annotation, 9b6–11b11, 21a7, 18a11, 18a25.

Liu Lifu. *Hongdao yu mingjiao: "Hongmingji" yanjiu.* Beijing: Zhongguo Shehui Kexue Chubanshe, 2004.

—. "Hongmingji" yanjiu. Gaoxion Xian Dashu Xiang: Foguangshan Wenjiao Jijinhui, 2004.

Makita, Tairyō, and Toshinori Ochiai, eds. *Nanatsudera koitsu kyōten kenkyū sōsho,* vol. 2. *Chūgoku senjutsu kyōten (sono 2).* Tokyo: Daitō Shuppansha, 1996.

Masuda, Koh, editor-in-chief. *Kenkyūsha's New Japanese-English Dictionary.* Tokyo: Kenkyusha Ltd., 1974, fourth edition.

Morgan, Evan, trans. *Tao, The Great Luminant: Essays from Huai nan tzu.* Shanghai: Kelly & Walsh Ltd., 1934.

Müller, F. Max, ed. *The Sacred Books of the East,* 50 vols. Oxford: Clarendon Press, 1879-1910.

Nienhauser, William H., Jr., ed. *The Grand Scribe's Records,* 9 vols. Bloomington, IN: Indiana University Press, 1994–2011.

Ogawa, Tamaki. *Rōshi Sōshi.* Tokyo: Chūō Kōronsha, 1998.

Ōta, Teizō, trans. *Kokuyaku issaikyō. Wa-Kan senjutsu bu. Gokyōbu 1.* Tokyo: Daitō Shuppansha, 1936. Japanese translation of the entire text of the *Hongmingji.*

Rosemont, Henry, trans. *The Chinese Classic of Family Reverence: A Philosophical Translation of the Xiaojing.* Honolulu: University of Hawai'i Press, 2009.

Sawada, Mizuho. *Ressenden Shinsenden.* Tokyo: Heibonsha, 1993.

Schmidt-Glintzer, Helwig. *Das Hung-ming chi und die Aufnahme des Buddhismus in China.* Wiesbaden: Steiner, 1976.

Wang Zhimei. *Cong "Hong ming ji" kan fo jiao Zhongguo hua.* Taibei: Taibei Xian Yonghe Shi: Hua mu lan wen hua gong zuo fang, 2008.

Watson, Burton, trans. *Han Feizi: Basic Writings.* New York: Columbia University Press, 2003.

Wong, Eva, trans. *Liezi: A Taoist Guide to Practical Living.* Boston: Shambhala Publications, 1995.

Yang, Hsien-yi, and Gladys Yang, trans. *Selections from Records of the Historian.* Peking: Foreign Languages Press, 1979.

Yoshikawa, Tadao, trans. *Gumyōshū Kōgumyōshū. Daijō butten: Chūgoku Nihon hen,* vol. 4. Tokyo: Chūō Kōronsha, 1988. T.2102.52:1a29–7a22, 16b7–17c25, 29c19–32b11, 34b3–c25, 70a26–72a19, 76c11–77a12, 77c1–79b11, 95a2–96b2.

Zürcher, Erik. *The Buddhist Conquest of China: The Spread and Adaptation of Buddhism in Early Medieval China.* Leiden: E. J. Brill, 1959. Pp. 160–163: T.2102.52:79b13–80b10; pp. 164–176: 86a23–89b2.

Index

D

E

F

G

H

I

N

T

X

Z

BDK English Tripiṭaka
(First Series)

Abbreviations

Ch.:	Chinese
Skt.:	Sanskrit
Jp.:	Japanese
Eng.:	Published title

	Title	Taishō No.
Skt.	Adhyardhaśatikā-prajñāpāramitā-sūtra	
Ch.	Renwangbanruoboluomijing (仁王般若波羅蜜經)	245
Skt.	Kāruṇikārājā-prajñāpāramitā-sūtra (?)	
Ch.	Banruoboluomiduoxingjing (般若波羅蜜多心經)	251
Skt.	Prajñāpāramitāhṛdaya-sūtra	
Ch.	Miaofalianhuajing (妙法蓮華經)	262
Skt.	Saddharmapuṇḍarīka-sūtra	
Eng.	*The Lotus Sutra* (Revised Second Edition, 2007)	
Ch.	Wuliangyijing (無量義經)	276
Eng.	*The Infinite Meanings Sutra* (in *Tiantai Lotus Texts,* 2013)	
Ch.	Guanpuxianpusaxingfajing (觀普賢菩薩行法經)	277
Eng.	*The Sutra Expounded by the Buddha on Practice of the Way through Contemplation of the Bodhisattva All-embracing Goodness* (in *Tiantai Lotus Texts,* 2013)	
Ch.	Dafangguangfohuayanjing (大方廣佛華嚴經)	279
Skt.	Avataṃsaka-sūtra	
Ch.	Shengmanshizihouyichengdafangbianfangguangjing (勝鬘師子吼一乘大方便方廣經)	353
Skt.	Śrīmālādevīsiṃhanāda-sūtra	
Eng.	*The Sutra of Queen Śrīmālā of the Lion's Roar* (2004)	
Ch.	Wuliangshoujing (無量壽經)	360
Skt.	Sukhāvatīvyūha	
Eng.	*The Larger Sutra on Amitāyus* (in *The Three Pure Land Sutras,* Revised Second Edition, 2003)	
Ch.	Guanwuliangshoufojing (觀無量壽佛經)	365
Skt.	Amitāyurdhyāna-sūtra	
Eng.	*The Sutra on Contemplation of Amitāyus* (in *The Three Pure Land Sutras,* Revised Second Edition, 2003)	
Ch.	Amituojing (阿彌陀經)	366
Skt.	Sukhāvatīvyūha	
Eng.	*The Smaller Sutra on Amitāyus* (in *The Three Pure Land Sutras,* Revised Second Edition, 2003)	
Ch.	Dabanniepanjing (大般涅槃經)	374

Title			Taishō No.
Skt.	Mahāparinirvāṇa-sūtra		
Eng.	*The Nirvana Sutra* (Volume I, 2013)		
Ch.	Fochuiboniepanlüeshuojiaojiejing (佛垂般涅槃略説教誡經)		389
Eng.	*The Bequeathed Teaching Sutra* (in *Apocryphal Scriptures,* 2005)		
Ch.	Dicangpusabenyuanjing (地藏菩薩本願經)		412
Skt.	Kṣitigarbhapraṇidhāna-sūtra (?)		
Ch.	Banzhousanmeijing (般舟三昧經)		418
Skt.	Pratyutpannabuddhasammukhāvasthitasamādhi-sūtra		
Eng.	*The Pratyutpanna Samādhi Sutra* (1998)		
Ch.	Yaoshiliuliguangrulaibenyuangongdejing (藥師琉璃光如來本願功德經)		450
Skt.	Bhaiṣajyaguruvaiḍūryaprabhāsapūrvapraṇidhānaviśeṣavistara		
Ch.	Milexiashengchengfojing (彌勒下生成佛經)		454
Skt.	Maitreyavyākaraṇa (?)		
Ch.	Wenshushiliwenjing (文殊師利問經)		468
Skt.	Mañjuśrīparipṛcchā (?)		
Ch.	Weimojiesuoshuojing (維摩詰所説經)		475
Skt.	Vimalakīrtinirdeśa-sūtra		
Eng.	*The Vimalakīrti Sutra* (2004)		
Ch.	Yueshangnüjing (月上女經)		480
Skt.	Candrottarādārikāparipṛcchā		
Ch.	Zuochansanmeijing (坐禪三昧經)		614
Ch.	Damoduoluochanjing (達磨多羅禪經)		618
Ch.	Yuedengsanmeijing (月燈三昧經)		639
Skt.	Samādhirājacandrapradīpa-sūtra		
Ch.	Shoulengyansanmeijing (首楞嚴三昧經)		642
Skt.	Śūraṅgamasamādhi-sūtra		
Eng.	*The Śūraṅgama Samādhi Sutra* (1998)		
Ch.	Jinguangmingzuishengwangjing (金光明最勝王經)		665
Skt.	Suvarṇaprabhāsa-sūtra		
Ch.	Rulengqiejing (入楞伽經)		671
Skt.	Laṅkāvatāra-sūtra		

Title		Taishō No.
Ch.	Jieshenmijing (解深密經)	676
Skt.	Saṃdhinirmocana-sūtra	
Eng.	*The Scripture on the Explication of Underlying Meaning* (2000)	
Ch.	Yulanpenjing (盂蘭盆經)	685
Skt.	Ullambana-sūtra (?)	
Eng.	*The Ullambana Sutra* (in *Apocryphal Scriptures,* 2005)	
Ch.	Sishierzhangjing (四十二章經)	784
Eng.	*The Sutra of Forty-two Sections* (in *Apocryphal Scriptures,* 2005)	
Ch.	Dafangguangyuanjuexiuduoluoliaoyijing (大方廣圓覺修多羅了義經)	842
Eng.	*The Sutra of Perfect Enlightenment* (in *Apocryphal Scriptures,* 2005)	
Ch.	Dabiluzhenachengfoshenbianjiachijing (大毘盧遮那成佛神變加持經)	848
Skt.	Mahāvairocanābhisambodhivikurvitādhiṣṭhānavaipulyasūtrendra-rājanāmadharmaparyāya	
Eng.	*The Vairocanābhisaṃbodhi Sutra* (2005)	
Ch.	Jinggangdingyiqierulaizhenshishedachengxianzhengdajiao-wangjing (金剛頂一切如來眞實攝大乘現證大教王經)	865
Skt.	Sarvatathāgatatattvasaṃgrahamahāyānābhisamayamahā*kalpa*rāja	
Eng.	*The Adamantine Pinnacle Sutra* (in *Two Esoteric Sutras,* 2001)	
Ch.	Suxidijieluojing (蘇悉地羯囉經)	893
Skt.	Susiddhikaramahātantrasādhanopāyika-paṭala	
Eng.	*The Susiddhikara Sutra* (in *Two Esoteric Sutras,* 2001)	
Ch.	Modengqiejing (摩登伽經)	1300
Skt.	Mātaṅgī-sūtra (?)	
Ch.	Mohesengqilü (摩訶僧祇律)	1425
Skt.	Mahāsāṃghika-vinaya (?)	
Ch.	Sifenlü (四分律)	1428
Skt.	Dharmaguptaka-vinaya (?)	
Ch.	Shanjianlüpiposha (善見律毘婆沙)	1462
Pāli	Samantapāsādikā	
Ch.	Fanwangjing (梵網經)	1484
Skt.	Brahmajāla-sūtra (?)	

Title		Taishō No.
Ch.	Youposaijiejing (優婆塞戒經)	1488
Skt.	Upāsakaśīla-sūtra (?)	
Eng.	*The Sutra on Upāsaka Precepts* (1994)	
Ch.	Miaofalianhuajingyoubotishe (妙法蓮華經憂波提舍)	1519
Skt.	Saddharmapuṇḍarīka-upadeśa	
Eng.	*The Commentary on the Lotus Sutra* (in *Tiantai Lotus Texts,* 2013)	
Ch.	Shih-chu-pi-p'o-sha-lun (十住毘婆沙論)	1521
Skt.	Daśabhūmika-vibhāṣā (?)	
Ch.	Fodijinglun (佛地經論)	1530
Skt.	Buddhabhūmisūtra-śāstra (?)	
Eng.	*The Interpretation of the Buddha Land* (2002)	
Ch.	Apidamojushelun (阿毘達磨俱舍論)	1558
Skt.	Abhidharmakośa-bhāṣya	
Ch.	Zhonglun (中論)	1564
Skt.	Madhyamaka-śāstra	
Ch.	Yüqieshidilun (瑜伽師地論)	1579
Skt.	Yogācārabhūmi	
Ch.	Chengweishilun (成唯識論)	1585
Eng.	*Demonstration of Consciousness Only* (in *Three Texts on Consciousness Only,* 1999)	
Ch.	Weishisanshilunsong (唯識三十論頌)	1586
Skt.	Triṃśikā	
Eng.	*The Thirty Verses on Consciousness Only* (in *Three Texts on Consciousness Only,* 1999)	
Ch.	Weishihershilun (唯識二十論)	1590
Skt.	Viṃśatikā	
Eng.	*The Treatise in Twenty Verses on Consciousness Only* (in *Three Texts on Consciousness Only,* 1999)	
Ch.	Shedachenglun (攝大乘論)	1593
Skt.	Mahāyānasaṃgraha	
Eng.	*The Summary of the Great Vehicle* (Revised Second Edition, 2003)	
Ch.	Bianzhongbianlun (辯中邊論)	1600
Skt.	Madhyāntavibhāga	

Title		Taishō No.
Ch.	Dachengzhuangyanjinglun (大乘莊嚴經論)	1604
Skt.	Mahāyānasūtrālaṃkāra	
Ch.	Dachengchengyelun (大乘成業論)	1609
Skt.	Karmasiddhiprakaraṇa	
Ch.	Jiujingyichengbaoxinglun (究竟一乘寶性論)	1611
Skt.	Ratnagotravibhāgamahāyānottaratantra-śāstra	
Ch.	Yinmingruzhenglilun (因明入正理論)	1630
Skt.	Nyāyapraveśa	
Ch.	Dachengjipusaxuelun (大乘集菩薩學論)	1636
Skt.	Śikṣāsamuccaya	
Ch.	Jingangzhenlun (金剛針論)	1642
Skt.	Vajrasūcī	
Ch.	Zhangsuozhilun (彰所知論)	1645
Eng.	*The Treatise on the Elucidation of the Knowable* (2004)	
Ch.	Putixingjing (菩提行經)	1662
Skt.	Bodhicaryāvatāra	
Ch.	Jingangdingyuqiezhongfaanouduoluosanmiaosanputixinlun (金剛頂瑜伽中發阿耨多羅三藐三菩提心論)	1665
Ch.	Dachengqixinlun (大乘起信論)	1666
Skt.	Mahāyānaśraddhotpāda-śāstra (?)	
Eng.	*The Awakening of Faith* (2005)	
Ch.	Shimoheyanlun (釋摩訶衍論)	1668
Ch.	Naxianbiqiujing (那先比丘經)	1670
Pāli	Milindapañhā	
Ch.	Banruoboluomiduoxinjingyuzan (般若波羅蜜多心經幽贊)	1710
Eng.	*A Comprehensive Commentary on the Heart Sutra (Prajñāpāramitā-hṛdaya-sūtra)* (2001)	
Ch.	Miaofalianhuajingxuanyi (妙法蓮華經玄義)	1716
Ch.	Guanwuliangshoufojingshu (觀無量壽佛經疏)	1753
Ch.	Sanlunxuanyi (三論玄義)	1852
Ch.	Dachengxuanlun (大乘玄論)	1853

Title		Taishō No.
Ch.	Zhaolun (肇論)	1858
Ch.	Huayanyichengjiaoyifenqizhang (華嚴一乘教義分齊章)	1866
Ch.	Yuanrenlun (原人論)	1886
Ch.	Mohezhiguan (摩訶止觀)	1911
Ch.	Xiuxizhiguanzuochanfayao (修習止觀坐禪法要)	1915
Ch.	Tiantaisijiaoyi (天台四教儀)	1931
Eng.	*A Guide to the Tiantai Fourfold Teachings* (in *Tiantai Lotus Texts,* 2013)	
Ch.	Guoqingbailu (國清百録)	1934
Ch.	Zhenzhoulinjihuizhaochanshiwulu (鎭州臨濟慧照禪師語録)	1985
Eng.	*The Recorded Sayings of Linji* (in *Three Chan Classics,* 1999)	
Ch.	Foguoyuanwuchanshibiyanlu (佛果圜悟禪師碧巖録)	2003
Eng.	*The Blue Cliff Record* (1998)	
Ch.	Wumenguan (無門關)	2005
Eng.	*Wumen's Gate* (in *Three Chan Classics,* 1999)	
Ch.	Liuzudashifabaotanjing (六祖大師法寶壇經)	2008
Eng.	*The Platform Sutra of the Sixth Patriarch* (2000)	
Ch.	Xinxinming (信心銘)	2010
Eng.	*The Faith-Mind Maxim* (in *Three Chan Classics,* 1999)	
Ch.	Huangboshanduanjichanshichuanxinfayao (黄檗山斷際禪師傳心法要)	2012A
Eng.	*Essentials of the Transmission of Mind* (in *Zen Texts,* 2005)	
Ch.	Yongjiazhengdaoge (永嘉證道歌)	2014
Ch.	Chixiubaizhangqinggui (勅修百丈清規)	2025
Eng.	*The Baizhang Zen Monastic Regulations* (2007)	
Ch.	Yibuzonglunlun (異部宗輪論)	2031
Skt.	Samayabhedoparacanacakra	
Eng.	*The Cycle of the Formation of the Schismatic Doctrines* (2004)	
Ch.	Ayuwangjing (阿育王經)	2043
Skt.	Aśokāvadāna	
Eng.	*The Biographical Scripture of King Aśoka* (1993)	

Title		Taishō No.
Ch.	Mamingpusachuan (馬鳴菩薩傳)	2046
Eng.	*The Life of Aśvaghoṣa Bodhisattva* (in *Lives of Great Monks and Nuns,* 2002)	
Ch.	Longshupusachuan (龍樹菩薩傳)	2047
Eng.	*The Life of Nāgārjuna Bodhisattva* (in *Lives of Great Monks and Nuns,* 2002)	
Ch.	Posoupandoufashichuan (婆藪槃豆法師傳)	2049
Eng.	*Biography of Dharma Master Vasubandhu* (in *Lives of Great Monks and Nuns,* 2002)	
Ch.	Datangdaciensisancangfashichuan (大唐大慈恩寺三藏法師傳)	2053
Eng.	*A Biography of the Tripiṭaka Master of the Great Ci'en Monastery of the Great Tang Dynasty* (1995)	
Ch.	Gaosengchuan (高僧傳)	2059
Ch.	Biqiunichuan (比丘尼傳)	2063
Eng.	*Biographies of Buddhist Nuns* (in *Lives of Great Monks and Nuns,* 2002)	
Ch.	Gaosengfaxianchuan (高僧法顯傳)	2085
Eng.	*The Journey of the Eminent Monk Faxian* (in *Lives of Great Monks and Nuns,* 2002)	
Ch.	Datangxiyuji (大唐西域記)	2087
Eng.	*The Great Tang Dynasty Record of the Western Regions* (1996)	
Ch.	Youfangjichao: Tangdaheshangdongzhengchuan (遊方記抄: 唐大和上東征傳)	2089-(7)
Ch.	Hongmingji (弘明集)	2102
Eng.	*The Collection for the Propagation and Clarification of Buddhism, Volume I* (2015)	
Ch.	Fayuanzhulin (法苑珠林)	2122
Ch.	Nanhaijiguineifachuan (南海寄歸内法傳)	2125
Eng.	*Buddhist Monastic Traditions of Southern Asia* (2000)	
Ch.	Fanyuzaming (梵語雑名)	2135
Jp.	Shōmangyōgisho (勝鬘經義疏)	2185
Eng.	*Prince Shōtoku's Commentary on the Śrīmālā Sutra* (2011)	

Title		Taishō No.
Jp.	Yuimakyōgisho (維摩經義疏)	2186
Eng.	*The Expository Commentary on the Vimalakīrti Sutra* (2012)	
Jp.	Hokkegisho (法華義疏)	2187
Jp.	Hannyashingyōhiken (般若心經秘鍵)	2203
Jp.	Daijōhossōkenjinshō (大乘法相研神章)	2309
Jp.	Kanjinkakumushō (觀心覺夢鈔)	2312
Jp.	Risshūkōyō (律宗綱要)	2348
Eng.	*The Essentials of the Vinaya Tradition* (1995)	
Jp.	Tendaihokkeshūgishū (天台法華宗義集)	2366
Eng.	*The Collected Teachings of the Tendai Lotus School* (1995)	
Jp.	Kenkairon (顯戒論)	2376
Jp.	Sangegakushōshiki (山家學生式)	2377
Jp.	Hizōhōyaku (秘藏寶鑰)	2426
Eng.	*The Precious Key to the Secret Treasury* (in *Shingon Texts*, 2004)	
Jp.	Benkenmitsunikyōron (辨顯密二教論)	2427
Eng.	*On the Differences between the Exoteric and Esoteric Teachings* (in *Shingon Texts*, 2004)	
Jp.	Sokushinjōbutsugi (即身成佛義)	2428
Eng.	*The Meaning of Becoming a Buddha in This Very Body* (in *Shingon Texts*, 2004)	
Jp.	Shōjijissōgi (聲字實相義)	2429
Eng.	*The Meanings of Sound, Sign, and Reality* (in *Shingon Texts*, 2004)	
Jp.	Unjigi (吽字義)	2430
Eng.	*The Meanings of the Word Hūṃ* (in *Shingon Texts*, 2004)	
Jp.	Gorinkujimyōhimitsushaku (五輪九字明秘密釋)	2514
Eng.	*The Illuminating Secret Commentary on the Five Cakras and the Nine Syllables* (in *Shingon Texts*, 2004)	
Jp.	Mitsugoninhotsurosangemon (密嚴院發露懺悔文)	2527
Eng.	*The Mitsugonin Confession* (in *Shingon Texts*, 2004)	
Jp.	Kōzengokokuron (興禪護國論)	2543
Eng.	*A Treatise on Letting Zen Flourish to Protect the State* (in *Zen Texts*, 2005)	

	Title	Taishō No.
Jp.	Fukanzazengi (普勧坐禪儀)	2580
Eng.	*A Universal Recommendation for True Zazen* (in *Zen Texts,* 2005)	
Jp.	Shōbōgenzō (正法眼藏)	2582
Eng.	*Shōbōgenzō: The True Dharma-eye Treasury* (Volume I, 2007) *Shōbōgenzō: The True Dharma-eye Treasury* (Volume II, 2008) *Shōbōgenzō: The True Dharma-eye Treasury* (Volume III, 2008) *Shōbōgenzō: The True Dharma-eye Treasury* (Volume IV, 2008)	
Jp.	Zazenyōjinki (坐禪用心記)	2586
Eng.	*Advice on the Practice of Zazen* (in *Zen Texts,* 2005)	
Jp.	Senchakuhongannenbutsushū (選擇本願念佛集)	2608
Eng.	*Senchaku Hongan Nembutsu Shū: A Collection of Passages on the Nembutsu Chosen in the Original Vow* (1997)	
Jp.	Kenjōdoshinjitsukyōgyōshōmonrui (顯淨土眞實教行証文類)	2646
Eng.	*Kyōgyōshinshō: On Teaching, Practice, Faith, and Enlightenment* (2003)	
Jp.	Tannishō (歎異抄)	2661
Eng.	*Tannishō: Passages Deploring Deviations of Faith* (1996)	
Jp.	Rennyoshōninofumi (蓮如上人御文)	2668
Eng.	*Rennyo Shōnin Ofumi: The Letters of Rennyo* (1996)	
Jp.	Ōjōyōshū (往生要集)	2682
Jp.	Risshōankokuron (立正安國論)	2688
Eng.	*Risshōankokuron or The Treatise on the Establishment of the Orthodox Teaching and the Peace of the Nation* (in *Two Nichiren Texts,* 2003)	
Jp.	Kaimokushō (開目抄)	2689
Eng.	*Kaimokushō or Liberation from Blindness* (2000)	
Jp.	Kanjinhonzonshō (觀心本尊抄)	2692
Eng.	*Kanjinhonzonshō or The Most Venerable One Revealed by Introspecting Our Minds for the First Time at the Beginning of the Fifth of the Five Five Hundred-year Ages* (in *Two Nichiren Texts,* 2003)	

Title		Taishō No.
Ch.	Fumuenzhongjing (父母恩重經)	2887
Eng.	*The Sutra on the Profundity of Filial Love* (in *Apocryphal Scriptures,* 2005)	
Jp.	Hasshūkōyō (八宗綱要)	extracanonical
Eng.	*The Essentials of the Eight Traditions* (1994)	
Jp.	Sangōshīki (三教指帰)	extracanonical
Jp.	Mappōtōmyōki (末法燈明記)	extracanonical
Eng.	*The Candle of the Latter Dharma* (1994)	
Jp.	Jūshichijōkenpō (十七條憲法)	extracanonical